H. P. Lovecraft: Art, Artifact, and Reality

THE HIPPOCAMPUS PRESS LIBRARY OF CRITICISM

S. T. Joshi, *Primal Sources: Essays on H. P. Lovecraft* (2003)

S. T. Joshi, *The Evolution of the Weird Tale* (2004)

Robert W. Waugh, *The Monster in the Mirror: Looking for H. P. Lovecraft* (2006)

Scott Connors, ed., *The Freedom of Fantastic Things: Selected Criticism on Clark Ashton Smith* (2006)

Ben Szumskyj, ed., *Two-Gun Bob: A Centennial Study of Robert E. Howard* (2006)

S. T. Joshi and Rosemary Pardoe, ed., *Warnings to the Curious: A Sheaf of Criticism on M. R. James* (2007)

S. T. Joshi, *Classics and Contemporaries* (2009)

Kenneth W. Faig, Jr., *The Unknown Lovecraft* (2009)

Massimo Berruti, *Dim-Remembered Stories: A Critical Study of R. H. Barlow* (2010)

Gary William Crawford, Jim Rockhill, and Brian J. Showers, ed., *Reflections in a Glass Darkly: Essays on J. Sheridan Le Fanu* (2011)

Robert W. Waugh, *A Monster of Voices: Speaking for H. P. Lovecraft* (2011)

Lovecraft Annual (2007–)

Dead Reckonings (2007–)

H. P. LOVECRAFT:

ART, ARTIFACT, AND REALITY

STEVEN J. MARICONDA

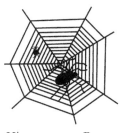

Hippocampus Press

New York

Cover art by Charles E. Burchfield (1893–1967)
Afterglow (July 8, 1916) watercolor with graphite on paper
19⅜ × 14 inches
Burchfield Penney Art Center, Gift of Tony Sisti, 1979
Reproduced with permission from the Charles E. Burchfield Foundation

Published by Hippocampus Press
P.O. Box 641, New York, NY 10156.
http://www.hippocampuspress.com

Cover design by Barbara Briggs Silbert.
Hippocampus Press logo designed by Anastasia Damianakos.

First Edition
1 3 5 7 9 8 6 4 2

ISBN 978-1-61498-064-3

To S. T. Joshi and David E. Schultz

Contents

CONTENTS

Introduction

Several decades have passed since I was compelled to write the first of these essays, specifically to refute the seemingly pervasive negative opinion of Lovecraft's style. It seemed to be a universally accepted truism in popular accounts of the day that Lovecraft was an embarrassment in prose; but after reading W. K. Wimsatt's *The Prose Style of Samuel Johnson*, I felt sure that I could construct a similarly compelling case in favor of the American author.

When I discovered a copy of S. T. Joshi's *H. P. Lovecraft: Four Decades of Criticism* (1980) in the Linderman Library of Lehigh University, I learned that there was a wider world of Lovecraft scholars who would be sympathetic with my thesis. As it turned out these individuals (much like Lovecraft) were gentlemen as well as scholars. Through the good offices of Robert M. Price and R. Alain Everts, I had the privilege to become acquainted with many of them.

Price, Everts, Peter Cannon, Donald R. Burleson, David E. Schultz, and S. T. Joshi were already involved with creating something of a grass-roots renaissance in Lovecraft studies. They provided much council and encouragement for my critical program, particularly Schultz and Joshi. The former had done much groundbreaking critical work in amateur journals on Lovecraft; the latter was fresh out of Brown University (where he spent much time studying Lovecraft's papers) and already envisioned a titanic program of publishing all of Lovecraft's work, including letters, in critical editions. Joshi, Price, and Everts published many of the essays and reviews here in their respective small-press journals, and Joshi was kind enough to include me in several of anthologies of literary criticism. In 1995, Marc A. Michaud collected several of the items (included here much revised) under the imprint of the Necronomicon Press.

As an avid reader of Lovecraft, I had always been struck by the manner in which a unique atmosphere flows from the very first sentence of his stories, almost as if a switch had been thrown. But statements in Lovecraft's letters made me realize that as a literary critic I could approach these tales as carefully crafted, orderly objects containing formal, observable patterns. This provided a level of confidence to undertake close textual analysis of the work. My focus in many of these essays is upon the connection between what the text says and the way it says it, viewing the two as constituting an organic unity.

Similarly, Lovecraft's statement in "Supernatural Horror in Literature" that "[a]tmosphere is the all-important thing, for the final criterion of authenticity is . . . the creation of a given sensation" impelled me to explore a reader-response critical approach to his work. Here, literature is considered to be something that meaningfully exists only in the mind of the reader, and the work is assessed primarily as a catalyst of mental events. This method seemed especially well-suited to that most notorious aspect of Lovecraft's fame, the Cthulhu Mythos.

Both the formal (or "New Criticism") and reader-response approaches involve close reading, and tend to exclude historical and biographical criticism. However, I found that consideration of the quality and effectiveness of Lovecraft's work could not discount those elements. On the most superficial level, Lovecraft joins Nathaniel Hawthorne, Sarah Orne Jewett, and Mary E. Wilkins Freeman as a master in using richly detailed New England local color—history, folkways, landscape, and architecture—as a foundation for supernatural incursions. But more specifically for my purposes, Lovecraft dovetailed the real and the unreal so seamlessly and pervasively that critical efforts to disassemble his text inevitably expose tailings of the actual. As I continue to discover nuggets of the real in Lovecraft, I become less able to say precisely what is not real.

While a dwindling number of uninformed Internet pundits still parrot the received wisdom that Lovecraft was not a good writer, further defense has recently come from unexpected districts—Continental metaphysics. Graham Harman is perhaps the clearest exponent of what has been dubbed Speculative Realism, arguing that all Being—including everything once separately classed as human and inhuman, natural and unnatural—is simply composed of objects. In his book *Weird Realism: Lovecraft and Philosophy* (Washington: Zer0 Books, 2012), Harman suggests that in Lovecraft's writing we *directly experience* "the explicit production of unparaphrasable real objects (Antarctic cities, Cthulhu idols) in the very midst of the sensual realm," with the former no less real and distinctive as objects than the latter. Of Lovecraft, Harman concludes: "I am happy to risk calling him one of [the 20th] century's greatest writers of fiction," largely based on close reading of 100 passages from the tales. It is an apt postscript here to say how pleased I am that he unknowingly arrived at the same conclusion as do these essays, by an unrelated and completely unanticipated path.

I. General Studies

H. P. Lovecraft: Consummate Prose Stylist

The problem of style in the fiction of H. P. Lovecraft is the primary problem of Lovecraft. He succeeds or fails as a literary artist largely by the extent to which his style engages the reader. His imaginative concepts are innovative—unique in the history of literature, even—but his style is polarizing. Enthusiasts see it as brilliant, others as awful. I propose that Lovecraft's style is purposeful, artful, and successful. Further, the degree to which Lovecraft endures is largely a function of the degree to which his style is compelling.

One rarely reads a review of Lovecraft without encountering the notion that his fiction is somehow marred by "verbosity" and excessive use of adjectives. Such criticism is inappropriate in light of Lovecraft's *intent*. His manner of writing is directly a function of his theory of the weird tale: *atmosphere* is paramount, and style is vital to the creation of atmosphere. Style is inseparable from the effects Lovecraft created. He manipulated mere words to conjure the ineffable from the commonplace, perhaps better than any other writer. To weave that peculiar atmosphere that we now know as "Lovecraftian," he wrote as the subject, tone, and narrative voice of each particular tale demanded. We know Lovecraft could write concisely when he wished: he was a highly literate individual. An amateur journalist at heart—that is, one who wrote for the sheer love of writing—he was a professional editor and ghost writer, and a mentor to other authors. But often—especially in the early part of his career—he mindfully adopted a highly colored, highly mannered approach to achieve his effects. Some of Lovecraft's stories, it is true, are inartfully written. Given their atmospheric effectiveness, the vast majority of his efforts are not. His writing, a unique medium as much poetry as fictional narrative, is informed by both purpose and intelligence. An analysis of Lovecraft's approach shows that he was a consummate stylist who penned some of the most successful prose in the history of weird fiction.

Reception

From the very beginning of Lovecraft's career, his style drew fire from critics. One of his first mature tales (1917) was attacked by an obscure group of amateur journalists in a discussion forum called "The Transatlantic Circulator." Lovecraft responded to the criticism in an essay "In Defence of 'Dagon'" (1921). The imaginative writer is "a painter of moods," Lovecraft said. He hoped his explanation of what he was "trying to do" would help the group understand: "I paint what I dream." The metaphor of the visual arts and the mention of dreams (an anticipation of surrealism) are instructive.

But the most damaging attacks came when Lovecraft was no longer around to answer them. Seven years after his death, the eminent Edmund Wilson unleashed a critical fusillade that set the tone for decades, dismissing Lovecraft's writing as "verbose and undistinguished" (47) and objecting to his use of adjectives. Many later critics blithely followed Wilson's lead. In *The Supernatural in Fiction* (1952), Peter Penzoldt characterized Lovecraft's prose as "artificial" (64). In the 1950s and early 1960s, such science fiction writers as Brian Aldiss and Avram Davidson jeered at his distinctive style (quoted in Chalker 25 and de Camp 439). British writer and philosopher Colin Wilson, while admitting that Lovecraft possessed "a gloomy imaginative power which compares with Poe," deemed him an "atrocious writer" (18). Lin Carter, himself the author of dubious Lovecraftian pastiches, lambasted Lovecraft's style as "stilted, artificial, affected" and "very overwritten, verbose, and swimming in adjectives" (xiii). Biographer L. Sprague de Camp called his prose "prolix." We find other typical negative comments about Lovecraft's style in *A Reader's Guide to Science Fiction* and its companion, *A Reader's Guide to Fantasy*. Here Baird Searles and company warn that Lovecraft's "verbosity" (*Science Fiction* 112) may put some readers off and describe his work as "purple to the point of ostentation" (*Fantasy* 212). This type of statement remains the common currency of reviews of Lovecraft's work. And yet, Lovecraft's *Tales* is one of the best-selling titles of the prestigious Library of America, whose mission is "to help preserve the nation's cultural heritage by publishing America's best and most significant writing in durable and authoritative editions." A recent comprehensive critical survey of the history of weird fiction confirms than Lovecraft is exceptional in terms of the reader response he was able to evoke.[1]

---

1. S. T. Joshi, *Unutterable Horror: A History of Supernatural Fiction* (Harrogate, UK: PS Publishing, 2012).

I. GENERAL STUDIES

Intent

The negative comments quoted above are remarkably short-sighted, and those who made them have not considered the need to re-frame the basis of their assessments. Atmosphere, not conciseness, was Lovecraft's primary goal. That goal, coupled with the care with which he composed his fiction, makes it evident that he wrote as he did by intent rather than through ineptitude.

In essays and letters, Lovecraft often commented on the supreme role of atmosphere in weird fiction. In "Supernatural Horror in Literature" he wrote:

> The true weird tale has . . . [a] certain atmosphere of breathless and unexplainable dread. . . . Atmosphere is the all-important thing, for the final criterion of authenticity is . . . the creation of a given sensation. . . . [T]he more completely and unifiedly a story conveys this atmosphere, the better it is as a work of art in the given medium. (*D* 368–69)

On another occasion he wrote specifically about the importance of atmosphere in his own work:

> I, for instance, have an absolute minimum of plot in the formal, academic sense, and depend almost entirely upon atmosphere. But in the end, atmosphere repays cultivation; because it is the final criterion of convincingness or unconvincingness in any tale whose major appeal is to the imagination. (*SL* 2.90)

In his attempt to create atmosphere, Lovecraft's most powerful and flexible tool was prose style. He wrote in a style best suited to his desired effect. He stressed the importance of carefully constructed prose to other writers of supernatural fiction:

> [N]o matter how prosaic the language of a weird tale may seem, it must always be carefully managed with a view to *atmospheric effect*. Effective weird-fictional language, through rhythm and associative word-values, must always have a certain undercurrent of menacing *tensity*. . . . Nothing kills a horror-tale so positively as a brisk, cheerful, casual, or otherwise colourless & incongruous style. (*SL* 3.212)

He was more explicit about technique to another correspondent:

> To make a story effective in the highest degree, the inner rhythms of the prose structure must be carefully fitted to the incidents as they march along; while each word must be chosen with infinite care—a care which considers

not only the dictionary meaning, but the subtle aura of associations which it has picked up through folk-usage and previous literary employment. In other words, prose must be created with just the same exactness, delicacy of ear, imaginative fertility, etc., as verse. (SL 3.355)

The last sentence is especially significant. Lovecraft thought of himself primarily as a poet prior to the resumption of his fictional efforts in 1917. He was thoroughly familiar with the devices of sound and rhythm that poetry employs, in Pope's words, to make "the sound . . . seem an Echo to the sense." He used his experience with these devices to great effect in his prose. In fact, it may be said that he never wholly left poetry because of the abundance of poetic devices in even his most realistic prose.

Lovecraft's regard for the power of style was reflected in his meticulous compositional habits. He called the revision phase of writing "a tedious, painstaking process" (SL 5.203). One should never, he wrote,

consider a rapidly written sentence as a finished product. It may be that four or five verbal transportations will be needed to produce the desired effect; or that wholesale substitutions of words of diverse length—often demanding still further textual changes for their perfect accommodation—will have to be effected. . . . [A]n artistically conceived prose manuscript must be in a perpetual state of flux; with unlimited opportunities for every kind of shifting, interpolation, and minute remodeling, and with no sentence or paragraph accepted more than tentatively until the very last word is set down. (SL 3.132)

We can see that the particulars of Lovecraft's writing were carefully measured. He attempted to create atmosphere in different ways, explicitly distinguishing "atmospheric impressionism" from "straightforward narrative prose" (SL 2.61). He approached each tale according to its subject matter. Part of the approach was the choice of narrative voice; another, the tone of the story—be it, say, "intense, clutching, delirious horror; delicate dream-like fantasy; realistic, scientific horror" or "very subtle adumbration" ([Notes on Weird Fiction]; CE 2.174).

The concept that the author's stated intent has no bearing on the merit of his product is not new, nor is it needed to support the argument here. At minimum we can say Lovecraft knew exactly what he was doing. It then becomes a question of how well he succeeded in terms of reader response. But before we turn to this, let us examine how he approached his task.

Development

I am fundamentally a *prose realist* whose prime dependence is on the building up of atmosphere through the slow, pedestrian method of multitudinous suggestive detail & dark scientific verisimilitude. Whatever I produce must be the sombre result of a deadly, literal seriousness, & almost pedantic approach. (*SL* 3.96)

Lovecraft made this declaration in a letter of December 1929, twelve years after he seriously undertook the writing of supernatural fiction. Both the strength and the validity of his conviction are evidenced by the tales he subsequently wrote: all are realistic, and many rank among his best. Lovecraft's early fiction is a heterogeneous mixture of styles ranging from ethereal phantasy to grim pseudo-realism, with an ever-increasing trend toward the latter; as Lovecraft himself noted, the above idea became a conscious one only around 1926, when he wrote "The Call of Cthulhu."

Even in Lovecraft's first five mature tales, we can see how he began to develop the stylistic method he later decided was best suited to supernatural fiction. There is a wide diversity of tone in these early attempts, almost as if he was experimenting for the most effective means to write forceful weird stories. In Lovecraft's fourth production, "The Green Meadow," we first see an inkling of many of the techniques he would later employ in his mature prose realism. His fifth attempt, "Beyond the Wall of Sleep," was fully based in what he would eventually settle on as the most successful stylistic formula for the horror tale.

This formula, which I will term "supernatural realism," may be said to consist of three components: (1) description of imaginative creations in very specific detail; (2) putting facts (including topical references) next to fictions, so as to make the latter seem more real; and (3) writing in a precise and erudite style that helps instill in the reader both trust in the narrator's judgment and terror regarding his experiences.

Related to the last component is Lovecraft's habit of making the narrator a man of science or an aesthete. Giving the narrator a position of intellectual authority is an explicit indicator to the reader that the narrator may be trusted to convey information with objectivity, just as the narrator's precise way of expressing himself (i.e., the prose style of the first-person narrative) is an implicit indicator that elicits such trust.

For convenience, the first two components of this supernatural realism may be classed as content; the third, as style. This realism, designed to foster a sense of the narrative's believability, was to serve Lovecraft well in such triumphs as "The Whisperer in Darkness" and "The Shadow over Innsmouth." As we will see, precursors of it appear in his work as early as 1919, and Lovecraft had discovered the essentials of the formula by 1920.

One other area that must concern us here is noticing how Lovecraft sometimes left room for natural explanations (delusion on the part of the narrator, primarily) for the supernormal events of his tales. As Lovecraft makes the credibility of his narrators greater and greater, the notion that all was a delusion on their part becomes less acceptable to the reader. All the evidence seems to point to a supernormal event—and though the narrator himself might cling desperately to the hope that the supernormal did not occur, the rational presentation of the tale makes the reader side with the evidence. This makes the tale seem much more real, and thus much more affecting.

Lovecraft's first mature attempt at the horror story came in June 1917. W. Paul Cook, much impressed with Lovecraft's "The Alchemist," a juvenile supernatural tale offered as a credential on application to the United Amateur Press Association, had urged his friend to try his hand again in the genre. The result was "The Tomb," a product much like "The Alchemist" in its resemblance to the work of Edgar Allan Poe. As a great student of Poe, Lovecraft once again had followed the stylistic approach with which he was most familiar and, thus, most comfortable.[2]

The narrator of "The Tomb," Jervas Dudley, is a young man of questionable sanity (reminiscent, of course, of Poe's "The Tell-Tale Heart"). He relates his story from the within a madhouse. Much of the tension of the tale results from questions regarding the narrator's credibility: Did he experience the events he relates? Or was it a delusion, as the other characters in the story insist?

The narrator's credibility is a factor of both what he says (content) and how he says it (style). As an example of content that affects the reader's perception of the narrator, take Jervas's statement of how in youth he "dwelt apart from the visible world" with the "presiding dryads" (D 4) of the forest. We immediately suspect the factuality of the rest of his story.

A second factor relative to credibility is the prose style of the narration. Obsessed with the eighteenth century, Jervas relates his tale in long sentences of rather archaic diction and vocabulary. Take the first sentence of the tale as an example: "In relating the circumstances which have led to my confine-

---

2. Pointed out by William Fulwiler, "A Double Dissection," *Crypt of Cthulhu* No. 38 (Eastertide 1986): 8–14.

I. GENERAL STUDIES

ment within this refuge for the demented, I am aware that my present position will create a natural doubt of the authenticity of my narrative" (*D* 3). The manner in which the information in this sentence is conveyed does not enhance the narrator's credibility. If the narrator was of keen mind, one may infer, he might have expressed himself in a more contemporary idiom than he does here.

Together, then, the content of the narration and its prose style decide how credible—and thus how real—the events of the tale seem to the reader. As we will see, Lovecraft eventually would strive to make the believability of his narrators, both in what they say and the way they say it, seem congruent and therefore impeccable.

In a very few of his later tales in the vein of supernatural realism, Lovecraft left open the question of whether supernormal events actually did occur. However, in those tales the possibility that an event did not take place—that it was all a delusion—seems less likely because the details of the tale are related by more trustworthy narrators. From the way they relate their experiences, the narrators initially appear to be exceptionally level-headed and intelligent, and we tend to feel that they are as objective as circumstances—and only as the circumstances—allow. Though each may have a small hope that the horrific occurrence was a delusion or dream, they are ultimately convinced of its existence by hard evidence—as is the reader.

In "The Tomb," we have the converse. Jervas Hyde does not cling to the hope that the supernormal event did not occur, but rather, that it *did*. His credibility is undermined by his eccentricity, which is evident in both what he says and the way he says it. Thus, the reader has a tendency think to dismiss the eerie phenomenon as only a delusion on his part. And this makes the tale rather less effective as a horror story.

One month after penning "The Tomb" Lovecraft wrote "Dagon." Perhaps a bit more confident, he tried a different approach. The narrator is not an eccentric "visionary and dreamer" but a morphine addict about to commit suicide; there is, however, an important "fact" in favor of his plausibility. Unlike Jervas, he was normal at the outset of his adventure: he was a supercargo, and by implication a practical seafaring man. This is reflected in the prose style; compare this opening sentence with that of "The Tomb": "I am writing this under an appreciable mental strain, since by tonight I shall be no more" (*D* 14). We sense immediately a more rational teller of the tale, since he at least recognizes his psychological condition. Still, his addiction and suicidal intent diminish his credibility; we question whether all he tells has actually occurred.

Lovecraft was edging toward the approach he would eventually adopt. To the reader, the possibility that the supernormal occurrence actually took place is low, but greater than it was in "The Tomb," because the narrator is slightly more credible. The increasingly greater credibility of the narrator, and correspondingly lesser possibility of the supernormal event being a mere delusion, continues in Lovecraft's succeeding tales.

"Polaris" (1918), Lovecraft's next story, though partially set in the real world, verges on pure phantasy and so concerns us only briefly here. Lovecraft wrote it in a style wholly new to him, one likely inspired by Poe's prose poems and Wilde's fairy tales, and perhaps by the King James Bible (see Joshi, "On 'Polaris'"). The narration is archaic and ornate, laced with parallelism and inversion.

The latter characteristic is found in the commencing sentence: "Into the north window of my chamber glows the Pole Star with uncanny light" (*D* 20). The atmosphere created by this sentence pointedly differs from that created by the same thought expressed as "The Pole Star glows with uncanny light into the north window of my chamber." Thus is the ethereal tone of the story immediately established; and, of course, this atmosphere gathers as the story unfolds.

In "Polaris" and other stories of its type, the effectiveness of the tale is not a factor of the narrator's believability. In phantasy, suspension of disbelief is taken for granted. Such tales do not attempt to convince us that the unknown lurks behind everyday life. Dunsany, for example, need not convince us that the lands "beyond the fields we know" actually exist; we happily accept his word. The euphony of the prose and the imaginative depth of the tale are paramount. Though Lovecraft abandoned this style, "because I don't think it natural to me" (*SL* 3.212), we must be thankful he continued to experiment with it long enough to create such jewels as "The White Ship" and "Celephaïs."

Lovecraft's stylistic range continues to be showcased in his next project, a collaboration with fellow amateur journalist Winifred Jackson, published as by Lewis Theobald, Jun. and Elizabeth Neville Berkeley. Lovecraft fleshed out Jackson's transcript of a dream into a sort of prose poem. He then added an introduction claiming that the text was found embedded in a large, recently fallen meteorite. Minor though "The Green Meadow" be in content and effect on the reader, it has an important bearing on Lovecraft's greatest fiction. Here for the first time in Lovecraft is strong pseudo-realism, the "prose realism" that he later would feel "is behind everything of importance that I write" (*SL* 3.96). The narrators of the introductory section are ostensibly the two translators of the manuscript. It is worthwhile to reproduce that section here in full.

The following very singular narrative, or record of impressions, was discovered under circumstances so extraordinary that they deserve careful description. On the evening of Wednesday, August 27, 1913, at about 8:30 o'clock, the population of the small seaside village of Potowonket, Maine, U. S. A., was aroused by a thunderous report accompanied by a blinding flash; and persons near the shore beheld a mammoth ball of fire dart from the heavens into the sea but a short distance out, sending up a prodigious column of water. The following Sunday a fishing party composed of John Richmond, Peter B. Carr, and Simon Canfield, caught in their trawl and dragged ashore a mass of metallic rock, weighing 360 pounds, and looking (as Mr. Canfield said) like a piece of slag. Most of the inhabitants agreed that this heavy body was none other than the fireball which had fallen from the sky four days before; and Dr. Richard M. Jones, the local scientific authority, allowed that it must be an aerolite or meteoric stone. In chipping off specimens to send to an expert Boston analyst, Dr. Jones discovered imbedded in the semi-metallic mass the strange book containing the ensuing tale, which is still in his possession.

In form the discovery resembles an ordinary notebook, about 5 × 3 inches in size, and containing thirty leaves. In material, however, it presents marked peculiarities. The covers are apparently of some dark stony substance unknown to geologists, and unbreakable by any mechanical means. No chemical reagent seems to act upon them. The leaves are much the same, save that they are lighter in colour, and so infinitely thin as to be quite flexible. The whole is bound by some process not very clear to those who have observed it; a process involving the adhesion of the leaf substance to the cover substance. These substances cannot now be separated, nor can the leaves be torn by any amount of force. The writing is *Greek of the purest classical quality,* and several students of palaeography declare that the characters are in a cursive hand used about the second century B.C. There is little in the text to determine the date. The mechanical mode of writing cannot be deduced beyond the fact that it must have resembled that of the modern slate and slate-pencil. During the course of the analytical efforts made by the late Prof. Chambers of Harvard, several pages, mostly at the conclusion of the narrative, were blurred to the point of utter effacement before being read; a circumstance forming a well-nigh irreparable loss. What remains of the contents was done into modern Greek letters by the palaeographer, Rutherford, and in this form submitted to the translators.

Prof. Mayfield of the Massachusetts Institute of Technology, who examined samples of the strange stone, declares it a true meteorite; an opinion in which Dr. von Winterfeldt of Heidelberg (interned in 1918 as a dangerous enemy alien) does not concur. Prof. Bradley of Columbia College adopts a less dogmatic ground; pointing out that certain utterly unknown ingredients are present in large quantities, and warning that no classification is as yet possible.

The presence, nature, and message of the strange book form so momentous a problem that no explanation can even be attempted. The text, so far as preserved, is here rendered as literally as our language permits, in the hope that some reader may eventually hit upon an interpretation and solve one of the greatest scientific mysteries of recent years.

—E. N. B. —L. T., Jr. (*HM* 3-4)

The content and style of this passage give it "an impersonal, unsmiling, minutely *reporting* quality" (*SL* 3.96) that Lovecraft later adopted as the best schema for the genre.

One important aspect of the passage is Lovecraft's *specificity*. The first paragraph, with its explicit details of place including the country, date, and time to the minute sets the tone for the whole passage. (Cf. "The Shadow out of Time": "It was on Thursday, May 14, 1908, that the queer amnesia came. . . . The collapse occurred about 10:20 a.m., while I was conducting a class in Political Economy VI" [*DH* 370].) There are many further small touches in the same vein. Note that the weight of the meteorite and the exact dimensions of the imaginary notebook are offered to the reader. Even given the middle initial of one of the witnesses is given.

This passage illustrates Lovecraft's facility in melding the real and the unreal. The mention of the two universities is a sly touch that would later become typical; Harvard's Widener Library, of course, would later become the location of a copy of the *Necronomicon*. In the mention of "chemical reagents" used to test the notebook we may, by comparing a similar situation in "The Colour out of Space" (1926), note how Lovecraft later went further with the tactic of providing specific facts next to his fictions:

Hot as it [i.e., the meteorite] was, they tested it in a crucible with all the proper reagents. Water did nothing. Hydrochloric acid was the same. Nitric acid and even aqua regia merely hissed and spattered against its torrid invulnerability. . . . There were ammonia and caustic soda, alcohol and ether, nauseous carbon disulphide and a dozen others; but . . . there was no change in the solvents to show that they had attacked the substance at all. (*DH* 58)

I. GENERAL STUDIES

Imaginary professors and scientists (as the four mentioned here) associated with actual institutions figure in some later tales such as "The Call of Cthulhu."

Another intertwining of fact and fancy here is the topical allusion to World War I. Lovecraft had used that conflict as a backdrop for "Dagon" and returned to it in "The Temple" and "Herbert West—Reanimator." As S. T. Joshi has shown, topical references abound in Lovecraft's stories.[3] They are, in fact, characteristic of Lovecraft's prose realism, and contribute much to the effect of plausibility in his tales. (The sheer number of topical annotations in the Penguin Classics editions of Lovecraft seems unprecedented for works of fiction, and further proves the point.)

The juxtaposition of fact and imaginative creation makes it very difficult for the reader to decide what the author is inventing. As a small example: is the town of Potowonket an actual place? (It is not, so far as I can determine, but its name resembles those of many towns in New England.) This uncertainty can extend to the more fantastic conceits of the narrative as well, and the borderline between reality and imagination becomes blurred. This has an unsettling effect on the reader.

As far as the style of the passage, Lovecraft's naturally erudite prose style—primarily a result of his intense early reading of Augustan non-fiction—serves him well in phrasing and word choice. In even the first sentence, which pauses to make the distinction that the "singular narrative" might more accurately be called a "record of impressions," we sense that the narrator is attempting to be as objective as possible. This precise style comes to the fore in the paragraph describing the notebook, in which there is a trace of Lovecraft's early scientific writing in the way the data are presented. Note the logical development of the information offered about the discovery: first of it "in form"; then "in material," first of the cover, then of the leaves; and finally of the writing itself.

"The Green Meadow," then, is the first hint of what was later to take force in Lovecraft's fiction. It calls to mind one of his celebrated precepts of the horror tale, which he wrote in a letter of 1930:

> My own rule is that no weird story can truly produce terror unless it is devised with all the care & verisimilitude of an actual *hoax*. The author must . . . build up a stark, simple account, full of homely corroborative details,

---

3. "Topical References in Lovecraft," *Extrapolation* 25 (Fall 1984): 247–65.

> just as if he were actually trying to "put across" a deception in real life—a deception clever enough to make adults believe. (*SL* 3.193)

Lovecraft's later efforts, happily, came progressively closer to being deceptive than did his collaboration with Mrs. Jackson.

"Beyond the Wall of Sleep" was Lovecraft's first effort wholly conceived in supernatural realism. The story evidently was inspired by a passage in an astronomy text, *Astronomy with the Naked Eye* (1908), by Garrett Serviss, noting a supernova observed in 1901. That Lovecraft set out from the inception of the tale to convince the reader of the narrator's credibility is reflected in the clinching point of the narrative:

> Lest you think me a biased witness, another pen must add this final testimony, which may perhaps supply the climax you expect. I will quote the following account of the star *Nova Persei* verbatim from the pages of that eminent astronomical authority, Professor Garrett P. Serviss. (*D* 35)

This use of a real event as the basis for a tale is echoed in the mention of the Vermont floods in "The Whisperer in Darkness" and the pivotal earthquake in "Cthulhu."

Lovecraft probably worked backward from the unusual astronomical occurrence, musing upon what weird causes might be ascribed to it. Once decided that the explosion would be made the result of a combat between two interstellar entities, he needed a means to have that fact made evident on earth; the visions of a "madman" would do. But the madman would have to be someone who ostensibly could not invent such cosmic vistas himself—a decadent mountain dweller, for example. (Lovecraft's reasoning here is somewhat problematic). The narrator—who ought to be perceived as an objective observer—could be his attendant at a sanitarium.

The difference in tone of the opening sentence from that of preceding stories is an immediate indication of Lovecraft's attempt to make the narrator seem plausible: "I have frequently wondered if the majority of mankind ever pause to reflect upon the occasionally titanic significance of dreams, and of the obscure world to which they belong" (*D* 25). Here we have the earliest instance where a Lovecraft tale is told by an apparently objective intellectual. The narrator is a scientist of sorts. We may note, for example, this assertion later in the tale: "It had long been my belief that human thought consists basically of atomic or molecular motion, convertible into ether waves or radiant energy like heat, light, and electricity" (*D* 31). This philosophical and scientific bias prefigures the outlook of the narrators of the classic tales of Lovecraft's later career, such as that of Nathaniel Wingate Peaslee of "The Shadow out of Time." Both in content and in style, the testimony of a rational person is conveyed by a person we are likely to believe. The narrator's believability is great, and so the tale seems that much more real and effective as horror.

It cannot be denied that "Beyond the Wall of Sleep" is a clumsy early attempt at the realistic approach. The narrator's plausibility is seriously compromised by his previous experiments with the telepathy machine he uses glimpse the cosmic vistas of the interstellar creature's mind. The machine is a peculiar device, even though Lovecraft tries to downplay that by couching its principle in pseudo-scientific jargon. The execution of the tale also is somewhat crude. Near the end, we find this declamation: "The climax? What plain tale of science can boast of such a rhetorical effect? I have merely set down certain things appealing to me as facts, allowing you to construe them as you will" (*D* 35). This overly obvious kind of pronouncement diminished as Lovecraft gained practice and became skilled in realism.

We can identify several examples of how Lovecraft set the stage of his tale with an implicit realism (again, somewhat awkwardly at stage in his career). The narrative proper begins thus:

> His name, as given on the records, was Joe Slater, or Slaader, and his appearance was that of a typical denizen of the Catskill Mountain region; one of those strange, repellent scions of a primitive Colonial peasant stock whose isolation for nearly three centuries in the hilly fastnesses of a little-traveled countryside has caused them to sink to a kind of barbaric degeneracy, rather than advance with their more fortunately placed brethren of the thickly settled districts. Among these odd folk, who correspond exactly to the decadent element of "white trash" in the South, law and morals are non-existent; and their general mental status is probably below that of any other section of native American people. (*D* 2)

In content, the alternate spelling of Slater's name constitutes a specific description of an imaginative creation. In the same sentence, fancy merges with fact as the cause of his people's decline is documented. The correlation of the Catskill hill people with their counterparts in the southern U.S. and the assessment of their level of intelligence imply a narrator who not only is precise but also is something of an amateur sociologist or historian. The phraseology and vocabulary again contribute to the detached tone. Words such as *denizen* and *scions* and phrases such as *general mental status* evoke precision—not to mention condescension. Long sentences with clauses set off by semicolons add to the effect. The narrator appears to be a person of some mental prowess—something of a sociologist, even—who perhaps could be trusted to tell his tale accurately and impartially.

The description of Slater himself that follows continues in this vein:

> Though well above the middle stature, and of somewhat brawny frame, he was given an absurd appearance of harmless stupidity by the pale, sleepy blueness of his small watery eyes, the scantiness of his neglected and never-shaven growth of yellow beard, and the listless drooping of his heavy nether lip. His age was unknown, since among his kind neither family records nor permanent family ties exist; but from the baldness of his head in front, and from the decayed condition of his teeth, the head surgeon put him down as a man of about forty. (D 26)

This passage recalls Lovecraft's later comment that he felt it necessary at times to describe a scene or event "as an entomologist might describe an insect" (SL 3.96).

In "Beyond the Wall of Sleep" we once more find the question left open of whether anything extraordinary actually occurred: "Dr. Fenton . . . denies the reality of everything I have related. He vows that I was broken down with nervous strain, and badly in need of a full vacation" (D 35). In this instance, much more so than in "The Tomb" and "Dagon," the reader is less likely to believe the convenient "out" of delusion on the narrator's part. This is because the credibility of the narrator seems greater—his "evidence" seems more solid, more objective—as a result of the style and content of his story. So it is for Lovecraft's later works; as he grows adept at the techniques he used to create such realism, the possibility of an actual supernormal intrusion seems greater, and the tales more terrifying.

Consider the case of "The Hound" (1922), a tale about a man stalked by a thing from a grave he defiled. The narrator is well versed in the Symbolists, the pre-Raphaelites, Huysmans, and Baudelaire. The great deal of pleasure he takes from grave-robbing and the cellar full of morbid objects he has assembled suggest that he is psychotic. He is about to commit suicide as a result of the thing's pursuit. Given these circumstances, the feverish, ornate prose of the tale is fitting. It certainly succeeds in creating atmosphere.

Contrast this with "The Temple" (1920), which only vaguely suggests its horror. Written by a German naval officer, the style of the tale is accordingly concise and restrained. It is very effective in inciting a feeling of unease—

specifically, the feeling of being in a submarine stranded on the ocean floor—and masterfully conveys the growing mental unbalance of the narrator.

This story was written two years *before* the "florid" "The Hound," proving that Lovecraft manipulated the ornateness of his style as the subject matter, narrative voice, and tone of each tale suggested. Each narrative performance must thus be judged not only at face value but also in relation to the tale as a whole. Under this exegesis, the terms "long-winded" and "florid" are meaningless. The question is whether the type of prose Lovecraft employed is well suited to the tale's particulars, whether it is well-written prose of its type, and, most important, whether the prose succeeds in creating atmosphere. Some of Lovecraft's tales, such as "The Lurking Fear," are overwritten even in context; others—like "Polaris"—are simply poorly written. However, more than three-quarters of Lovecraft's fictional output stands as a formidable array of effective and consummately turned prose. Highlights are numerous. The insidious "The Rats in the Walls," the evocative "The Colour out of Space," the dignified and eruditely horrific *The Case of Charles Dexter Ward,* and the icily scientific *At the Mountains of Madness* form only a fraction of the vast body of Lovecraft's stylistic achievement.

Approach

Critics have noted that Lovecraft's infamous pantheon of "gods"—actually primal beings incomprehensible and indifferent to humans—is a fictional reflection of his materialistic conception of a purposeless universe governed by a fixed and only partially knowable set of laws. For example, his conviction that "the cosmos in a mindless vortex; a seething ocean of blind forces" (*SL* 1.156) is brilliantly symbolized by the "blind idiot god, Azathoth, Lord of All Things," who sprawls at the center of Ultimate Chaos "encircled by his flopping horde of mindless and amorphous dancers" (*DH* 110). But if Lovecraft's outlook dictated his fiction's themes, it also explicitly influenced his stylistic approach; for the realistic narrative voice and detail found in his tales may likewise be traced to his philosophical stance. His rationalistic worldview eliminated the possibility of religion and caused him to seek another imaginative outlet—one that supplemented rather than contradicted reality. This imaginative outlet was fantasy fiction. But only fantasy fiction of a certain type would satisfy him; a type in which reality was first convincingly and accurately portrayed before the "supplementing" took place. The need for such portrayal was the primary force behind Lovecraft's prose realism.

Writing weird fiction gave Lovecraft an essential "imaginative refuge" from what he viewed as a directionless cosmos. He felt that

> objective phaenomena—endless and predictable repetitions of the same old stuff over and over again—form only the very beginning of what is needed to keep [a] sense of significance, harmony, and personal adjustment to infinity satisfied. All sensitive men have to call in unreality in some form or other or go mad from ennui. That is why religion continues to hang on . . . (*SL* 3.139)

His objectivity, however, prevented him from embracing religion as the solution to his dilemma. He saw religion as "insulting to the intellect in its outright denial of plain facts and objective probabilities" and as having "no foundation in reality" (*SL* 3.139f.). Left to his own devices by his unyielding rationalism, Lovecraft turned to that form of "unreality" to which he had been inclined since youth: the creation of, imaginative fiction. However, he found that for this fiction to be satisfying, it had to be firmly rooted in the real world, and to avoid contradicting what we know to be true about it:

> I do not share the real mystic's *contempt* for facts and objective conditions, even though I fail to find them interesting and satisfying. *On the contrary,* I am forced to respect them highly, and allow for them in every system of imaginative refuge I formulate. . . . I get no kick at all from *postulating what isn't so,* as religionists and idealists do. . . . My big kick comes from *taking reality just as it is*—accepting all the limitations of the most orthodox science—and then permitting my symbolising faculty to *build outward* from the existing facts; rearing a structure of *indefinite promise and possibility* whose topless towers are in no cosmos or dimension penetrable by the contradicting-power of the tyrannous and inexorable intellect. But the whole secret of the kick is *that I know damn well it isn't so.* (*SL* 3.140)

In concluding that the fantastic element of his fiction had to "*supplement,* rather than *contradict,* reality" (*SL* 3.140), Lovecraft set himself the task of creating as realistic a background as possible for his tales. The degree of his success is attested to by our reaction to tales such as *At the Mountains of Madness,* where the central events of the story seem frighteningly plausible. He laid the foundation of his best tales with a verisimilitude approaching that of the "true" school of literary realists. His dictum that "No avenue can lead us away from the immediate to the remote . . . unless it really does begin at the immediate—& not at any false, cheap, or conventional conception of the immediate" (*SL* 3.195) echoes in the very convincingness of his work, from "The Rats in the Walls" to "The Shadow out of Time."

So where did Lovecraft find the models for his prosodic approach? Influences may be roughly classed into two groups. One group is those writers whom he more or less consciously took as models; horror authors such as Edgar Allan Poe, Nathaniel Hawthorne, M. R. James, and Ambrose Bierce, who had likewise anchored their tales in realistic detail. Poe, however, left him a far broader legacy than the others mentioned. Lovecraft's psychological realism, in which the terrible mental reaction of a character (usually the first-person narrator) to the horror is documented by the use of vocabulary and syntax, is derived from his early favorite.

The second influence is far more subtle, and one that Lovecraft himself in some ways had very little control over. His writing was shaped by youthful influences exceedingly apt to its later role of fostering the believability of his narratives. As seen in examining the humble beginnings in "The Green Meadow," his prose was a product primarily of his avid early reading of eighteenth-century essayists, historians, and scientists. These writers, employing vocabulary and syntax that seem pedantic to the modern reader, lent Lovecraft exactly the erudite tone and precision of style necessary for him to delineate realistic scenes with an authority and convincingness which instills in the reader a subtle sense of confidence. This sense of confidence leaves us especially vulnerable for the supernormal intrusion of horror at the end. Ironically, Lovecraft's style was influenced by exactly the "right" writers for its later purpose.

So while Lovecraft willfully followed and expanded upon the approach of Poe and certain other "supernatural realists," the influence of the eighteenth-century prose stylists became an unconscious, inherent baseline for his writing. It is the element that is constant in all his prose, be it essay, letter, or fiction.

Paramount among what I will term the conscious influences on Lovecraft's rendering of prose realism was his "God of Fiction," Edgar Allan Poe. Lovecraft lauded Poe for establishing "a new standard of realism in the annals of literary horror," and followed his example of "consummate craftsmanship" ("Supernatural Horror in Literature" [*D* 396]) by carefully researching and laying out the background of his tales. A good example of Poe's background realism is "The Gold-Bug," with its description not only of Sullivan's Island, but also of the intricacies of cryptography and entomology. So impressed with these tales as a child, Lovecraft closely followed Poe in his meticulous planning and emphasis on accurate description.

Poe also left Lovecraft a far more important legacy in the area of realism—that of psychological realism. In addition to carefully thought-out character motivation, Lovecraft learned from Poe the importance of documenting with his prose the mental effects of horror upon his characters. First-person narration is best suited to this, and was thus favored by Poe in such tales as "The Fall of the House of Usher" and "The Pit and the Pendulum." In these stories the emotional excitement of the narrator—and the frenzy of the style—grows as the horrible events of the tale unfold. This first-person viewpoint, its prose a finely tuned reflection of the narrator's psychic state, is found in nearly three-quarters of Lovecraft's original fiction as well.[4]

Lovecraft's quest for realistic backgrounds also contributed to his frequent use of New England, which he knew and loved so well, as a fictional setting; to the point where some critics have called him a local colorist. For this approach we can thank not only Poe but, as Donald R. Burleson has shown, Nathaniel Hawthorne (*Critical Study* 218). The scholarly antiquarianism of M. R. James, whom Lovecraft read at a rather late date, doubtless also reinforced the latter's tendency to include references to actual books (such as the cryptographic reference materials mentioned in "The Dunwich Horror") and other historical detail in his stories.

Technique

Beyond Lovecraft's obvious attention to detail, mixing of factual information with fantastic imagination, psychological accuracy, use of "local color," and so on, there is a more basic element that binds these into a convincing whole: syntax, diction, and word choice. Style is the fabric of the approach that his philosophical and literary orientation impelled him to take with his fiction. For in Lovecraft's prose style lies the realism that we perceive but do not observe when we read his stories, and the atmosphere to which we respond. All readers of Lovecraft know the peculiar tone of his narration; the surety, the authoritative voice of his narrators as they recount their incredible tales. In reading we acquire a subtle trust in the narrator, as much for how he expresses things as for what he is expressing. The deliberate, erudite word choice and phrasing make the reader sense that the narrator is a man of caution and intelligence; this instills in the reader a certain respect for the events to follow. The message

---

4. See note 6 for a list of HPL's stories told in the first person.

I. GENERAL STUDIES

of Lovecraft's style is that the narrator's voice is the voice of sanity—sanity that is threatened by monstrous intrusions from "Outside."

The force behind the unique and subtle credibility of Lovecraft's narration is what S. T. Joshi has termed the "precision" of his writing (*H. P. Lovecraft* 62). Precision is manifest in vocabulary and grammar alike, and it serves to reflect both the objective and subjective reactions of the narrator. That the precision and authoritative tone ring true, in an almost subconscious manner, reflects the fact that these qualities are inherent to his style. Lovecraft's unique ideolect was shaped, as is anyone's, by the linguistic stimuli of his youth. As we have seen, the bulk of those stimuli consisted of volumes in his ancestral library written in the eighteenth century. At about age six he "began to choose only such books as were very old—with the 'long s,'" and selected as his guide to composition Abner Alden's *The Reader* (1802), "which was in the 'long s', and reflected in all its completeness the Georgian rhetorical tradition of Addison, Pope, and Johnson" (*SL* 2.107f.). Lovecraft himself noted the strength of these influences in his "Some Notes on a Nonentity" (1933):

> I used to spend hours in the attic poring over the long-s'd books banished from the library downstairs and unconsciously absorbing the style of Pope and Dr. Johnson as a natural mode of expression. This absorption was doubly strong because of the ill health which rendered school attendance rare and irregular. (*CE* 5.208)

Lovecraft's style forever after bore the indelible imprint of those early studies. Louis T. Milic, in *Stylists on Style,* articulates this effect:

> The child acquires language in uneven increments. He learns a great deal during the third year and again when he first goes to school. In general, however, the curve of language learning describes a downward trend. The more he has learned about his language, the less he is able to change. The longer he speaks or writes, the more fixed become the patterns in his active repertory. The older he gets, the less he can modify his style. . . . This progressive hardening or "set" of the style also helps explain why the writer seems so much at the mercy of his medium. (8)

Milic stresses the inviolability of a writer's ideolect—and, by implication, the early linguistic influences that shape it:

> The writer's choice is not really free. . . . [H]is stylistic options are limited by the resources of his ideolect (his active repertory of lexicon and syntax) and by the way this ideolect functions below the surface of his consciousness. Thus, though a writer may state his stylistic preferences, cultivate rhetorical

choices he considers effective, or even pattern his style upon models, the essence of his expression, that which is inescapably unique to him, is governed by factors over which he has little control. (10)

This passage has great implications on any assessment of Lovecraft's stylistic influences. It is clear that the writers whom Lovecraft absorbed in his early years—primarily Johnson, Addison, Steele, and Gibbon[5] (and Poe, to whom he became devoted at age eight)—are those who shaped his prose style. We can also minimize the *stylistic* effect of Lord Dunsany (whom Lovecraft did not read until he was nearly thirty years old), Machen, et al.

The traits characteristic of the eighteenth-century writers central to Lovecraft's style include "philosophick" vocabulary, parallelism, inverted syntax, chiasmus (an inverted symmetry among the elements of two parallel phrases), and antithesis.

Lovecraft's detractors have been quick to vilify his tendency to use "big words," rather than express himself as simply as possible. Yet this tendency, directly inherited from his influences, did much to give his writing a subtle, pervasive sense of authority. Referring to Samuel Johnson, W. K. Wimsatt, Jr., describes the effect of the use of general or abstract words that have a scientific or philosophical flavor:

> There are certain words for delineating objects which may not denote these any more generically than other words denoting the same objects, but which suggest that the objects are to be thought of as a class rather than individuals; they emphasize by their tone the aspect under which the class is concerned and have little or no connotation of complete appearance or the physical accidentals which clothe individuals of the class. These terms speak as having been coined by men who knew more accurately than common men the precise aspect, or complex of aspects, that constitute the class, who named classes only after studying them with the advantage of vast preliminary erudition. (60)

Thus, we find in Lovecraft's stories such words as the celebrated "rugose" and "squamous," and to good effect regarding the confidence we have in the narrator's intelligence and judgment. Wimsatt notes, too, that the same sort of impression is made upon the reader by more basic word choices made by the writer—the use of "frequently," for example, in place of "often."

---

5. HPL conveniently identifies these authors as his primary eighteenth-century prose influences at *SL* 1.11.

Also worth a second glance among Lovecraft's eighteenth-century-derived traits is a syntactical element of extreme frequency and importance in his prose. This is parallelism, the repetition of syntactically similar elements. A single sentence from "Hypnos" supplies several examples:

> And when he opened his immense, sunken, and wildly luminous black eyes I knew he would be thenceforth my only friend—the only friend of one who had never possessed a friend before—for I saw that such eyes must have looked fully upon the grandeur and the terror of realms beyond normal consciousness and reality; realms which I had cherished in fancy, but vainly sought. (*D* 165)

On the simplest level of parallel, there are the words coupled with "and," which is very frequent in Lovecraft. These doubled words, which are a salient characteristic of Johnson's style as well, can be roughly divided into four classes. (See Wimsatt 20; examples are from "Hypnos.") They may describe:

- exact range (i.e., "the grandeur and the terror")
- illustrative range ("[his voice was] the music of deep viols and of crystalline spheres" [*D* 165])
- different aspects of an object ("low and damnably insistent whine" [*D* 169])
- overlapping aspects of an object ("the strange and hideous thing" [*D* 170])

The last two classes, especially, make for increased emphasis, and predominate in Lovecraft as well as in Johnson (Wimsatt 22). It is sometimes difficult to distinguish among these four types, as in this example from "The Shunned House" (1924): "He was at once a devil and a multitude, a charnel-house and a pageant" (*MM* 258).

Another type of parallel important and frequent enough in Lovecraft to mention and evidently derived from this school of writing is anaphora, where the parallel elements begin with the same words or phrase. In the first-quoted sentence from "Hypnos," an example is the phrase beginning with the word "realms." This parallelism likewise makes for increased emphasis, as does the chiasmus centered on the words "only friend."

If in the last analysis Lovecraft had relatively little control over the fabric of his ideolect, he was well aware of its natural erudition and was able to make stylistic choices that reinforced his desired effect on the reader. In many tales, he underscored this feeling of credibility by giving his narrators positions of responsibility and intelligence; thus the predominance of academics, writers, and men of science we find relating Lovecraft's fantastic narratives.[6] Here (and in his third-person narration also) we get the impression

6. In the following list of HPL's first-person narratives, occupations of the narrators, when stated, are in parentheses; those inferred are in brackets.

Dagon (supercargo)
Polaris
Beyond the Wall of Sleep (medical intern)
The Transition of Juan Romero (ex-military officer)
The White Ship (lighthouse keeper)
The Statement of Randolph Carter
The Cats of Ulthar
The Temple (Lieutenant-Commander of German Navy)
The Street
From Beyond
Nyarlathotep
The Picture in the House [genealogist]
Ex Oblivione
The Nameless City [archaeologist]
The Moon-Bog
The Outsider
The Music of Erich Zann (student of metaphysics)
Hypnos (sculptor)
What the Moon Brings
The Hound
The Lurking Fear (reporter)
The Rats in the Walls (retired manufacturer)
The Unnamable (weird author)
The Festival
The Shunned House [antiquarian]
He (poet)
In the Vault
Cool Air (journalist)
The Call of Cthulhu [anthropologist?]
Pickman's Model [writer?]
The Silver Key
The Colour out of Space (surveyor)
The Whisperer in Darkness (professor of literature)
At the Mountains of Madness (geologist)
The Shadow over Innsmouth [businessman; antiquarian]
The Thing on the Doorstep (architect)
The Shadow out of Time (professor of economics)

We should note that HPL's style gives us the impression that his narrators are men of

that the storyteller is intelligent enough to be able to distinguish between fact and fallacy, and is not one to be frightened without cause. And when we watch as the narrator becomes more and more upset—sometimes to the point of breaking down entirely—we are most affected by these series of events.

Lovecraft also drew attention to the intelligence—and, by extension, the reliability—of his narrators by contrasting their exposition with that of (ostensibly) common people, and also individuals who have come in contact with outside forces and been utterly deranged as a result. An example of the first kind is found in "Cool Air" (1926):

> Anxious to stop the matter at its source, I hastened to the basement to tell the landlady; and was assured by her that the trouble would quickly be set right.
>
> "Doctair Muñoz," she cried as she rushed upstairs ahead of me, "he have speel hees chemicals. . . . He nevair go out, only on roof, and my boy Esteban he breeng heem hees food and laundry and mediceens and chemicals. My Gawd, the sal-ammoniac that man use for keep heem cool!"
>
> Mrs. Herrero disappeared up the staircase to the fourth floor, and I returned to my room. (*DH* 200-201)

Similarly, there is the clinical description of Joe Slater's attack in "Beyond the Wall of Sleep" (1919—a pivotal tale in the development of Lovecraft's prose realism), which contrasts so strikingly with Slater's ravings:

> Rushing out into the snow, he had flung his arms aloft and commenced a series of leaps directly upward in the air; the while shouting his determination to reach some 'big, big cabin with brightness in the roof and walls and floor, and the loud queer music far away'. As two men of moderate size sought to restrain him, he had struggled with maniacal force and fury, screaming of his desire and need to find and kill a certain 'thing that shines and shakes and laughs'. At length, after temporarily felling one of his detainers with a sudden blow, he had flung himself upon the other in a daemoniac ecstasy of bloodthirstiness, shrieking fiendishly that he would 'jump high in the air and burn his way through anything that stopped him'. (*D* 27)

These two passages seem almost grotesque—bathetic—in their contrast between the reserve and intellect of the narrator and the lack of control of the other characters; but this contrast reinforces Lovecraft's point: that the narrator is one of exceptional erudition and judgment, and whose word is to be trusted.

---

intelligence and judgment even when they are not explicitly identified as such.

We can conclude that Lovecraft's desire for realism in his weird fiction had a large philosophical component. To him, an intellectually acceptable imaginative refuge had to be based solidly in objective fact. Religion did not meet this criterion, earning his disdain because of it. In setting out to create his own fictions, however, he did his utmost to show that their fantastic—though often theoretically possible—events took place in the world that our science knows.

In technique, for both physical and psychological realism, he found his primary model in his literary idol, Edgar Allan Poe. But a great deal of the effectiveness of his realism is derived from other, more unconscious sources, the eighteenth-century writers in whom he immersed himself all through his early life. These elements of philosophical thought, adopted technique, and unconscious influence form a very fortuitous combination. They are the basis of the realism that helps make Lovecraft's tales so credibly terrifying.

Illustrations and Examples

We've seen that as Lovecraft grew experienced in writing weird fiction, he became progressively convinced that "a solidly realistic framework is needed in order to build up preparation for the unreal element" (*SL* 3.192–93). The prose that he used to put across "The Call of Cthulhu" and most of its successors is correspondingly subdued and can hardly be called "purple." Even when Lovecraft chose a strictly realistic approach to a narrative, he used careful construction and an extraordinary amount of poetic devices to create mood. We can see this in one of his last tales, "The Haunter of the Dark" (1935). "Haunter" is one of his stories available as a recording, and hearing it read aloud makes it easier to detect some of the techniques he used.

In the story, Lovecraft tried to capture the feelings of strangeness incited in him by a distant view of an old, deserted edifice (see *SL* 5.224). He chose a third-person narrator to relate "dispassionately" (*DH* 93) the story of the last days of the weird artist Robert Blake. This is a departure from the usual first-person narration, which enabled him to build atmosphere with subjective as well as objective description and to employ his prose to reflect the rising alarm of the narrator (see Joshi, *H. P. Lovecraft* 62). In constructing "Haunter," Lovecraft felt that atmosphere could be more effectively sustained by modulating the viewpoint, tone, and tension. He accomplished this by switching back and forth from the narrator's "objective" commentary to the quotations from Blake's diary and Providence newspaper accounts of the events.

There are even passages of the narrative that are related at third hand, such as the paragraph of dialogue of an Irish policeman whom Blake speaks with in the church square:

> There had been a bad sect there in the ould days—an outlaw sect that called up awful things from some unknown gulf of night. It had taken a good priest to exorcise what had come, though there did be those who said that merely the light could do it. If Father O'Malley were alive there would be many the thing he could tell. . . . Some day the city would step in and take the property for lack of heirs, but little good would come of anybody's touching it. Better it be left alone for the years to topple, lest things be stirred that ought to rest forever in their black abyss. (*DH* 97–98)

Lovecraft had greater opportunity for more obviously poetic atmosphere-building as he moved farther away from the first-hand relation of events.

Another example of narrative distance in the story is the history of the Shining Trapezohedron, transcribed from the cryptographic church record (*DH* 106). This passage illustrates yet another device Lovecraft often used: a sequence of outré and exotic places, names, or books. The recitation of such words has an incantatory and hypnotic effect. These proper nouns are frequently preceded by epithets—"dark Yuggoth," "the abhorred *Necronomicon*"— that surround them with a subtle aura of dread. Related to Lovecraft's use of epithets is his coining of compound descriptives such as "sky-reaching" monoliths (*DH* 104) or "bird-shunned" shadows (*DH* 105). Aside from lending a sense of urgency, these terms imply that the nature of what is being described evokes unprecedented nomenclature.

Similarly, Lovecraft combined several words into more potently atmospheric phrases. In this and in longer passages as well, he used two important techniques: alliteration (repetition of consonant sounds) and assonance (repetition of vowel sounds). Lovecraft could be extremely deft with these devices, and he used them frequently. The narrator tells us that Blake "painted seven canvases; studies of nameless, unhuman monsters, and profoundly alien, non-terrestrial landscapes" (*DH* 94). The repetition of the *s* and the sonorant *m*, *n*, *l*, and *r* combines with the tense vowel sounds *a* and *e* to give this sentence an atmospherically affecting quality. Lovecraft sometimes used alliteration and assonance in onomatopoeia, where the sound of the words is strongly suggestive of the object or action being described: "At the sharp click of that closing a soft stirring sound seemed to come from the steeple's eternal blackness overhead, beyond the trap-door" (*DH* 205). In this effective sentence we hear the awakening of the Haunter of the Dark.

Lovecraft also employed sentence structure and syntax onomatopoeically:

> And yet that stirring in the steeple frightened him horribly, so that he plunged almost wildly down the spiral stairs, across the ghoulish nave, into the vaulted basement, out amidst the gathering dusk of the deserted square, and down through the teeming, fear-haunted alleys and avenues of Federal Hill toward the sane central streets and the home-like brick sidewalks of the college district. (*DH* 105)

This sentence conveys a feeling of frantic motion through its parallel structure, the repetition of phrases that duplicate one another in their main grammatical features. Lovecraft frequently used parallel structure to gain atmospheric effect:

> They were the black, forbidden things which most sane people have never even heard of, or have heard of only in furtive, timorous whispers; the banned and dreaded repositories of equivocal secrets and immemorial formulae which have trickled down the stream of time from the days of man's youth, and the dim, fabulous days before man was. (*DH* 100)

One of his favorite types of parallel structure is also here: anaphora, in which the parallel phrases all begin with the same words:

> He felt entangled with something—something which was not in the stone, but which had looked through it at him—something which would ceaselessly follow him with a cognition that was not physical sight. (*DH* 104)

The climactic order of the information in the structures adds to the effect. Between the first and second phrases we see another atmospheric device, chiasmus (or symmetry), the inverted relationship between the syntactical elements of parallel phrases.

Parallel structure can also be used to delay the completion of grammatical structure (closure) of the sentence. Until closure is reached, the reader experiences an expectation of it as grammatical tension. Grammatical tension varies with the types of structures used, the number of structures kept open, and the degree of interrupting material included (Eastman 165–66). Low-tension syntax resolves all structures quickly, and Lovecraft used it for "objective" or terse statements. Movement between high- and low-tension syntax serves to build atmosphere in this passage:

It was then that his nerves broke down [low tension]. Thereafter, lounging exhaustedly about in a dressing-gown, he did little but stare from his west window, shiver at the threat of thunder, and make wild entries in his diary [high tension].

    The great storm broke just before midnight on August 8th [low tension]. Lightning struck repeatedly in all parts of the city, and two remarkable fireballs were reported. The rain was torrential, while a constant fusillade of thunder brought sleeplessness to thousands. Blake was utterly frantic in his fear for the lighting system, and tried to telephone the company around 1 a.m., though by that time service had been temporarily cut off in the interest of safety. He recorded everything in his diary—the large, nervous, often undecipherable hieroglyphs telling their own story of growing frenzy and despair, and of entries scrawled blindly in the dark [high tension]. (*DH* 110–11)

The tensest possible syntax is called periodic, because grammatical closure is delayed to the final segment of the sentence (Eastman 166). Lovecraft powerfully employs this syntax near the end of his tale:

Excessive imagination and neurotic unbalance on Blake's part, aggravated by knowledge of the evil bygone cult whose startling traces he had uncovered, form the dominant interpretation given those final frenzied jottings. (*DH* 114)

The passive voice and placement of the noun and verb at the end add substantially to the tension of the sentence.

    Another method Lovecraft used to create a mood was rhythm. As we know from poetry, the cadence of words and phrases has a profound effect on the reader's state of mind. Lovecraft created atmospheric rhythm with both sentence structure and word choice. He attempted to relate each incident with appropriate accentuation, as in the passage in which Blake gazes into the Shining Trapezohedron:

Before he realised it, he was looking at the stone again, and letting its curious influence call up a nebulous pageantry in his mind. He saw processions of robed, hooded figures whose outlines were not human, and looked on endless leagues of desert lined with carved, sky-reaching monoliths. He saw towers and walls in nighted depths under the sea, and vortices of space where wisps of black mist floated before thin shimmerings of cold purple

haze. And beyond all else he glimpsed an infinite gulf of darkness, where
solid and semi-solid forms were known only by their windy stirrings, and
cloudy patterns of force seemed to superimpose order on chaos and hold
forth a key to all the paradoxes and arcana of the worlds we know.

Then all at once the spell was broken by an access of gnawing, inde-
terminate panic fear. (*DH* 104)

Lovecraft weaves a dream-mood with the paired dactyls (´ ˘ ˘) and a "procession" of trochees (´ ˘). These rhythms and the lengthening clauses of the sentences create an ever-deepening feeling of somnolence. He cuts this mood off
sharply at the beginning of the following paragraph with four iambs (˘ ´).

In Lovecraft's fiction we often encounter a verbatim transcription of the
chaotic thoughts of a character. In the first-person narration that predomi-
nates in Lovecraft, the entire tale, of course, is a record of the narrator's
thoughts. The tale closes with the final diary entry of Robert Blake, recording
his impressions during the last minutes of his life. This is one of many instances in which the rational, self-possessed voice of the narrator breaks down
into a grammatically fragmented discourse recording the dissociated contents
of his mind, occasionally reaching downward to a deeper level of consciousness at which images are used to represent sensations and emotions. In these
instances Lovecraft employs stream-of-consciousness techniques. These techniques take three forms: interior monologue, impressionistic description, and
stream-of-consciousness dialogue.

Stream-of-consciousness techniques are clearly derived from the high modernist literature of Joyce, Eliot, and Gertrude Stein, which Lovecraft so disliked. It at first seems paradoxical that this literary traditionalist who
considered himself "fundamentally a *prose realist*" (*SL* 3.96) would employ
such a radical and impressionistic group of techniques in his tales. It was, in
fact, Lovecraft's very regard for realism that led him to incorporate stream-of-
consciousness into his work. He deplored the high modernists not because
he disbelieved in their assumption that man's mental life is made up of a disjointed, illogical flow of thoughts; rather, he felt they took this assumption to
extremes, employing their approach to such a disproportionate extent that
the result was a "grotesque chaos" more akin to science than art (*SL* 2.251,
248). He actually welcomed the techniques of these writers when used pru-
dently to step away from the Victorian artificiality he despised in literature:

I myself think that the extreme methods of Joyce, Eliot, and their congeners do indeed transcend the limits of real art; though I believe they are destined to exert a strong influence upon art itself. Literary art, I think, must continue to adhere to the practice of recording outward happenings in consecutive order; but it must from now on realise the complex and irrational motivation of all these happenings, and must refrain from attributing them to simple, obvious, and artificially rationalised causes.

Hinting that he had considered the matter in light of his own fictional attempts, he continued:

> Just how much of the subconscious hodge-podge behind any outward event ought to be recorded by a literary artist is still a very perplexing question. It must be decided independently in each particular case by the author's own judgment and aesthetic sense—and I for one believe that it can be done in such a manner as to leave the main current of Western-European literary tradition undisturbed in its aesthetic essentials. (SL 2.249)

Lovecraft assimilated stream-of-consciousness techniques into his fiction because they were well suited to his attempts at realistic psychological portraiture. Lovecraft's frequent complaint was that the characters of cheap weird fiction responded unrealistically to the bizarre events they encountered. The writer, he felt, "must see that the characters react . . . with adequate emotion" (SL 3.193). This is why Lovecraft found stream-of-consciousness techniques so useful. His wonders were of a uniquely alien kind, which, realistically, would leave an individual totally stunned, his rational flow of thought disrupted. These techniques were a perfect way to adequately reflect such a mental state. They typically occur at a high point in the narrative, after an intrusion from outside has taken place and sent the character's mind reeling, to show just how profound a shock he has received.

Lovecraft also exploited these techniques as powerful atmospheric devices. They gave him an opportunity to abandon his rational, controlled narrative style and to "play" in a more extended emotional and imaginative range. He was able to use more colorful and openly poetic words and images, and more obvious alliteration and assonance. He could create rhythmic tension with short phrases punctuated by ellipses or dashes. The stream-of-consciousness passages in Lovecraft's stories show a great deal of artistry. They bring the tales to a nearly unbearable pitch, culminating in a quite disturbing effect upon the reader. Lovecraft's use of these techniques in weird fiction is an innovation.

Though founded upon certain of Poe's tales—for example, "The Tell-Tale Heart"—they are characteristic of no other fantastic writer up to his time.

Stream-of-consciousness devices in Lovecraft may be grouped into three categories. Direct and indirect interior monologues focus on the internal contents of a character's mind. Impressionistic description delineates a physical object or event outside the narrator's mind. Stream-of-consciousness dialogue contains verbalized elements of both interior monologue and impressionistic description, predominantly the latter.

The direct interior monologue occurs in first-person narrative, when the interior self of the narrator is portrayed directly as though the reader is overhearing an articulation of the associational flow of thought in the character's mind. This can record the narrator's thoughts on one or more levels, ranging from the wholly conscious (though chaotic) to the subconscious, where symbols or images express themselves. An example of the latter kind, where the unconscious is documented with shattering effect, is Blake's final diary entry in "The Haunter of the Dark" (1935):

> Sense of distance gone—far is near and near is far. No light—no glass—see that steeple—that tower—window—can hear—Roderick Usher—am mad or going mad—the thing is stirring and fumbling in the tower— (*DH* 115)

S. T. Joshi has pointed out that the reference to "Roderick Usher" is symbolic of the psychic union between Blake and the entity in the steeple (*H. P. Lovecraft* 42). A higher-level direct interior monologue is Wilmarth's breakdown in the penultimate paragraph of "The Whisperer in Darkness" (1930), in which only the conscious elements are told:

> Sorcerer, emissary, changeling, outsider . . . that hideous repressed buzzing . . . and all the time in that fresh, shiny cylinder on the shelf . . . poor devil . . . "Prodigious surgical, biological, chemical, and mechanical skill . . ." (*DH* 271)

The direct interior monologue was the first technique Lovecraft employed to document a character's stream-of-consciousness, in the opening of the prose-poem "Nyarlathotep" (1920).

An interior monologue can also be indirect, when a third-person narrator selects from and comments upon a character's stream of thoughts and associations. Indirect interior monologue is thus limited to a rather more conscious level than one given directly and uncensored. Walter Gilman's mind racing through the horrors of his recent past near the end of "The Dreams in the Witch House" (1932) is an example: "The roaring twilight abysses—the green hillside—the blistering terrace—the pulls from the stars—the ultimate black vortices . . . what did all this mean?" (MM 289).

Another stream-of-consciousness technique is simply an impressionistic description of an object or scene by the first-person narrator. Here, the main features of a particular physical object or event are suggested with a few broad brush strokes of sense-data that reflect the impression made upon the narrator at a single instant. The implication is that the thing being described is so upsetting to the narrator that his rational grammar breaks down, and fragmented phrases and images well up from just beneath his controlling consciousness. A fine example is the protagonist's description of the ape-things at the climax of "The Lurking Fear" (1922):

> Shrieking, slithering, torrential shadows of red viscous madness chasing one another through endless, ensanguined corridors of purple fulgurous sky . . . formless phantasms and kaleidoscopic mutations of a ghoulish, remembered scene; forests of monstrous overnourished oaks with serpent roots twisting and sucking unnamable juices from an earth verminous with millions of cannibal devils; mound-like tentacles groping from underground nuclei of polypous perversion . . . (D 198)

Lovecraft parodied this device the following year with a hilarious impressionistic description of World War I from the viewpoint of a necrophiliac in "The Loved Dead." (It is instructive to contrast this with the direct interior monologue of the tale's final paragraph, where impressionistic description gives way to the recording of an internal, emotional experience on several levels.)

Stream-of-consciousness is sometimes present in Lovecraft's dialogue, when a character other than the narrator verbalizes the jumbled thoughts resultant from some horror he has experienced. This dialogue is usually an impressionistic description of the horror, but occasionally descends to a more internal level closer to interior monologue, as in Nahum Gardner's death speech in "The Colour out of Space" (1927):

> ". . . evil water . . . Zenas never come back from the well . . . can't git away . . . draws ye . . . ye know summat's comin', but 'taint no use . . . I seen it time an' agin senct Zenas was took . . . whar's Nabby, Ammi? . . . my head's no good . . . dun't know how long senct I fed her . . . it'll git her ef we ain't keerful . . . jest a colour . . ." (DH 71–72)

Edward Derby's ravings in "The Thing on the Doorstep" (1933) are another example of stream-of-consciousness dialogue.

It is to Lovecraft's credit that he was open-minded enough to recognize the validity of stream-of-consciousness techniques despite his personal dislike of modernist literature. He lent a great deal of vividness and force to his narratives by adapting these devices to his own purposes. They realistically convey a sense of horrified disorientation and constitute many of the most distinctive and atmospherically potent passages in all his work. Indeed, the effect of several of these stream-of-consciousness passages, such as that at the climax of "The Rats in the Walls," has been rarely equaled in supernatural fiction.

In "The Haunter of the Dark," the author gives us a disturbing glimpse directly into the mind of Robert Blake as the character attempts to resist psychic possession by the thing in the steeple. Blake wavers between full sentences and dissociated fragments of thought, the punctuation becoming ever more abrupt, until the final, horrific sentence: "I see it—coming here—hell-wind—titan blur—black wings—Yog-Sothoth save me—the three-lobed burning eye . . ." (DH 115).

Effect

Lovecraft's stylistic choices are on the whole highly effective, but it is not to be thought that the intangible impact of his stories rests merely on the mechanical application of a series of linguistic gimmicks. As he wrote to Clark Ashton Smith:

> As for the *unconscious* element in composition . . . I agree with you that it is really very considerable. In fact, I think it may be fairly said that no first-rate story can ever be written without the author's actually experiencing the moods & visions concerned in a sort of oneiroscopic way. Unless there is actual emotion & pseudo-memory behind a tale, something will inevitably be lacking, no matter how deft, expert, & mature the craftsmanship may be. Emotion makes itself felt in the unconscious choice of words, management of rhythms, & disposal of stresses in the flow of narration; whilst an image or idea of natural or spontaneous occurrence is a thousandfold more vivid than any which can be arbitrarily invented or consciously adopted from external sources. (SL 3.212–13)[7]

---

7. See also SL 2.112 and 4.264.

In this lies the true power of Lovecraft's prose, for few authors have conceived their work as sincerely and acutely as he.

All assessments of Lovecraft's style must address this fact: the bulk of his stories are *atmospherically effective*. Impeccably executed, his approach to prose is not intrinsically worse than any other. He wrote as he did for carefully considered reasons, leveraging a naturally erudite style into an effective instrument to create weird atmosphere. Though he was obviously capable of writing them, simple sentences with few adjectives were often incompatible with Lovecraft's desired effect and the particulars of his tales. He plumbed the depths of fear, dream, time, and space as few others have, and nothing other than the unique style we now know as "Lovecraftian" could have better conveyed the intense philosophical and psychological conceptions that were his concerns. With his prose Lovecraft achieved that which he had set out to do—to excite in the reader "a profound sense of dread, and of contact with unknown spheres and powers; a subtle attitude of awed listening, as if for the beating of black wings or the scratching of outside shapes and entities on the known universe's utmost rim" ("Supernatural Horror in Literature" [D 368-69]).

Lovecraft's Concept of "Background"

The elements of cosmic outsideness and New England local color in H. P. Lovecraft's fiction may be traced, paradoxically enough, to the same source: his philosophy of cosmic indifferentism. Lovecraft's universe is a purposeless mechanism that mankind's limited sensory apparatus can never fully comprehend. The cosmic horror of his fiction—one of unknowable forces that sweep men aside as indifferently as men do ants—is based upon this philosophy.

If Lovecraft found intellectual and imaginative satisfaction in this formulation, one inevitably wonders how he managed to find any emotional solace in it. Closer examination shows that the same skeptical analysis behind Lovecraft's metaphysics led him to the concept of relative values, and to his one great source of emotional fulfillment: his "background," the rich heritage of New England tradition and culture in which he set his greatest tales of cosmic intrusion. The concept of *background* is a central one in Lovecraft's life and work, and our understanding of both may be increased by examining it.

As is often the case with Lovecraft's thought, it is well to approach the issue from the perspective of his *Weltanschauung*—what Freud tidily summarized as an "intellectual construction which gives a unified solution of all the problems of our existence in virtue of a comprehensive hypothesis, a construction, therefore, in which no question is left open and in which everything in which we are interested finds a place. . . . When one believes in such a thing, one feels secure in life, one knows what one ought to strive after, and how one ought to organise one's emotions and interests to the best purpose."

The seeds of Lovecraft's world view seem to have been, in a sense, innate—he was a born analyst, by nature inclined to approach the world on an intellectual level. Few toddlers take an early interest in science, and not many undertake independent laboratory work at age eight. Lovecraft equally early applied the same sort of rigorous approach to metaphysics. At five years,

Lovecraft was asking if God was a myth in the manner of Santa Claus. Soon after he was cross-examining his Sunday School teachers so vehemently that they were undoubtedly glad to see him go when his mother allowed him to discontinue attendance at age twelve. By seventeen, following on the heels of profound study of astronomy and other natural sciences, he had adopted the essentials of his philosophical orientation. Following Democritus, Epicurus, and Lucretius, he saw himself as a "mechanistic materialist" who saw the cosmos as "a meaningless affair of endless cycles of alternate electronic condensation and dispersal—a thing without beginning, permanent direction, or ending, and consisting wholly of blind force operating according to fixed and eternal patterns inherent in entity" (SL 3.124-25).[1] This outlook eliminated the possibility of deity and afterlife, but the positivist Lovecraft found he could come to no other conclusion. The most current science of the day, after all, provided no evidence to support idealism—religious or otherwise—instead tidily explaining the origin of theism with anthropological and psychological theory.

But Lovecraft's philosophy left him spiritually adrift in a universe that cared neither for him nor anything else, an emotionally daunting situation at best. Joseph Wood Krutch, in *The Modern Temper* (1929) (which Lovecraft thought of highly), expressed the problem this way:

> The world of modern science is one in which the intellect alone can rejoice. The mind leaps, and leaps perhaps with a sort of elation, through the immensities of space, but the spirit, frightened and cowed, longs to have once more above its head the inverted bowl beyond which may lie whatever paradise its desires may create. . . . Thus man seems caught in a dilemma which his intellect has devised. (12-13)

The Providence writer's mind certainly did leap with elation through space, but nonetheless realized that his emotional ground would have to be found elsewhere.

The same sense of rationality or objectivity that created Lovecraft's emotional dilemma, however, also provided its solution. Though human concerns are of no importance to the universe at large, this need not mean that they are of no value to the individual psyche:

---

1. For a groundbreaking and thorough treatment of HPL's metaphysics, see S. T. Joshi's *H. P. Lovecraft: The Decline of the West* 1-30. Note especially 4ff., where Joshi explains why HPL was "remarkably careless" for grouping Democritus with Epicurus and Lucretius.

> I have the cynic's and the analyst's inability to recognise the difference in *value* between the two types of consciousness-impacts, *real* and *unreal* . . . [and] to retain the illusion that their actual vast physical difference gives them any difference *in value* as psychological agents impinging on man's consciousness. My one standard of value is imaginative suggesting-power or symbolising-quality. (SL 3.125–26)

Here we have Lovecraft's pragmatic adoption of relative values: "What gives us relative painlessness and contentment we may arbitrarily call 'good' and vice versa" (SL 2.356). That such an adoption is required amidst the bleak cosmos of modern science was also evident to Krutch: "The most ardent lover of truth, the most resolute determination to follow nature no matter to what black abyss she may lead, need not blind one to the fact that many of the lost illusions had, to speak the language of science, a survival value" (13).

Lovecraft claimed that "*the satisfaction of our own emotions* is the one solid thing which we can ever get out of life" (SL 3.21). This need not lead us to believe that he was a hedonist or amoralist, for the notion was moderated by his Apollonian insistence that such satisfaction might take place only by the "intelligent manipulation" of the "raw material" of emotion (*Letters to Alfred Galpin* 174). So Lovecraft cultivated those emotional stimuli that gave him pleasure, but that did not conflict with his intellectual perception. He meanwhile tried to rationally minimize the effects of their unpleasant counterparts.

But where did Lovecraft, who found human beings no more or less interesting than any other phenomenon, find his emotional sustenance? The answer, documented explicitly in innumerable letters and implicitly in the bulk of his fiction, poetry, and essays, is his "background," a term he used to describe his cultural heritage in its broadest dimension:

> No one thinks or feels or appreciates or lives a mental-emotional-imaginative life at all, except in terms of the artificial reference-points supply'd him by the enveloping body of race tradition and heritage into which he is born. We form an emotionally realisable picture of the external world, and an emotionally endurable set of illusions as to value and direction in existence, solely and exclusively through the arbitrary concepts and folkways bequeathed to us through our traditional culture-stream. (SL 3.207)

As far as specifics go, Lovecraft saw his background as consisting of layers of different intensity, most distantly what he considered to be his "Aryan" heritage, followed in increasing strength by his Western-European heritage, his Teuton-Celtic heritage, his Anglo-Saxon heritage, and his Anglo-American heritage (SL 3.208). He especially revered the life of the eighteenth century of old and New England. His father's forebears were English country-gentry, or so he liked to believe. Lovecraft was only the second generation of his paternal family branch in the United States; and at times he whimsically claimed that as the grandson of an Englishman he was by rights a British citizen.[2] His mother's ancestry was a long line of New England Yankees, the first of whom crossed the Atlantic at the astoundingly early date of 1630 and settled in Watertown, Massachusetts (SL 3.363).

Lovecraft believed his background was not merely the simple, familiar traditions passed down from father to son. Aside from components normally associated with tradition such as social customs, attitudes, and institutions, he described background as including "material from my immediate blood-ancestry and personal milieu—habit-patterns, spontaneous likes and dislikes, standards and associations, geographical points of view. . . . These things are physical phenomena—gland functionings and nerve patterns" (SL 3.331). Here Lovecraft implies something beyond the mere influence of his upbringing: the action of environmental factors upon his heredity. He thought his ancestors' agrestic lifestyles had, to some extent, affected his psychological makeup:

> My instincts were formed by the functioning of a certain line of germ-plasm
> through a certain set of geographical and social environing conditions . . .
> and so I continue to react spontaneously and unconsciously in the manner
> of my forefathers, liking the same superficial forms and types and attitudes
> they liked, except when such things conflict with the fundamental laws of
> truth and beauty. (SL 2.333)

Lovecraft goes out on a limb here, venturing into a sort of vague Lamarckism (not unknown in the decades following Darwin).

If the degree of effect of hereditary factors upon Lovecraft's psychological makeup is debatable, there can be no question of the very real influence of his early environment. His upbringing greatly contributed to his acute sense of background. Born in Providence, Rhode Island, and raised there from three years of age, he always felt a mystic identification with the town. The colonial atmosphere of Providence, founded in 1636 by Roger Williams, was then preeminent—especially so in the East Side neighborhood where Lovecraft grew up. Among the antique public buildings of the city were the Col-

---

2. de Camp 21. Typically, de Camp does not document where he got this information.

ony House (1761), University Hall at Brown University (1770), the Brick Schoolhouse (1769), the Market House (1773), the First Baptist Church (1775), the St. John's and Round Top churches (both c. 1810), the Golden Ball Inn (1783), and the old Brick Row warehouses (1816) (*SL* 2.108). There were also many private residences and mansions dating from 1750 onward, and a few—farmhouses overtaken by the city, primarily—built before that date.

As S. T. Joshi has written, it is difficult to realize just how *distant* we are from Lovecraft's time (*H. P. Lovecraft* 7); this is particularly true regarding the milieu of the Providence Lovecraft knew in youth. Many vestiges of past life survived there. Houses were still lit by gaslight. The city's horse-drawn public transport was discontinued only in 1894; and in 1897 over six hundred schooners and several barques still entered the port of Providence, docking at the waterfront at the base of College Hill (*SL* 5.65; Field 2.566, 488).

Added to the effect of the town itself was that of the environment of the house where he grew up. Whipple Phillips's large Queen Anne mansion had been built in the 1870s, but contained many relics of the later 1700s. Most important among the latter was a large library of long-s'd books stored in the attic trunk-room, whence from age six onward Lovecraft often went alone and by candlelight to immerse himself in the atmosphere of the colonial era. He thrived on the work of Addison, Dryden, Johnson, Pope, Steele, and Swift. His interest did not stop there, however. Lovecraft was also familiar with more obscure British and American writers, such as John Oldham (1653–1683), Samuel Garth (1661–1719), Thomas Parnell (1679–1718), Edward Young (1683–1765), Thomas Tickell (1686–1740), James Thomson (1700–1748), Timothy Dwight (1752–1817), and Joel Barlow (1754–1812), making him something of a specialist in the literature of the period.

The maturing Lovecraft began to look at the world from the perspective of the Georgian era. He took as his model for composition *The Reader* (1797), by Abner Alden, who had taught in an East Kingston, R.I., school at the turn of the century (Field 2.357). He began writing the date two hundred years earlier, and wrote with the archaic long s (*SL* 2.107).

Defending his emotional kinship with the period in later life, he explained its lure in more impersonal terms:

> What the eighteenth century really was, was the *final* phase of that perfectly unmechanised aera which as a whole gave us our most satisfying life. . . . Its hold upon moderns is due mainly to its *proximity*. . . . [I]t is the nearest to us of all the purely pre-mechanical periods; the only one with which we have

any semblance of personal contact (surviving houses and household effects in large quantities; association [for Americans] with high historic tension; fact that we can still talk with old men who in their youth talked with living survivors; vestigial customs and speech-forms in greater number than from earlier periods, etc., etc.) and whose ways are in any manner familiar to us save through sheer archaeological reconstruction. (SL 3.50)

This *"proximity"* Lovecraft felt most potently in youth, both in the houses, churches, and brick sidewalks of Providence, and the conservative mores of his family. It served to create in him a strong sense of background that would sustain him emotionally throughout his life.

Aside from the purely old New England ways of life, there was also a strong agrestic or pastoral component in Lovecraft's upbringing; and thus was his ideal of the English squire expanded to the notion of that of gentleman-farmer. Providence was at the turn of the century a city of only 175,000; and Lovecraft's house was not far from the wooded countryside, where he loved to wander. In his neighborhood were several small farmsteads that strongly affected him. He later boasted that he "knew the old New England country as well as if I had been a farmer's boy." More astonishing is the little-known fact that Whipple Phillips himself pastured milk cows and planted potatoes and corn on the property of 454 Angell Street (SL 3.217). Lovecraft avidly read all the old *Farmer's Almanacs* he could find around the house—he continued to be a collector throughout his lifetime—and became devoted to the pastorals of Thomson and Bloomfield, of Virgil and Hesiod.

Lovecraft valued his background highly, and the concept figures greatly in his thought. His racialist stance, for example, was partly based in his wish to keep his culture-stream—his one last emotional anchor—safe from erosion by an influx of foreign tradition. (See SL 3.207: "A native culture-heritage is the most priceless and indispensable thing any person has—*and he who weakens the grasp of a people upon their inheritance is most nefariously a traitor to the human species.*") More importantly for our purposes, background played an important part in Lovecraft's thoughts on the nature of art:

My theory of aesthetics is a compound one. To me beauty as we know it, consists of two elements; one absolute and objective, and based on rhythm and symmetry; and one relative and subjective, based on traditional associations with the hereditary culture-stream of the beholder. The second element is probably strongest with me, since my notions of enjoyment are invariably bound up with strange recallings of the past. (SL 2.229)

This passage has important repercussions in both Lovecraft's fiction and poetry. There is, in his finest work, an adherence to the traditional values of simplicity, proportion, and restraint; in these qualities we may trace the influence of the ancient classics filtered through the refined sensibilities of the Georgian age. But more explicitly, the substance of his art is often concerned with "recallings of the past."

Lovecraft's poetry provides some obvious examples. His work in this medium has often been condemned as soulless imitation of Augustan verse. This is true to a point, as he himself realized:

> I wrote only as a means of re-creating around me the atmosphere of my beloved 18th century favourites . . . everything succumbed to my one intense purpose of thinking and dreaming myself back into that world of periwigs and long s's which for some odd reason seemed to me the normal world. (SL 2.315)

Lovecraft here admits that recapturing the ethos of his background was not merely one motive for writing, but the primary driver for picking up his pen. The poetry is reflective of Lovecraft's background both in its form (rhymed couplets in the manner of Pope) and, often, in its subject matter; examples include "On a New England Village Seen by Moonlight" (1913), "An American to Mother England" (1916), and "Old Christmas" (1917). The last, a seemingly interminable 324-line paean to the traditions of his ancestors, begins with an invocation of background:

> Would that some Druid, wise in mystic lore,
> Might waft me backward to the scenes of yore;
> Midst happier years my wand'ring soul detain,
> And let me dwell in ANNA's virtuous reign:
> Warm in the honest glow of pure content,
> And share the boons of rustic merriment.
> Awake, Pierian Muse! and call to view
> The snow-clad groves and plains my grandsires knew . . . (AT 283)

Happily, Lovecraft largely shed his affected approach to poetry in the mid-1920s. It is ironic that when he eventually composed a verse on his concept of "Background," in the *Fungi from Yuggoth* (1929–30), he did so not in his beloved Augustan couplets but in a simple and understated sonnet form very much his own as a mature artist.

The background concept can help us explicate another of the *Fungi*, "Continuity." Lovecraft writes that certain objects hint "of locked dimensions harbouring years gone by" (l. 7), concluding:

> It moves me most when slanting sunbeams glow
> On old farm buildings set against a hill,
> And paint with life the shapes which linger still
> From centuries less a dream than this we know.
> In that strange light I feel I am not far
> From the fixt mass whose sides the ages are. (*AT* 94, ll. 9–14)

Lovecraft at such times felt an almost mystical sense of *identity* with his native and hereditary tradition. One such instance was his first sight, from high ground, of the colonial seaport Marblehead, Massachusetts, in 1922: "In a flash all the past of New England—all the past of old England—all the past of Anglo-Saxondom and the Western World—swept over me and identified with me the stupendous totality of all things in such a way as it never did before and never will again" (*SL* 3.126). Note the emphasis on the sense of unity, the feeling that one may "merge oneself with the whole historic stream and be wholly emancipated from the transient and the ephemeral" (*SL* 3.220). This acute *realization* of background, typically incited by regional scenic vistas, is what Lovecraft labeled "continuity." It is Lovecraft's personal "shock of recognition," his own most sought after emotional epiphany.

Turning to Lovecraft's fiction, we may better understand his use of realistic local color when we recall his emphasis on the importance of background in aesthetics. An author, he felt, "does best in founding his elements of incident and colour on a life and background to which he has a real and deep-seated relation" (*SL* 2.100). As he viewed it, the creative process is more natural—and the result more powerful—when an author uses the raw materials he knows best: the social customs, attitudes, institutions, geographical points of view, and other components of his background. The subjective or associative component is also vital to the work from the reader's perspective—the latter may relate more poignantly to the events of a tale when realistic detail is used, for such details will be instantly recognizable and set off a chain of personal associations in his mind. Hence the unique kind of sincerity that the reader often feels in Lovecraft's most artistically accomplished tales—think, for example, of "The Shunned House."

The New England background figures in many of Lovecraft's stories to varying extent. In a few (such as "From Beyond" [1920]), it has little or no role in the tale. For the most part, though, the local color of the region plays a pivotal part in the proceedings. The first tale to exploit the approach was "The Picture in the House" (1920), whose first paragraph suggests that in certain isolated dwellings common in desolate areas of the region, "strength, solitude, grotesqueness, and ignorance combine to form the perfection of the hideous" (*DH* 116). The narrator of the tale is forced by a storm to seek shelter in such a dwelling—despite his bias, acquired from "legends" he has heard, against such places. He finds that the interior, with its relics of Revolutionary days, would but for its condition be "a collector's paradise" (*DH* 118). The occupant soon descends from the floor above; with his ragged clothing and "weak voice full of fawning respect" which speaks "an extreme form of Yankee dialect" (*DH* 120), he at first seems merely a New England eccentric. We soon discover, though, that he is nothing less than a cannibal who is several hundreds of years old.

In this tale we see Lovecraft using elements of his background in the local color of the story. In later works he would make yet more extensive use of the history, folklore, speech, dress, mannerisms, beliefs, and topography of New England and its people. Tales such as "The Shunned House" (1924) and *The Case of Charles Dexter Ward* (1927) are inextricably intertwined with regional history. The latter is mixed so deftly with the events of these tales that scholarship has not yet been fully able to decide exactly what is fact and what fiction.

"The Colour out of Space" (1927), "The Dunwich Horror" (1928), "The Whisperer in Darkness" (1930), "The Shadow over Innsmouth" (1931), "The Haunter of the Dark" (1935), and others also make pivotal use of New England locales. They describe, with an insight only a native can possess, the loneliness and grandeur of the primal countryside, as well as villages spanning from the "ridiculously old" (*DH* 158) Dunwich to contemporary Providence.

Special note should be made of Lovecraft's use of regional characters. It has often been said that Lovecraft was unable to draw convincing characters, but this is belied by many of his rural portraits. The farmer Nahum Gardner in "The Colour out of Space" is one among many vivid Lovecraftian figures. He is one who has "always walked uprightly in the Lord's ways, so far as he knew" (*DH* 66), and we can feel nothing but horror as this simple man and his family are destroyed by an alien and incomprehensible force which alights upon his "trim white . . . house amidst its fertile grounds and orchards" (*DH* 57). Note also the use here of local customs as a narrative device; for soon after the advent of the strange meteorite the Gardners become "far from steady in their churchgoing or their attendance at the various social events of the countryside" (*DH* 61).

Few authors have used dialect as felicitously as Lovecraft did at his best; the finest example of this perhaps being the speech of the aged Zadok Allen of "Innsmouth." Allen, possessed of "a great tendency to philosophise in sententious village fashion" (*DH* 328), speaks in a distinctive (even if now extinct) grammar, vocabulary, and pronunciation of the region. This is in opposition to the ticket agent at the beginning of the tale, "whose speech shewed him to be no local man" (*DH* 305). Dialect also plays an important role in the verisimilitude of "The Picture in the House," "The Dunwich Horror," and "The Colour out of Space."[3]

How can we reconcile the seemingly disparate elements of cosmic horror and background in Lovecraft's fiction? The answer may be found in his explanation of the difference between his brand of cosmicism and that of his fellow fantaisistes Clark Ashton Smith and Donald Wandrei. The latter two authors often began and wholly conducted their tales in other dimensions or the far reaches of space; but Lovecraft felt his cosmic voyagings were most affecting when shown relative to the small realm of mankind, and to New England in particular. Again he refers to background as the basis of his excursions, this time not merely emotional but also imaginative:

> I recognise the impossibility of any correlation of the individual and the universal without an immediate visible world as a background—or starting-place for a system of outward-extending points of reference. I cannot think of any individual as existing except as part of a pattern—and the pattern's most visible and tangible areas are of course the individual's immediate environment; the soil and culture-stream from which he springs, and the milieu of ideas, impressions, traditions, landscapes, and architecture through which he must necessarily peer in order to reach the "outside" . . . I begin with the individual and think outward—appreciating the sensation of spatial and temporal liberation only when I can scale it against the known terrestrial scene. . . . With me, the very quality of being cosmically sensitive breeds an exaggerated attachment to the familiar and immediate—Old Providence, the woods and hills, the ancient ways and thoughts of New England. (*SL* 3.220–21)

---

3. A full examination of local color in HPL's fiction is beyond the scope of this paper; for a more expansive treatment, see Jason C. Eckhardt's "The Cosmic Yankee" (in *An Epicure in the Terrible*).

The cosmic vistas of Lovecraft's tales, then, are made even more meaningful when juxtaposed with the solid, familiar scenes and traditions of his regional background. The terrible alienness of his outside beings and realms is emphasized by their antipodal difference from the narratives' settings.

Let us now briefly retrace our steps. Lovecraft's bleak philosophy, born of his scientific disposition, inspired the cosmic horror of his tales. It also led him to the concept of relative values, which reinforced the role of his background—tradition in its largest sense—as an emotional anchor. His aesthetic sense was satisfied most by art that conjured associative images from the fund of his background; and he believed an artist must use his background as raw material for his art for the latter to be truly powerful. Thus did he choose New England local color as the basis for the realism he thought vital to the effectiveness of the weird tale. Aside from adding to the believability of his narratives, Lovecraft felt that the homely regional background best contrasted with his vast cosmic vistas, making the horror of the latter even more poignant.

To summarize the essence of background itself, we can surely do no better than Lovecraft himself did:

> I never can be tied to raw, new things,
> For I first saw the light in an old town,
> Where from my window huddled roofs sloped down
> To a quaint harbour rich with visionings.
> Streets with carved doorways where the sunset beams
> Flooded old fanlights and small windowpanes,
> And Georgian steeples topped with gilded vanes—
> These were the sights that shaped my childhood dreams.
>
> Such treasures, left from times of cautious leaven,
> Cannot but loose the hold of flimsier wraiths
> That flit with shifting ways and muddled faiths
> Across the changeless walls of earth and heaven.
> They cut the moment's thongs and leave me free
> To stand alone before eternity. (AT 92)

[I would like to thank David E. Schultz and Sam Gafford for their suggestions regarding this essay.]

I. GENERAL STUDIES

Toward a Reader-Response Approach to the Lovecraft Mythos

I. *The Lovecraft Mythos: The Great Not-To-Be-Named*

Over the past eight decades, readers and critics alike have discussed and written about the Lovecraft Mythos more than any other aspect of the author's work. Despite this, the Mythos remains the most poorly understood facet of Lovecraft's oeuvre. Opinions about its meaning and importance vary wildly. A numerically large contingent of readers and a particularly vehement set of critics believe it is the most significant thing about Lovecraft. They spend much time not merely categorizing Lovecraft's Mythos entities, but also inventing their own entities, writing stories about them, participating in role-playing games that involve them, reading comic books about them, watching movies that feature them, posting in internet forums about them, making jokes about them, and even believing in their literal existence. Mainstream reference works, forced by space constraints to convey Lovecraft's legacy in a few sentences, often mention the Mythos as the centerpiece of his fiction. Arrayed against this Mythos-focused faction are the leading Lovecraft scholars—including such notables as S. T. Joshi and David E. Schultz—who see the Mythos simply as background elements which Lovecraft drew upon to add highlights to his cosmic montage. These latter scholars have amassed such a Promethean understanding of Lovecraft through primary research that it is striking to note how well the Mythos-focused contingent has flourished in the face of their arguments.

Despite the inordinate scrutiny given it since Lovecraft's death in 1937, the Mythos has succeeded in evading explication or even definition. One indication of this is the still-ongoing attempt at taxonomy that was begun half a century ago. It is instructive to compare the attempt by Francis T. Laney (1942) to encompass and define Mythos entities with similar efforts by Bernadette Bosky (1982), Robert M. Price (1983, 1991b), and others. There are basic disagreements about what to include and what to exclude. Among those elements that are included, there is a basic inability to find a common definition of meaning or even basic attributes.

A good example of the latter is the entity called Nyarlathotep. Price describes this entity as "variously depicted but seems in general to be a messenger or harbinger of Azathoth, almost an antichrist who brings fatal knowledge of the end of all things to those unwise enough to summon him or seek him out. He may appear in human or monstrous form" (Price 1991b, 252). The use of so many qualifiers in this brief passage by Price—the scholar who more than anyone has specialized in the Mythos—is instructive. Of the same entity, Laney says: "The noxious Nyarlathotep, a mad, faceless god, forever howls blindly in the darkness, though somewhat lulled by the monotonous piping of two amorphous idiot flute players. He is also known as a mighty messenger, and bringer of strange joy to Yuggoth. Father of the million favored ones is another of his titles" (Laney 30). Given the small and well-bounded set of source material required to create such a definition, the lack of congruence between the two attempts is striking. And neither writer addresses Nyarlathotep's role in "The Whisperer in Darkness" (1930), where Lovecraft implies the entity is a crablike being who has donned a mask and robe to participate in a rather cosmic practical joke on an unsuspecting human being.

It is more convenient for systematizers to ignore such things, and ignore them they do. Examples abound. Shub-Niggurath is said to be "friendly to man" in "Out of the Aeons" (*HM* 273), but Price instead cites Lovecraft's joke letter to an adolescent fan and soberly instructs us that Shub-Niggurath is a "cloud-like entity" (Price 1991b, 252). Yog-Sothoth, clearly inimical to the human race in "The Dunwich Horror," is shown to be benign in "Through the Gates of the Silver Key." Unable to codify this type of discrepancy, taxonomers can only ignore it. Characterizations of Cthulhu, likewise, focus on the tentacled devil-god of "The Call of Cthulhu," but never, ever refer to the "spirit of universal harmony anciently symbolised as the octopus-headed god who had brought all men down from the stars" (*HM* 136). Nigguratl-Yig (in "The Electric Executioner"), though apparently derived from Yig ("The Curse of Yig" and others) and Shub-Niggurath ("The Whisperer in Darkness" and others), is likewise too bothersome to deal with. Yet Price and Will Murray have built a miniature critical cottage industry around Nug and Yeb, drawing most of their information on these entities (mentioned in Heald's "Out of the Aeons," de Castro's "The Last Test," and Zealia Bishop's "The Mound") from joking allusions in private correspondence (Price 1985a, 44).

Equally unsuccessful are attempts to decide which Lovecraft stories contribute to or belong to the Mythos. Assessments range from three of them (including one story that mentions no entities [Murray 1986, 30]) to all of them (Mosig 4). These attempts have led to some especially futile attempts at sub-distinguishing among "Yog-Sothoth Cycle of Myth," "Arkham Cycle," and other types of tales. Similarly confounding is the question of where the Mythos begins and ends. Some commentators have gone back to before Lovecraft was born, drafting the hapless Ambrose Bierce (we can only wish we might read the cynic's response to being drafted). Most of these same pundits agree the Mythos is still being supplemented by contemporary writers (mostly adolescents who enjoy creating odd-sounding names).

Mythos-oriented commentators have jumped through logical hoops to explain their inability to codify the Mythos. In the case of specific entities, they simply ignore information that doesn't fit. Sometimes they come up with situation-specific band-aids, as when they simply throw up their hands and label the inscrutable Nyarlathotep a shape-shifter. On a broader level, Murray remarks blithely that "a creative writer is not going to let the fact that he said something in print in one story hold him back from revising that concept in a later story, to make it better, to push it in another direction" (Murray 1984, 18). And, of course, the easiest out of all: that real myth patterns are inconsistent across various accounts, so Lovecraft must have made these rationally irreconcilable characterizations on purpose.

The work of a single scholar, Robert M. Price, serves to show that interpretative issues regarding the Mythos are impossible to pin down. Why does Price, who is one of the brightest critics in the field—he possesses multiple Ph.D.s in religious studies—find it so difficult to explain the Mythos? The body of material he has to work with is relatively small, has well-defined boundaries, and is rich in easily accessible source material. At first, Price suggested that Lovecraft originally conceived the Mythos entities as gods and subsequently transformed them to alien beings (Price 1986); he later rescinded this and concluded that they were always aliens (Price 1991a, 21). Despite this change of position, Price later published a genealogy of Mythos entities, an approach that has no meaning (a genealogy of aliens?) under his current exegesis (Price 1993b, 30).

Similarly, Price has been unsuccessful in enumerating which tales do and do not "belong" to the Mythos. In his paper "H. P. Lovecraft and the

Cthulhu Mythos," whose stated object is "to bring increased clarity to the Cthulhu Mythos debate," he proposed three myth cycles: the Dunsanian cycle, the Arkham cycle, and the Cthulhu cycle. After noting that "a piece of lore may be transferred between [sic] the three cycles," he concludes: "The stories draw on various bodies of lore indiscriminately, but that does not mean we cannot discriminate between the bodies of lore" (5). Price dodges the obvious question: if lore is interchangeable and used indiscriminately, why bother to set up the dichotomy? Price later reversed himself and posited that all Lovecraft stories draw from a large single body of lore (Panel Discussion 28); still later, he claimed that the stories themselves rather than the lore should be considered the Mythos (Price 1993a, 19). The various genealogies of Mythos entities Price has published mutate from appearance to appearance; at the conclusion of the most recent effort, which includes entities mentioned in no Lovecraft story or letter, he concludes sheepishly: "In compiling this genealogy I have rejected previous attempts, thinking it better to start fresh" (Price 1993b, 30).

All this indicates that the Mythos escapes categorization and explication. Critic Stanley Fish, citing a commentary on Milton, speaks of a similar situation: a set of interpretative issues that cannot be agreed upon by diverse editors, even though—as with Price's theories—"every position taken is supported wholly by convincing evidence." Fish concludes that

> these are problems that apparently cannot be solved, at least not by the methods traditionally brought to bear on them. What I would like to argue is that they are not *meant* to be solved, but to be experienced (they signify), and that consequently any procedure that attempts to determine which of a number of readings is correct will necessarily fail. What this means is that the commentators and editors have been asking the wrong questions and that a new set of questions based on a new set of assumptions must be formulated. (Fish 1980a, 164–65)

Later in this article I would like to suggest a few new assumptions under which we might henceforth consider the Mythos.

Not only has the Mythos escaped categorization and explication, it has even escaped naming. Derleth began during Lovecraft's lifetime by proposing "The Mythology of Hastur," which Lovecraft politely shrugged off. After Lovecraft's death, Derleth used "Cthulhu Mythology" and, more widely, "Cthulhu Mythos." Later, after Derleth died and scholars began to distinguish between Lovecraft's apparent intent as indicated in his tales and letters and Derleth's obfuscations, other names were proposed for part or all of it. Tierney offered the "Derleth Mythos"; Mosig, the "Yog-Sothoth Cycle of Myth"; and Burleson and Joshi, the "Lovecraft Mythos." Other names are to be expected in the future.

As mentioned, Lovecraft himself refused to give it a name. Mythos-oriented scholars have not interpreted this fact to mean that whatever the Mythos is, it is not something of a nature that can or should be named. This, in turn, calls to mind something mentioned in a Lovecraft story but never commented upon by Mythos-oriented critics: the *Magnum Innominandum*, the Great-Not-To-Be-Named. Perhaps this is what the Mythos should be called.

In conclusion, a survey of Mythos-related criticism reveals that the Cthulhu Mythos cannot be defined or bounded. The meaning of the Lovecraft Mythos is that it is beyond meaning. Not only can it not be explicated on a rational level, it cannot even be named.

II. *Yet Another Interpretation: The Mythos as Symbol*

Most Mythos criticism has taken the entities Lovecraft uses to be literal beings. One of the new set of assumptions I propose is that Lovecraft considered these entities to be symbolic rather than representative. A symbol combines a literal referent with a cluster of abstract or suggestive aspects. With this approach, literal catalogues of the attributes of various entities ("Cthulhu is large octopoid creature who smells real bad and likes to eat boats for lunch") would be superseded by attempts to understand the complex of emotional meanings associated with the entities. To date, no critic has done extensive study of the Mythos as symbol.[1]

Lovecraft left some clues that he created the Mythos because he needed his own, more powerful and aesthetically refined set of symbols than traditional myth and folklore. He often attributed the idea for a personal myth cycle to Lord Dunsany,[2] who he said "weaves a strangely potent fantastic

---

1. On specific entities, Donald R. Burleson has done good work in this area; for example, he sees Cthulhu as "most significant . . . for his effects in absence," concluding that Cthulhu is "an allegorization of the textually necessary absence of a center" (81). Derleth made some feeble and unsuccessful efforts to tie the HPL Mythos to the Christian Mythos. Others have made general statements about what the Mythos as a whole is meant to symbolize.

2. "Regarding the solemnly cited myth cycle of Cthulhu, Yog-Sothoth, R'lyeh, Nyarlathotep, Nug, Yeb, Shub-Niggurath, etc., etc.,–let me confess that this is a synthetic concoction of my own, like the populous and varied pantheon of Lord Dunsany's Pegāna" (HPL

beauty which has its roots in primitive myth and folklore" (*SL* 2.227). Taken to task by a colleague about his use of a personal myth cycle, Lovecraft defended himself this way:

> I really agree that Yog-Sothoth is basically an immature conception, & unfitted for really serious literature. The fact is, I have never approached really serious literature as yet. But I consider the use of actual folk myths as even more childish than the use of new artificial myths, since in employing the former one is forced to retain many blatant puerilities & contradictions of experience which could be subtilised or smoothed over if the supernaturalism were modeled to order for the given case. The only permanently artistic use of Yog-Sothothery, I think, is in symbolic or associative phantasy of the frankly poetic type; in which fixed dream-patterns of the natural organism are given embodiment & crystallization. (*SL* 3.293)

The impetus for this "symbolic phantasy" came from Lovecraft's enchantment with the natural world. He wrote to composer Harold Farnese about how he tried to effect or embody his imaginative impulses:

> In my own efforts to crystallise this spaceward outreaching, I try to utilize as many as possible of the elements which have, under earlier mental and emotional conditions, given man a symbolic feeling of the unreal, the ethereal, & the mystical—choosing those least attacked by realistic mental and emotional conditions of the present. Darkness—sunset—dreams—mists—fever—madness—the tomb—the hills—the sea—the sky—the wind—all these, & many other things have seemed to me to retain a certain imaginative potency despite our actual scientific analyses of them. Accordingly I have tried to weave them into a kind of shadowy phantasmagoria which may have the same sort of vague coherence as a cycle of traditional myth or legend—with nebulous backgrounds of Elder Forces & trans-galactic entities which lurk about this infinitesimal planet, (& of course about others as well), establishing outposts thereon, & occasionally brushing aside other accidental forms of life (like human beings) in order to take up full habitation. This is essentially the sort of notion prevalent in most racial mythologies—but an artificial mythology can become subtler & more plausible than a natural one, because it can recognize & adapt itself to the information and moods of the present. The best artificial mythology, of course, is Lord Dunsany's elaborate & consistently developed pantheon of Pegāna's gods. (*SL* 4.70ff)

---

to R. E. Howard, 14 August 1930; *SL* 3.166).

I. GENERAL STUDIES

Here Lovecraft makes what must be the clearest *précis* in print about the genesis and function of the Mythos. It is a set of simple steps.

1. Lovecraft sought a means to embody his imaginative impulses.

2. To do this, he identified those elements of reality which powerfully symbolize the unreal.

3. Having identified these elements, he created a "phantasmagoria" (a constantly shifting complex succession of things seen or imagined, or, literally, an assembly of phantasies) with the "vague coherence" of a cycle of traditional myth or legend.[3]

The passage cited above is, to my mind, by far the most important piece of primary information about the Mythos we have, even more so than the widely cited and discussed "All my stories" passage from a 1927 letter to *Weird Tales* editor Farnsworth Wright. The recommendation that we approach the Mythos as a set of symbols that are beyond "meaning" rather than literal representations of scary monsters with odd-sounding names is consistent with traditional approaches to myth itself. D. H. Lawrence put it this way:

> Myth is descriptive narrative using images. But myth is never an argument, it never has a didactic or moral purpose, you can draw no conclusion from it. Myth is an attempt to narrate a whole human experience, of which the purpose is too deep, going too deep in the blood and soul, for mental explanation or description. And the images of myth are symbols. They don't "mean something." They stand for units of human feeling, human experience. A complex of emotional experience is a symbol. And the power of a symbol is to arouse the deep emotional self, and the dynamic self, beyond comprehension. Many ages of accumulated experience still throb within a symbol. And we throb in response. (31)

These "units of human experience" will tend to vary from one human to another, based on their respective life experiences. Henri Peyre, in a well-known book on Symbolism, puts it this way:

> [A symbol] is a sign that as such demands deciphering. This sign represents or evokes in a concrete manner what is innate within it, the thing signified

---

3. HPL makes similar statements elsewhere, for example: "The fact is, I rather prefer purely original weird concepts as opposed to those derived from genuine folklore. Authentic folk-beliefs are likely to be insipid, ill-proportioned, freakish, and in general far less aesthetically effective than concepts formed by an author with a specific artistic purpose in mind" (HPL to E. Hoffmann Price, 29 May 1935; *SL* 4.169).

and more or less hidden. The two meanings, one concrete and the other ulterior and perhaps profound, are fused into a single entity in the symbol. The meaning beneath appearances is not necessarily a single one; the symbol is not a riddle within which human ingeniousness (that of an artist, a priest, a legislator, or a prophet) . . . has been pleased to enclose a certain meaning which would otherwise be too clear. . . . Within the symbol there is therefore a polyvalence, a multiplicity of meanings, certain ones addressed to all, others to the initiated alone. . . . Each person, on beholding a sign or symbol, may according to his turn of mind (concrete, esthetic, oneiric, metaphysical, artistic) extract from it the meaning that is most enriching for him or her. (8)

The notion that each person—in our scenario, each reader of Lovecraft—will extract a different meaning from the Mythos leads me to my next assumption: that the Mythos is most productively examined from the perspective of the reader's response to it.

III. *The Weird Tales Mythos*

For the bulk of his writing career, the majority of Lovecraft's fiction was submitted to and ultimately published in *Weird Tales* magazine. In considering the Lovecraft Mythos, *Weird Tales* is important for two reasons. Firstly, the very fact that *Weird Tales* was Lovecraft's primary fictional market shaped the manner in which the Mythos developed. Secondly, from the reader-response perspective (which will be further examined in section IV), the readership of *Weird Tales* was the first community of readers to experience the unfolding of the Mythos as it happened. As such, their experience of it is of historical interest.

In this section, I wish to examine how *Weird Tales* itself, and the circumstances of Lovecraft's perception of the magazine as his primary market, shaped the way the Mythos came to life. We can identify three factors which contributed to the development of the Mythos in *Weird Tales*.

First, Lovecraft knew that he would submit most if not all of what he wrote to *Weird Tales*. Lovecraft knew that editor Farnsworth Wright was generally inclined to accept his work (this was particularly true prior to 1930). In *Weird Tales*, Lovecraft knew that he had a captive audience. He took advantage of this well-defined forum, which offered a fairly well-bounded set of fairly faithful readers, as a place in which to create a new universe.[4]

---

4. Cf. HPL's own loyalty to early pulps *All-Story* and the *Argosy*. HPL claimed to have read *every issue* of the former magazine published between 1905 and 1914 ("To the *All-Story*

Secondly, starting in the mid-1920s, Lovecraft ghostwrote stories which he often knew were intended for *Weird Tales* but which would be published under other names (Adolphe de Castro, Hazel Heald, Zealia Bishop). This ability to put tales in front of the same readers of his signed tales broadened Lovecraft's "power base" and enhanced his ability to make the Mythos seem real. He realized that by using the Mythos in tales signed by others, he could add credibility to the Mythos and create among the reader community a unique set of sensations—awe, puzzlement, perhaps thrills—unachievable by any set of tales signed by a single author.

Thirdly, Lovecraft was in touch by mail with other major *Weird Tales* contributors. He could thus encourage their use of his Mythos properties and ask permission to appropriate post facto any entities or locales used in their stories. Again, Lovecraft's use of elements coined by such *Weird Tales* titans as Robert E. Howard and Clark Ashton Smith—writers highly regarded by the readership—leveraged the effectiveness of the Mythos in ways unavailable to any author operating autonomously, even one publishing tales in parallel under other names.

Why did Lovecraft undertake the use the Mythos in ghostwritten tales and encourage its use by writers who published in the magazine? Two reasons: the sheer fun of it, and the ability to lend realism to his creation. "It rather amuses the different writers to use one another's synthetic demons & imaginary books in their stories. This pooling of resources tends to build up quite a pseudo-convincing background of dark mythology, legendry, & bibliography," he wrote to a correspondent in 1934. He adds disingenuously: "of course none of us has the least wish actually to mislead readers" (*SL* 4.346). This was, in fact, his exact objective.[5]

Consider Lovecraft's compositional environment during the period of roughly 1925–35, when he created the Mythos using *Weird Tales*. A table that shows a chronology of the writing dates interwoven with the publication

---

Weekly," MW 496). He was also a prominent part of the *Argosy*'s community of readers, and was at one point something of a celebrity feature in its letter column (see de Camp 76–80). His sense of the continuity and community of the *Weird Tales* readership was undoubtedly fostered by these experiences.

5. There are many similar passages in *Selected Letters*, for example: "For the fun of building up a convincing cycle of synthetic folklore, all our gang frequently allude to the pet demons of others. . . . Thus our black pantheon acquires an extensive publicity and pseudo-authoritativeness it would otherwise not get. . . . All this gives it a sort of air of verisimilitude" (HPL to W. F. Anger, 14 August 1934; *SL* 5.16).

dates of Lovecraft's stories is useful here. It helps examine how his use of the Mythos in a certain tale *being written* for *Weird Tales* may have been affected by his knowledge that other tales had been or were *about to be published* in *Weird Tales* (see Appendix). There is little activity in the Mythos prior to 1926, primarily sporadic use of Abdul Alhazred and the *Necronomicon*. The inflection point for the development of the Mythos seems to have been "The Call of Cthulhu"—not the writing of the story, but its placement in *Weird Tales*.

As we have seen, Lovecraft's power over the *Weird Tales* readership was factorially increased by a fortuitous circumstance: his ghostwriting of horror tales for others' *Weird Tales* placements. Sometime in 1927, subsequent to the writing of "The Call of Cthulhu," Lovecraft revised Adolphe de Castro's "The Last Test" (item 54). Lovecraft, who was particularly bored with the revision of this tale, dropped some Mythos names into the story as expletives in a speech of one of the characters, without detail or explanation. It appears that Lovecraft knew that "Call" was to be published in *Weird Tales* (item 56) and that de Castro planned to submit his tale to *Weird Tales* as well. He therefore saw an opportunity to create some unusual reactions among the *Weird Tales* readership. He admitted as much in a letter:

> The reason for its echoes in Dr. de Castro's work is that the latter gentleman is a revision-client of mine—into whose tales I have stuck these glancing references for sheer fun. If any other clients of mine get work placed in W.T., you will perhaps find a still-wider spread of the cult of Azathoth, Cthulhu, and the Great Old Ones! (*SL* 3.166)

Lovecraft implies a cause-and-effect relationship between use of Mythos names in revision tales and their anticipated placement in *Weird Tales*.

We can see a similar relationship between Lovecraft's use of the Mythos in the composition of certain tales and his knowledge of stories that had been accepted for publication or had already published in the magazine. As Lovecraft was writing "The Dunwich Horror" in the summer of 1928 (item 60), he was aware that "The Last Test" was to be published in *Weird Tales* (item 61) and that he planned to submit "Dunwich" to *Weird Tales* as well. He thus seeded the story with six Mythos names. In writing "The Curse of Yig" sometime in 1928 for Zealia Bishop (item 58), Lovecraft refrained from loading on the Mythos names. This may be because he did not know if Bishop planned to submit the tale to *Weird Tales*. However, once "The Curse of Yig" was published in *Weird Tales* in November 1929 (item 66), Lovecraft knew that the *next* story he wrote for Bishop was likely to be published there as well. He thus loaded "The Mound" (item 67) with over a dozen Mythos names. (As it happened, this story was rejected by editor Farnsworth Wright.)

Of course, Lovecraft also measured the Mythos element in his signed offerings by the knowledge of what *Weird Tales* readers had previously seen. He wrote the *Fungi from Yuggoth* sonnet cycle with *Weird Tales* primarily in mind, mentioning four Mythos names in four separate sonnets (items 68–77).

The use of Mythos elements in "The Whisperer in Darkness" proves that Lovecraft had an eye on the reactions of the *Weird Tales* readers to his ongoing creation. Here we see a very different approach to use of Mythos names than in any of the previous signed fiction. Over two dozen names appear, and for the first time Lovecraft aggressively pulls from no less than five other writers (Howard, Dunsany, Bierce, Long, Chambers), past and present, for names. What caused this shift? A letter from a *Weird Tales* reader published in March 1930 clearly provides the answer. One N. J. O'Neail wrote to the letter column, "The Eyrie":

> I was very much interested in tracing the apparent connection between the characters of Kathulos, in Robert E. Howard's "Skull-Face," and that of Cthulhu, in Mr. Lovecraft's "The Call of Cthulhu." Can you inform me whether there is any legend or tradition surrounding that character? And also Yog-Sothoth? Mr. Lovecraft links the latter up with Cthulhu in "The Dunwich Horror" and Adolphe de Castro also refers to Yog-Sothoth in "The Last Test." Both these stories also contain references to Abdul Alhazred the mad Arab, and his *Necronomicon*. I am sure this is a subject in which many readers besides myself would be interested; something which could be reviewed in a series of articles similar to those [on common folk beliefs] written by Alvin F. Harlow. (Joshi, *Weird Writer in Our Midst* 71)

O'Neail's letter appears to have had a profound effect upon the manner in which Lovecraft subsequently developed the Mythos. As it happened, Lovecraft was just beginning his correspondence with Robert E. Howard—who is mentioned by O'Neail's letter—when the letter was printed. Five months later Lovecraft wrote Howard:

> [Frank Belknap] Long has alluded to the *Necronomicon* in some things of his—in fact, I think it is rather good fun to have this artificial mythology given an air of verisimilitude by wide citation. I ought, though, to write Mr. O'Neail and disabuse him of the idea that there is a large blind spot in his mythological erudition! (*SL* 3.166)

The manner in which and extent to which Lovecraft used Mythos names in "The Whisperer in Darkness" (item 83)—including a tip of the hat to both O'Neail and correspondent Howard by his use of the latter's "Kathulos"—shows that he was cognizant of its impact upon the readership. The effect upon a *Weird Tales* reader of encountering sixteen Mythos names created by six authors strung together in an independent clause leads us to the consideration of a reader-response approach to the Cthulhu Mythos.

IV. *Toward a Reader-Response Approach to the Lovecraft Mythos*

As mentioned at the outset of this paper, one of the most remarkable things about the Mythos is that no two scholars can seem to agree upon what it is. Even the single scholar who specializes in it cannot seem to choose among several theories he has successively proposed and discarded. Critic Stanley Fish, writing of texts in general and the phenomenon of multiple conclusions drawn from exactly the same evidence, remarks: "[these critical analyses] assume that meaning is embedded in the artifact [and therefore] will always point in as many directions as there are interpreters." Not only can an analysis prove something, it can prove anything. The text will not accept any single interpretation and will remain determinedly evasive (Fish 1980a, 166). Fish's assessment of how differing groups choose those interpretative strategies which prove their critical stance is reminiscent of the factionalism of Mythos criticism, with Robert M. Price accusing others of a critical heterodoxy even as he creates one of his own. Giving the example of Augustine's "rule of faith" for interpreting the Scriptures to find God's love for us throughout, even if it involves figurative interpretation, Fish continues:

> Interpretive communities are made up of those who share interpretive strategies not for reading (in the conventional sense) but for writing texts, for constituting their properties and assigning their intentions. In other words these strategies exist prior to the act of reading and therefore determine the shape of what is read rather than, as is usually assumed, the other way around. . . . [I]f a community believes in the existence of only one text, then the single strategy its members employ will be forever writing it. The first community will accuse the members of the second of being reductive, and they in turn will call their accusers superficial. The assumption of each community will be that the other is not correctly perceiving the "true text," but the truth will be that each perceives the text (or texts) its interpretive strategies demand and call into being. (Fish 1980a, 182)

On the basis of the evasiveness of the Lovecraft Mythos and its inability to yield to any critical faction, I would therefore propose a reader response approach to its meaning. Fish explains the reader-response approach this way:

> The concept is simply the rigorous and disinterested asking of the question, what does this word, phrase, sentence, paragraph, chapter, novel, play, poem, *do?*; and the execution involves *an analysis of the developing responses of the reader in relation to the words as they succeed one another in time.* . . . The category of response includes any and all of the activities provoked by a string of words: the projection of syntactical and/or lexical probabilities; their subsequent occurrence or non-occurrence; attitudes toward persons, or things, or ideas referred to; the reversal or questioning of those attitudes; and much more. . . . [T]he analyst . . . in his observations must take into account all that has happened (in the reader's mind) at previous moments, each of which was in turn its subject to the accumulating pressures of its predecessors. . . . [I]n an utterance of any length . . . the report of what happens to the reader is always a report of what has happened to that point [and] includes the reader's set toward future experiences but not those experiences. (Fish 1980b, 73–74)

Thus, it is the experience of an utterance—or of a sequence of utterances, or paragraphs, or stories—that is its meaning.

No one has yet considered exactly what the reaction of a reader might be as he or she encounters the name Cthulhu or Yog-Sothoth for the first time. Under the reader-response approach, we would focus on instances in the experience in reading Lovecraft when attention is compelled because an expectation has been fulfilled or disappointed by the appearance of an unpredictable element such as a Mythos name (Fish 1980b, 94). One approach of particular interest would be to concentrate on a very specific interpretative community: the readership of *Weird Tales* as the Mythos was experienced for the first time.[6] Discarding the auctorial intent upon which the earlier parts of this essay are based, we would instead concentrate on how a typical reader would react to Mythos-related cues found in stories appearing

---

6. Of course, there are a number of interpretative communities with which one might conduct a reader-response analysis in mind, for example, HPL critics who have read the stories dozens of times. But the *Weird Tales* readership was the first such community to experience the Mythos. And, if we fall back to auctorial intent, it is apparent from HPL's letters and the contents lists for prospective story collections he drew up near the end of his life that he never expected any interpretative community to reread his stories with the idea of collating the Mythos.

in *Weird Tales* bylined by Lovecraft or otherwise. The reader's activities would be at the center of the analyses, since they reflect the meaning—the experience—of the Mythos. The meaning they have is a consequence of making and revising assumptions, rendering and regretting judgments, coming to and abandoning conclusions, giving and withdrawing approval, specifying causes, asking questions, supplying answers, and solving puzzles (Fish 1980b, 172).

While conducting this exegesis is beyond the scope of this paper, it is likely that we would conclude that the Lovecraft Mythos means the reversal of expectations, the refusal of reality to adhere to preconceived schemas. Meanwhile, we can touch on some of the ideas that the reader-response approach to the Lovecraft Mythos implies.

When considering reader response to the Mythos, we might first consider what the reader experiences when he or she encounters a Mythos name in a story for the first time. Lovecraft said he created his Mythos names to evoke Arabic, Hebraic, Oriental, Celtic, and non-human sources:

> [A]s to those artificial names of unearthly places and gods and persons and entities—there are different ways of coining them. To a large extent they are designed to suggest—either closely or remotely—certain names in actual history or folklore which have weird or sinister associations with them. Thus "Yuggoth" has a sort of Arabic or Hebraic cast, to suggest certain words passed down from antiquity in the magical formulae contained in Moorish and Jewish manuscripts. Other synthetic names like "Nug" and "Yeb" suggest the dark and mysterious tone of Tartar or Thibetan folklore. Dunsany is the greatest of all name-coiners, and he seems to have three distinct models—the Oriental (either Assyrian or Babylonian, or Hebrew from the Bible), the classical (from Homer mostly), and the Celtic (from the Arthurian cycle, etc.). . . . I myself sometimes follow Dunsany's plan, but I also have a way strictly my own—which I use for devising non-human names, as of the localities and inhabitants of other planets. . . . The sounds ought not to follow any human language-pattern, and ought not to be derived from—or adapted to— the human speech-equipment at all. In other words, the whole design ought to be alien to both the ideas and the tongue of mankind—a series of sounds of different origins and associations, and capable only in part of reproduction by the human throat and palate and mouth. Just how far, and in what direction, such a sound-system ought to differ from human speech, must of course depend on how far and in what direction the imaginary users are represented as differing. . . . Usually my stories assume that the non-human sounds were known to certain human scholars in elder days, and recorded in secret manuscripts like the Necronomicon, the Pnakotic Manuscripts,

etc. In that case I likewise assume that the . . . ancient authors of these manuscripts gave the non-human names an unconscious twist in the direction of their own respective languages—as always occurs when scholars and writers encounter an utterly alien nomenclature and try to represent it to their own people. (HPL to Duane Rimel, 14 February 1934, *SL* 4.386ff)

He went on to remark that it is certainly advantageous now and then to introduce a coined word that has been shaped with great care from just the right associational sources (*SL* 4.386ff).

Aside from the reaction of a *Weird Tales* reader to a specific instance of Mythos nomenclature, we must consider how the Lovecraft Mythos appeared to a *Weird Tales* reader as it developed over the decade following 1925. This approach looks at the experience of the Mythos, and its resulting meaning to a reader, not at a point in time but over a time series. Studying the chronological publication information in the Appendix gives a sense of how the Lovecraft Mythos would have unfolded to a hypothetical *Weird Tales* reader.[7] For example, readers who read Lovecraft's sonnet "Nyarlathotep" (pub. Jan. 1930) would have last seen the name in a de Castro tale, "The Last Test" (pub. Nov. 1928), and perhaps dimly recall its prior appearance in "The Rats in the Walls" (pub. March 1924). As Wolfgang Iser, another pioneer of the reader-response approach, comments:

> Whatever we have read sinks into our memory and is foreshortened. It may later be evoked again and set against a different background with the result that the reader is enabled to develop hitherto unforeseeable connections. The memory evoked, however, can never reassume its original shape, for this would mean that memory and perception were identical, which is manifestly not so. The new background brings to light new aspects of what we had committed to memory; conversely these, in turn, shed their light on the new background, thus arousing more complex anticipations. Thus, the reader, in establishing these inter-relations between past, present, and future, actually causes the text to reveal its potential multiplicity of connections. (54)

Of course, not every reader of *Weird Tales* would have read every issue. Any single reader might have missed issues, skipped stories, and so on. But the implied reader for a reader-response analysis of the Lovecraft Mythos among the interpretative community of *Weird Tales* readers would likely have seen

---

7. For this exercise to be meaningful, the Appendix would have to be fleshed out with stories written by others—Robert E. Howard, Clark Ashton Smith, Frank Belknap Long, etc.—published in *Weird Tales*. I leave this task to some future Lovecraft scholar.

some combination of tales signed by Lovecraft, ghostwritten by Lovecraft, and written by Lovecraft's correspondents.

How can we characterize the interpretative community of *Weird Tales* readers? Lovecraft, speaking of coining Mythos names, realized that they were a heterogeneous group, remarking: "It really is a perplexing question to determine just what will strike the sensible reader right, & what will impress him as childish & meaningless stage paraphernalia. No two readers, of course, are alike, so one must use his own judgment about how wide a circle to aim at" (*SL* 4.70f). So who was the circle of readers—or to use the reader-response term, the implied reader—Lovecraft aimed at? Without doing any primary research, we can take Lovecraft's word for it: the bulk of *Weird Tales* readers were "crude and unimaginative illiterates" (*SL* 4.53). Elsewhere he was more expansive if no less harsh:

> [Pulp magazine editors] aim to please the very lowest grade of readers, probably because these constitute a large numerical majority. When you glance at the advertisements in these magazines . . . you can see what a hopelessly vulgar and stupid rabble comprise the bulk of the clientele. These yaps and nitwits probably can't grasp anything even remotely approaching subtlety. (*Uncollected Letters* 34)

Elsewhere he called *Weird Tales* readers "zippy morons" and suggested to Frank Long that his sense of these implied readers had affected his use of Mythos names: "It ruins one's style to have a publick of tame-souled half-wits hanging over one's head as one writes" (*SL* 2.79). However, despite all this there is evidence that Lovecraft believed that there was another, more intelligent implied reader of *Weird Tales*. He contrasts a small group of elite readers with what he termed "the Eyrie-bombarding proletariat": "It seems to me that there is little doubt but that *Weird Tales* is bought and read by large numbers of persons infinitely above the pulp-hound level—persons who relish Machen and Blackwood and M. R. James, and who would welcome a periodical of the Machen-Blackwood-James degree of maturity and fastidiousness if such were published" (*SL* 5.322). The response of this more literate section of the *Weird Tales* readership must have reacted in quite a different way than the "zippy morons" to this infamous passage to "The Whisperer in Darkness":

> I found myself faced by names and terms that I had heard elsewhere in the most hideous of connexions—Yuggoth, Great Cthulhu, Tsathoggua, Yog-Sothoth, R'lyeh, Nyarlathotep, Azathoth, Hastur, Yian, Leng, the Lake of Hali, Bethmoora, the Yellow Sign, L'mur-Kathulos, Bran, and the Magnum

Innominandum—and was drawn back through nameless aeons and inconceivable dimensions to worlds of elder, outer entity at which the crazed author of the *Necronomicon* had only guessed in the vaguest way. (*DH* 223)

Readers familiar with Dunsany ("Bethmoora"), Bierce ("Hali"), and Chambers ("the Yellow Sign") would have a much different experience of this passage—one of amusement, no doubt—than that of N. J. O'Neail, who had written in perplexity a few months before about the possible relation of Cthulhu and Kathulos.

The original meaning of the Lovecraft Mythos, then, lies in an examination of the way in which the *Weird Tales* readership—its original interpretative community—experienced it. Each successive interpretative community, including modern-day Lovecraft scholars and Mythos fans, will have a slightly different experience of it; thus, for them, it will have a slightly different meaning. The reader-response approach is a useful one to take in examining the Mythos, for it has tenaciously evaded explication, definition, and even naming. Without realizing it, a spectator at the 1986 World Fantasy Convention panel discussion on "What Is the Lovecraft Mythos?" perhaps came closest to the spirit of the reader-response approach. Speaking of the Mythos and her first reading of the tales, she remarked: "I think that's the magic of Lovecraft. I can still remember reading my first story; I didn't understand who the creatures were, and the names were strange to me, but that's what made it exciting" (Panel Discussion 24).

APPENDIX: Lovecraft Compositions and Publications during the *Weird Tales* Period

	Title	M	Y	Act	PP	Elements Used
1	The Rats in the Walls	9	23	wrtg		Nyarlathotep
2	The Unnamable	9	23	wrtg		
3	Ashes (Eddy)		23	wrtg		
4	The Ghost-Eater (Eddy)		23	wrtg		
5	The Loved Dead (Eddy)	?	23	wrtg		
6	The Festival	?	23	wrtg		Alhazred; *Necronomicon*
7	Dagon	10	23	pub	WT	Dagon
8	The Horror at Martin's Beach (Greene)	11	23	pub	WT	
9	Deaf, Dumb and Blind (Eddy)	?	24	wrtg		
10	The Picture in the House	1	24	pub	WT	
11	The Hound	2	24	pub	WT	Alhazred; Long; *Necronomicon*
12	Under the Pyramids (Houdini)	3	24	wrtg		
13	The Rats in the Walls	3	24	pub	WT	Nyarlathotep
14	Ashes	3	24	pub	WT	
15	Arthur Jermyn	4	24	pub	WI'	
16	The Ghost-Eater (Eddy)	4	24	pub	WT	
17	Hypnos	5–7	24	pub	WT	
18	The Loved Dead (Eddy)	5–7	24	pub	WT	
19	Under the Pyramids (Houdini)	5–7	24	pub	WT	
20	The Shunned House	10	24	wrtg		
21	The Festival	1	25	pub	WT	Alhazred; *Necronomicon*
22	The Statement of Randolph Carter	2	25	pub	WT	
23	Deaf, Dumb and Blind (Eddy)	4	25	pub	WT	
24	The Music of Erich Zann	5	25	pub	WI	
25	The Unnamable	7	25	pub	WT	
26	The Horror at Red Hook	8	25	wrtg		
27	He	8	25	wrtg		
28	In the Vault	9	25	wrtg		
29	The Temple	9	25	pub	WT	
30	In the Vault	11	25	pub	Ty	
31	The Tomb	1	26	pub	WI	
32	The Cats of Ulthar	2	26	pub	WT	
33	Cool Air	3	26	wrtg		
34	The Outsider	4	26	pub	WT	
35	Polaris	5	26	pub	NA	
36	The Moon Bog	6	26	pub	WT	
37	Nyarlathotep	7	26	pub	NA	Nyarlathotep
38	The Call of Cthulhu	Su	26	wrtg		
39	The Terrible Old Man	8	26	pub	WT	
40	He	9	26	pub	WT	

	Title	M	Y	Act	PP	Elements Used
41	The Strange High House in the Mist	9	26	wrtg		Elder Ones
42	Two Black Bottles (Talman)	10	26	wrtg		
43	Pickman's Model		26	wrtg		
44	The Silver Key	?	26	wrtg		
45	The Dream Quest of Unknown Kadath	1	27	wrtg		Azathoth; Elder Ones; Leng; Nyarlathotep
46	The Horror at Red Hook	1	27	pub	WT	
47	The Case of Charles Dexter Ward	3	27	wrtg		Alhazred; *Necronomicon*; Yog-Sothoth
48	The Colour out of Space	3	27	wrtg		
49	The White Ship	3	27	pub	WT	
50	The Green Meadow	Sp	27	pub	Va	
51	Two Black Bottles (Talman)	8	27	pub	WT	
52	The Colour out of Space	9	27	pub	AS	
53	Pickman's Model	10	27	pub	WT	
54	The Last Test (de Castro)	?	27	wrtg		Alhazred; Irem; Nug; Nyarlathotep; Olathoë; Pnakotic Mss.; Yeb; Yog-Sothoth
55	History of the *Necronomicon*	?	27	wrtg		Alhazred; Cthulhu; *Necronomicon*; Yog-Sothoth
56	The Call of Cthulhu	2	28	pub	WT	Alhazred; Cthulhu; Great Old Ones; Irem; *Necronomicon*; R'lyeh
57	Cool Air	3	28	pub	TM	
58	The Curse of Yig (Bishop)	?	28	wrtg		Yig
59	The Lurking Fear	6	28	pub	WT	
60	The Dunwich Horror	Su	28	wrtg		Alhazred; Cthulhu; *Necronomicon*; Old Ones; Shub-Niggurath; Yog-Sothoth
61	The Last Test (de Castro)	11	28	pub	WT	Alhazred; Irem; Nug; Nyarlathotep; Olathoë; Pnakotic Mss.; Yeb; Yog-Sothoth
62	The Silver Key	1	29	pub	WT	
63	The Dunwich Horror	4	29	pub	WT	Alhazred; Cthulhu; *Necronomicon*; Old Ones; Shub-Niggurath; Yog-Sothoth
64	The Electric Executioner (de Castro)	?	29	wrtg		Cthulhu (Cthulhutl); R'lyeh; Yig
65	The Hound	9	29	pub	WT	Alhazred; Leng; *Necronomicon*
66	The Curse of Yig (Bishop)	11	29	pub	WT	Yig
67	The Mound (Bishop)	1	30	wrtg		Azathoth; Cthulhu (Tulu); gnophkehs; K'n-Yan; Nug; Nyarlathotep; Olathoë; Old Ones; N'Kai; Relex; Shub-Niggurath; Tsathoggua; Yeb; Yig; Yoth

APPENDIX: Lovecraft Compositions and Publications during the *Weird Tales* Period

	Title	M	Y	Act	PP	Elements Used
68	The Courtyard (verse)	1	30	wrtg		
69	Hesperia (verse)	1	30	wrtg		
70	Star-Winds (verse)	1	30	wrtg		Yuggoth
71	Antarktos (verse)	1	30	wrtg		Elder Ones
72	The Bells (verse)	1	30	wrtg		
73	Nyarlathotep (verse)	1	30	wrtg		Nyarlathotep
74	Azathoth (verse)	1	30	wrtg		Azathoth
75	Mirage (verse)	1	30	wrtg		
76	The Elder Pharos (verse)	1	30	wrtg		
77	Alienation (verse)	1	30	wrtg		
78	Recapture	1	30	wrtg		
79	Recapture	5	30	pub	WT	
80	Medusa's Coil (Bishop)	5	30	wrtg		Cthulhu (Clooloo); Elder Ones; Mu; *Necronomicon*; Rlyeh; Shub-Niggurath; Yuggoth
81	The Rats in the Walls	6	30	pub	WT	Nyarlathotep
82	The Electric Executioner (de Castro)	8	30	pub	WT	Cthulhu (Cthulhutl); R'lyeh; Yig
83	The Whisperer in Darkness	9	30	wrtg		Alhazred; Azathoth; Bethmoora; Black Goat/Woods; Bran; Cthulhu; Hastur; Hounds of Tindalos; K'n-Yan; Lake of Hali; Leng; L'mur-Kathulos; Magnum Innominandum; N'Kai; *Necronomicon*; Pnakotic Mss.; R'lyeh; Shub-Niggurath; Tsathoggua; Yellow Sign; Yig; Yog-Sothoth
84	The Courtyard (verse)	9	30	pub	WT	
85	Star-Winds (verse)	9	30	pub	WT	
86	Hesperia (verse)	10	30	pub	WT	Yuggoth
87	Antarktos (verse)	11	30	pub	WT	Elder Ones
88	The Bells (verse)	12	30	pub	WT	
89	Nyarlathotep (verse)	1	31	pub	WT	Nyarlathotep
90	Azathoth (verse)	1	31	pub	WT	Azathoth
91	Mirage (verse)	2–3	31	pub	WT	
92	The Elder Pharos (verse)	2–3	31	pub	WT	
93	The Outsider	6–7	31	pub	WT	
94	Alienation (verse)	4–5	31	pub	WT	
95	At the Mountains of Madness	3	31	wrtg		Alhazred; Cthulhu; Elder Ones; Great Old Ones; Leng; *Necronomicon*; Olathoë; Old Ones; Pnakotic Mss.; R'lyeh; Tsathoggua; Yog-Sothoth

I. GENERAL STUDIES

	Title	M	Y	Act	PP	Elements Used
96	The Whisperer in Darkness	8	31	pub	WT	Alhazred; Azathoth; Bethmoora; Black Goat/Woods; Bran; Cthulhu; Hastur; Hounds of Tindalos; K'n-Yan; Lake of Hali; Leng; L'mur-Kathulos; Magnum Innominandum; N'Kai; *Necronomicon*; Pnakotic Mss.; R'lyeh; Shub-Niggurath; Tsathoggua; Yellow Sign; Yig; Yog-Sothoth
97	The Strange High House in the Mist	10	31	pub	WT	Elder Ones
98	The Trap (Whitehead)		31	wrtg		
99	The Shadow over Innsmouth	12	31	wrtg		Cthulhu; Dagon
100	The Dreams in the Witch House	2	32	wrtg		Alhazred; Azathoth; *Black Book*; *Book of Eibon*; *Necronomicon*; Nyarlathotep; Shub-Niggurath; *Unaussprechlichen Kulten*
101	The Trap (Whitehead)	3	32	pub	ST	
102	The Man of Stone (Heald)		32	wrtg		Black Goat; *Book of Eibon*; R'lyeh; Shub-Niggurath; Tsathoggua; Yoth
103	In the Vault	4	32	pub	WT	
104	Winged Death (Heald)	Su	32	wrtg		Cthulhu (Clulu); Tsathoggua (Tsadogwa)
105	The Man of Stone (Heald)	10	32	pub	WS	Black Goat; *Book of Eibon*; R'lyeh; Shub-Niggurath; Tsathoggua; Yoth
106	The Music of Erich Zann	10	32	pub	ES	
107	The Horror in the Museum (Heald)	10	32	wrtg		Azathoth; *Book of Eibon*; Chaugnar Faugn; Cthulhu; Gnoph-Keh; Leng; *Necronomicon*; Old Ones; Pnakotic Mss.; Rhan-Tegoth; Shub-Niggurath; Tsathoggua; *Unaussprechlichen Kulten*; Yog-Sothoth; Yuggoth
108	The Cats of Ulthar	2	33	pub	WT	
109	Through the Gates of the Silver Key	3	33	wrtg		Alhazred; Cthulhu; Irem; Leng; *Necronomicon*; Pnakotic Mss.; R'lyeh; Tsathoggua; Yian-Ho; Yog-Sothoth; Yuggoth
110	Out of the Aeons (Heald)	?	33	wrtg		Alhazred; Black Book; *Book of Eibon*; Elder Ones; Ghatanothoa; Leng; *Unaussprechlichen Kulten (Nameless Cults)*; Mu; *Necronomicon*; Nug; Pnakotic Mss.; Shub-Niggurath; Tsathoggua; Yeb; Yig; Yuggoth

APPENDIX: Lovecraft Compositions and Publications during the *Weird Tales* Period

Title	M	Y	Act	PP	Elements Used
111 The Dreams in the Witch House	7	33	pub	WT	Alhazred; Azathoth; *Black Book*; *Book of Eibon*; *Necronomi-*
112 The Horror in the Museum (Heald)	7	33	pub	WT	*con*; Nyarlathotep; Shub-Niggurath; *Unaussprechlichen Kulten* Azathoth; *Book of Eibon*; Chaugnar Faugn; Cthulhu; Gnoph-Keh; Leng; *Necronomicon*; Old Ones; Pnakotic Mss.; Rhan-Tegoth; Shub-Niggurath; Tsathoggua; *Unaussprechlichen Kulten*; Yog-Sothoth; Yuggoth
113 The Thing on the Doorstep	8	33	wrtg		Alhazred; Azathoth; *Book of Eibon*; *Necronomicon*; Shub-Niggurath; *Unaussprechlichen Kulten*
114 The Festival	10	33	pub	WT	Alhazred; *Necronomicon*
115 The Other Gods	11	33	pub	FF	
116 The Horror in the Burying Ground (Heald)	7	33	wrtg		
117 Polaris	2	34	pub	FF	
118 Winged Death (Heald)	3	34	pub	WT	Cthulhu (Clulu); Tsathoggua (Tsadogwa)
119 Celephaïs	5	34	pub	MT	
120 From Beyond	6	34	pub	FF	
121 Through the Gates of the Silver Key	7	34	pub	WT	Alhazred; Cthulhu; Irem; Leng; *Necronomicon*; Pnakotic Mss.; R'lyeh; Tsathoggua; Yian-Ho; Yog-Sothoth; Yuggoth
122 Beyond the Wall of Sleep	10	34	pub	FF	
123 The Other Gods	10	34	pub	TSS	
124 The Music of Erich Zann	11	34	pub	WT	
125 Till A' the Seas" (Barlow)	1	35	wrtg		
126 The Shadow out of Time	3	35	wrtg		Alhazred; *Book of Eibon*; *Cultes de Goules*; *De Vermis Mysteriis*; *Necronomicon*; Old Ones; Nyarlathotep; Pnakotic Mss.; *Tsathoggua*; *Unaussprechlichen Kulten*
127 The Doom that Came to Sarnath	3-4	35	pub	MT	
128 Out of the Aeons (Heald)	4	35	pub	WT	Alhazred; *Black Book*; *Book of Eibon*; Elder Ones; Ghatanothoa; Leng; *Unaussprechlichen Kulten (Nameless Cults)*; Mu; *Necronomicon*; Nug; Pnakotic Mss.; Shub-Niggurath; Tsathoggua; Yeb; Yig; Yuggoth

APPENDIX: Lovecraft Compositions and Publications during the *Weird Tales* Period

	Title	M	Y	Act	PP	Elements Used
129	Arthur Jermyn	5	35	pub	WT	
130	The Quest of Iranon	7-8	35	pub	Ga	
131	The Challenge from Beyond	8	35	wrtg		Eltdown Shards
132	The Challenge from Beyond	9	35	pub	FM	Eltdown Shards
133	The Disinterment (Rimel)	2	35	wrtg		
134	The Diary of Alonzo Typer (Lumley)	10	35	wrtg		*Book of Dzyan; Book of Eibon* (*Livre d'Eibon*); *De Vermis Mysteriis;* Pnakotic Mss.; Shub-Niggurath; Yian-Ho
135	The Haunter of the Dark	11	35	wrtg		Azathoth; *Book of Dzyan; Book of Eibon* (*Liber Ivonis*); *Cultes des Goules; De Vermis Mysteriis; Necronomicon;* Nyarlathotep; Old Ones; Pnakotic Mss.; *Unaussprechlichen Kulten;* Yog-Sothoth; Yuggoth

Key to PP (place of publication) codes:

AS	*Amazing Stories*		ST	*Strange Tales of Mystery and Terror*
ES	*Evening Standard* (London)		TM	*Tales of Magic and Mystery*
FF	*Fantasy Fan*		TSS	*True Supernatural Stories*
FM	*Fantasy Magazine*		Va	*Vagrant*
GA	*Galleon*		WS	*Wonder Stories*
MT	*Marvel Tales*		WT	*Weird Tales*
NA	*National Amateur*			

Lovecraft's Cosmic Imagery

H. P. Lovecraft's weird tales are distinguished by their unique cosmic orientation—the horror stems not from traditional supernatural themes, but from the concept of an indifferent and unknowable universe. During his career Lovecraft evolved a characteristic set of imagery to convey cosmic horror, imagery reflecting his view of the universe as a vast, purposeless machine. Before we examine that imagery, let us consider how the central tenet of Lovecraft's worldview—that the universe is governed by an immutable and only partially knowable set of laws—provided both the motivation for his art and an infinite canvas upon which to create it.

First, the laws governing the universe are fixed. There is no purpose or direction to the cosmos, for it is only a well-oiled Newtonian machine. Lovecraft accepted this concept intellectually, but found it imaginatively stifling, insisting that "a highly organised man can't exist endurably without mental expansions beyond objective reality" (SL 3.140). He was therefore compelled to create fiction which, by incorporating his imaginings as *extensions* rather than *negations* of reality, accommodated both his intellectual and his emotional needs.

Lovecraft had the opportunity to create such fiction because of the second part of the proposition above, that the universe's laws are only partially knowable: "Absolute reality is forever beyond us—we cannot form even the vaguest conception of what such a thing would be like, for we have no terms to envisage entity apart from those subjective aspects which reside wholly in our own physiology and psychology" (SL 2.301). This gave his imagination free reign to create the alien realms and entities that are the sources of his horror. "If one must weave cobwebs of empty aether," he said, "let them supply a decorative element to those cosmic spaces which would otherwise be an ambiguous and tantalizing void" (SL 3.147).

Lovecraft did not seriously attempt weird fiction until he was twenty-six, when his philosophy was solidly established. It is clear from a letter of September 1932 that his aesthetic of the weird was a direct outgrowth of the worldview outlined above:

> It is true that we no longer credit the existence of discarnate intelligence & superphysical forces around us, & that consequently the traditional "Gothick" tale of spectres and vampires has lost a large part of its power to move our emotions. But in spite of this disillusion there remain two factors largely unaffected—& in one case actually increased—by the change: first, a sense of impatient rebellion against the rigid & ineluctable tyranny of time, space, & natural laws—a sense which drives the imagination to devise all sorts of plausible hypothetical defeats of that tyranny—& second, a burning curiosity concerning the vast reaches of unplumbed and unplumbable cosmic spaces which press down tantalizingly on all sides of our pitifully tiny sphere of the known. (SL 4.70)

But Lovecraft the philosopher had set Lovecraft the artist a formidable task: to depict with mere words that which forever lies beyond the sphere of the known. Over the course of his twenty-year career he made great strides in his attempt to imagine the unimaginable, to describe the indescribable. From the clumsy attempts at conveying the outré in "Dagon" (1917) to the magnificent cosmic montage in "The Haunter of the Dark" (1935), he shows substantial artistic progress, refining and expanding the imagery he used to achieve his purpose. Examining these image patterns will lend the reader a greater understanding of Lovecraft's intent and a greater appreciation both of the scope of his imagination and of his skill as stylist.

We should pause to note Lovecraft's assertion that imagery played a central role in art. Fiction and poetry, he said, "must be read wholly for imagery and not for ideas" (SL 2.118). His own motive for authorship was "a literary ambition confined altogether to the recording of certain images connected with bizarrerie" (SL 2.111). Lovecraft also wrote of "a wish to get on paper some of the images . . . constantly running through my mind" (SL 2.107). We will see that he drew upon his conception of the universe in his fiction to create imagery conveying its vastness, its magnificence, and ultimately, its terror.

The narrator of "Hypnos" (1922) may have been speaking for Lovecraft when he decried "that chief of torments—inarticulateness" (D 166). The author was captivated by the wonders of the universe from adolescence, and he never ceased refining and clarifying his imaginative vision. Throughout his life, Lovecraft's letters to more traditionally inclined correspondents are filled with passages describing his conception of the cosmos. The universe is simply "blind force operating according to fixed & eternal patterns inherent in entity" (SL 2.124–25). In another early letter he described the cosmos as a "ceaseless and boundless rearrangement of electrons, atoms, and molecules which constitute the blind but regular mechanical patterns of cosmic activity" (SL 2.41).

This mental picture of the cosmos is the basis for one of the most pervasive motifs in the fiction, that of *kaleidoscopic* imagery. The technique of showing a rapidly shifting panorama of images first appears in "Beyond the Wall of Sleep" (1919), Lovecraft's earliest attempt to depict the vast Outside. The story is mediocre, but the narrator's dream-visions have impressive impact: "Walls, columns, and architraves of living fire blazed effulgently. . . . Blending with this display of palatial magnificence, or rather, supplanting it at times in kaleidoscopic rotation, were glimpses of wide plains and graceful valleys, high mountains, and inviting grottoes" (*D* 32). Note that Lovecraft pauses to clarify the way in which these visions are perceived, a rhetorical device that both adds to the prose realism and enforces the meaning. In a story written the following year, "From Beyond" (1920), there is a similar exponent. Here an experimental machine invokes a vision that "was wholly kaleidoscopic, . . . [a] jumble of sights, sounds, and sense-impressions" (*D* 95).

More impressive than these stories is "The Shunned House" (1924), in which Lovecraft successfully grafts a transdimensional entity onto a homely Providence dwelling. This entity is reminiscent of a vampire in that it saps the life-force of other beings; but, in an innovative twist, it is also mentally invasive upon its victims. The narrator speculates upon the far-reaching nature of the phenomenon, using the language of Einsteinian physics and quantum mechanics. Near the climax of the tale, during the vigil of the narrator and his uncle in the house's basement, the elderly man experiences a disturbing dream-vision that again embodies Lovecraft's conception of the universe as characterized by "kaleidoscopic pattern-seething" (SL 3.230):

> There was a suggestion of queerly disordered pictures superimposed one upon another; an arrangement in which the essentials of time as well as space seemed dissolved and mixed in the most illogical fashion. In this kaleidoscopic vortex of phantasmal images were occasional snapshots, if one might use the term, of singular clearness but unaccountable heterogeneity. (MM 255–56)[1]

---

1. The importance of this passage was first pointed out by David E. Schultz in his essay "The Lack of Continuity in *Fungi from Yuggoth*" 15. Schultz contends that HPL's sonnet

The wording of this descriptive passage recalls numerous passages in Lovecraft's letters, notably his pronouncement to the Gallomo correspondence club that "the cosmos is a mindless vortex" (SL 1.156). Happily, he here does not offer a succession of architectural and landscape images (cf. "Beyond the Wall of Sleep") as examples of what Elihu Whipple saw. Instead, he implies a disturbing *diversity* of possibilities with the closing antithesis. The device of the kaleidoscope enabled Lovecraft to convey both the meaningless, never-ending interactions of matter and the incomprehensible extent of the universe.

Lovecraft grew more and more adventurous in the use of his cosmic kaleidoscope. The hallucinatory "ride on a comet's tail" that the sailor Johansen experienced during his return voyage from R'lyeh in "The Call of Cthulhu" (1926) is a notable example. Even this is exceeded by the "bizarre conceptions" that composed Danforth's ravings at the end of At the Mountains of Madness (1931). Lovecraft's bold use of a kaleidoscopic coda for this most far-reaching of tales (a use about which colleagues and editors alike expressed reservations) indicates how central this motif was to his imagination. It also reminds us of the astonishing and surrealistic sequence of visions that concludes his experiment in the prose poem "Nyarlathotep" (1920).

It may be noted that Lovecraft's boundless kaleidoscopic excursions take place largely within the human consciousness itself: "As I gazed, I perceived that my own brain held the key to these enchanting metamorphoses" ("Beyond the Wall of Sleep," D 32).[2] This approach represents the defeat of those sensory limitations that Lovecraft the dreamer found so repressive. Perhaps the Providence gentleman secretly hoped, like Lord Northam in the fragment "The Descendent" (1926?), that "he held within his own half-explored brain that cryptic link which would awaken him to elder and future lives in forgotten dimensions; which would bind him to the stars, and to the infinities and eternities beyond them" (D 362).

Both in association with kaleidoscopic imagery and independently of it, Lovecraft often employs *sound* to convey horror. This thread is evident in his *Commonplace Book*; for example:

[14] Hideous sound in the dark.

---

sequence is not a connected narrative but "a congeries of dreams and memories." He supports this ingenious theory by citing this passage and also the passage from "Beyond the Wall of Sleep" above.

2. Cf. Crawford Tillinghast's boast in "From Beyond" (1920): "'We shall overleap time, space, and dimensions, and without bodily motion peer to the bottom of creation'" (D 91).

[39] Sounds—possibly musical—heard in the night from other world or realms of being. (CE 5.220, 221)

Certainly Lovecraft's enthusiasm for M. P. Shiel's "The House of Sounds" — with its famous enigma, "Can you not hear the *sound of the world?*"—stems from his imaginative affinity for sound imagery.

Just as Lovecraft's unfortunate protagonists do not see the word-pictures quoted above with their eyes, they do not hear the outré sounds with their ears. Perception takes place in the brain, and is not derived from information gathered through the usual sense-organs. Karl Heinrich, commander of the German submarine and discoverer of an antediluvian undersea city in "The Temple" (1920), is the victim of an "aural delusion." A sedative removes his impression that a "wild yet beautiful chant or choral hymn" (D 70) is coming from the temple outside his ship. The narrator of "Beyond the Wall of Sleep," similarly, experiences "a weird lyric melody" of "chords, vibrations, and harmonic ecstasies" (D 32) to accompany his dream-vision.

Sometimes Lovecraft's sounds take the form of a simple drone: for example the "infinitely faint, subtly vibrant, and unmistakably musical" sound that held "a quality of surpassing wildness" (D 93–94) in "From Beyond." Similar images appear in both "The Music of Erich Zann" (1921) ("an exquisitely low and infinitely distant musical note" [DH 89]) and "Hypnos" ("a low and damnably insistent whine from very far away" [D 169]). Note the adjectives associated with sound in these stories: faint, low, vibrant, droning, wild, insistent, deliberate, purposeful, clamoring, mocking, calling. This is Lovecraft's music of the spheres, but it is more of a discord—an aural representation of a chaos of atoms.

It is this chaos, indeed, that echoes symbolically in the voice of great Cthulhu—"a subterrene voice or intelligence shouting monotonously in enigmatical sense-impacts uninscribable save as gibberish" (DH 129). We cannot understand the import of these sounds. To us they can never have meaning, for we do not possess the "sense-equipment" (a term Lovecraft was fond of using in letters)[3] to interpret them.

---

3. S. T. Joshi has noted the influence of Hugh Elliot's *Modern Science and Materialism* (New York: Longmans, Green & Co., 1919) on HPL's thought regarding man's sensory limitations. Cf. pp. 2–3: "Let us first ask why it is that all past efforts to solve ultimate riddles have failed, and why it is that they must continue to fail. It is, in the first place, due to the fact that all knowledge is based on sense-impressions, and cannot, therefore, go beyond what the senses perceive. . . . Now, supposing that we happened to have a thousand senses instead of five, it is clear that our conception of the universe would be

In the later fiction, Lovecraft modified his sound exponent, introducing the element of *rhythm*.[4] Fictional imagery again echoes the author's conception of the universe, here as explained in a letter to Elizabeth Toldridge of 26 November 1929:

> One of the fixed conditions of this infinite & eternal entity [i.e., the cosmos] is pattern or rhythm—certain regular relationships of part to part within the fabric of the unchanging whole; & specialized aspects of this rhythm appear to be the basis of our notions of time, space, motion, matter, & change. (SL 2.86)

The rhythm motif is explicated and fully worked out in "The Dreams in the Witch House" (1932). This story is best thought of as Lovecraft's Magnificent Failure—its uneven execution is not equal to its breathtaking conceptions, which are some of the most original in imaginative literature. Walter Gilman has a fever, one symptom of which is hearing so sensitized that it gives him a sense of "strident pandemonium" (MM 261). The choice of the noun, with its overtones of cosmic chaos, is no accident. Soon Gilman experiences strange dreams (actually entries into other dimensions) accompanied by a "shrieking, roaring confusion of sound . . . past all analysis as to pitch, timbre, or rhythm" and having "obscure, relentlessly inevitable fluctuations" (MM 268). In the same way that he connects Keziah Mason's witchcraft with non-Euclidian mathematics, Lovecraft links sound—again symbolic of the "sound" of the universe itself—with the ritual of the Black Mass: "the chants of the Sabbat were patterned on this faintly overhead pulsing which no earthly ear could endure in its unveiled spatial fulness" (MM 293). One of the things Gilman dreads most of all is experiencing "the monstrous burst of Walpurgis-rhythm in whose cosmic timbre would be concentrated all the primal, ultimate space-time seethings which lie behind the massed spheres of matter and sometimes break forth in measured reverberations that penetrate faintly every layer of entity" (MM 291).

Even more important to Lovecraft's fiction than the rhythm motif was the other component he mentioned to Toldridge: that of *pattern*. The idea of pattern, and the related ideas of proportion, symmetry, and geometry, combine to form the most important motif of Lovecraft's cosmic imagery. In *The Case*

---

extremely different from what it now is."

4. An early precursor of this rhythm element is found the section of "The Poe-et's Nightmare" (1916) called "Aletheia Phrikodes" ["The Hideous Truth"]: "A touch of rhythm celestial reach'd my soul, / Thrilling me more with horror than with joy" (AT 44).

of Charles Dexter Ward (1927), Dr. Willett is sent temporarily insane by something he sees in Joseph Curwen's underground laboratory. For this reaction Lovecraft offers the following explanation: "There is about certain outlines and entities a power of symbolism and suggestion which acts frightfully on a sensitive thinker's perspective and whispers terrible hints of obscure cosmic relationships and unnamable realities behind the protective illusions of common vision" (MM 207). Similarly, "the *general outline*" of the bas-relief of Cthulhu is the "most shockingly frightful" (*DH* 127) aspect of the object. The "general shape" of the black stone in "The Whisperer in Darkness" (1930), too, "almost defies the power of language" (*DH* 222). Of the ichthyic designs on a piece of bizarre jewelry in "The Shadow over Innsmouth" (1931), the narrator notes that "every contour" invoked "the ultimate quintessence of unknown and inhuman evil" (*DH* 312).[5]

What could make a simple outline so disturbing? An outline is merely a line bounding a geometrical figure. It is geometry, indeed, that is the very source of these objects' horror. The black stone's cutting was guided by unknown and "outlandish geometrical principles," while on the jewelry "the patterns all hinted of remote secrets and unimaginable abysses in time and space."

The issue of geometry and symmetry in Lovecraft is a complex one. Let us begin by recalling Lovecraft's belief that humankind's aesthetic sense consists of two elements: "one absolute and objective, and based on rhythm and symmetry; and the other subjective" (SL 2.229). In his essay "Some Causes of Self-Immolation" (1931), Lovecraft lists eleven instincts and their associated emotions (e.g., nutrition and hunger). To this classification, credited to William McDougall, he adds: "The present writer feels convinced that one basic instinct . . . ought to be added to this list; namely, an instinct for symmetry in the abstract, based upon habituation to the ceaseless rhythms and regularities (astronomical and otherwise) of the terrestrial environment" (CE 5.79).

Lovecraft, then, thought that a craving for symmetry was inbred in the human race. He also believed that the universe itself is possessed of symmetry, that it operates in a predictable way. Recall his description of the cosmos to Elizabeth Toldridge—"regular relationships of part to part." Such fixed relations imply order and symmetry. Perhaps as a result, Lovecraft tended to

---

5. Note also the disturbing "contours, dimensions, [and] proportions" (MM 56) of the Old Ones' city in *At the Mountains of Madness*. The city's layout, like its counterparts in "The Nameless City" (1921) and "The Shadow out of Time" (1934–35), here reflects the non-human nature of its builders.

I. GENERAL STUDIES

envision the universe in terms of geometry. Relating a dream in which he was a participant in a sort of séance, Lovecraft wrote that his vision "began to take in vast vistas of space—represented by aggregates of gigantic cubes scattered along a gulf of violet radiation" (*Dreams and Fancies* 38). The use of the word "represented" is insightful. Lovecraft, of course, did not literally believe the universe was a collection of cubes; rather, the image is a mental construct or metaphor that helps us envision its underlying order or fabric. Using related imagery, the crablike space beings in "The Whisperer in Darkness" (1931) reveal to a startled Albert Wilmarth the place of our cosmos in "the unending chain of linked cosmos-atoms" (*DH* 256).[6] Walter Gilman's alternate dimensions, too, are populated by "prisms, labyrinths, clusters of cubes and planes, and Cyclopean buildings" (MM 267).

If geometry informs the universe, then mastery of geometry is the key to the universe's domination. Keziah Mason uses the unusual angles of her room in the Witch House to enter other dimensions. Wilbur Whateley of "The Dunwich Horror" (1928) needs to "learn all the angles of the planes" in preparation for his attempt to "clear off the earth" (*DH* 184).

The discoveries of Max Planck and Albert Einstein did not move Lovecraft, "a mechanistic materialist of the line of Leucippus, Democritus, Epicurus, and Lucretius—and in modern times, Nietzsche and Haeckel" (SL 2.160), away from his position that the universe operated in an orderly fashion. Lovecraft contended (as did Einstein) that the irregularities indicated by quantum physics need not mean the universe operates randomly:

> What most physicists take the quantum theory, at present, to mean, is *not that any cosmic uncertainty exists* as to which of several courses a given reaction will take; but in certain instances *no conceivable channel of information can ever tell human beings which course will be taken*, or by what course a certain observed result came about. (*SL* 3.228)

More than one hundred years after Lovecraft's birth, scientific thought tends to disagree. But Lovecraft's mechanistic universe was intact—except in his fiction, where he used *asymmetry* to symbolize "that most terrible conception of the human brain—a malign and particular suspension or defeat of those fixed

---

6. We might note that Henry Akeley, who allows himself to be lured by the aliens, was (like Walter Gilman) "a notable student of mathematics" (*DH* 215). This aptitude is amusing when we recall HPL's comment to Frank Belknap Long on 22 November 1930—less than a month after finishing the tale—that "only train'd mathematicians are able to conduct original research into the question of 'what is anything?'" (*SL* 3.223).

laws of Nature which are our only safeguard against the assaults of chaos and the daemons of unplumbed space" (*D* 263). If the universe operated according to an intelligible Euclidian geometry, then the existence of objects adhering to non-Euclidian geometry was profoundly unnatural.[7]

The Old Ones of *At the Mountains of Madness* possess both knowledge of higher mathematics and experience in transcosmic voyaging. Their architectural designs, Lovecraft tell us, "displayed a profound use of mathematical principles, and were made up of obscurely symmetrical curves and angles" (MM 56). (The brilliant adjectival pair "obscurely symmetrical" shows yet again Lovecraft's brilliance as stylist, as the narrator clings to the hope if finding order in chaos.)

The spectacular description of the city itself that opens chapter five, too, revolves around its geometrical characteristics: "The general shape of these things [the buildings] tended to be conical, pyramidal, or terraced; though there were many perfect cylinders, perfect cubes, clusters of cubes, and other rectangular forms, and a peculiar sprinkling of angled edifices" (MM 46). But a violation of known natural law is immediately evident to Dyer and Danforth, because the designs embody "monstrous perversions of geometrical laws" (MM 30). Similar to this is the city of R'lyeh—whose geometry was "*all wrong*" (*DH* 143)—as well as the Great Race's city in "The Shadow out of Time." These edifices are not designed using the familiar geometry we know, but are instead made up of "geometrical forms for which even an Euclid could scarcely find a name" (MM 51). Even the physiology of these cities' inhabitants does not follow familiar bilateral symmetry but instead adheres to a five-pointed radial plan.[8] Non-Euclidian geometry is also evoked in "The Dreams in the Witch House"; this is both what Walter Gilman is studying and what Keziah Mason has used to move among dimensions.

It is insightful to note how Lovecraft bemoaned the movement of modern (terrestrial) architecture away from familiar forms and toward purely geomet-

---

7. Donald R. Burleson, a HPL scholar who also holds a master's degree in mathematics, explains the idea of non-Euclidian geometry this way: "Non-Euclidian geometry involves eschewing the Euclidian Parallel Postulate—which is independent of the other postulates of Euclid and states given a line and a point not on the line, there is exactly one line through the given point parallel to the given line—in favor of some other axiomatic assumption, e.g., that there are *two* such lines, or none at all, giving rise to such alternative geometries as the Lobachevskian or the Riemannian." ("A Note on HPL, Mathematics, and the Outer Spheres.")

8. I owe this observation to David E. Schultz.

rical forms. In "A Living Heritage: Roman Architecture in Today's America" (1935), he protested these "new decorative designs of cones and cubes and triangles and segments" as "problems in Euclid" (CE 5.123). His plaint helps to explain why his fantastic cities are so disturbing:

> Our longing for familiar symbols—our homesickness, as it were, of things we have known—is in reality the most authentic possible expression of the [human] race's persistent life-force. It is the pitiful struggle of the ego against that ineluctable change which means decay and engulfment in the illimitable dark. (CE 5.121)

Just as Lovecraft railed against Picasso, Brancusi, Modigliani, the architect Raymond Mathewson Hood, and other modernists in his letters, he used modern art as a cue for otherworldly intrusions in his fiction. The Cthulhu bas-relief recalls "the vagaries of cubism and futurism" (DH 127); and when the unfortunate Johansen described the undersea city "without knowing what futurism is like, [he] achieved something very close to it" (DH 150).

The elements of asymmetry, otherworldly sound, and kaleidoscopic vision all fuse in Lovecraft's concept of Ultimate Chaos. Ultimate Chaos is the Hell of the Lovecraftian cosmology, the essence and center of his cosmically indifferent universe. This concept mutated as Lovecraft developed it. Its embryonic appearance was in the climactic final sentence of "Nyarlathotep":

> And through this revolting graveyard of the universe the muffled, maddening beating of drums, and the thin, monotonous whine of blasphemous flutes from inconceivable, unlighted chambers beyond time; the detestable pounding and piping whereunto dance slowly, awkwardly, and absurdly the gigantic, tenebrous ultimate gods—the blind, voiceless, mindless gargoyles whose soul is Nyarlathotep. (MW 34)

A variant of this imagery is found in "The Rats in the Walls" (1923). (Nyarlathotep is later supplanted by Azathoth, the blind idiot god that is the symbolic figurehead of Lovecraft's cosmos.) Lovecraft returns to this verbal icon in several stories, as well as in the sonnet "Azathoth" (1930), always to invoke the very nadir of terror. Of all the secrets that Wilmarth learns from the Outside Ones about time and space, nothing evokes in him more "loathing" than the revelation about "the monstrous nuclear chaos beyond angled space which the Necronomicon had mercifully cloaked under the name of Azathoth" (DH 256).

Lovecraft most fully explored this important motif in "The Dreams in the Witch House." Keziah Mason insists Gilman must go "to the throne of

Azathoth at the centre of ultimate Chaos" (MM 272). Lovecraft ventures to depict this abortive journey:

> There were suggestions of the vague, twilight abysses, and of still vaster, blacker abysses beyond them—abysses in which all fixed suggestions of form were absent. He had been taken there by the bubble-congeries and the little polyhedron [Keziah Mason and Brown Jenkin, respectively] which always dogged him; but they, like himself, had changed to wisps of milky, barely luminous mist in this farther void of ultimate blackness. . . . Eventually there had been a hint of vast, leaping shadows, of a monstrous, half-acoustic pulsing, and of the thin, monotonous piping of an unseen flute—but that was all. (MM 282)

We can see a hierarchy of horrors here: first certain bizarre phenomena are perceived; then all form itself is lost, and there is only blackness and chaos. This progression is maintained and used to powerful advantage in Lovecraft's fictional swan song, "The Haunter of the Dark" (1935). Robert Blake, writer and painter of fantasy, discovers a church used by a strange cult. The latter worships the entity of the story's title, which shows them other worlds and galaxies and is invoked by staring into an oddly angled stone called the Shining Trapezohedron. As Blake first examines the stained-glass windows of the church, he notices that "one seemed to shew merely a dark space with spirals of scattered luminosity scattered about in it" (DH 100). When Blake discovers the Shining Trapezohedron in the bell tower room, he makes a kaleidoscopic mental excursion to the center of the Lovecraftian universe:

> Before he realised it, he was looking at the stone again, and letting its curious influence call up a nebulous pageantry in his mind. He saw processions of robed, hooded figures whose outlines were not human, and looked on endless leagues of desert lined with carved, sky-reaching monoliths. He saw towers and walls in nighted depths under the sea, and vortices of space where wisps of black mist floated before thin shimmerings of cold purple haze. And beyond all else he glimpsed an infinite gulf of darkness, where solid and semisolid forms were known only by their windy stirrings, and cloudy patterns of force seemed to superimpose order on chaos and hold forth a key to all the paradoxes and arcana of the worlds we know. (DH 104)

Perhaps it is this same "infinite gulf of darkness" past even Ultimate Chaos that Crawford Tillinghast experienced as his visions from beyond "gradually gave way to a more horrible conception; that of utter absolute solitude in infinite, sightless, soundless space" (*D* 93). Certainly it is the same "chaos and pandemonium" that the music of Erich Zann invoked, finally causing the narrator to flee from "the blackness of space illimitable; unimagined space alive with motion and music, and having no semblance to anything on earth" (*DH* 90).

We have seen that Lovecraft's worldview provided both the motivation to write supernatural fiction and the opportunity for unlimited speculation as to the vistas that lie forever beyond our ken. It also set him the challenge to envision and describe such vistas. The resulting cosmic imagery in Lovecraft's fiction is a natural and cohesive outgrowth of his philosophical position as expressed in letters and essays. Kaleidoscopic visions, uncanny drones, alien rhythms, disturbing outlines and proportions, geometrical figures and patterns, asymmetry, and Ultimate Chaos and the black void beyond: all are motifs he wove through his fiction to convey cosmic horror. Such imagery is the concentrated essence of Lovecraft's unique artistic achievement, the purest expression of his imaginative genius.

H. P. Lovecraft: Art, Artifact, and Reality

Of the value provided us by art, H. P. Lovecraft wrote, "there is nothing more important in the universe" (SL 3.20). It is thus hardly surprising that art and artists play a role in more than two-thirds of his stories. Art in Lovecraft functions as a way to expand the parallax, so to speak, of human perception. Man has sensory limitations inherent in his physiology and psychology; and he is able, Lovecraft thought, to perceive reality only dimly through the veil of these limitations. Art expands our understanding of the cosmos by allowing us to perceive reality through the vision of another. In some stories the author took this concept one step further: he used non-human art objects to provide his protagonists an even more transcendent understanding of existence. Contemplation of these alien artifacts enables Lovecraft's characters to perceive reality surreptitiously through the vision of beings with completely different senses and emotions. The resulting enhanced understanding of the universe is inevitably a revelation of terror.

We can group the tales that use art and artifacts into several non-exclusive categories. One type of story uses artifacts of human origin—though of an admittedly bizarre nature—to hint of realms beyond our ken. A second group of stories focuses on human artists and how their sensitivity to the most subtle aspects of existence imperils their very sanity. A third group uses non-human artifacts to expand the parallax of human perception even further, much to the detriment of the protagonists.

I. *Artifacts of Human Origin*

In two early tales Lovecraft used strange artifacts of human origin to suggest that reality is not what it seems. "The Temple" (1920) is the first of these. When a World War I German submarine surfaces after sinking a freighter, a man's body is found clutching the rail of the warship. The body is thrown overboard, but the crew retains "a very odd bit of ivory carved to represent a youths head crowned with laurel" apparently "of great age and artistic value" found in the man's pocket. The object is referred to as a "souvenir" (*D* 60): something that serves as a reminder, in this case a reminder that our civilization is only the most recent this planet has seen.

After an explosion and mutiny the narrator, a hard-headed Prussian materialist, is left alone on the drifting, submerged vessel. He becomes strangely obsessed with the art object: "I could not forget the youthful, beautiful head with its leafy crown, though I am not by nature an artist." The psychic equilibrium of one who greatly prides scientific knowledge is being slowly undermined, for the object both encapsulates a "terrible antiquity" (*D* 66) and foreshadows its actuality in the present. The submarine settles to the ocean floor in the midst of an ancient city, whose architecture and decoration are of "inexpressible beauty": "The art is of the most phenomenal perfection" (*D* 67). Friezes pay homage to a male youth, and soon the narrator is startled to realize that *"the head of the radiant god in the sculptures on the rock temple is the same as that carven bit of ivory which the dead sailor bought back from the sea"* (*D* 69). Put differently, the existence of the artifact implies the existence of another plane of entity on our own planet. As James K. Feibleman states:

> Works of art suggest to the appreciator more than he is capable of experiencing without their aid. They point beyond the limits of experience. . . . The purpose of art is not to give pleasure, though assuredly it may do that, but to intensify the senses and give depth to experience. (78)

The narrator concludes that he must don a diving suit and use the last of its air to explore the carven secrets of the rock temple. In doing so he symbolically renounces our familiar realm of being to enter another of "unfathomed waters and uncounted years" (*D* 72).

"The Hound," written two years later, features a similar talisman. Because of a "frightful emotional need" for aesthetic fulfillment, the graverobber-protagonists have assembled an art museum in the cellar of their house. But this is no ordinary salon: the display mixes statues and paintings, "all of fiendish subjects" (*D* 172), with human remains featured in niches and showcases. The latter human artifacts—"human" here in the sense both of manipulator and material manipulated—serve to represent the most bizarre aspects of reality as we commonly know it.

But there is a reality even more bizarre lying in wait. Upon opening an ancient grave the two men find around the corpse's neck "an amulet of curious and exotic design" of an "oddly conventionalised figure of a crouching winged hound" (*D* 174). The art object is "conventionalised"; that is, it employs a mode of artistic representation that simplifies or provides symbols or substitutes for a natural form. But in this case the figure symbolizes something "alien . . . to all art and literature which sane and balanced readers know," for it is not merely a symbol but a "soul-symbol." The soul-symbol either belongs to or represents "the corpse-eating cult of inaccessible Leng."

There is yet more ambiguity in the narrator's explanation of the object. Its "lineaments" (contours) were "drawn from some obscure supernatural manifestation of the souls" (*D* 174) of the cultists. The phrase "drawn from" is vague. In one sense we can read it to mean that the souls literally (physically) created the object. We can also read it to mean that the object's contours were attracted from another realm of existence.

The two men are eventually pursued by a demon that takes various forms; and when one is killed, the narrator tries to return the amulet to the grave before he suffers the same fate. In doing so, he metaphorically attempts to bury (put out of mind) the symbol of a world more terrible than one he had ever sought or even suspected. The only alternative to repressing such aesthetic insight is that experienced by his companion: death.

II. *Human Artists*

A handful of Lovecraft's stories focus on human artists: sculptors, painters, musicians, and poets. Lovecraft defined the successful human artist as one with the ability to

> pin down in some permanent and intelligible medium a sort of idea of what he sees in Nature that no one else sees. In other words, to make the other fellow grasp, though skilled selective care in interpretive reproduction or symbolism, some inkling of what only the artist himself could possibly see in the actual objective scene itself. (SL 2.298; Lovecraft's italics)

Art provides us insight into life which we could not otherwise achieve. When the artist successfully encapsulates his vision in a finished aesthetic product, we apprehend existence more fully:

> Besides the joy of discovering untapped wells in ourselves, there is *the joy of capturing another's vision*—the sense of expansion and adventure inherent in viewing Nature through a larger proportion of the total eyes of mankind. We derive from this process a feeling of magnification in the cosmos—of having approached the universe a trifle more closely, and banished a little

of our inevitable insignificance. Instead of being merely one person, we have become two persons. (SL 2.300)[1]

In the first of Lovecraft's tales to feature an artist, "Hypnos" (1922), the artist-protagonist is literally depicted as two persons. The unnamed narrator, a sculptor, encounters a man unconscious in the midst of a crowd. The man's state—unconscious—is descriptive of his position or function within the narrator's psyche. The man personifies the aesthetic sensitivity in the sculptor's personality, inspiring him to create new works.[2] The sculptor even describes the man in the language of aesthetics: his visage was "beautiful," with a brow "white as the marble of Pentelicus"; he was "a faun's statue out of antique Hellas"; "his voice was music." On the basis of the man's appearance, the sculptor takes him as his "only friend" (*D* 165). The sculptor has become in touch with his subconscious Self in pursuit of his art.

The two begin experiments in dream, indescribable save as *"plungings"* and *"soarings"* through what seem to be other dimensions. The character of these dreams parallels Lovecraft's description of his own most sought-after aesthetic experiences:

> There must always be a sense of . . . *soaring outward* toward the discovery of stupendous, cosmic, inconceivable things, and toward the envisagement and comprehension of awesome rhythms and patterns and symmetries too Titanic, too unparticled, too trans-galactic, and too overpowering for the relatively flat, tame, and local name of "Beauty." (*SL* 2.127)

In the context of the tale we may consider the dream as a work similar to the work of art, but uncontrolled and lacking the force and beauty of art (see Feibleman 17). But here the artist, tragically, does not have the discipline to

---

1. Note that while in letters HPL portrays the expanded perception made possible by art as a pleasurable sensation, in the tale it is always horrific. Instead of "banishing our insignificance," non-human art actually underscores it. This is not a contradiction, I think, but rather a question of degree. While the insight provided by traditional human art is welcome, the insight provided by outré and non-human art is so revealing as to be emotionally oppressive and even maddening. HPL's fictive treatment of the effects of knowledge is similar. Knowledge in and of itself is not intrinsically dangerous; what is dangerous is "the inability of the human mind to endure certain kinds of knowledge, especially that which reveals our insignificant place in the cosmos" (Joshi, *Decline of the West* 107–11). This is the kind of knowledge that outré and non-human art provides.

2. Given HPL's reverence for Edgar Allan Poe, this reading is consistent with Peter Cannon's conjecture that the friend is modelled physically after Poe (see Cannon, *H. P. Lovecraft* 32).

gain control of his muse. The sculptor—apparently because of the flawed, narcissistic personal character hinted at by his Bohemian dress—goes astray, allowing the friend to lead him deep into the realm of art and even beyond it.[3] The friend has "designs which [involve] the rulership of the visible universe and more" (D 166); metaphorically, the desire to understand existence completely. The sculptor's subconscious Self has become dominated by the Super-ego.

In a dream-excursion the friend succeeds in traversing a "sticky, clammy mass." He thus passes beyond art into a realm offering an even higher degree of metaphysical knowledge about the universe. His ability to apprehend directly a reality beyond ordinary knowing has been indeed enhanced—to such an extent that "vistas of unvisitable hells gleamed for a second in black eyes crazed with fright" (D 167). The mind of the sculptor (to borrow a phrase from "The Call of Cthulhu") has metaphorically "correlate[d] all its contents" (DH 125) with dire results.

Afterwards the two men try to stay awake to avoid further such insights. The narrator can no longer create art: "I had no means to purchase new materials, or energy to fashion them even had I possessed them" (D 168). His expanded understanding of the mechanistic nature of the universe has frozen his aesthetic sensibility. In the end the friend is literally frozen into a statue by a beam of light from outer space.

In "The Call of Cthulhu" (1926) another sculptor, Henry Anthony Wilcox, fares better than the sculptor of "Hypnos." Because of an aesthetic receptiveness, Wilcox's muse comes to him fully formed; because of a strong personal character, he is able to take full advantage of this event. After a vivid dream-vision, the sculptor had "found himself working, chilled and clad only in his nightclothes, when waking had stolen bewilderingly over him" (DH 129). In contrast to the uncontrolled imaginings of the sculptor in "Hypnos," Wilcox's vision is controlled—by Great Cthulhu himself. The bas-relief that results from Wilcox's midnight inspiration is a fully realized work of art, one that manifests reality as perceived by a non-human entity.

When Cthulhu withdraws his influence Wilcox, unlike the sculptor in "Hypnos," not only survives but actually benefits from his augmented understanding of the universe. He is able to do so only because of a superior character (while again depicted as a person of neurotic and excited "aspect,"

---

3. HPL's distaste for Bohemian artist-types is well documented in published and unpublished correspondence; see, for example, Letters to Richard F. Searight 72.

Wilcox is "of an excellent family" [DH 128]) and unwillingness to push the boundary of perception even further. As it is, the vision Cthulhu sends leaves a "subconscious residuum," says the narrator, that "influenced his art profoundly, and he shewed me a morbid statue whose contours almost made me shake with the potency of its black suggestion" (DH 143). Wilcox retains only a vestige of the perceptual insight given him by Cthulhu; enough to make his aesthetic product more powerful, but not so much as to cause madness.

Thurston, the narrator who prides himself on his scientific mien, remarks tellingly that in retrospect "only the ingrained scepticism then forming my [mechanistic] philosophy can account for my continued distrust for the artist" (DH 130). "The artist" can be read as singular (Wilcox) or plural (artists in general). Art, Lovecraft says, provides an understanding of existence fuller than science alone can convey. Newspaper cuttings, for example, reveal that around the same time as Wilcox's dream, similar visions were experienced by others—but only those persons who are aesthetically sensitive: "It was from the artists and poets that the pertinent answers came," answers to questions about the essence of entity. As Lovecraft put it in a letter of 1931:

> Reason as we may, we cannot destroy a normal perception of the highly limited & fragmentary nature of our visible world of perception & experience as scaled against the outside abyss of unthinkable galaxies & unplumbed dimensions . . . & this perception cannot fail to act potently upon the natural instinct of *pure curiosity*. . . . In types where this urge cannot be gratified by actual research in pure science, or by the actual exploration of unknown parts of the earth, it is inevitable that a symbolic aesthetic outlet will be demanded. (SL 3.294–95)

The ability of the artist to apprehend and communicate what science cannot is clear when the narrator remarks that "average people in society and business . . . gave an almost completely negative result" when queried about transcendent (and ultimately true) visions; and "scientific men" were but "little more affected" (DH 131).

Later in the story, the narrator offers a detailed description of Wilcox's dream-product, a bas-relief covered with prehistoric writing. "Above [the] apparent hieroglyphics was a figure of evidently pictorial intent, though its impressionistic execution forbade a very clear idea of its nature" (DH 127). The narrator, the story soon reveals, has it backwards. The figure does *not* depict something by evoking subjective impressions rather than by recreating objective reality: that is, the technique is *not* impressionistic. Instead, as Lovecraft punningly hints, it represents—quite literally—another "nature" (i.e., reality).[4] The style of the object does not hinder our ability to comprehend its subject; it is the subject itself that is incomprehensible. By contemplating Wilcox's bas-relief, the narrator comes one step closer (as he says at the outset of the tale) to that "piecing together of dissociated knowledge" which opens up "terrifying vistas of reality" (*DH* 124). Lovecraft used similar phraseology to a correspondent:

> The constant discovery of different people's subjective impressions of things, as contained in genuine art, forms a slow, gradual approach, or faint approximation of an approach, to *the mystic substance of absolute reality itself*— the stark, cosmic reality which lurks behind our varying subjective perceptions. (*SL* 2.301–2)

Wilcox's art-object is only one among many in Lovecraft's work which reveals that "stark, cosmic reality" is a different and more terrible one than that which we as individuals can see. Richard Upton Pickman, perhaps Lovecraft's most memorable protagonist, is said to possess "profound art and profound insight into Nature." The second, of course, is a prerequisite to the first; but the "Nature" into which Pickman has insight is not one that can be perceived by other people.

Discoursing on the aesthetic of the fantastic, the narrator of "Pickman's Model" (1926) posits that "the really weird artist has a kind of vision which makes models, or summons up what amounts to actual scenes from the spectral world he lives in" (*DH* 13–14). Pickman certainly has "vision"—not in the sense of an act of imagination, as the narrator may believe, but in the literal sense of an act of seeing the real qualities of an object. More obviously, this painter does make "models"—not visions that serve as a pattern for his art, but rather miniature representations in oil of things that exist. Thus the narrator can truly call Pickman a "realist" because he depicts a world that, while actual, is simply beyond the grasp of the mass of humanity. It is a world as "real" and elegant as that known by our science; a "stable, mechanistic, and well-established horror-world which he saw fully, brilliantly, squarely, and unfalteringly" (*DH* 21).

---

4. Cf. a similar usage of the word "nature" in "The Dreams in the Witch House" (1932). In a dream Walter Gilman finds himself on a balustraded terrace above an alien landscape. At intervals along the railing are decorative figures "of grotesque design and exquisite workmanship" whose "nature utterly defied conjecture" (MM 277). It is apparent that this "nature" (reality) actually exists.

I. GENERAL STUDIES

Erich Zann is another of Lovecraft's artists whose aesthetic skill enlarges our understanding of entity. The narrator is a student of metaphysics, yet he has much to learn about the true nature of the cosmos from Zann's art. Overhearing Zann playing a viol, he is "haunted by the weirdness of his music. Knowing little of the art myself, I was yet certain that none of his harmonies had any relation to music I had heard before, and concluded he was a composer of highly original genius" (*DH* 85). The concept of genius represents the aesthetic part of the personality, that part which can beget (*gignere*) what is immortal. An individual who is a "genius," according to Otto Rank, therefore embodies the same process and achievement which in its religious form takes the image of God:

> Artistically, it [the notion of genius] implies the individual style, which indeed still holds on to the exemplars that later appear in aesthetic as formulated law, but which is already free and autonomous in its divine creative power and is creating new forms out of itself. The artist, liberated from God, himself becomes god, soon overleaps the collective forms of style and their abstract formulation in aesthetic and constructs new forms of an individual nature, which cannot therefore, be subsumed under laws. (24)

The "satyr-like" (*DH* 85) Zann (as is hinted more blatantly of Pickman), then, may himself be only partly human. Robert M. Price first proposed this reading, suggesting that Zann's music is "bought whole and unchanged from a realm in which it fitted into a realm, our own, where it did not" (Price, "Erich Zann" 13). We may read the description of Zann's playing, "a blind, mechanical, unrecognisable orgy that no pen could even suggest" (*DH* 90), as a literal description of the true aspect of the cosmos itself.

Zann's music holds "vibrations suggesting nothing on this globe of earth," and indeed his art expresses an existence to which humans are not privy. Upon seeing the musician's humble rooms, the narrator casually remarks: "Evidently Erich Zann's world of beauty lay in some far cosmos of the imagination" (*DH* 85). The apparent metaphors are not after all, wholly figurative: Zann's music embodies a universe that, though our own, is alien to us.

The concept of "genius" comes originally from early Roman times, when it meant a personal protecting spirit. This sense is seen, finally, in Zann's disposition regarding what lay beyond his garret window. He first glances there "as if fearful of some intruder," and at the end of the tale the narrator discovers that the motive behind his playing "was stark fear. He was trying to . . . ward something off . . . —what, I could not imagine, awesome though I felt it must be" (*DH* 89). The quasi-human Zann attempts to maintain his own vision of reality in the face of another—and wholly unhuman and unimaginable—vision dispatched by some Outside entity. But he cannot ward off a realization of the ultimate ground of existence, one heralded by a "calm, deliberate, purposeful, mocking note from far away in the West" that represents "only the blackness of space illimitable" (*DH* 89–90).

What Wilcox, Pickman, and Zann have in common is their ability to broaden our experience of the world. They help us overcome, ever so slightly, the limitations of our five senses. While we can perceive entity only through this sensory filter, these artists provide us with a slightly different way of looking at the world:

> We have only extremely fragmentary and illusory specialised projections to go by, and can form no idea of any principle of reference by which to define or envisage such a thing as absolute entity or reality apart from its few sensory manifestations. All we can do is to judge the relationships which those manifestations bear toward one another, and accept our fractional vision as having some fixed proportion or relationship to whatever the inconceivable whole may be. The mind of man can never—*this is the one absolute certainty in our knowledge*—get any further than this, since the limits of the five senses are a fixed and insurmountable barrier beyond which we have no possible avenue of access. Religion pretends to satisfy by assuming man's possession of mystic information-channels apart from the senses, but we are outgrowing the possibilities of this benign delusion. Only the subtler illusion of art is left—the illusion of our ability to command slightly different points of view within the human radius gives us a triangulation-base large enough to permit mensurational guesses regarding absolute reality. (SL 2.301–2)

But Lovecraft, in his fiction, found a way to go further, to expand the "triangulation base"—by expanding our perspective beyond the "human radius."

III. *Non-Human Artifacts*

S. T. Joshi has pointed out how Lovecraft often invokes human artists to convey that "*any* fictional work—even the work of a genius—cannot rival the horrors concealed on the underside of reality" (*Decline of the West* 114).[5] For example, the alien impersonator of Akeley in "The Whisperer in Darkness"

---

5. A glance through Joshi's *An Index to the Fiction and Poetry of H. P. Lovecraft* (West Warwick, RI: Necronomicon Press, 1992) shows mentions of no less than eighteen different (human) authors and thirteen different (human) painters in HPL.

(1930) attempts to entice Wilmarth by saying that a visit to the planet Yuggoth "ought to be enough to make any man a Dante or a Poe if he can keep sane long enough to tell what he has seen" (*DH* 254). The conundrum, of course, is that no human artist can stay sane long enough. After Wilmarth discovers the aliens' plot, he flees through the Vermont woods; the ride, he says, "was a piece of delirium out of Poe or Rimbaud or the drawings of Doré" (*DH* 271). If Wilmarth must take recourse to Poe in describing this anticlimactic and relatively mundane trip, we may assume, he would not have been able to withstand the sanity-blasting vistas of Yuggoth.

So while the most accomplished human art broadens our understanding of the cosmos and of our place within it, the magnitude of this broadening is still relatively trivial: "it is absurd to fancy that the narrow range of visions afforded by different artists within the human species could give even the merest hint of ultimate reality known to us only from the restricted point of view (or closely related points of view) of mankind with its local and limited range of sense-equipment" (*SL* 2.301–2). The points of view embodied in human art are too similar for any great revelations into the nature of reality, this similarity resulting from "our membership in the same organic species, in the same race-stock, [and] in the same civilisation" (*SL* 2.298) as the artist. However, Lovecraft found it simple to hurdle these barriers in his fiction. He uses a variety of artifacts to show us reality—conveyed through artistic media—from the perspective of other "organic species." The reality that is thus revealed is one of extreme terror.[6]

"The Haunter of the Dark" (1935) shows the limitations of human art by positioning it as the most superficial of a series of three nested levels. In taking up the tale, the reader encounters a human artist who writes weird fiction (Lovecraft) who tells of a human artist who writes weirder fiction (Robert Blake) who discovers a non-human artifact (the Shining Trapezohedron) that offers yet weirder cosmic visions. These visions are horrible beyond not

---

6. A word of definition may be in order at this point. Art objects are a subclass of artifacts. Art objects reflect the conscious use of skill and creative imagination in the production of aesthetic objects. The work of art is an artifact aimed at having a specific effect on man, not to accomplish something else in the way of reducing man's needs (as a tool might) but directly itself in terms of its emotional impact. An artifact, by contrast, is more broadly defined as an object showing human modification, or a product of civilization or artistic endeavor created to serve human needs (Feibleman 48, 52). Artifacts, according to George Santayana, are "things which would not only betray the agent's habits, but would have served and expressed his intent" (301).

merely what Lovecraft can conceive; they are horrible beyond what his human artist-protagonist Blake could possibly conceive.

The story abounds in self-reflexive elements which almost collapse in upon one another. One such element is Lovecraft's use (rare in his work) of third-person narration. He immediately forces an awareness of the narrator upon the reader: "let us summarise the dark chain of events from the expressed point of view of their chief actor" (*DH* 93). It is as if Lovecraft himself will tell us the story of Blake. Lovecraft thus explicitly places himself in the role of the human weird artist who will broaden our "triangulation base" and give us a greater insight into the horror of reality. Another self-referential element is the epigraph for the tale:

> I have seen the dark universe yawning
> > Where the black planets roll without aim—
> Where they roll in their horror unheeded
> > Without knowledge or lustre or name.
> > > —*Nemesis*. (*DH* 92)

It is unusual for an author to quote one of his own poems as a motto for a tale. The typical reader must wonder whether the quatrain is to be taken as the work of Robert Blake—"a writer and painter wholly devoted to the field of myth, dream, terror, and superstition" (*DH* 93)—or as the work of Howard Lovecraft. By compounding his identity with Blake, Lovecraft reminds us how little even he (Lovecraft) can approach "the mystic substance of reality itself." Lovecraft, the artist, will attempt to expand our understanding of reality. But this understanding is just as superficial as the understanding that Blake, the artist, can provide his readers compared to the horrible revelations of the Shining Trapezohedron. The horror we experience in reading Lovecraft's story must be trivial compared to the revelations that actually lie beyond Lovecraft's telling—and beyond even Blake's telling.

Having become obsessed with a great abandoned church visible on the horizon from his study window, Blake is unable to make progress with his "long-planned novel" about a "survival of the witch-cult in Maine" (*DH* 95–96). This is a work within a work, but as frightening as Lovecraft might imply it to be, its impact could never be more than mundane relative to the non-human artifacts that embody the objective world independent of our perception.

Soon Blake strikes out to visit the church. Inside, he pauses to offer an aesthetic critique of its stained-glass windows:

The designs were largely conventional, and his knowledge of obscure symbolism told him much concerning some of the ancient patterns. The few saints depicted bore expressions distinctly open to criticism, while one of the windows seems to shew merely a dark space with spirals of curious luminosity scattered about in it. (*DH* 100)

Note the progression of conventional to unconventional: the last work of art mentioned hints at the real terror which neither Lovecraft nor Blake, as human artists, can begin either to perceive or to portray.

In the tower Blake finds a "curiously angled stone pillar" atop which is a "metal box of peculiarly asymmetrical form." On the box, again, are "odd bas-reliefs" whose "figurings were of a monstrous and utterly alien kind." Within it is an object that is "either a very remarkable crystal of some sort, or an artificial object of carved and highly-polished mineral matter" (*DH* 101–2). This object, the Shining Trapezohedron, may or may not be an artifact shaped by an alien artisan; it encapsulates a universe so bizarre that it is difficult for a human—even a human artist—to say.

The worshippers of the Shining Trapezohedron, according to the notes Blake finds in the church steeple, say that "it shews them heaven & other worlds" (*DH* 103). The object thus functions as a way to transcend sensory limitations and expand one's understanding of the cosmos, as human art does but on such a scale as to be frightening. (Thus Blake's "final frenzied jottings," more terrifying than any story he ever wrote, record that his "senses [are] transfigured" [*DH* 114–15].) The visions inspired by the Shining Trapezohedron make the visions recorded in Blake's paintings—"nameless, inhuman monsters, and profoundly alien, non-terrestrial landscapes" (*DH* 94)— seem positively trite. His final Trapezohedron-inspired perception of "a vast, unplumbed abyss of night wherein whirled suns and worlds of an even profounder blackness" (*DH* 110) echoes the epigraph and hints at the true nature of a universe which we can know only dimly even with the help of art.

Several other tales also revolve around artifacts created by non-human races that provide us a broader parallax of perception. "Dagon" (1917), Lovecraft's second mature tale, sets the precedent. The narrator, shipwrecked on split of newly-risen sea-bed, discovers "an array of bas-reliefs whose subjects would have excited the envy of a Doré" and were "grotesque beyond the imagining of a Poe or a Bulwer" (*D* 18). If art, as Feibleman puts it, "consists of symbols somehow standing for true values—in a word, little representations of larger segments of the world" (227), these bas-reliefs are little segments of a world not merely unseen but also unimaginable by these most accomplished human artists. Even the terror of Poe, "penetrating to every festering horror in the gaily painted mockery called existence" ("Supernatural Horror in Literature" [D 398]), is reduced to insignificance.

"The Call of Cthulhu" (1926), which has been called an expansion and recapitulation of "Dagon," also features non-human artifacts (see Schultz, "From Microcosm to Macrocosm" 206, 210–11). Wilcox's dream-object is mirrored in three similar objects. The first of these to come to light is a statuette of "exquisitely artistic workmanship" seized by police at a Louisiana voodoo ritual. To the scholars that view it, it initially seems that "centuries and even thousands of years seemed recorded in its dim and greenish surface of unplaceable stone." But they soon recognize that the object manifests an alien reality rather than an ancient world: "not one link did it shew with any known type of art belonging to civilization's youth—or indeed to any other time." The object is alien not only in its aesthetic technique (style) but in the meaning it conveys (substance): "totally separate and apart, its very material was a mystery" (DH 134). The second object of the non-human triad is a bas-relief worshipped by Greenland Eskimos, "rough[ly] parallel in all essential features" (DH 135) to the Louisiana image. The third object, again of "balefully exquisite workmanship" (DH 148), is an idol recovered from the yacht Alert in the Pacific Ocean.

All who have the misfortune to view these idols with their "air of genuinely abysmal antiquity" (DH 134) experience an embodiment of the horror of the Great Old Ones, beings who "had come from the stars, and had bought Their images [i.e., their art and its implications about the cosmos] with Them" (DH 148). When the cultist Castro says that "the carven idol was great Cthulhu" he means it literally as well as figuratively—the idol encapsulates the bizarre, non-Euclidean cosmos in which the octopoid god and his brethren dwell. "They had shape—for did not this star-fashioned image prove it?" (DH 139–40). The image is "star-fashioned," a manifestation of the very universe itself. It imposes form on the non-human reality of the Great Old Ones.

At the Mountains of Madness (1931) employs human artifacts (the work of Poe, Dunsany, and Nicholas Roerich), alien artifacts (the murals of the Old Ones), and even ultra-alien artifacts (the murals of the shoggoths) in its meditation on the nature of reality. The expedition's scientists must take continual recourse to analogies with the most fantastic human art, yet can convey only the merest hints of the strangeness of their discoveries. At first it is a case of life imitating art—that is, weird art. Only seven pages into the story, on the first leg of the voyage toward Antarctic peaks, the narrator notes that "something about the scene reminded me of the strange and disturbing Asian paintings of Nicholas Roerich" (MM 7). On the next page, a passage from Poe's "Ulalume" is quoted upon the sight of Mt. Erebus, with the narrator noting that the mountain "had undoubtedly been the source of Poe's image."[7] The line between weird art and reality begins to blur: the locale evoked the writing of the poem and the quoting of the poem is evoked by the locale. Three pages later, objective reality bleeds into the vision of an artist "supreme in the creation of a gorgeous and languorous world of iridescently exotic vision" ("Supernatural Horror in Literature" [D 429]), Lord Dunsany: "often the whole white world would dissolve into a gold, silver, and scarlet land of Dunsanian dreams" (MM 11). And when the protagonists see the cubelike dwellings of the Old Ones, an entire geographic region is subsumed into the domain of fantastic (human) art: "There was indeed something hauntingly Roerich-like about this whole unearthly continent of mountainous mystery" (MM 29). The mentions of Roerich (six in all over a period of 100 pages) become positively obtrusive, but we must not attribute them to hasty writing on the part of the meticulous author. They underscore, heavily, the central role art plays in this tale.

The strangeness conveyed by these human artifacts, once again, pales in light of the alien art—"mature, accomplished, and aesthetically evolved to the highest degree of civilized mastery" (MM 56)—created by the Archaean race called the Old Ones. Most of the narrator's information about this race and their epoch is drawn from the mural sculptures that abound in their ruined city.[8] Roerich and Poe are forgotten as the narrator goes on for four paragraphs in praise of the Old Ones' art:

> Beneath their [i.e., the murals'] strict conventionalisation one could grasp
> the minute and accurate observation and graphic skill of the artists; and in-
> deed, the very conventions themselves served to symbolise and accentuate
> the real essence of vital differentiation of every object delineated. We felt,

7. An interesting point of Poe scholarship: this connection was first made by HPL in his tale. See Thomas Ollive Mabbott, ed., *The Poems of Edgar Allan Poe* (Cambridge, MA: Harvard University Press, 1978), 421.

8. This, of course, recalls the non-human art featured in "The Nameless City" (1921). The main action occurs in an ancient hall that is "a monument of the most magnificent and exotic art. Rich, vivid, and daringly fantastic designs and pictures formed a continuous scheme of mural paintings whose lines and colours were beyond description" (D 104).

too, that besides these recognisable excellences there were others lurking beyond the reach of our perceptions. Certain touches here and there gave vague hints of latent symbols and stimuli which another mental and emotional background, and a fuller or different sensory equipment, might have made of profound and poignant significance to us. (MM 57)

These alien artists possess a different set of sense-equipment than we do, and as a result their art tells us something about the cosmos we otherwise could not know. "In delicacy of execution," too, "no sculpture I have ever seen could approach it" (MM 56). This perhaps reflects the different physiognomies of the Old Ones—five arms each ending in twenty-five tentacles (MM 21).

It is not, however, the physical differences alone of the alien sculptors that give their art such tremendous impact for the human observers. There is another element: "Their method of design . . . embodied an analytical psychology beyond that of any known race of antiquity" (MM 56–57). This recalls to mind Lovecraft's pronouncement on his theory of aesthetics:

> To me beauty as we know it, consists of two elements; one absolute and objective, and based on rhythm and symmetry; and one relative and subjective, based on traditional associations with the hereditary culture-stream of the beholder. The second element is probably strongest with me . . . (SL 2.229)

At first it seems strange that humans could be so moved by art that is by definition lacking in the second, subjective element. We may conclude that there is enough of an overlap in the outlook of this particular alien race and the human race for the explorers to feel the great depth of the Old Ones' art. Thus the narrator's remark that the murals possessed "an artistic force that moved us profoundly" (MM 56) foreshadows the sympathy of his later exclamation: "whatever they had been, they were men!" (MM 96). The shoggoths, which supplant by the Old Ones as the objects of our fear, certainly are *not* men. Art is used as a cue for the redirection of the explorers' terror, as the murals reflect a subtle change from the supreme artistic accomplishments in those murals first seen by the explorers: "This new and degenerate work was coarse, bold, and wholly lacking in delicacy of detail." It seemed "more like a parody than a perpetuation" of the Old Ones' work. Apparently, "some subtly but profoundly alien element had been added to the aesthetic feeling behind the technique" (MM 92). Unlike the Old Ones, the shoggoths are so antipodally alien that the explorers feel no empathy for whatever for their "aesthetic feeling." These "multicellular protoplasmic masses" (MM 62) can have no art as we know it; as Lovecraft remarked in a 1933 letter, our art is "more intrinsically removed from the unevolved protoplasmic stage of organic reaction that any other human manifestation except pure reason" (SL 4.223).

The presence of the Deep Ones in "The Shadow over Innsmouth" (1931) first manifests itself in the form of an artifact. The narrator (called Robert Olmstead in the notes for the tale) hears of Innsmouth from a railroad ticket clerk in nearby Newburyport. Upon researching the shadow-haunted town he discovers that a specimen of the jewelry for which it is famous is displayed at the local Historical Society. When he sees the item, a tiara, he states: "It took no excessive sensitiveness to beauty to make me literally gasp at the strange, unearthly splendour of the alien, opulent phantasy that rested there on a purple velvet cushion." Note the verbally exact (literal) use of the word "gasp": to pant, to desire eagerly. The semi-human Olmstead has a revelation of his aesthetic connection with the alien art.

As usual, the non-human artifact is represented as an outstanding artistic success from the perspective of style: "It clearly belonged to some settled technique of infinite maturity and perfection, yet that technique was utterly remote from any—Eastern or Western, ancient or modern—which I had ever heard of or seen exemplified." But the narrator's pleasure is not unalloyed: "there was a curiously disturbing element hardly to be classified or accounted for" (*DH* 311), just as it will be difficult for the reader to classify or account for the existence of the amphibious fish-frog-men inhabitants of the town.

I have elsewhere discussed the importance of pattern in Lovecraft's cosmic imagery (see "Lovecraft's Cosmic Imagery"). Corresponding to the first part of Lovecraft's twofold aesthetic theory—the "absolute and objective [factor,] . . . based on rhythm and symmetry"—Lovecraft used pattern throughout his work to symbolize the mechanistic nature of the cosmos. According to Rank, this tendency is also apparent in primitive art forms:

> The potential extension to infinity which is common in these primitive art-forms (music and ornament) expresses the externalizing impulse par excellence. Ornament in line and melody in music are not only abstractions of what is seen and felt in space and time, but abbreviations of the infinite, in spatial form in once case, in temporal in the other. (351)

Because Rank groups together ornament and music, we can read in the compositions of Erich Zann the same cosmic symbolism:

> Both these [music and ornament] have rhythm as a principle of form, which is manifest in music as temporal and in ornament as spatial repetition. . . . In their developed forms they display still more clearly than the metaphori-

cal speech the fundamental essence of metaphor: namely, *extension into the infinite*. For while metaphors of speech only succeed in retaining and recalling some past by association with the present, rhythmic ornament, in drawing or music, tends to connect the whole past as such, in abstract form, with the future, since a rhythmic line or a tone succession can in principle be continued into infinity. (Rank 350)

Thus the tiara attests to the perpetual existence of another level of entity: "the patterns all hinted of remote secrets and unimaginable abysses in time and space," and every contour was "overflowing with the ultimate quintessence of unknown and inhuman evil" (*DH* 311–12). Zann's music, similarly, is "a kind of fugue, with recurrent passages of the most captivating quality" (*DH* 86). It too forms an extension into the infinite, for ultimately it causes the narrator "almost [to] see shadowy satyrs and Bacchanals dancing and whirling insanely through seething abysses of clouds and smoke and lightning" (*DH* 89).

In a discarded draft of "Innsmouth" the jewelry plays an even more central role in the narrative than it does in the finished tale. Following the encounter with the railway clerk, Olmstead discovers at the local library a sales brochure for the Marsh Refining Company. He is so impressed with "the strangeness and beauty of the designs" that he visits the offices of the Company posing as a jewelry buyer (*MW* 63).[9] His deeply felt reaction is similar to that in the final version, but even more extreme: "when I beheld the glittering marvels before me I could scarcely walk steadily or talk coherently" (*MW* 64). Olmstead's physical reactions cunningly foreshadow the revelation that he is descended from the alien Innsmouth stock, with their "flopping, hopping" (*DH* 360) gait and "hoarse barkings and loose-syllabled croakings [which] bore so little resemblance to human speech" (*DH* 345). In this case, Lovecraft hints, the subjective aesthetic element—the "traditional associations with the hereditary culture stream of the beholder"—is intensely strong because the narrator belongs to the Deep Ones' culture stream. His aesthetic empathy to non-human art is thus much different, and far stronger, than that of Lovecraft's other, wholly human narrators.

---

9. As a biographical aside, this episode and Olmstead's ultimate fate are uncanny echoes of HPL's father, Winfield Scott Lovecraft. The elder Lovecraft was a traveling sales representative for the Gorham Silver Company, he went violently mad in 1893 and died five years later under restraint.

The carven heads, amulets, bas-reliefs, idols, statuettes, paintings, music, murals, and jewelry that populate Lovecraft's stories serve as prisms that focus the light of reality, enabling us to see it as it truly is. These objects impound the perception of other races in a form that enable us to *know*; they force us to confront the universe anew through a physiology and psychology which humans have been mercifully denied. They impound Lovecraft's message about the mechanistic universe, and place it upon a shelf for us to gaze upon in terror.

Lovecraft's artifacts, both human and non-human, have a strange fascination for the reader as much as for his protagonists. They possess what Lovecraft in a letter called "a perverse and macabre impressiveness which is itself a shadowy form of beauty" (*Letters to Richard F. Searight* 51). Always described in terms of the highest critical praise—delicate, exquisite, marvelous—the non-human artifacts especially hint at such impressiveness, one that will thankfully never be ours to experience fully. Our sensations as we gaze in awe upon the museum-housed artifacts of Egypt, Greece, and Rome must be a mere shadow of what Lovecraft's characters feel as they encounter such things as the Cthulhu idol, the Innsmouth tiara, or the Old Ones' murals. For in these artifacts, as in the cryptical arabesques of the Silver Key, there "stand symbolised all the aims and mysteries of a blindly impersonal cosmos" (MM 420).

H. P. Lovecraft: Reluctant American Modernist

Introduction

Was H. P. Lovecraft a lurker at the threshold of the American Modernist movement? Shall we class him with Poe, Machen, and Dunsany, or with T. S. Eliot, Eugene O'Neill, and Sherwood Anderson? Our typical impression of Lovecraft is the periwigged antiquarian, the Anglophile, the one who wished he had been born in England in the eighteenth century. We tend not to think of him as a characteristically American author, and certainly not as an author in step with the Modernist movement of the early part of the 20th century.

Lovecraft himself encouraged the impression that he was a cultural and artistic outsider in his letters and essays: the violent attacks on the "new" poetry, on non-representational fiction like *Ulysses*, on contemporary architecture and painting, and so on. Writing in October 1921, for example, he claimed that "so far as I touch art at all, I am not only a non-modern but a violent anti-modern" (*Letters to Alfred Galpin* 113). My intent is to demonstrate that Lovecraft was, in fact, very much an American Modernist in the same way that we consider Eliot, Hart Crane, Theodore Dreiser, and other writers of the second American Renaissance of the 1920s' American Modernists.

I won't claim, though, that other American Moderns influenced Lovecraft's work. I would like to. The only reason I won't do so is that I can't—he never read most of them. What I do hope to show, instead, is that Lovecraft was a product of the same social and cultural forces that the American Moderns were, and these common influences inform their respective artistic products. The revolt against Victorianism; the intense interest in subjective states of consciousness and the estrangement of the self; the concern with the city and the machine; and above all, the sense of anxiety and disorientation in the face of Freud, Darwin, Nietzsche, the tide of immigration and the First

World War—these and other factors are at the center of Lovecraft's work, just as they are at that of the American Moderns.

I. *Lurker at the Threshold of the American Modernist Movement*

Cleveland 1922

Cast your mind back now to the roaring '20s. The thirty-two-year-old Howard Lovecraft visited his friend Samuel Loveman in Cleveland in early August 1922. En route he got his first glimpse of mid-America, noting with interest that "the villages are insufferably dismal—like 'Main Street'" (*SL* 1.191). The allusion to Sinclair Lewis's novel was apt, for Lovecraft was about to enter the world of American Modernism.

It was in Cleveland that Lovecraft first met Hart Crane, a member of Loveman's circle of artist friends who was to become one of the greatest American poets of the era. Crane, though only twenty-three years old, was already deeply immersed in the Modernist movement, both its art and its social scene. He was reading Eliot, Wallace Stevens, Cocteau, Rimbaud, Laforgue, Verlaine, Apollinaire. He was in touch with people like Ezra Pound and Allan Tate. He was deeply involved with the work of Modern painters like Picasso and DeChirico. His work, including the two major poems "Black Tambourine" and "Chaplinesque," had been published in leading Modernist organs like the *Dial*, the *Pagan*, *Gargoyle*, *Bruno's Weekly*, the *Little Review*, and the *Double Dealer*.

So Lovecraft arrived at an exciting moment. Crane was in the midst of writing his first great long poem, "For the Marriage of Faustus and Helen." He had just played host to Sherwood Anderson, already famous as the author of *Winesburg, Ohio*. In addition, Crane was consumed in reading the smuggled-in copy of the newly published *Ulysses* he had received only weeks before.

Crane, however, was not the radical Modern that some might have perceived him. Just as Lovecraft was passionate about the Georgians—Pope, Dryden, Johnson, Addison, and Swift—Crane intensely admired the Elizabethans—Donne, Marlowe, Webster, and Vaughan. In fact, more than one commentator has remarked that Crane was among the most traditional of the Modernists.

Lovecraft felt right at home in the Cleveland scene. On 9 August 1922, he wrote to his aunt:

We held a meeting here [last night] of all the members of Loveman's literary circle, at which the conversation covered every branch of aesthetics. . . . It gave me a novel sensation to be 'lionised' so much beyond my deserts by men as able as the painter Summers, Loveman, Galpin, &c. I met some new figures—Crane the poet, [and others]. . . . All the circle say they like my stories—which duly inflates me with pride. . . . Tonight Galpin, Crane, [and] I . . . are going to a concert held in the museum art building.[1]

Crane was already developing some unusual habits of composition in the bedroom study in the turret of his Victorian home on Euclid Avenue. Quaffing red wine and playing classical music over and over on the Victrola, he would declaim his lines aloud as he cobbled them together from notes he kept over long periods of time. Lovecraft couldn't resist writing a parody of this "egotistical young aesthete." He called the parody "Plaster-All," after Crane's poem "Pastorale." The parody, written in the first person as by Hart Crane, is notable for its remarkably intimate knowledge of Crane—his home, the layout of his tower bedroom, his social milieu, his Modernist connections, and so on. The poem concludes:

> The wind wails
> Around the corner of Euclid and 115th St.,
> The trees shiver
> Like brass, or cymbals of some such metal,
> It rains and then it ceases,
> But I, seated on my Aztec carpets,
> And playing Debussy
> On the wheezy Victrola
> (What Rhythms! What Rhythms!)
> Conjure for myself
> An entire world,
> Made of myself, by myself, for myself!
> Knowing myself
> To be myself. (AT 256)

Despite this, Lovecraft would ultimately have high praise for Crane's venture into poetic modernism.

---

1. HPL to L. D. Clark, 9 August 1922 (ms., JHL).

I. GENERAL STUDIES

New York 1924–1926

A few years later Lovecraft eloped from Providence to New York to marry, find work, and seek more congenial literary society. He dived into the cultural and social scene with both feet. He saw *All God's Chillun Got Wings* and *The Emperor Jones*, and acknowledged O'Neill "a great dramatist—perhaps the only American dramatist of note now living." The theme of atavism in *The Emperor Jones*, which he called "a thing of terror, ably presented," influenced Lovecraft's "The Rats in the Walls." In September 1924 he notes a visit to the galleries of Grand Central Terminal, which were "designed to display the best work of Modern American artists. . . . I observed some excellent items."[2] In November he called on his visiting friend Arthur Sechrist at the Brevoort Hotel, long famous as the haunt of bohemian artists. The two then went to a typical bohemian gathering at the home of one of Sechrist's friends at the corner of 9th Avenue and 14th Street, in the heart of the West Village.[3] In addition to this round of social gatherings, Lovecraft continued to sample Modernist literature, reading Waldo Frank's difficult impressionistic novel *City Block* in February 1925.

But Lovecraft's primary connection to the Modernist movement during this period, again, was Hart Crane. Samuel Loveman had moved to New York, and he was the point of contact between Lovecraft and Crane. The center of Crane's social scene was in Brooklyn at 106–108–110 Columbia Heights. Three contiguous brick dwellings had been turned into a sort of art colony, with the basement and first floors made into large studio areas by tearing out dividing walls. Apartments were on the other floors, John Dos Passos (later famous for *Manhattan Transfer* and the *U.S.A.* trilogy) was also living at the Columbia Heights address at the time, and Modernist notables like the painter Marsden Hartley were frequent visitors.[4] A room on the fourth (upper) floor of the building was, coincidentally, the location from which the disabled Washington Roebling had observed the completion of the Brooklyn Bridge. It was this room that became Loveman's and then Crane's, playing an important part in the inspiration of the latter's greatest work.

On 19 September 1924, Lovecraft and Loveman visited Crane at the Columbia Heights address. From the bedroom study window, Lovecraft was enthralled by the same view that would inspire Crane:

---

2. HPL to Lillian D. Clark, 29–30 September 1924 (ms., JHL).

3. HPL to Lillian D. Clark, 11 November 1924 (ms., JHL).

4. HPL to Lillian D. Clark, 11 November 1924 (ms., JHL).

I nearly swooned with aesthetic exaltation when I beheld the panorama—the evening scene with innumerable lights in the skyscrapers, shimmering reflections and bobbing ships' lights on the water, and at the extreme left and right, the flaming Statue of Liberty and the scintillant arc of the Brooklyn Bridge, respectively. But even this was not the climax. That came when we went out on the flat roof . . . and saw the thing in all its unlimited and unglassed magnificence. . . . Crane is writing a long poem on Brooklyn Bridge in a modern medium, which may some time be printed in *The Dial.* (SL 1.352)

More than fifty years later Loveman recalled the personal dynamic between Lovecraft and Crane. "Without preliminaries, [they] met one evening at my apartment, and there followed a beautiful discussion on astronomy. . . . They talked rapidly; Hart with a certain amount of deference toward Howard. Later, each complimented one another to me."[5]

On 12 October 1924, Lovecraft records another visit to Columbia Heights.

We found Crane in & sober—but boasting over a two day spree he had just slept off, during which he had been picked up dead drunk from the street in Greenwich village by the eminent Modernist poet E. E. Cumming—whom he knows well—& put in a homeward taxi. Poor Crane! I hope he'll sober up with the years, for there's really good stuff & a bit of genius in him. . . . After some conversation we all went out for a scenic walk through the ancient narrow hill streets that wind about the Brooklyn shore. There is a dark charm in this decaying waterfront, & the culmination of our tour was the . . . Fulton Ferry, which we reached about 9 o'clock, in the best season to enjoy the flaming arc of the Brooklyn Bridge in conjunction with the constellation of Manhattan lights across the river, & the glimmering beacons of slow moving shipping on the lapping tides. (SL 1.358)

Meanwhile, Lovecraft was on the verge of making another important Modernist connection. On 29 November 1924, Lovecraft wrote to his aunt that Loveman had invited him to his apartment to meet "[a] literary man of some prominence—Allan Tate, of the *Nation*, whom they want me to meet with a view of gradually getting my stories before suitably influential & conceivably appreciative eyes. . . . I shall be rather interested to meet this Tate, of whom I've heard before."[6] Tate, a prominent critic and poet, was later to be-

---

5. Samuel Loveman to Alfred Galpin, 30 March 1971 (Hart Crane Papers, Columbia University).
6. HPL to Lillian D. Clark, 29 November 1924 (ms., JHL).

come known as a member of the Southern Agrarian group, whose rather conservative version of Modernism is reminiscent of Lovecraft's.

There is no record, unfortunately, that this meeting ever occurred. On the very same day Lovecraft wrote to his aunt, however, Crane attended an event that shows how close Lovecraft physically was to the center of the Modernist movement. That evening Crane went to a party at the home of well-known critic Paul Rosenfeld. In attendance were an astonishing "Who's Who" of the American Modernists—people like Alfred Steiglitz, Georgia O'Keefe, Jean Toomer, Paul Strand, Alfred Kreymborg, Marianne Moore, Van Wyck Brooks, Edmund Wilson, and Lewis Mumford. Crane wrote: "There was music by Copeland, a modern composer, and after that the [poetry] readings by Miss Moore, myself, Kreymborg, and Jean Catel. . . . I began by reading three of my shorter poems: 'Chaplinesque,' 'Sunday Morning Apples,' . . . [and] 'Paraphrase.' As I was urged to read '[For the Marriage of] Faustus and Helen,' I finally did so. Kreymborg came to me afterward and said it was magnificent, and even the conservative Van Wyck Brooks clapped his hands" (Hart Crane to Grace Hart Crane, 30 November 1924; *Complete Poems and Selected Letters* 403–4).

American literary history, perhaps, might have been different had Lovecraft attended this gathering. In fact, he had no contact with Crane, who was shuttling back and forth to a vacation home in New York state, until the next year. On 14 October 1925, again at Sam Loveman's apartment, Lovecraft met with Crane. The poet, he said, "was just back from the country and only about one-quarter 'lit up' by his beloved booze. Poor Crane! A real poet and a man of taste, descendant of an ancient Connecticut family, & a gentleman to the fingertips, but the slave of dissipated habits which will soon ruin both his constitution & his still striking handsomeness!" (*Letters from New York* 223).

Just before he moved back to Providence, Lovecraft had another brush with the mainstream of the second American Renaissance. Lovecraft met amateur journalist Vrest Orton around Christmas 1925. Orton offered other connections to the Modernist movement. He worked at the *American Mercury* and knew H. L. Mencken. And, as Orton later recalled, "I knew Theodore Dreiser about whom I was then writing a small book, and could have introduced Howard but he would not have it. He said Dreiser was not a good wielder of the English tongue. . . . I had also visited Edna St. Vincent Millay in her narrow house on Bedford Street . . . and I considered her then . . . America's greatest lyric poet. When I invited Howard to go with me to meet here he said he did not have the proper clothes" (Cannon, *Lovecraft Remem-*

bered 344). Lovecraft would later call Dreiser "the greatest novelist America had yet produced" (*SL* 3.195) and Millay an "excellent minor" poet (*SL* 4.110).

The final time Lovecraft saw Crane was in May 1930, when Lovecraft was visiting New York.

> There appeared that tragically drink-riddled but now eminent friend of Loveman's whom I met in Cleveland in 1922, & once or twice in New York—Hart Crane, whose new book, *The Bridge,* has made him one of the most celebrated and talked-of figures of contemporary American letters. . . . When he entered, his discourse was of alcoholics in various phases—& of the correct amount of whiskey one ought to drink in order to speak well in public—but as soon as a bit of poetic & philosophic discussion sprang up, this sordid side of his strange dual personality slipped off like a cloak, & left him as a man of great scholarship, intelligence, & aesthetic taste, who can argue as interestingly & profoundly as anyone I have ever seen. Poor devil—he has "arrived" at last as a standard American poet seriously regard by all reviewers & critics; yet at the very crest of his fame he is on the verge of psychological, physical, and financial disintegration, & with no certainty of ever having the inspiration to write a major work of literature again. After about three hours of acute & intelligent argument poor Crane left—to hunt up a new supply of whisky & banish reality for the rest of the night. (*SL* 3.151)

Lovecraft's comments are unusually complimentary, and unfortunately highly prescient. Two years later Crane, who considered himself written out, committed suicide by jumping off an ocean liner en route from Mexico to the U.S.

II. *Was Lovecraft a Modernist?*

Lovecraft's physical proximity to the American Modernist movement, which we have just reviewed, may show he was exposed to its ideas. But it does not by itself prove he was an American Modernist. We may now to consider the question of whether Lovecraft the artist may be considered a Modernist.

The lives of many American Moderns, both writers and painters, tended to follow a similar pattern. A period of conventional or classically oriented work would be followed by a period of flamboyant experimentation. In many instances, as with T. S. Eliot or the painter Thomas Hart Benton, the latter phase would be impelled by a travel—a trip abroad, or to the metropolis. Lovecraft himself remarked as much in a letter of February 1925:

> A careful survey of the writings of the most vigorous and receptive minds of the country reveals a great and increasing sense of frustration and mental

starvation, so that large numbers of the most desirable persons have been forced to reside in Europe in order to escape the deadening and devastating influence of a half-baked, commerce-ridden machine culture. In my next letter I will send you a magazine cutting . . . very pertinent to this subject—a letter from an American in Paris, explaining why he cannot endure the ordeal of living in his own land. . . .[7]

The final phase after this aesthetic expansion would be a pulling back into a uniquely personal art that solidly reflected the author's native environment yet consolidated elements of highly experimental approaches to art.

If we look at Lovecraft's career we see the same familiar pattern. Early artistic isolation and reliance on classical models—for this, think of the poetry of the 1915–19 period. Then an effort to break out his attempt to join the war effort, as Hemingway, E. E. Cummings, and others had succeeded in doing. This corresponds to Lovecraft's artistic pilgrimage to New York in the early 1920s, and his entrance into a decadent phase—think here of things like "The Hound" and the early prose poems. And finally, his return to New England in the late 1920s and his creation of his most characteristic work—realistic, flavored with local color, but containing those surreal, modernist flights of fancy we call Lovecraftian.

One reason why Lovecraft has not been considered an American Modernist, I think, lies largely in his own misreading of what Modernism was. In a June 1933 letter, for example, he states that "the modernist's case rests utterly & pathetically on the flimsy faddist assumption that true beauty is a perfectly simple & definite thing—a geometrical property based wholly on abstract arrangements & entirely independent of all associative factors" (SL 4.211). This is too narrow a characterization to be correct. Similarly, in a 1928 letter he said Modernism eliminated "all anchors of inheritance & all traditional feelings & associations." The latter claim is not consistently true, as T. S. Eliot's essay "Tradition and the Individual Talent" alone shows.

Whatever his interpretation of Modernism, Lovecraft's real objection to the concept was its overreliance on non-representational style and form. It was his hatred of what he called the "Advanced Moderns"—the Imagists, the Dadaists, Gertrude Stein, and e. e. cummings—that caused him to condemn Modernism as a whole. But again, his statement in a 1927 letter that the "keynote of the modern doctrine is the dissociation of ideas and resolving

---

7. HPL to Woodburn Harris, 25 February–1 March 1929 (ms., JHL).

cerebral contents into its actual chaotic components" (*ES* 1.59–60) is clearly too general and vague to be correct.

So what is Modernism? We will need a common definition if we are to gauge Lovecraft's relation to it. Unfortunately, there is no common definition. We may, however, compile a list of characteristics of Modernist art from several sources:

- a quality of abstraction and self-conscious artifice
- a breaking away from familiar functions of language and conventions of form
- a turn toward style and technique
- a sense of formal desperation
- a disestablishment of communal reality and conventional notions of causality
- a linguistic chaos which ensues when public notions of language have been discredited and when all realities have become subjective fictions
- a remarkably high degree of self-signature
- a disenchantment with culture and civilization itself
- a fascination with evolving aesthetic, psychological, and historical consciousness
- a concern to objectify the subjective
- a concern to defamiliarize and dehumanize the expected
- a tendency to see uncertainty as the only certain thing
- a belief in perception as plural, in life as multiple, in reality as insubstantial
- a rage against prevalent traditions [i.e., Victorianism]
- a presentation of the individual as isolated from humanity
- an attention to toward individual or subjective experience
- a sense of the threat of the void and weight of vast numbers
- a use of myth, to quote T. S. Eliot on James Joyce, as a way of "controlling, of ordering, of giving a shape and significance to the immense paradox of futility and anarchy which is contemporary history" (*Selected Prose* 126)

To me, almost all these describe Lovecraft's work. Barton St. Armand, I think, was correct when he claimed that Eliot and Lovecraft were "brothers beneath the skin" in their "disgust with modern civilization, a horror of the mob, and a firm belief in the coming collapse of the West" ("H. P. Lovecraft's *Waste Paper*" 43).

Aside from the themes that I mentioned earlier and which we will discuss in more depth, what Lovecraft and the Moderns had most fundamentally in common was a hatred of the hypocrisies and falsities of Victorian literature. "It is time," he wrote in a 1923 editorial, "definitely to challenge the sterile and exhausted Victorian ideal which blighted Anglo-Saxon culture for three quarters of a century and produced a milky 'poetry' of shop-worn sentimentalities and puffy platitudes [and] a dull-grey prose fiction of misplaced didacticism and insipid artificiality" (*CE* 2.70).

Attracted by Modernism's anti-Victorianism but repelled by the formal chaos of the "Advanced Moderns," Lovecraft exhibited a deep ambivalence toward Modernism. He initially oscillated between attacking and endorsing it. Starting in 1917 he published a string of essays in the amateur press, like "The Vers Libre Epidemic," that attacked modern poetry. In 1919 he wrote a poem called "Amissa Minerva" in which he not only lambasted modern poetry but attacked specific poets like Carl Sandburg and Edgar Lee Masters by name. In an editorial of March 1923 he called *The Waste Land* "practically meaningless" (*CE* 2.64). Despite this, he continued to show a keen interest in the Eliot poem, and when it was published in book form he avidly sought it out to examine the explanatory footnotes that were not published in the *Dial*. He also was interested enough to write a very good parody of the poem, called "Waste Paper." But if Lovecraft disliked *The Waste Land*, he again had something in common with many other Modernists. William Carlos Williams, for example, saw it as a disastrous setback toward academic poetry, and even Hart Crane was repulsed by its negativity.

In the 1923 editorial mentioned earlier, Lovecraft made the following remarkable statement one that explicitly aligns himself with Modernism over against Victorianism:

> What is art but a matter of impressions, of pictures, emotions, and symmetrical sensations? It must have poignancy and beauty, but nothing else counts. *It may or may not have coherence.* If concerned with large externals or simple fancies, or produced in a simple age, it is likely to be of a clear and continuous pattern; but if concerned with individual reactions to life in a complex and analytical age, as most modern art is, it tends to break up into

detached transcripts of hidden sensation and offer a loosely joined fabric which demands from the spectator a discriminating duplication of the artist s mood. (CE 2.71; my italics)

Aside from hatred of Victorianism, the other fundamental commonality between Lovecraft and the Moderns was an intense interest in subjective states of consciousness. In July 1932 he wrote:

> The poet is a man desperately driven to express in some way a series of insistent, unplaced impressions which relentlessly haunt him. Often he cannot tell what they mean, but they are none the less real to him. His task is to set down the vague symbols of these impressions as they come to him—leaving all interpretations to others. In former times, poets sought an appearance of clearness by falsifying their moods just enough to make them correspond with known and simple things. Nowadays the sincere artist scorns such artificialities and subterfuges, and is determined to say what is in him regardless of his audience. We realise in this age as never before the confused, irrelevant hodge-podge of complexities which constitutes our real inner cerebral life behind the mask of conventional simplicity and coherence. . . . [We] must not forget that in many cases a powerful and clear-cut primary image may exist without being referable to any single source in reality. In such cases, the want of a concrete interpretation ought not to chain the poet down to silence. Perhaps his readers can interpret what he cannot—and perhaps there are as many possible (and equally valid) interpretations as there are different persons in the world. One must use one's taste, sense of proportion, and individual judgment in appraising such matters.[8]

Finally, in October 1931 he made the statement that most firmly aligns him with the Modernist aesthetic: "Modern art does not emulate photography, but tries to incorporate some essence of the subjective—some hint of the inward & unreal perspective through which the artist individually & uniquely views his subject. . . . Modern art tries to shew what an artist sees when he looks at a thing. It is not, except nominally, a portrait of the object. Essentially it is a diagram of the artist's mood" (SL 3.419). This echoes Lovecraft's many statements in letters and essays that his sole objective in writing was to create a mood. In the 1921 essay "The Defence Reopens!," for example, Lovecraft contrasted romanticism, which calls on emotion, with realism, which calls on reason. He placed his own work in a third category—the imaginative, which he said "finds strange relations and associations among the objects of visible

---

8. HPL to Maurice W. Moe, 12 July 1932 (ms., JHL).

I. GENERAL STUDIES

and invisible Nature" (CE 5.47). As an imaginative artist, he considered himself a "painter of moods" (CE 5.47), just as he describes the Modernists.

In concluding we may make a brief inventory of comments to show that despite all the fiery polemics and rhetoric of his youthful letters and essays, Lovecraft had a remarkable number of good things to say about Modernist works of art.

Hart Crane's *The Bridge* "is really a thing of astonishing merit." (SL 3.152)

Theodore Dreiser "is really a titanic figure–*the* novelist of the United States." (SL 3.155)

Sherwood Anderson is "a real & important artist." (SL 4.125)

Ulysses is "an important landmark in the history of prose expression." "There is no more powerful and penetrant writer living than Joyce when he is not pursuing his [aesthetic] theory to . . . ultimate extremes." (SL 4.14)

"I admire Sinclair Lewis intensely, for he has the artist's capacity to apply the appropriate emotions [i.e., satire] to the objects he treats." (SL 3.241)

Edgar Lee Masters is "powerful whether you call him poetry or prose." (SL 4.110)

"Robert Frost is the real stuff." (SL 4.110)

Finally, in 1932: "*Verse* is spectacularly and paradoxically *improving;* so that I do not know any age since that of Elizabeth in which poets have enjoy'd a better medium of expression." (SL 4.33)

So if we consider Lovecraft to be a Modernist, where are his Modernist works? In general, examples of Lovecraft stories marked by Modernism include things like "Nyarlathotep," *At the Mountains of Madness*, "The Shadow over Innsmouth," "The Dreams in the Witch House," "The Haunter of the Dark," and "The Outsider." In these and other stories Lovecraft firmly announces himself as a Modernist in his use of narrative strategies and handling of time (or more precisely, duration). Take for example "The Outsider." At least one commentator claimed could this pass for a lost tale of Poe. Quite to the contrary, the story's differences from Poe illustrate just how "modern" is Lovecraft. Foremost is the concern we see in "The Outsider" with *the Self* and its alienation from wholeness and from the world. Another Modernist marker is the insubstantiality of reality. The story seamlessly moves from real to surreal. It opens in a castle in a forest, but when the Outsider emerges from his tower we discover the opening has been set *below ground.* It closes in flight over Egypt and elsewhere, with the protagonist transported with ghouls on the night wind. In between these points, perhaps, the narrative is Poesque, but we leave the story with a sense of cultural and social alienation that could only be conveyed by a Modernist author. A similar concern with the self permeates almost all Lovecraft's work, which in part explains the prevalence of first-person point of view narration. Thus the use of stream-of-consciousness techniques in stories as diverse as "The Lurking Fear" and "The Haunter of the Dark."

III. *Characteristically Modernist Elements in Lovecraft's Work*

In this last section I would like to touch briefly on five elements that tie Lovecraft's work most strongly to the Modernists. These include problems of form and style; use of the "Waste Land" theme; racialism; urban figuration; and machine imagery.

A. *"Fiction is not the medium for what I really want to do": Problems of Form and Style*

We see a concern with problems of form and style in all of Lovecraft's fiction. S. T. Joshi has already pointed out Lovecraft's experiments with form in his longer stories, where we find nested narratives and disrupted time sequences. "The Call of Cthulhu" and *The Case of Charles Dexter Ward* illustrate how Lovecraft pushed narrative structure to extremes.

Language and its function, too, are paramount throughout Lovecraft's work. He began his career as a poet, but realized (rightly) he didn't have talent for the form. When he moved to prose, he still emphasized the importance of language in the creation of mood and claimed that "prose must be created with just the same exactness, delicacy of ear, imaginative fertility, etc., as verse" (SL 3.355). In his search for a usable medium he experimented with the prose poem from early in his career, creating one of his most powerful works, "Nyarlathotep," in that form. Significantly, the prose poem—a form which Lovecraft endorsed—is considered the forerunner of free verse, a form he purported to oppose.

This was Lovecraft's formal problem. Prose, he said, was meant to convey ideas. But Lovecraft wanted to convey moods. "Verse," he said, "*was never meant* to convey *ideas*, but only *moods, images, and sensations.*"[9] What Lovecraft was compelled to write, then, was something between prose and poetry.

Late in his career, Lovecraft was still searching for answer to the problems of form and style. The year prior to his death he complained that "Fiction is not the medium for what I really want to do. (Just what the right medium would be, I don't know—perhaps the cheapened and hackneyed term 'prose poem' would hint in the general direction)" (SL 5.230).

B. "Shall I at Least Set My Lands in Order?": Lovecraft's Waste Land

In undertaking our examination of the Waste Land theme, consider the following quotation.

> Almost half way between West Egg and New York the motor road hastily joins the railroad and runs beside it for a quarter of a mile, so as to shrink away from a certain desolate area of the land. This is a valley of ashes—a fantastic farm where ashes grow like wheat into ridges and hills and grotesque gardens; where ashes take the form of houses and chimney and rising smoke and, finally, with a transcendent effort, of ash-grey men who move dimly and already crumbling through the powdery ash.

This passage is not from Lovecraft, but from Chapter II of F. Scott Fitzgerald's *The Great Gatsby*. The Waste Land concept we see here, according to Warren French, is "World War One's no-man's land, a land of dead fragments of dead civilizations and the fading hopes of dying religions" (*The Twenties* 2). This pervasive sense of loss and futility following the Great War informs works by Modernist authors such as Sherwood Anderson, Fitzgerald, Hemingway, Dreiser, Faulkner, Dos Passos, Steinbeck, Frost, Cummings, and Crane.

"The Rats in the Walls" is the Lovecraft story that most strongly exhibits the Waste Land mood. As Barton St. Armand has shown, the final ravings of de la Poer are clearly modeled after the end of *The Waste Land*. Less superficially, the story speaks deeply to issues raised by the First World War. Imagery of the trenches, of dismemberment, of bodies piled high, is pervasive in the story. There is also imagery directly influenced by Eliot's poem—the coarse vegetation, the rats, the sprouting corpses, the clairvoyant, the wind under the door, the references to Atys, and so on.

---

9. HPL to Maurice W. Moe, 9 August [1930?] (ms., JHL).

We also find Waste Land imagery and World War related imagery in several of Lovecraft's other stories. "Dagon" features a risen sea-bottom and a creature whose puny talons will drag war-weakened humanity under. "The Temple" speaks of a German submarine commander displaced from his martial culture into another that is utterly silent and static. One chapter of "Herbert West—Reanimator" depicts a landscape of horrible dismemberments of the war wounded, in a manner that intends to be parodic but is best characterized as obscene. The "blasted heath" in "The Colour out of Space" is of course the most frightening example of a Lovecraftian Waste Land, with the life force literally sucked out of its inhabitants.

C. "Stinking Viscous Slime": Lovecraft's "Alien" Races

In his various biographical studies, S. T. Joshi has astutely pointed out that racism underpins everything Lovecraft wrote. Sadly, this places Lovecraft in the company of American artists and thinkers of the early part of this century people like Eliot, Fitzgerald, Cummings, Pound, and Mencken.

The general attitude in American regarding immigrants in the first three decades of this century is so extreme as to be difficult to believe. In the aftermath of World War I the enemy was no longer the German nation but the so-called "radicals," which was really a code word for "immigrants." Laws like the Espionage and Sedition Acts of 1917 and 1918 were vague enough to give law enforcement officers sweeping power. In November 1919, for example, the police in fifteen cities made raids on the suspected headquarters of radical immigrants. Mostly what they raided were settlement houses, and they left behind broken furniture, smashed typewriters, and ripped documents. People were beaten, arrested, and held without cause. In January 1920, during the Palmer Raids, over 4,000 people were arrested and held on mere suspicion in thirty-three cites in pool halls, restaurants, bowling alleys, schools, and homes. In the end only 500 were deported. This sort of mania, backed up by specious scientific theories about the biological superiority of the great white race, informs much of Lovecraft's fiction.

The prose poem "The Street," which reflects this climate precisely, was directly inspired by the Boston Police Strike of 1919. Lovecraft speaks of "swarthy, sinister faces with furtive eyes and odd features, whose owners spoke unfamiliar words and placed signs in known and unknown characters upon most of the musty houses" (D 346). These foreigners plan an uprising in which "millions of brainless, besotted beasts would stretch forth their noisome talons from the slums of a thousand cities, burning, slaying, and destroying till the land of our fathers should be no more" (*D* 347).

Joshi has explored Lovecraft's racism, which had a pseudo-scientific basis widely believed at the time, in depth. Instead of rehearsing that, I would like to read a remarkable passage from a March 1924 letter in which Lovecraft recounts a walk through the Lower East Side. The content speaks volumes about Lovecraft as a person; the style speaks volumes about how racism could energize his art.

> The organic things—Italo-Semitico-Mongoloid—inhabiting that awful cesspool could not by any stretch of the imagination be called human. They were monstrous and nebulous adumbrations of the pithecanthropid and amoebal; vaguely moulded from some stinking viscous slime of earth's corruption, and slithering and oozing in and out on the filthy streets or in and out of windows and doorways suggestive of nothing but infesting worms or deep-sea unnamabilities. They—or the degenerate gelatinous fermentation of which they were composed—seem'd to ooze, seep, and trickle thro' the gaping cracks in the horrible houses . . . and I thought of some avenue of Cyclopean and unwholesome vats, crammed to the vomiting point with gangrenous vileness, and about to burst and inundate the world in one leprous cataclysm of semi-fluid rottenness. From that nightmare of perverse infection I could not carry away the memory of any living face. The individually grotesque was lost in the collectively devastating; which left on the eye only the broad, phantasmal lineaments of the morbid soul of disintegration and decay . . . a yellow leering mask with sour, sticky, acid ichors oozing at eyes, ears, nose, and mouth, and abnormally bubbling from monstrous and unbelievable sores at every point. (*SL* 1.333–34)

Malcolm Bradbury said that a Modernist work will typically exhibit "a node of linguistic energy" (*Modernism: 1890–1930* 50), and I presume this is one such node. We find similar paranoid-manic rhetoric in "The Horror at Red Hook," "He," and "The Street," where the buildings themselves spontaneously implode to symbolize the impending collapse of American culture. Even a tale like "The Shadow over Innsmouth," which may not appear racist on its surface, betrays itself. The shambling, grunting fish-men of the city are simply placeholders for immigrants. We must conclude this when the narrator overhears them speaking "in a language I could have sworn was not English" (*DH* 341). He does not say, "in a language I could have sworn was not human."

D. "Impious Pyramids Flung Savagely to the Moon": Urban Horror

Urban figuration is another characteristic of Modernist art, seen in writers like Eliot and William Carlos Williams as well as visual artists like Steiglitz, Joseph Stella, Charles Sheeler, Charles Demuth, and many others. In Lovecraft we find it in stories like "He," "Cool Air," "The Horror at Red Hook," "Pickman's Model," and many others.

We may recall the famous first lines of "The Love Song of J. Alfred Prufrock," which has the city stretched out beneath the sky "like a patient etherised upon a table" (*Collected Poems* 3). In Lovecraft's story "He," the patient has expired: "This city of stone and stridor . . . is in fact quite dead, its sprawling body imperfectly embalmed and infested with queer animate things which have nothing to do with it as it was in life" (*D* 267). This in turn reminds us of the passage in *The Waste Land* where Eliot observes the crowds of London pedestrians and (paraphrasing Dante) remarks, "so many, / I had not thought death had undone so many" (*Collected Poems* 55).

A characteristic element of urban figuration is the use of the passing stranger, or *passant*, to symbolize the city. The passant typically takes the form of a woman. In "He," the male protagonist is picked up by a man—cloaked, hatted, and with "a noble, even a handsome, elderly countenance" (*D* 269). The homosexual overtones are obvious as they return to the man's home so that the protagonist may be initiated. The man takes the narrator's hand and leads him to the window, telling him that he, the narrator, "would be tickled by a better sight of sartain other years than your fancy affords you" (*D* 272). He gets a glimpse of the future New York:

> I saw the heavens verminous with strange flying things, and beneath them a hellish black city of giant stone terraces with impious pyramids flung savagely to the moon, and devil-lights burning from unnumbered windows. And swarming loathsomely on aërial galleries I saw the yellow, squint-eyed people of that city, robed horribly in orange and red, and dancing insanely to the pounding of fevered kettle drums, the clatter of obscene crotala, and the maniacal moaning of muted horns whose ceaseless dirges rose and fell ululantly like the waves of an unhallowed ocean of bitumen. (*D* 273–74)

Again we see the fear of immigrants, but what is more interesting to me here is the auditory imagery. It exactly describes the early work of Edgard Varèse, particularly *Amériques*. This piece was composed from 1918 to 1921, soon after Varese's arrival in New York, and reflected his fascination with the street sounds he heard from his window. The work consists of massive planes of sound colliding with one another, and uses the slowly oscillating tones of a siren and a wide array of arcane percussive instruments—including crotales, small brass disks with thick centers and specific pitches and arranged in two chromatic octaves.

One other item I have to call attention to is the scene at the beginning of "The Horror at Red Hook." A New York detective is recovering from dealing with devil worshippers—read, immigrants—in New York, and has been sent to a country village to recover. He walks to an adjoining town where he encounters a tall building. The mere sight of this mini-skyscraper causes him to fall into a hysterical fit. In real life, Lovecraft's attitude toward the skyscraper was as ambivalent as his attitude toward modern art in general. He liked the "tall & fantastic" "needle pointed" Chrysler Building (*SL* 4.21), and made it a point in September 1924 to visit "the exquisite black & gold American Radiator building—which was designed by a Pawtucket architect. It is, in a sense, an experiment in a wholly new style—as [Hart] Crane heatedly maintains—but its ethereal verticality clearly shews its legitimate descent from the gothic."[10] Ironically, Lovecraft later savaged the Rhode Island architect Raymond Hood, alluded to here in his 1935 essay "Heritage or Modernism: Common Sense in Art Forms" (in *MW*). Yet in a 1929 letter he would blithely write: "The skyscraper has a charm of its own in its proper place, achieving an exotic and almost fairylike effect when seen in masses from a distance."[11] But for the purposes of his fiction, he made the skyscraper a symbol of everything he found fearful about the city.

E. *"Prodigious Mechanical Skill": The Horror of Technology*

The Modernists' concern with technology is generally traced to 1907 publication of *The Education of Henry Adams,* and runs like a thread through the work of people like Carl Sandburg, Sherwood Anderson, D. H. Lawrence, Eugene O'Neill, and T. S. Eliot. Concern with technology and its impact is also evident in Lovecraft. In "The Whisperer in Darkness," for example, machinery is seen literally to dehumanize, as mechanical sensory devices enable surgically removed brains to survive. At the end Akeley, the hero, remains alive but is no longer a person. He is a construction consisting of wires, metal

---

10. HPL to Lillian D. Clark, 29–30 September 1924 (ms., JHL).
11 HPL to Woodburn Harris, 25 February–1 March 1929 (ms., JHL).

cylinders, a tall machine with two glass lenses on top, a box with vacuum tubes and a sounding board, and a box with a metal disc on top.

The notion of human brings as mechanical apparatus here echoes the "machine portraits" of Francis Picabia. He depicted various colleagues as conglomerations of springs, bellows, gearshift levers, horns, sparkplugs, headlamps, and light bulbs. The horror of technology and the machine is also seen in "The Statement of Randolph Carter," "Beyond the Wall of Sleep," "From Beyond," and other stories.

In closing, consider one of the greatest passages in Lovecraft, from the prose poem "Nyarlathotep." The story is about technology, and the passage goes back to the Modernist characteristics discussed at the beginning of this essay—a quality of abstraction and self-conscious artifice, a breaking away from familiar functions of language, a turn toward style, a high degree of self signature, a disenchantment with civilization, and a sense of the threat of the void. A sort of mad scientist (apparently modeled on Nicola Tesla) goes from city to city giving a demonstration of electrical machinery that causes the physical and mental disintegration of the city. At the end, the city's residents—including the narrator—group into columns and march like automata into oblivion. The narrative suddenly cuts away into an abstract, nonrepresentational Chaos:

> Screamingly sentient, dumbly delirious, only the gods that were can tell. A sickened, sensitive shadow writhing in hands that are not hands, and whirled blindly past ghastly midnights of rotting creation, corpses of dead worlds with sores that were cities, charnel winds that brush the pallid stars and make them flicker low. Beyond the worlds vague ghosts of monstrous things; half-seen columns of unsanctified temples that rest on nameless rocks beneath space and reach up to dizzy vacua above the spheres of light and darkness. And through this revolting graveyard of the universe the muffled, maddening beating of drums, and the thin, monotonous whine of blasphemous flutes from inconceivable, unlighted chambers beyond time; the detestable pounding and piping whereunto dance slowly, awkwardly, and absurdly the gigantic, tenebrous ultimate gods the blind, voiceless, mindless gargoyles whose soul is Nyarlathotep. (MW 34)

"Expect Great Revelations":
Lovecraft Criticism in His Centennial Year

From a critical perspective, Howard Phillips Lovecraft had a good hundredth birthday. In 1990 more people were aware of him, more people were reading him, and more excellent critical and biographical work was published than in any previous year. Lovecraft studies reached a turning point, entering a new phase characterized by greater critical rigor, specialization, and reliance on primary sources. The assortment of published works lent an unprecedented diversity of insight into Lovecraft as a man and as an artist. Many brought to light startling new interpretations that not only improve our understanding but also necessitate a refashioning of our very image of Lovecraft.

Peter Cannon unknowingly brought an era to a close with his *H. P. Lovecraft*, Twayne's 594th entry in its United States authors series (1989). This is the last in a series of general books about Lovecraft in English in the 1980s, following S. T. Joshi (1982), Donald R. Burleson (1983), and Maurice Lévy (trans. 1988). It was—by virtue of its extensive plot summary, comprehensive collation of existing Lovecraft scholarship, copious annotation, and avoidance of heavy critical or philosophical analysis—the best book-length introduction to Lovecraft to date for the general reader. The work was given an oddly mixed reception by other Lovecraft scholars (in a group of reviews published in *Lovecraft Studies* Nos. 19/20), possibly because these scholars had different expectations from the author and publisher.

There were, in fact, some discoveries in the book. Cannon was the first to notice, sixty-seven years after the fact, that Edgar Allan Poe is the protagonist of "Hypnos." This is one of those revelations that, once it has been pointed out, seems perfectly obvious—and all the more dramatic for it. The author does not attempt to explicate why Lovecraft put Poe in the story, instead simply assuming *hommage*. Cannon raised another interesting point in his analysis of "The Hound" (1922), a tale that Lovecraft denounced eight years after its writing (p. 33): why did Lovecraft forget—or deny—its origin as a literary in-joke for Rheinhart Kleiner and Frank Belknap Long? The subsection on decadence, which pointed the way for further work on this topic by S. T. Joshi and David E. Schultz in 1990, was another notable feature of Cannon's introduction.

But *H. P. Lovecraft's* comprehensiveness made this type of volume obsolete: no more general overviews of Lovecraft would be required for the foreseeable future. And as Cannon was busy putting a capstone on this approach, two other Lovecraft scholars were building a foundation for the future. Both Joshi and Burleson, each with one general study already in print, published challenging specialized treatments of Lovecraft.

Joshi's *H. P. Lovecraft: The Decline of the West* was the first full-length philosophical study of the author. The volume features sections on Lovecraft's philosophy and his fiction; each section is divided into parallel subsections on metaphysics, ethics, aesthetics, and politics. A background in classical philology and solid grounding in philosophy made the leading Lovecraft scholar especially well qualified for the task; but these skills were enhanced by the maniacal *diligence* that characterizes so much of his work.

The author—fresh from completing *The Weird Tale* (University of Texas Press, 1990), which required him to read all of Machen, Dunsany, Blackwood, and Bierce (he was probably the first person to do so)—went back and absorbed Lovecraft's philosophical influences. Haeckel, Hugh Elliot, Santayana, Joseph Wood Krutch, Nietzsche: every reader of *Selected Letters* is familiar with these names, which Lovecraft tosses off so glibly. But only Joshi is so bold as to confront Lovecraft on his own terms:

> When [Lovecraft] wrote that "my philosophical position [is] that of a mechanistic materialist of the line of Leucippus, Democritus, Epicurus, and Lucretius—and in modern times, Nietzsche and Haeckel" (SL 11.60), he was being remarkably careless. Only the first two of these thinkers can be called mechanistic materialists, and even they differ so significantly from Lovecraft and all other modern materialists that any resemblance is fortuitous. (7)

He takes Lovecraft to task, too, for blithely advising an elderly correspondent: "Begin with [Santayana's] *Scepticism and Animal Faith* and then proceed to the five-volume *Life of Reason.*" Unfortunately, the former *supplants* the latter, so reading them in that order makes little sense (5-6).

The finest sections of the book are on Lovecraft's metaphysics. Most important is Section II.B, "The Defence of Materialism," in which Joshi documents how Lovecraft synthesized his worldview and later assimilated Einstein's theories and quantum physics into a modified materialism. But Lovecraft refused to admit the apparent conclusion of quantum physics: that the movement of certain subatomic particles is inherently random, so that we can only establish statistical averages of how a certain reaction will transpire:

> The point Lovecraft is trying to establish is that the "uncertainty" of quantum theory is not *ontological* but *epistemological*; that it is only our inherent inability to predict the behaviour of sub-atomic particles that results in uncertainty. (20)

This belief, I think, is a critical lynchpin in Lovecraft's outlook. He thought that the universe was inherently orderly and symmetrical, operating uniformly according to a series of laws. One can tell this even from the language Lovecraft uses in letters—e.g., the "cosmos of pattern'd energy" (*SL* 2.261). I think this was a kind of psychological necessity for him. Consequently, a source of horror in his stories is the hint that the universe may in fact operate randomly after all—that all is Ultimate Chaos.

Joshi does not examine this particular issue, possibly because he has more than enough material to cover elsewhere. He does well, for example, in cataloguing the many, sometimes confusing, allusions to materialism in the fiction. The narrators' materialism (e.g., Francis Thurston's "absolute materialism" in "The Call of Cthulhu") is contrasted with the "informed and sceptical materialism of the mature Lovecraft" (81). Another significant subsection on Lovecraft's "monsters" concludes: "The materiality of all the entities in Lovecraft's fiction . . . is the trump card for the assertion of a unity between Lovecraft's philosophy and his fiction" (83). Simple as this may seem in retrospect, it was the first time any critic has pointed it out.

Another useful chapter is that on aesthetics, in which we find discussion of Lovecraft's temporary adoption of decadence (47ff.) and an unexcelled section on "The Theory of the Weird" (51–56). Joshi refined the latter to perfection over a series of articles and sections of previous books. So too with the section on politics (59–80), which includes a definitive discussion of Lovecraft's "racialism." New to the reader will be the fine "Dunsanianism and Its End" (115–19), in which the author disproves Lovecraft's statement that "Dunsany is *myself*" (*SL* 1.243). Another innovative section proposes the idea of "ethical fascism" in Lovecraft, where authorities try to rewrite history to hide the events that Lovecraft documents in his tales (130).

Despite these strengths, one occasionally gets the sense of Joshi struggling with the vast amount of information he needs to assimilate and convey. The volume would have benefited from summaries at the end of each section and at the end of the book. In addition, some interesting areas, such as Lovecraft's outlook on religion (or what might be characterized as a quasi-rational mysticism) are only lightly covered.

Perhaps this is an inherent problem in a volume of this ambitious scope, the first comprehensive study of *all* of Lovecraft's thought. Joshi himself expresses doubt in his Preface: "Perhaps another entire book on the subject will be needed in the future." *Several* books—and several dozen essays—will been needed in the future, both to expand on ideas Joshi briefly mentions and to summarize and consolidate his findings. (The first edition's 8½" by 11" format, appropriately, reminds us of a workbook.) But we should applaud the author for undertaking this daunting task. He alone had both the audacity to accept the challenge and the expertise to succeed.

As early as the 1980s, one of Joshi's personal goals included a wish "to take Lovecraft away from the world of fantasy fandom and to establish him definitively in the broader world of scholarly literary criticism" ("The Development of Lovecraftian Studies, 1971–1982 [Part IIB]," *Lovecraft Studies No. 11* [Fall 1985]: 60). As evidenced in his concluding address to the Lovecraft Centennial Conference in August 1990, he has now modified this aim, wishing a broader base of both academic and popular acceptance. Joshi has also urged Lovecraft critics to refocus their efforts. Concluding a chapter on Lovecraft in the outstanding *The Weird Tale* he wrote:

> I no longer have any interest in much of the nuts-and-bolts work that takes up so much time in Lovecraft scholarship. . . . [U]nless some broader conclusion is made, it is all so much useless intellectual baggage—and brings us no closer to what Lovecraft's stories are really about. Whereas mainstream critics must struggle to absorb Lovecraft's letters and essays to understand the fiction, it may be advisable for the inner circle of Lovecraft scholars momentarily to forget this body of peripheral material and read again the stories as stories. (229)

One of this "inner circle" to take up the gauntlet with a vengeance is Donald R. Burleson. His *Lovecraft: Disturbing the Universe* (University Press of Kentucky, 1990) uses a poststructuralist approach, one in which "the 'meaning' of a text can never be totalized or encapsulated or reached, because the nature of language is such that there are always elements of indeterminacy and is such that texts do not have edges or borders" (5). In his methodological introduction, Burleson emphasizes that "the *manner* of functioning of texts within language is problematic. Texts tend to unravel themselves, tend to subvert their own 'ruling' logic. It is the purpose of deconstructive reading to discover how this self-subversion comes about." He also handily dispenses with authorial intent, a notion that Joshi vigorously defends in his introduction to *The Decline of the West*. Burleson thus became the first critic to free himself of the ponderous baggage that Lovecraft commentators carried around for years: five volumes of letters plus tens of thousands more unpublished, several hundred articles, Cthulhu Mythos concordances, and other miscellany. The startling fact is that Burleson wrote a book without a single footnote—and not because he didn't attribute his findings. He took an approach that as revolutionary as it was simple—to concentrate on (of all things) *the text itself*. This was a breakthrough in Lovecraft studies.

Unfortunately, Burleson didn't accomplish his achievement without resistance. His volume was preceded by a string of poorly received deconstructionist essays published primarily in, of all places, *Crypt of Cthulhu*. The ironies here are many. *Crypt*, though it publishes a broad range of material, tends to position itself as a light, fan-oriented publication. Burleson became the target of a firestorm of negative reaction in the letters column, attacked not only for his approach but also his abilities. The nadir was Darrell Schweitzer's implication that Burleson was incompetent as a deconstructionist, suggesting that he was *"doing it wrong"* (*Crypt* No. 68 [Hallowmas 1989]: 58). Burleson responded with some level-headed and well-reasoned letters (*Crypt* Nos. 61 and 64) and an excellent essay, "Why (Not) Deconstruct Lovecraft?" (*Crypt* No. 66 [Lammas 1989]: 44–47).

Disturbing the Universe gets off to a strong start with a fine chapter on "The Statement of Randolph Carter." This story has always seemed somehow archetypal in the Lovecraft oeuvre. The author held it among his favorites, and it has a unique atmosphere that perhaps stems from its origin in a dream. But no commentator has ever been able to point out much of interest in it. Burleson's close reading of the story's very first sentence ("I repeat to you, gentlemen, that your inquisition is fruitless") immediately reveals a tremendous amount of depth in the text:

> Carter [the narrator] says that the interrogation "is fruitless" (barren of results), he suggests that the interrogation is *already* barren of definite results. . . . The text anticipates itself, sees itself as already written and already

read. And by beginning with "I repeat," the text even says that it has said *before* that the interrogation is, and always will be devoid of establishable results: always already fruitless.

Those who have seen the Strange Company folio reproduction of Lovecraft's handwritten manuscript (1976) can perhaps especially appreciate this insight. The insistent use of "I" in the opening of this story seems accentuated in this holograph format. Burleson's analysis, which continues with an examination of Harley Warren's "absence," is a triumph that proves the usefulness of his approach straight from the start. No mention is made that Warren was based upon Samuel Loveman—this type of tired historical-biographical tidbit is rendered obsolete here and throughout the volume. It's replaced by a dogged, heads-down determination to *read* what Lovecraft *wrote.*

There are similar small triumphs scattered throughout the book. In his analysis of "The Nameless City," Burleson catches some contradictory adjectives that heighten the sense of the city's treachery. Lovecraft describes the place as "inarticulate" (unassembled, but also unable coherently to express one's thoughts) and "unvocal" (quiet, but also unable to speak). These seemingly commonplace adjectives take on a confounding meaning when we think of how the city's murals "tell" the narrator a detailed and distinct saga.

Another example of Burleson's brilliance in dissecting Lovecraft's word choice and syntax is his analysis of the penultimate sentence of "The Terrible Old Man": "He was by nature reserved, and when one is aged and feeble one's reserve is doubly strong." The word "reserve," taken by most readers in the sense of "withdrawal," also signifies "that which is kept in readiness for use when needed." This reading makes the story much more frightening, for it intensifies the sense of the Terrible Old Man's unnatural tenacity.

The volume, however, is not without some flaws. A few chapters, like those on "The Cats of Ulthar" and "The Call of Cthulhu," seem less substantial than others. Burleson's wanderings into the outer reaches of deconstruction—especially the use of etymology to trace the Indo-European roots of key words—create a few awkward moments. At times he seems unable to summarize his findings; and the chapters' concluding paragraphs, with their talk of "indeterminacy" and "self-subversion," begin to sound a bit redundant. Some of his most provocative analysis of Lovecraft's style, too, could have been accomplished without the theoretical baggage of deconstruction.

Regardless of these shortfalls, Burleson made a profound statement by being a Lovecraft scholar employing a specific, and radically innovative critical methodology. The bulk of Lovecraft criticism, historically, had been appreciative, or impressionistic— more commentary than criticism. There had been other approaches—chiefly historical-biographical, followed by philosophical (primarily Joshi), and to a lesser extent Jungian (primarily Dirk W. Mosig). But Burleson, along with Joshi, "upped the ante" for other critics: their rigorous adoption of explicit critical-interpretative perspectives challenge all others in the field to write criticism of higher quality.

Robert M. Price, who in contrast to Joshi and Burleson often approaches Lovecraft as entertaining reading rather than "serious" literature, was likewise well represented during the Centennial year. In *The Horror of It All: Encrusted Gems from the "Crypt of Cthulhu"* (Starmont House, 1990), he offered a mixed bag from his long-running periodical. The contents range from insubstantial (Price's "Gol-Goroth, a Forgotten Old One"), to groundbreaking (Schultz's "The Origin of Lovecraft's 'Black Magic' Quote") to hilarious (Price's classic "Lovecraft as I Seem to Remember Him").

Encrusted Gems, unfortunately, didn't begin to do justice to his often-excellent magazine. Started in 1981, *Crypt* surpassed the *Fantasy Fan* and the *Acolyte as* the finest Lovecraft fan magazine. *The Horror of It All's* objective is to present a "cross section of *Crypt.*" By doing so, it tends to highlight the magazine's weaknesses—disposable articles on Mythos minutiae and lame amateur fiction—rather than its strengths. We may hope that future volumes will preserve the numerous important critical articles by Faig, Behrends, Schultz, Murray, and others, the original work by Campbell and Ligotti, and even the spirited debates in the letters columns, that made the magazine such valuable reading.

Price's contributions to the critical field are occasionally more problematic. His *H. P. Lovecraft and the Cthulhu Mythos* (Starmont House, 1990), which collects his essays from *Crypt* and elsewhere, is varied in both approach and quality. There are some outstanding pieces here on general topics. "Lovecraft's Use of Theosophy," for example, was the first article to delineate the influence of Blavatsky and Scott-Elliot. "The Humor at Red Hook" is clearly correct in its radical autobiographical reading of Lovecraft's 1925 story.

But the book is primarily a showcase for Price's work on the Mythos. "Demythologizing Cthulhu," which well displays its author's erudition with a dazzling exercise in hermeneutics, makes for fascinating and enlightening reading. The title essay, though, is on much shakier ground. Price begins promisingly by noting that Lovecraft's tales don't "belong" to the Mythos but merely use elements of it in varying degrees, dissolving the categorization of stories into "Cthulhu," "Dunsanian," and "New England horror" tales. However, he does a 180-degree turn by introducing another, equally awkward, schema. He postulates a "Dunsanian canon" (merely from Lovecraft's mentions of his Dunsany-influenced period!); an "Arkham cycle"; and a "Cthulhu cycle," which confusingly is "defined over against the Dunsanian canon." Price then implicitly disproves his own hypothesis by mentioning exceptions to this schema: "[Rarely a piece of lore may be transferred between the three cycles" (87). So why force-fit this schema, which adds no value to our comprehension of Lovecraft? A second problem manifests itself when Price brings things like the *Book of Iod* and the *Ghorl Nigral* under Lovecraft's imprimatur. Though Lovecraft politely did not affront his young correspondents when they proposed these things, it is a leap to claim he thought they had value of any kind, imaginative or otherwise.

Happily, the author modified the conclusions of these two articles. However, his weakest Mythos effort to date came in an article in the *H. P. Lovecraft Centennial Guidebook* (Montilla Publications, 1990). "The Lovecraft Mythos & Monsters" was the most regressive piece of Lovecraft criticism published over the course of the year. It was also the most potentially damaging, because of its place of publication—many of two hundred attendees of the Brown University-sponsored Centennial conference probably do not have enough familiarity with Lovecraft's work to see through its numerous misinterpretations.

The article begins by pointing out how Lovecraft was intentionally inconsistent with the details of his various entities. But then Price explicitly aligns himself with those who have done most to obfuscate Lovecraft's vision—Francis T. Laney, Derleth, Lin Carter, and Brian Lumley. He finds it, he says, "irresistible to try to provide for the interested reader, perhaps new to Lovecraft, if not a systematic outline, at least a summarizing overview of his mythology." Despite the disclaimer he proceeds to create this self-same systematic outline (a three-tier hierarchy of entities), one which has only a tangential resemblance to Lovecraft's work. The unsuspecting reader, for example, is soberly instructed that in the highest tier of the pantheon, right alongside Azathoth, is "the Nameless Mist." This will confuse the most seasoned critic until he remembers Lovecraft's mock-genealogy of his own family in a 1933 letter to James F. Morton (*SL* 4.183). Price never places the claim in context for the uninformed: this entity never appeared in the fiction! (Why not draft into the Mythos, too, the offspring of Cthulhu and Yog-

Sothoth, Shaurash-ho and Yabon, mentioned in this chart?) This article's lapses in logic, distortions, and apparent hidden agenda seriously misrepresent Lovecraft's intentions.

This is not to demean Price's acuity and contribution to the field. His "Lovecraft's 'Artificial Mythology'" (in *An Epicure in the Terrible* and written, oddly, before "Mythos & Monsters") is of very high caliber. Here he assays the religious implications of the Mythos, thoroughly covers the notion of "cosmic indifference," refrains from dragging in superfluous items, and clearly distinguishes between Lovecraft's work and others. This article, along with his excellent "Erich Zann and the Rue d'Auseil" (*Lovecraft Studies* Nos. 22/23) and many others, mark his major contributions to the field.

In 1990 some of the most extraordinary insight into Lovecraft as author—insight that causes us to reshape our understanding of him—came from Will Murray. His "Lovecraft and the Pulp Magazine Tradition" (in *An Epicure in the Terrible*) and "Lovecraft and *Strange Tales*" (*Crypt of Cthulhu* No. 74 [Lammas 1990]) are models of Lovecraft historical-biographical scholarship. Murray, consolidating primary and secondary research, proves Lovecraft *did* pursue pulp markets at times despite his eternal protestations—until now generally accepted—that he wrote only for himself.

Murray asks us to consider whether "The Colour out of Space" was "expressly written for *Amazing Stories*" (112); I think this is unlikely in light of Lovecraft's shock when that magazine accepted it and ignorance of its payment rate (SL 2.148). More solid—and more startling—is the hypothesis that Lovecraft had *Strange Tales* in mind when plotting the chase scenes for "The Shadow over Innsmouth." Murray concludes that the Providence author had "outgrown his pulp markets but never successfully aspired beyond them" (129).

The most significant biographical contribution in 1990 was made by the eminent Kenneth W. Faig. His long monograph *The Parents of Howard Phillips Lovecraft* (Necronomicon Press) consolidates the little secondary information we know about Winfield and Sarah Lovecraft, and adds his own primary research to the picture. The essay sheds a tremendous amount of light on the elder Lovecrafts as personalities, and on their relationship with and effect upon their son. This volume is a must for anyone who seeks to understand Lovecraft the man.

The section on the shadowy Winfield Lovecraft—whereabouts unknown 1853–1889, died 1898—is most fascinating of all. It forces us to seriously reconsider the environment that the precocious and sensitive Howard experienced from 1892 until his father's death. The elder Lovecraft, a traveling salesman, went mad in a hotel room in April 1893 and was confined in a Providence hospital until he died five years later. Faig contravenes Lovecraft's statement that his father was "never able again to move and or foot, or to utter a sound" (*SL* 1.33). If Winfield Lovecraft was paralyzed, he reasons, why was he returned to Providence "under restraint"; why was he described as "an insane person" when Albert A. Baker was appointed his legal guardian in 1893; and how was he able to survive five years after his return?

Faig concludes not only that the elder Lovecraft was conscious, but also that Lovecraft knew his father was mad and not simply comatose. Was the son—as we have been conditioned to believe—completely insulated from his father's madness? Or did Lovecraft witness his father's terrible outbursts? The latter now appears to be possible—a conclusion which has a profound effect upon our understanding of Howard Phillips Lovecraft.[1]

Faig presented a condensed version of his monograph in the biographical section of *An Epicure in the Terrible: A Centennial Anthology of Essays in Honor of H. P. Lovecraft* (Fairleigh Dickinson University Press, 1991; rev. ed. rpt. Hippocampus Press, 2011), edited by David E. Schultz and S. T. Joshi. The latter collection represented the top Lovecraft scholars at the top of their form. Section I complemented Faig's article with Jason Eckhardt's first-rate "The Cosmic Yankee" (the first real study of Lovecraft as local colorist) and Murray's piece on Lovecraft as pulp writer.

The section of "Thematic Studies" contained a definitive overview by Burleson covering the themes of denied primacy, merciful ignorance, illusory surface appearances, unwholesome survival, and oneiric objectivism. Stefan Dziemianowicz's long "Outsiders and Aliens: The Uses of Isolation in Lovecraft's Fiction" surveyed how Lovecraft's narrators changed with his adoption of a progressively cosmic outlook.

David E. Schultz picked up this thread with "From Microcosm to Macrocosm: The Growth of Lovecraft's Cosmic Vision." Schultz (whose analogous presentation was a high point of the Centennial Conference) offered his strongest essay to date—a historical-biographical analysis of Lovecraft's shift from being a "macabre" writer to the "cosmic" writer, a movement that is

---

1. John McInnis, in his essays "'The Colour out of Space' as the History of Lovecraft's Immediate Family' (presented at the Lovecraft Centennial Conference) and "Father Images in 'Hypnos'" (*Fantasy Commentator* 7, No. 1 [Fall 1990]) claims that HPL witnessed attacks of madness that Winfield Lovecraft—who was briefly confined at 454 Angell Street—experienced prior to 1893. His source of information is inadequately documented. McInnis ought to come forth with more a more substantive essay to document his claims.

unique in literature. This idea, articulated here for the first time, was an important step forward in understanding the artistic growth of Lovecraft. It is still to be hoped that he will follow up with a book-length analysis of Lovecraft's 1924–1926 "New York Exile," which contributed so much to the latter's artistic progression.

The book concluded with a series of comparative and genre studies. The best of these is Barton St. Armand's "Synchronistic Worlds: Lovecraft and Borges," which contrasts Borges's celebration of reality with the reality-supplementing of the American author, providing many interesting citations from Borges work along the way. Of further interest in this section is R. Boerem's "Lovecraft and the Tradition of the Gentleman Narrator" and Norman R. Gayford's "The Artist as Antaeus: Lovecraft and Modernism," which ranges far afield—across the work of Padraic Colum, Eugene O'Neill, W. B. Yeats, T. S. Eliot, Sherwood Anderson, and Upton Sinclair—to place Lovecraft in the context of the twentieth century.

In all, *An Epicure in the Terrible* was an exceptional showcase. Not only were the individual pieces strong, but the essays seemed to compliment and expand upon each other. This anthology superseded Joshi's *Four Decades of Criticism* as the key collection of articles on Lovecraft.

The one hundredth year of Lovecraft, then, was an important one for the understanding of his legacy. Murray, Faig, and Schultz reshaped our perception of Lovecraft the man and author; Joshi and Burleson lent new insight into Lovecraft's work and thought, and pointed the way to critical work in the second hundred years. We missed the contribution of some veteran Lovecraft scholars—notably R. Alain Everts and William Fulwiler—but were favored by the presence of others—St. Armand and Boerem. There were refreshing contributions, too, from newcomers like Gayford and Robert H. Waugh. Yet this year's revelations about Lovecraft raised as many points of interest as they explained, reaffirming as they did his standing as a prominent American author.

II. Essays on Specific Works

On "Amissa Minerva"

"Amissa Minerva," a poem of 92 lines written in rhymed couplets, is an insightful reminder of both the depth of H. P. Lovecraft's literary erudition—regarding contemporary as well as classical literature—and the skill of his satirical verse. Though not reprinted since its original appearance in the obscure journal The *Toledo Amateur* for more than six decades, it ranks with the best of Lovecraft's poetical satires. In content it reflects the vital interest Lovecraft had in the poetic art, and his support of classical literary standards, and his ambivalent position on Modern art.

Lovecraft has at often been represented as one who separated himself from his time, retreating into a world of fantasy and outlandish "gods." This notion, of course, is belied by even a cursory examination of his many essays and letters on contemporary politics, science, and art. Lovecraft, ever an interested spectator of the cultural developments of his era, noted around him the rise of the machine-age, with its emphasis on quantity rather than quality, and a Spenglerian decline of Western culture which he felt would eventually usher in a new age of barbarism.

In literary matters, he found a corresponding decline of the classical qualities of "simplicity, moderation, and elegance of taste" in the both the prosodic and poetical specimens of his contemporaries:

> We moderns have overreached ourselves, and we are blundering along with a dislocated sense of values amidst a battle of heavy formalities and false emotions which find reflection in the vague, hectic, hurried, and impressionistic language of decadence. (CE 2.38)

Note how Lovecraft classes himself with the moderns.

One may easily imagine the mixed horror and amusement of Lovecraft as he watched the emergence of the "new poetry," not long after the turn of the century. At the forefront of the movement was the Chicago periodical *Poetry: A Magazine of Verse*, whose first issue was published in October 1912.

By 1915, the magazine had featured the work of Ezra Pound, "H. D." (Hilda Doolittle), Vachel Lindsay, Amy Lowell, William Carlos Williams, Robert Frost, Carl Sandburg, Wallace Stevens, and T. S. Eliot. These poets, generally of the opinion that traditional poetic forms and subjects were played out and bereft of relevance to the present day, set about to create what they saw as a more vital poetry using freer rhythms to address topics closer to everyday experience. Various "schools" of poets (e.g., Vorticists, Cubists) sprang up, each with slightly varying credos, and volumes such as *Some Imagist Poets* (1915) began to come forth.

Though it is unknown whether Lovecraft followed these developments in *Poetry* or on some other periodical such as the *Dial*, his reaction to it is well documented. In a letter to fellow amateur-journalist and poet Rheinhart Kleiner of 23 August 1916, Lovecraft made this pronouncement:

> I have lately been amusing myself by a perusal of some of the *Imagism* nonsense of the day. As a species of pathological phenomena it is interesting. The authors are evidently of approximately harmless characteristics, since so far as I know, they are all at large; but their work indicates that most of them are dangerously near the asylum gates—uncomfortably close to the padded cell. There is absolutely no artistic principle in their effusions; ugliness replaces beauty, and chaos supplies the vacant chair of sense. Some of the stuff, though, would mean something if neatly arranged and read as prose. Of the major portion no criticism is necessary, or even possible. It is a product of hopelessly decayed taste, and arouses a feeling of sympathetic sadness, rather than contempt. Since *Imagism* has no relation to poesy, I think no lover of the muse need entertain apprehension of his art from this quarter. (*SL* 1.24–25)

Upon examining some of his contributions of the period to amateur journals, however, we find that Lovecraft must have felt something approaching "apprehension." A spate of essays in his *Conservative*, the first of which was "Metrical Regularity," appearing in the July 1915 number, contain attacks on the new poetry of varying degrees of detail and violence. Lovecraft next led off the October issue of that year with a Pope-like poetic satire on "The State of Poetry," blasting a variety of contemporary ills ranging from faulty attempts at rhyming to inappropriate subject matter.

"The Vers Libre Epidemic" (January 1917) divided the new poets into those who wrote poetically but lacked metrical dress, and those who left not only meter but sense by the wayside (cf. note on Amy Lowell in the Annotation). Lovecraft reiterated his conviction that the new schools had "no relation to poesy," though in a rather more pointed fashion:

These pitiful creatures are naturally divided into various types and schools, each professing certain "artistic" principles based on the analogy of poetic thought to other aesthetic sources such as form, sound, motion, and colour; but they are fundamentally similar in their utter want of a sense of proportion and of proportionate values. . . . These radicals are animated by mental and emotional processes other than poetic. They are not in any sense poets, and their work, being wholly alien to poetry, cannot be cited as an indication of poetical decadence. It is rather a type of intellectual and aesthetic decadence of which vers libre is only one manifestation. (CE 2.20)

One of his last amateur articles to address the new poetry was "The Despised Pastoral" (in the *Conservative* of July 1918), where Lovecraft was explicit regarding his view on the nature of true poetry—it should be a description of "ideal beauty, or the straightforward presentation of pleasing images for no other purpose than to delight the fancy" (CE 2.22).

The next year saw the publication of "Amissa Minerva" in The *Toledo Amateur*, which more or less restates in rhyme the points Lovecraft presented had presented in previous essays. The poem is of especial interest in the immensity of its scope: Lovecraft deftly surveys the whole of poetic history from Homer to Carl Sandburg in 92 lines with a surety that bespeaks both a long and thoughtful study of the art and a supreme skill in its execution.

In theme the poem takes the form of an impassioned plea to Minerva, Roman goddess of all concerned with intellect and craft, to reinstate the powers of poetry to modern bards. In this it echoes the notion expressed in an essay of Lovecraft's that was published the same year, "The Case for Classicism": "The literary genius of Greece and Rome, developed under peculiarly favourable circumstances, may fairly be said to have completed the art and science of expression" (CE 2.37).

There is fascinating schema of literary influences at work in the poem. Lovecraft is writing in the preeminently precise and polished idiom of his acknowledged model in verse, Alexander Pope. The satire is twice influenced by classical models—once through the direct influence of Lovecraft's classical reading, and once through Lovecraft's reading of Augustan satire, which was in its turn influenced by classical models. Lovecraft thus sings the praises of these poets as he demonstrates the virtues of their style and satiric manner.

In all, we may say that Pope's work is the primary influence on the poem (as indeed it is on the bulk of Lovecraft's poetry). Lovecraft's favorite poet, Pope translated the *Iliad* and *Odyssey* into the "resounding couplets" Lovecraft favored most, and also did some "Imitations" of the great satirist

Horace. Pope's satires (which were primarily influenced by Horace) certainly had effect here, though Lovecraft's satire is rather more personal and biting, in the manner of a Juvenal.

As far as specifics go, the first section of Pope's celebrated *An Essay on Criticism* is the obvious antecedent in the theme of "Amissa Minerva." Pope warns both critics and poets not to stray far from the "natural" precepts established by classical authors:

> Moderns, beware! or if you must offend
> Against the precept, ne'er transgress its end;
> Let it be seldom, and compell'd by need;
> And have, at least, their precedent to plead. (ll. 163–66)

The ending of the first section of the *Essay* (ll. 181–200), in the form of an evocation to the ancient bards, is very similar to Lovecraft's conclusion:

> Still green with bays each altar stands,
> Above the reach of sacrilegious hands;
> Secure from flames, from envy's fiercer rage,
> Destructive war, and all-involving age.
> See from each clime the learn'd their incense bring!
> Hear in all tongues consenting paeans ring!
> In praise so just let every voice be join'd,
> And fill the general chorus of mankind.
> Hail, bards triumphant! born in happier days;
> Immortal heirs of universal praise!
> Whose honours with increase of ages grow,
> As streams roll down enlarging as they flow;
> 0 may some spark of your celestial fire,
> The last, the meanest of your sons inspire,
> . . . .
> To teach vain wits a science little known,
> To admire superior sense, and doubt their own!

Lovecraft's version differs from Pope's in that it addresses Minerva rather than the ancient bards, and laments the temporary absence of the classical standards rather than lauding their steadfastness.

The satiric aspect of "Amissa Minerva" does not come fully to the fore until the last section, after Lovecraft has identified the standards to which modern poetry should be compared. Making a brief resume of the best poets of

II. ESSAYS ON SPECIFIC WORKS

western civilization, he pauses to enumerate the follies of the new poetry. Lovecraft then lays into the various moderns with some lines with a stinging wit that rivals the best of his satiric poetry (e.g., "The Dead Bookworm" [1919], the hilarious "Power of Wine" [1915], and "An Epistle to Francis, Ld. Belknap" [1929]).

To conclude, the combined encapsulation here of the progress and aesthetics of poetry, coupled with the amusing satire of the poem, make it unfortunate that it has not been reprinted before a wider audience. It is to be hoped that it will someday be part of a volume showcasing the poetic satires of Lovecraft.

Amissa Minerva

"Humano capiti cervicem pictor equinam
Jungere si velit, et varias inducere plumas
Undique collatis membris, ut turpiter atrum
Desinat in piscem mulier formosa superne;
Spectatum admissi risum teneatis amici?"
                              —Horace, *Ars Poetica.*

In ancient times, when bards without pretence
Knelt down to beauty, and deferr'd to sense,
Bright Nature glow'd in well-selected dress,
And pleas'd us with a double loveliness.
'Twas then great Homer warm'd the list'ning heart,   5
And gentle Maro cheer'd the soul with art:
Then Horace made the laws of writing known,
And what he preach'd attended in his own;
With care reflected, and with wisdom taught
Each turn of poesy and rule of thought.   10
In various fashions various authors writ,
Yet none but strove for melody and wit;
Dulness was eas'd, and worth sublimely grac'd,
With even numbers, and harmonious taste.
Succeeding times an equal genius bore,   15
Yet the skill'd bard attends the rules of yore;
Unchang'd they reign, tho' novel themes abound,
Their goal exalted, and their spirit sound.
Thus lofty Shakespeare struck the living lyre,

And Milton sang with scarce inferior fire;   20
Thus facile Pope our modern tongue refin'd,
And Horace's to Homer's talents join'd:
Thus Thomson the revolving year review'd,
And shew'd the changing charms of wold and wood;
Thus gentle Goldsmith and the dismal Dean   25
With classic ease serv'd up their smiles or spleen.
Cowper's sad Muse enervate art display'd,
And Wordsworth's prattle pain'd the Heav'nly Maid;
Yet thro' it all the poet throng she led,
Beauty and truth still beaming bright ahead.   30
Immortal Keats th' Olympian impulse knew,
And hapless Poe kept Helicon in view.
Sweet Tennyson melodic murmurs roll'd,
And shining Swinburne felt the flame of old:
So from on high the noble notes we hear,   35
When hark! they fade—they pause—they disappear!

Engulfing folly! Spawn of febrile earth!
Destructive monster of unnatural birth!
Aonia weeps as thy foul dictates sway
The public fancy and the poet's lay.   40

True art, like Nature, variously glows,
And ev'ry side in gen'rous measure shews;
Surveys the scene with calm appraising eye,
And sings its choicest features as they lie.
No odd perspective lends eccentric tone,   45
Nor aimless musing takes its flight alone;
The idle fancy and the vagrant mind,
In science, not in art, their province find.
Artistic souls the earthly picture scan;
Paint what hath shone to centuries of man;   50
Psychology the mental wand'rer views,
And Aesculapius claims him, not the Muse!
Yet see on ev'ry hand the antic train
That swarm uncheck'd, and gibber o'er the plain.
Here Librist, Cubist, Spectrist forms arise;   55

With foetid vapours cloud the crystal skies;
Or led by transient madness, rend the air
With shrieks of bliss and whinings of despair.
Exempt from wit, each dullard pours his ink
In odes to bathtubs, or the kitchen sink;   60
Bent on effect, they search their souls for themes,
And spout disease, or colic-troubled dreams.
See to what depths a Lowell can descend;
How Masters can his guideless force expend;
Hear morbid Gould inflict a limping tune,   65
Or striving Sandburg bay the suff'ring moon.
Distress'd we watch the clownish chorus chant
Unmeaning nonsense and abhorrent cant;
When thro' the gloom some reason is diffus'd,
We mourn to think of so much sense unus'd!   70

Undying Pallas, whose all-pow'rful rule
Exalts the artist and condemns the fool,
Whose gentle will made Grecian genius shine,
And gave to Rome her majesty divine,
Pardon the erring race which bade thee fly   75
So lately to thine own Olympian sky:
Descend once more to these celestial meads,
To kindle art, and ease our mortal needs.
Instruct each bard in bright forgotten truth,
And from his follies save aspiring youth;   80
Unfold again the heav'n-imparted code
That shapes the lyric, pastoral, and ode.
Pierian skill a second time confer
On feeble man, so prone to sink and err,
And with kind patience teach his race anew   85
To choose the good, the beautiful, the true.
These boons, Athena, in thy mercy send
To bless the few who still would call thee friend;
The faithful few who with threnetic lays
Implore thy succour, and diffuse thy praise: 90
Offspring of Jove, may thy forgiving care
Reward our smoking altars and our pray'r!

Notes

Title: Latin for "Minerva Lost." Minerva, daughter of Jupiter (cf. l. 92) was one of the primary Roman divinities. She was, among other things, the goddess of wisdom, thinking and inventive power personified. As a maiden divinity whose father was a supreme god, the Romans identified her with the Greek Athena (cf. l. 87), who likewise was concerned with human wit and cleverness. Minerva was worshipped as the patroness of all the arts and trades, and at her festival she was particularly invoked by all who desired to distinguish themselves in these disciplines. (The latter practice is reflected in the last stanza of the poem.) Cf. Horace's *Ars Poetica* 385–86: "But you will do nothing against Minerva's will; such is your judgment, such your good sense."

Epigraph: Horace, *Ars Poetica* 1–5: "If a painter chose to join a human head to the neck of a horse, and to spread feathers of many a hue over limbs picked up now here now there, so that what at the top is a lovely woman ends below in a black and ugly fish; could you, my friends, if favored with a private view, refrain from laughing?"

5 Homer] Lovecraft thought Homer (9th–8th? cent. B.C.E.) the greatest poet (see below). He was an early devotee of The *Odyssey*, and at age seven wrote "The Poem of Ulysses; or, The New Odyssey."

6 Maro] "Foremost of the Augustans, and next to Homer perhaps the world's greatest poet, was P. Vergilius Maro (70–19 B.C.E.), commonly known as Virgil. Born of honest rural stock in the tiny village of Andes, near Mantua, Virgil has often been affectionately termed 'the Mantuan Swain.' His education took place at Cremona and Rome, and at the age of twenty-two he commenced the Eclogues or pastoral poems modeled after the Greek Theocritus, which form the earliest of his surviving efforts. Being dispossessed of his farm when the countryside was apportioned to the soldiery who had battled against Brutus, Virgil was reimbursed by the generous Emperor Augustus, whose praises he sang in his later eclogues. At the suggestion of his friend and patron Maecenas, Virgil next exercised his Muse in the composition of an agricultural poem called the 'Georgics', whose precepts are sound, and whose poetry is exquisitely finished. But the poet's crowning work is his 'Æneid', a sublime epic in twelve books designed to glorify the Roman people and Caesar's line by tracing them back to Æneas, a mythical survivor of conquered Troy who was said to have settled Italy" ("The Literature of Rome," CE 2.27).

7 Horace] "Most modern in spirit of all classic authors—so modern, in fact, that nearly every bard of today makes occasional translations or imitations of his witty lines—is the lyricist and satirist Q. Horatius Flaccus (65–8 B.C.E.), commonly called Horace. . . . As a poet Horace is always subjective and auto-biographical. . . . His works consist of satires, which are without exception mild, tolerant, and written as if by a man of the world who shares the follies he ridicules; epodes, or individual satires; and odes, from which he derives the greatest fame. The odes are of extreme literary excellence, and so vividly reflect the light, trivial, fundamental commonplaces of human nature, that they have survived with unimpaired popularity to the present day" ("The Literature of Rome," CE 2.27–28). The allusion in ll. 7–10 is, of course, to the Ars Poetica.

8 Cf. Pope's comment on Horace in An Essay on Criticism, l. 660: "His precepts teach but what his works inspire."

16–18 Cf. "The Case for Classicism" (1919): "Indeed, those modern periods have been most cultivated, in which the models of antiquity have been most faithfully followed" (CE 2.37).

19 Shakespeare] Lovecraft thought Shakespeare (1564–1616) "is certainly a splendid exemplification of genius, and the most natural reproducer of Nature and mankind in literary history. In variety and range he stands alone" (HPL to Alfred Galpin, 5 November 1918; Letters to Alfred Galpin 50).

20 Milton] John Milton (1608–1674). Lovecraft considered him, along with Virgil and Wordsworth, among the "foremost artists" (SL 5.55). Elsewhere he remarked, "I don't see how you . . . can argue away the distinctive charm of the large part of his work. He has the power of evoking unlimited images for person of active imagination" (SL 4.158). Lovecraft thought that Dore's illustrations to Milton's Paradise Lost had inspired his dreams of the creatures he called "night-gaunts," which he later wrote of in his sonnet sequence Fungi From Yuggoth.

21 Pope] Alexander Pope (1688–1744) was, along with Poe, one of Lovecraft's "prime favourites" (SL 1.72). The latter wrote in "The Allowable Rhyme" (1915): "Delicately attuned to the subtlest harmonies of poetical construction, Alexander Pope bought English prosody to its zenith, and still stands alone on the heights" (CE 2.14). Pope is the primary influence upon the bulk of Lovecraft's poetry (see Introduction). The allusion in l. 22 reflects the fact that Pope wrote both mock-epic (and didactic) poetry in the manner

of Homer (in addition to making celebrated translations of the *Iliad* and *Odyssey*), as well as satires in the manner of Horace.

23 Thomson] James Thomson (1700–1748). His *Seasons* was a perennial favorite of Lovecraft (see, for example, *SL* 2.317).

25 Goldsmith] Cf. "The Allowable Rhyme": "In Oliver Goldsmith [1730–1774] there rose one who, though retaining the familiar classical diction of Pope, yet advanced further still toward what he deemed ideal polish by virtually abandoning the allowable rhyme" (*CE* 2.15).

Dean] Jonathan Swift (1667–1745), Dean of St. Patrick's Cathedral in Dublin. Lovecraft favored his prose above his poetry.

27 Cowper] William Cowper (1731–1800). It might be noted that Lovecraft, certainly the greatest epistolarian of the twentieth century, found Cowper's missives "most interesting of all letters" (*SL* 1.88).

28 Wordsworth] William Wordsworth (1770–1851).

31 Keats] Keats (1795–1821), along with Shelley, represented to Lovecraft "the absolute zenith of the poetic art" (*SL* 4.109–10). The allusion at 1. 30 is to Keats's famous lines, "Beauty is truth, truth beauty;—that is all / Ye know on earth, and all ye need to know" from "Ode on a Grecian Urn." Note, however, how in a letter to Alfred Galpin of 27 May 1918 Lovecraft elaborated that "Beauty is certainly the prime object [of poetry]; Truth is to be considered only when coincident with Beauty—which is not so often as the late J. Keats believed" (*Letters to Alfred Galpin* 21).

32 Poe] The influence of Edgar Allan Poe (1809–1849) upon Lovecraft (predominantly his fiction) is vast in nature and scope, and may perhaps be best summarized here with Lovecraft's celebrated remark, "Poe has probably influenced me more than any other one person" (*SL* 3.378).

Helicon] A famous mountain of antiquity in Boeotia, sacred to Apollo and the Muses. On the summit was the grove of the Muses, with statutes of those divinities.

33 Tennyson] Alfred, Lord Tennyson (1809–1892) "drew no pictures beyond the commonplace vision of the stolid bourgeoisie . . . and derives his fame

mainly from a marvelous gift of rhythmical melody and an ability to please the unimaginative mind" (*SL* 1.137).

34 Swinburne] "Of [Charles Algernon] Swinburne [1837–1909], I like the earlier things, though of course he babbled himself out in repetition" (*SL* 1.109).

47–52 Cf. *SL* 2.249: "One application of modern psychology which you may have noticed is the new *'stream-of-consciousness'* school of literature, which has undoubtedly gained surprisingly in the last decade. This school recognizes as a fundamental principle the newly discovered fact that our minds are really full at all times of a thousand irrelevant and dissociated threads of imagery and ideation . . . against it we may argue that art concerns only *results* and harmonic impression patterns—a definition which would classify stream-of-consciousness writing as mere prosaic *science* or *philosophy* rather than genuine aesthetic creation." Lovecraft's view of reliance upon such techniques as primarily of psychological interest accounts for the reference to Aesculapius, the Graeco-Roman god of medicine, at l. 52.

55 Librist, Cubist, Spectrist] These terms refer, respectively, to three schools of the "new poetry." Librist refers to vers libre, or free verse. Cubist poetry, like cubist painting, attempted to take the elements of an experience, fragment them, and reassemble them in a new and insightful manner. Spectrist poetry was a mock school of literature invented by Witter Bynner and Arthur Davidson Ficke, who wrote "Spectric" poems and articles about the supposed school's principles in 1915–16. Meant as a satire on the Imagists, Vorticists, et al., the school actually attained a following for nearly two years; a volume entitled *Spectra: A Book of Poetic Experiments* emerged in 1916. Bynner did not reveal the hoax until some thirty years later. In "The Vers Libre Epidemic" (1917), Lovecraft provided this example of the work of an anonymous "so-called Spectrist" (*CE* 2.20), taken from a New York City newspaper:

> Her soul was freckled
> Like the bald head
> Of a jaundiced Jewish banker.
> Her fair and featurous face
> Writhed like
> An Albino boa-constrictor.

She thought she resembled the Mona Lisa.
This demonstrates the futility of thinking.

60 odes to bathtubs, or the kitchen sink] This is likely an illusion to Gertrude Stein's *Tender Buttons* (1914), which consists of impressionistic descriptions of food and common household objects such as a seltzer bottle and dinner plates. Cf. also Lovecraft's "The State of Poetry" (1915), ll. 54–55: "His earthly fancy never mounts the sky, / But draws its source from kennel, barn, or sty."

63 Lowell] Amy Lowell (1874–1925). The allusion becomes clear when we read Lovecraft's later description of her as one who had "discarded the late XIX century tradition for the imagistic thought of the early XX century" (*SL* 3.115–16). In "The Vers Libre Epidemic" we find this amusing tirade directed at her work: "[A] wholly erratic school of free poets is that represented by Amy Lowell at her worst; a motley horde of hysterical and half-witted rhapsodists whose basic principle is the recording of their momentary moods and psychopathic phenomena in whatever amorphous and meaningless phrases may come to their tongues or pens at the moment of inspiration (or epileptic) seizure" (*CE* 2.20).

64 Masters] Edgar Lee Masters (1868–1950), best know for his *Spoon River Anthology* (1915). Later in life Lovecraft admitted that Masters was "powerful whether you call him poetry or prose" (*SL* 4.110).

65 Gould] Gerald Gould (1885–1936) was an English journalist, reviewer, essayist and poet. Lovecraft may have seen his work in the *Atlantic Monthly*, the *Egoist*, *Coterie*, or the *Little Review*.

66 Sandburg] Carl Sandburg (1878–1967), whose *Chicago Poems* had been published in 1916.

71 Pallas] An epithet of Athena, whose meaning is probably related to the Greek word for "young girl" or "maiden." Traditionally, however, it was bestowed because a giant named Pallas was among those Athena vanquished in the battle between the Olympians and the Giants.

83 Pierian] Referring to Pieria, in antiquity a country in Macedonia whose inhabitants were early worshippers of the Muses.

89 threnetic] Of or pertaining to a threnody (a dirge); i.e., mournful.

"The Hound"—A Dead Dog?

Critics have been quick to dismiss H. P. Lovecraft's "The Hound" (1922) as an overwritten imitation of Edgar Allan Poe. Even the author himself, a decade after it was written, wryly called it a "dead dog" (Barlow, *On Lovecraft and Life* 16). There is, however, something of interest in "The Hound": it is the major fictional reflection of Lovecraft's interest in decadent literature in general and in Joris-Karl Huysmans in particular. The story also displays Lovecraft's early tendency toward literary dilettantism. He assimilated and employed Decadent elements with startling speed. Startling, too, is his later disavowal (either a memory lapse or conscious denial) of the story's apparent intent.

When "The Hound" was written in 1922, Lovecraft was just emerging from his personal and literary shell. After years sequestered in his Providence home, saturating himself in Graeco-Roman classics, eighteenth-century literature, and Poe, Lovecraft had broken out in 1914 by joining the United Amateur Press Association. This event, coupled with the death of a dearly loved but oppressive mother in 1921, saw Lovecraft broadening his horizons with a vengeance. His literary skill and personal charm had earned him a place in the highest tier of amateur journalism of the day, elected President of the United (1917) and appointed President of the National Amateur Press Association (1922).

New acquaintances, new literary influences, and travel came quickly. All these affected his literary productions. While in Boston for an amateur convention in November 1919, for example, he saw a lecture by Lord Dunsany; a spate of Dunsanian tales promptly followed.

In September 1922 Lovecraft was visiting New York City for the second time, spending time with (among others) Frank Belknap Long, one of his closest and most influential friends. Long, another amateur journalist, had begun to exchange letters with Lovecraft in 1920. Long impressed Lovecraft as "a sincere and intelligent disciple of Poe, Baudelaire, and the French decadents" (SL 1.80). Their early correspondence is peppered with exchanges about these topics.

The French Decadents were a school of late nineteenth- and early twentieth-century authors who held that art was superior to nature, and that the greatest beauty was that of dying or decaying things. Joris-Karl Huysmans consolidated and explored this outlook in the 1884 novel A Rebours (Against the Grain), summarizing his narrator's attitude this way:

> Artifice, besides, seemed to Des Esseintes the final distinctive mark of man's genius.
> Nature had had her day, as he put it. By the disgusting sameness of her landscapes and skies, she had once for all wearied the considerate patience of æsthetes. Really, what dulness! . . . What a monotonous storehouse of fields and trees! What a banal agency of mountains and seas! (47)

Lovecraft was immersed in this school of literature in 1922, through not only Long's influence but also that of fellow amateurs Samuel Loveman and Alfred Galpin. To the latter he had written in June: "My aunt tells me that the Gallic stuff has safely arrived at #598 [Angell Street]. . . . Thanks for the kind words anent that first attempt at Baudelairian translation" (letter to Alfred Galpin, 30 June 1922; Letters to Alfred Galpin 120). Lovecraft, then, was so enthusiastic about the Decadent school that he attempted to translate some of Baudelaire—despite the fact that he never learned French.

This same enthusiasm seems to be the stimulus for the writing of "The Hound." Lovecraft and Long discussed Huysmans when they first met in Manhattan in April 1922, alone and in company with their other amateur friends, Rheinhart Kleiner and James F. Morton. The first American edition of A Rebours had just been published in New York by Lieber & Lewis, in a translation by John Howard. Long apparently lent Lovecraft the book on this trip or during the September visit. Lovecraft enjoyed A Rebours; five years later he wrote: "I read it and thought it excellent. Huysmans shewed the aesthete and decadent at his extreme development, and his work has really become a classic of its kind—the definitive epitomisation of the neo-hedonistic philosophy of the 'nineties" (letter to August Derleth, 9 February 1927; ES 1.68). Lovecraft, always fond of noting how he favored atmosphere over plot in weird fiction, found Huysmans—who "was not a lover of the story for its own sake"[1]—a sympathetic counterpart.[2]

---

1. "Huysmans is a great figure—there is no question about that. He summarised a certain aesthetic attitude better than any other one person, & was an exceedingly potent influence

The spirited discussions about Decadence among Lovecraft's acquaintances were fresh in his mind when he and Rheinhart Kleiner made an antiquarian exploration to the Dutch Reformed Church in Flatbush on 16 September:

> That evening, Kleiner and I investigated the principal antiquity of this sec-
> tion—the old Dutch Reformed Church—and were well repaid for our
> quest. . . . Around the old pile is a hoary churchyard, with interments dat-
> ing from around 1730 to the middle of the nineteenth century. . . . From
> one of the crumbling gravestones—dated 1747—I chipped a small piece to
> carry away. It lies before me as I write—and ought to suggest some sort of
> horror-story. I must place it under my pillow as I sleep. . . . Who can say
> what thing might not come out of the centuried earth to exact vengeance
> for his desecrated tomb? And should it come, who can say what it might
> now resemble? (SL 1.98)

He composed "The Hound" almost immediately after his visit to the church.[3] Following the line of thought in his letter, he created the story of two men stalked by a thing, resembling a gigantic hound, from a grave they defiled. Lovecraft used Kleiner as one of the protagonists, St. John. This was the nick-name Lovecraft often used for Kleiner in the salutation of letters, referring to the eighteenth-century philosopher Henry St. John, Viscount Bolingbroke. By extension, we can safely assume that Lovecraft cast himself in the role of the narrator.

---

on later writers of his school. You will find 'A Rebours' worth going a good deal of trouble to get—though that, of course, is more philosophy than fiction. Huysmans was not a lover of the story for its own sake." HPL to August Derleth, 11 March 1927; ES 1.74.

2. By examining HPL's letters we can determine what works of Huysmans he read. We have seen that HPL first read *A Rebours* when Frank Belknap Long lent him his copy dur-ing the first or second New York City visit. In 1932 HPL bought his own copy (SL 4.91). Long also lent HPL *En Route* (HPL to August Derleth, 2 March 1927; ES 1.72). HPL owned a copy of *Là-Bas* in translation (HPL to August Derleth, 16 March 1927; ES 1.75). August Derleth promised to lend HPL a copy of *Down Stream* (HPL to August Derleth, 24 June 1927; ES 1.96), but I have no evidence that he ever did.

3. HPL wrote "The Hound" while he was still in New York. See HPL to Edwin Baird, quoted in the March 1924 issue of *Weird Tales*, rpt. in S. T. Joshi and Marc A. Michaud, ed., *H. P. Lovecraft in "The Eyrie"* (West Warwick, RI: Necronomicon Press, 1979), 19. The story must have been composed in October 1922 rather than September as is com-monly accepted; see HPL to Annie E. P. Gamwell, 3 October 1922 (ms., JHL): "Sunday [1 October] . . . in the [Dutch Reformed Church] graveyard I chipped another piece from a hoary tombstone . . . I must summon from their deeps the ghouls of midnight."

"The Hound," then, is a thinly disguised literary joke written for the benefit of Kleiner and their circle. The playful nature of the story becomes apparent in its very first paragraph, as Lovecraft zestily dispatches his friend in the third sentence:

> In my tortured ears there sounds unceasingly a nightmare whirring and flapping, and a faint, distant baying as of some gigantic hound. It is not dream—it is not, I fear, even madness—for too much has already happened to give me these merciful doubts. St. John is a mangled corpse; I alone know why, and such is my knowledge that I am about to blow out my brains for fear I shall be mangled in the same way. Down unlit and illimitable corridors of eldritch phantasy sweeps the black, shapeless Nemesis that drives me to self-annihilation. (*D* 171)

The style is another element that immediately alerts us to the story's design. The author had penned the delicate "Music of Erich Zann," with its sober and concise prose, a scant nine months before. But he used a highly-colored style to complement the theme of "The Hound," one which is taken directly from *A Rebours*. The protagonist, a graverobber, cites the reason for his aberrant behavior:

> Wearied with the commonplaces of a prosaic world, where even the joys of romance and adventure soon grow stale, St. John and I had followed enthusiastically every aesthetic and intellectual movement which promised respite from our devastating ennui. (*D* 171)

This motivation is identical to one that drives the plot of Huysmans's *A Rebours*. The novel's prologue documents the youth of Duc Jean des Esseintes, and his growing disillusionment with religion, sex, Parisian society, and academics in turn:

> Whatever he attempted proved vain; an unconquerable ennui oppressed him. . . . [H]e dreamed of and practiced perverse loves and pleasures. This was the end! As though satisfied with having exhausted everything, as though completely surrendering to fatigue, his senses fell into a lethargy . . . (25)

Des Esseintes retires in seclusion to the suburbs of Paris and undertakes a series of episodic attempts to amuse himself with, among other things, elaborately decorated chambers, a gilded and bejeweled tortoise, bizarre flowers and plants, recherché literature and art, and a "mouth organ" that dispenses "inner symphonies" (82) of liqueurs. But eventually, he realizes how far from the normal he has strayed:

II. ESSAYS ON SPECIFIC WORKS

> In short, since leaving Paris, Des Esseintes was removing himself further
> and further from reality, especially from the contemporary world which he
> held in an ever-growing detestation. This hatred had inevitably reacted on
> his literary and artistic tastes . . . (267)

A *Rebours* exhibits what John Taylor calls "the subordination of the experience of external reality to that of inner . . . reality," of a reality "which is, so
far as possible, pure sensation" (72–73). Lovecraft took this rationale to its
extreme, using it both as a basis for the writing style and as a reason why the
narrator and St. John engage in such bizarre behavior:

> Only the sombre philosophy of the Decadents could hold us, and this we
> found potent only by increasing gradually the depth and diabolism of our
> penetrations. Baudelaire and Huysmans were soon exhausted of thrills, till
> finally there remained for us only the more direct stimuli of unnatural per-
> sonal experiences and adventures. It was this frightful emotional need
> which led us eventually to . . . the abhorred practice of grave-robbing. (*D*
> 171–72)

The introductory paragraphs of "The Hound" are a succinct restatement of
Des Esseintes's dilemma. What follows is a more grotesque version of his attempted solution. In fact, it is so grotesque that it crosses the border from
pastiche into parody: Lovecraft seems intent on going Huysmans one better.

Des Esseintes, for example, possesses a "volume, bound in sealskin. The
book was 'The Adventures of Arthur Gordon Pym', specially printed for him
on laid paper, each sheet carefully selected, with a sea-gull watermark" (44).
But Lovecraft's protagonist tells of "a locked portfolio, bound in tanned human skin, [which] held certain unknown and unnamable drawings which it
was rumoured Goya had perpetrated but dared not acknowledge" (*D* 172).

Similarly, Huysmans regales us with a gruesome description of engravings
by the Dutchman Jan Luyken:

> [There were] horrible prints . . . pregnant with human sufferings, showing
> bodies roasting on fires, skulls split open with swords, trepaned with nails
> and gashed with saws, intestines separated from the abdomen and twisted
> on spools, fingernails slowly extracted with pincers, eyes gouged, limbs dis-
> located and deliberately broken, and bones bared of flesh and agonizingly
> scraped by sheets of metal. (103)

Lovecraft can only top this with a description of the charnel museum, very
much in the style of Huysmans but teetering on the brink of the absurd:

> Around the walls of this repellent chamber were cases of antique mummies alternating with comely, life-like bodies perfectly stuffed and cured by the taxidermist's art, and with headstones snatched from the oldest churchyards of the world. Niches here and there contained skulls of all shapes, and heads preserved in various stages of dissolution. There one might find the rotting, bald pates of famous noblemen, and the fresh and radiantly golden heads of new-buried children. (*D* 172)

The incongruous adjectives here—"comely," "perfectly," "fresh," "radiantly golden," and especially the coinage "new-buried"—show us that we are now in the realm of parody. Lovecraft's later description of *A Rebours* as "a veritable text-book of aestheticism carried to a reductio ad absurdum" (letter to August Derleth, [2 April 1927]; *ES* 1.79) indicates that although he enjoyed the book he never completely agreed with its rationale. But for the sake of parody he took this "reductio ad absurdum" even further in "The Hound."

The reader can find a fuller exposition of the Decadent influence on Lovecraft in Barton St. Armand's *H. P. Lovecraft: New England Decadent*. St. Armand's case for the mature Lovecraft as a writer of the Decadent school, however, has been handily demolished by S. T. Joshi, who identified 1921–26 as the period of possible Decadent influence and severely qualified its extent (see Joshi's review of St. Armand's book; *Lovecraft Studies* No. 3 [Fall 1980]: 35–38). Joshi's position is clearly correct: in a letter to Long five months before writing "The Hound," Lovecraft implicitly qualifies his devotion to the Decadents by contrasting them with Poe: "[Poe] is the father of most of the redeeming features of decadent literature, and differs from the actual decadents in that they have failed to comprehend the magnificent and ultra-human point of view upon which his creations are based" (*SL* 1.173). I believe that the many Poe allusions in "The Hound"—the "oblong box" exhumed, the "knock at my chamber door," and the "red death" brought by the Hound—are a message to Long that although the Decadents amused him, it was Poe whom he held in high esteem.

Lovecraft initially held "The Hound" in some regard, for it was one of his five initial submissions to *Weird Tales*. As time went by, however, he disliked the story more and more. In 1930 he wrote to August Derleth: "'The Hound' is the worst piece of mine to get into print" (letter to August Derleth, 18 February 1930; *ES* 1.247). Similarly, to Clark Ashton Smith he complained: "There is too much sonorous rhetoric & stock imagery, & not enough substance, in this piece of junk" (*SL* 3.192). To these and other correspondents, he never mentions the origin of the story as a display of literary versatility written specifically as an amusement for a group of friends. Citing the letter to Smith, Peter Cannon first pointed out that Lovecraft seems to have forgotten his original intent (*H. P. Lovecraft* 33). If Lovecraft did not forget it, he certainly disavowed it. But Lovecraft's own criticism shows that in "The Hound"—perhaps without realizing it—he achieved what C. Hugh Holman described as the paradigm of a Decadent work:

> [A Decadent] work of art [is one] in which a declining seriousness of purpose or loss of adequate subject matter is combined with an increasing skill and even virtuosity of technique and form to produce an overly intense sensationalism or effect. (147–48)

"Hypnos": Art, Philosophy, and Insanity

"Hypnos" (1922), one of H. P. Lovecraft's earliest and most obscure efforts, is of interest in its vivid depiction of the dangers of being an artist. Specifically, it shows how a failure to discern the functions of art, science, and philosophy can lead one from genius to madness.

One reason that "Hypnos" is so little discussed, perhaps, is that its literal meaning is elusive. On first reading the story seems somewhat unfocused and imagistically confused. I believe, however, that with more reflective analysis we may class it with other outstanding early tales—such as "The Outsider" (1921) and "The Music of Erich Zann" (1921)—in which Lovecraft worked in a deliberately impressionistic manner.

We can best approach "Hypnos" by laying out a point-by-point summary of its incidents.

1. A sculptor aids a man who has fallen unconscious in a railway station.
2. The sculptor is impressed by the man's beauty and decides he will take the man as his "only friend."
3. They commence "studies" in dream work, in which they experience magnificent cosmic vistas and the friend's face is seen by the sculptor as youthful.
4. The sculptor creates works with the friend as his model.
5. The friend expresses an intent to rule the universe.
6. During a dream episode, the friend breaks through a barrier which the sculptor cannot pass into another, horrifying realm.
7. Frightened at what he sees, the friend advises that the dream work cease and that they must now try to remain conscious.
8. The two men age rapidly and unaccountably.
9. The friend shows a fear of the constellation Corona Borealis.
10. The friend accidentally falls asleep.

11. The sculptor hears a drone from the direction of Corona Borealis.
12. The friend is struck by a beam of light from that direction which turns him into a statue.
13. The sculptor is told the friend was imaginary, and the statue is a youthful self-portrait of the sculptor.

With the events of the narrative itemized this way, let us consider "Hypnos" as a cautionary tale for those seeking refuge in the realms of aesthetics and metaphysics.

When the sculptor first discovers the friend at the train station, the latter has fallen in the midst of "a crowd of the vulgarly curious" (D 164). Lovecraft depicts the refinement he felt inherent in an aesthetic sensibility by contrasting the friend with the average person. At the outset of the story the friend symbolically represents this sensibility in its most vital form. He is even described in the language of aesthetics: his visage was "beautiful," with a brow "white as the marble of Pentelicus"; he was "a faun's statue out of antique Hellas"; "[h]is voice was music."[1]

---

1. HPL based the elements of the sculptor on his friend and fellow amateur journalist Samuel Loveman (1889–1976). Loveman, whom HPL considered "a glorious pagan" (SL 1.166), was a poet and classicist noted primarily for the long poem *The Hermaphrodite*. HPL had been Loveman's sponsor in 1917 for the latter's second advent into the United Amateur Press Association, and considered him the finest poet in amateur journalism (SL 1.51). Four months before penning "Hypnos," HPL wrote to Frank Belknap Long: "Loveman . . . is a romantic figure, about whose poverty, suffering, genius, and divine melancholy one might write a moving volume. He is one step in advance of his beloved vagabonds and bohemians—for he has pride, honour, and character" (SL 1.166).

Sonia Haft Greene states that HPL "described his [Loveman's] character and temperament in one of his stories called 'The Statement of Randolph Carter', into which there is woven a substantial amount of subtle praise and, I might say, admiration" (*Private Life* 11). It is true that Harley Warren is patterned after Loveman, because "Statement" is based an a dream HPL had involving the two men (SL 1.94). However, I postulate that Ms. Greene is actually referring here to "Hypnos." "Statement" contains very little about the character and temperament of Warren. It simply relates the events of the dream almost verbatim. Also, Ms. Greene was present when HPL debuted "Hypnos" on 6 April 1922, by reading it aloud to Loveman and several other friends (SL 1.176). "Statement," on the other hand, was written several years before she met HPL.

The passage cited ("his voice was music") recalls HPL's comment in a contemporary letter that "Loveman makes language a thing of music" (SL 1.176). The neurosis of the sculptor is also reminiscent of HPL's associate: "The sensitiveness of Loveman is painful—his nerves and emotions are highly organised. A kind word is balm to him, and a cruel word crushes him wholly" (SL 1.176). There is also a Loveman tie-in with the story's classical sculpture motif. Writing to Lillian D. Clark after a 1925 visit to the Metropoli-

By using the motif of Greek sculpture Lovecraft hints of the educative ideology of that ancient tradition, which held that "men should learn from works of art and try themselves to become as beautiful and perfect as the statues around them" (Rank 54). Ironically, this literally happens at the end of the story.

Clearly, the tale's twist ending (incident 13) is meant to convey that the sculptor's friend not a person at all, but rather a projection of some part of the sculptor's personality. This is interesting because the very reason why the sculptor is attracted to the friend is the latter's superior ability to perceive the universe:

> And when he opened his . . . eyes I knew he would henceforth be my only friend—the only friend of one who had never possessed a friend before—for I saw that such eyes must have looked fully upon the grandeur and the terror of realms beyond normal consciousness and reality; realms which I had cherished in fancy, but vainly sought. (D 165)

The friend represents that part of the sculptor's personality that has access to the creative powers of the subconscious. This is borne out by the fact that when the sculptor first encounters the friend the latter is "unconscious" (D 164). The artist needs to draw upon his subconscious mind in order to create true art; that is, he needs to be able to access "realms beyond normal consciousness and reality" to achieve a true aesthetic product. The friend helps the sculptor access "realms which I cherished in fancy" (i.e., the imagination), acting in the role of genius or muse. According to Otto Rank:

> The idea of the "Genius" comes originally from early Roman times, when it means the personal protecting spirit . . . and corresponds to the Egyptian "ka" and Greek "daimon." Without discussing this notion of a psychical double of man, which is represented in different forms in the different doctrines of the soul, let us note here that the Roman Genius . . . acquired the literal meaning of "begetter." (20)

---

tan Museum of Art, HPL mentions a hallway of Graeco-Roman antiquities in which is displayed "the famous athlete's head which Loveman worships as the marble embodiment of his poetic 'Hermaphrodite'" (19–23 August 1925; JHL).

Aside from this internal evidence, S. T. Joshi discovered a typescript of "Hypnos" in the possession of Mara Kirk Hart with the dedication "To S. L." written under the title on page one. The fact that HPL dedicated "Hypnos" to Loveman seems to support the theory put forth here.

The friend is the "begetter" of the sculptor's art. After the initial meeting with the friend, the sculptor experiences a burst of creative inspiration: "I chiselled busts of him and carved miniature heads in ivory to immortalise his different expressions" (D 165). The word "expression" has a double meaning in this context. At first we may take it only in the sense of "a facial aspect indicative of feeling." But it also carries the connotation of "aesthetic expression": something that, having in some way taken shape and definition in the psyche of the sculptor, is outwardly objectified for others with the help of an external sign (in this case, the resulting marble sculpture).

The two men then embark on a series of adventures in dream-visions (incident 3). A dream is a work similar to the work of art, but uncontrolled and lacking the permanence, and hence the great beauty, of art (Feibleman 17). These visions represent the imagining that must precede the controlled imagining involved with creation of the artistic product. At first the sculptor and the friend achieve spectacular success: "Human utterance can best convey the general character of our experiences by calling them *plungings* or *soarings*" (D 166). Lovecraft used similar imagery in a letter to James F. Morton as he attempted to explain the essence of his own most profound aesthetic experiences:

> There must always be a sense of . . . *soaring outward* toward the discovery of stupendous, cosmic, inconceivable things, and toward the envisagement and comprehension of awesome rhythms and pattern and symmetries too Titanic, too unparticled, too trans-galactic, and too overpowering for the relatively flat, tame, and local name of "beauty". When a city or landscape or experience can give me this sense of untrammelled and starward soaring, I account it worth my while to go after it. (SL 3.127)

In "Hypnos," however, the friend oversteps his bounds (incident 5). Taken with the godlike stature inherent in the role of artist, the friend seeks not merely to depict the universe but instead to control it. "No god or daemon could have aspired to discoveries and conquests like those which we planned," the sculptor boasts. The friend is no longer content with helping create new forms of an individual nature. Instead, he attempts to shape the very cosmos to his will: "He had designs which involved the rulership of the visible universe and more; designs whereby the earth and the stars would move at his command, and the destinies of all living things be his" (D 166). The "design" is of a universe which moves like a machine, with all outcomes already destined.

The friend thus leaves the proper domain of the artist, now seeking truth instead of beauty. He has moved out of the realm of art and into the realm of science and philosophy, a transgression symbolized in his penetration of an obstacle through which the sculptor cannot pass (incident 6). The friend's orientation is no longer toward classical aesthetics, but rather toward Einsteinian physics (hence Lovecraft's allusion to the scientist as the "man with Oriental eyes" [D 165] near the tale's outset). His "perceptions of infinity" have given way to "vistas of unimaginable hells" (D 167) as he confronts his realization of a meaningless, mechanistic universe.

Lovecraft often warned his writer associates not to confuse the functions of art and philosophy: "Poetry and art for *beauty*—but science and philosophy for *truth*" (SL 2.23). But the friend is unable to maintain this distinction. By doing so he imperils his very existence: "In many cases," Lovecraft wrote, "the truth may cause suicidal or nearly suicidal depression" (SL 1.65; see also Joshi, *Decline of the West* 111).

As depicted in the story, Lovecraft did not perceive the barrier between art and philosophy to be conceptually difficult to traverse. A few years before writing "Hypnos" he blithely advised a disillusioned and ill-adapted amateur poet: "Having failed to derive satisfaction from contemplating yourself as a highly organised centre of impressions and sensations, try contemplating yourself as a speck of dust in the midst of infinite creation. . . . Be a scientist instead of a litterateur" (SL 1.86). The friend does just this, but with disastrous results.

Lovecraft, of course, was both artist and philosopher; we need not conclude that attempts to fulfill both roles must necessarily result in the crisis experienced by the sculptor. The latter has here made the error of confounding the roles of the two disciplines, apparently because he lacks strength of personal character. Based on the sculptor's lack of normal relations with other people, we may safely conclude that he is meant to represent a neurotic type. The friend's physical appearance (black clothing, small beard, flowing hair), which symbolically reflects the narrator's disposition, conveys this neurosis. The costume is that of the artist-poseur type which Lovecraft loathed as insincere. Soon after completing the story the author remarked in a letter, "I despise Bohemians, who think it essential to art to lead wild lives" (SL 1.229).

After the friend breaks through the barrier, the two men age visibly. They have lost the childlike sense of wonder necessary to achieve aesthetic product. Lovecraft continually advised his associates, especially fellow weird writer Frank Belknap Long, never to lose this orientation:

II. ESSAYS ON SPECIFIC WORKS

I wou'd advise any young man, to purge his mind clear of extravagant notions of divinity and perfection, and his veins clear of extravagant emotions. . . . I would furthermore . . . have him exalt the pleasures of pride and strength . . . rather than sink into the empty ticklings and melancholy introspections of languid feebleness, effeminacy, and decay. (SL 2.261)

The sculptor in "Hypnos" has been unable to avoid the pitfalls outlined here. Instead, he has been seared by "Aletheia Phrikodes" ("the hideous truth"; cf. Lovecraft's 1916 poem of the same name). As a result he can no longer create art: "My statues and ivory heads were all sold, and I had no means to purchase new materials, or energy to fashion them even had I possessed them" (D 168).

The stars, too, have ceased to be a source of aesthetic wonder. The constellation Corona Borealis is no longer symbolic of the classical myth of Dionysus and Ariadne; it is simply a group of unrelated, infinitely distant gaseous globes. The "spangled night sky" (D 166) is now merely an outpost of cosmic indifference. It is the source of a power that strikes down the friend as the sculptor's mind races, not with thoughts of beauty but of metaphysics: "clocks—time—space—infinity" (D 169).

All that is left is a bust depicting the sculptor as he had been at age twenty-five when, we can assume, the naive wonder requisite for artistic creation had not been blasted away (incident 12). This statue is the only legacy of an aesthetic sense despoiled by "the mad ambitions of knowledge and philosophy" (D 170). The sculptor has failed to fulfill the potential of the artist: to immortalize his mortal life. Instead of artistically transforming death into life, as it were, he has misguidedly transformed life into death. Such, Lovecraft cautions, is may be the result of the "tragic life" that fuses "art, philosophy, and insanity" (D 170).

Curious Myths of the Middle Ages and "The Rats in the Walls"

The great variety of sources for H. P. Lovecraft's fiction reflects the fact that he was always alert for suitable images and ideas. He was quick to note any seemingly apt incident encountered in his personal life, in dreams, and in printed matter for possible fictional use. *Curious Myths of the Middle Ages* should be numbered among the many books from which Lovecraft obtained fictional material, for internal evidence indicates it influenced "The Rats in the Walls" (1923). There are marked similarities between two of the myths presented in the book and aspects of Lovecraft's tale.

Curious Myths of the Middle Ages was written by Sabine Baring-Gould (1834–1924), a parson, folklorist, historian, and archaeologist (see Shepherd, "Introduction" to *Curious Myths* vi). Each of the book's twenty-four chapters deals with a particular medieval superstition and its variants and antecedents. It was first published in two parts in 1866 and 1868, and went into many editions over the succeeding years because of its great popularity (Shepherd viii). Lovecraft alludes to the work in the second chapter of "Supernatural Horror in Literature":

> In this fertile soil [i.e., the Middle Ages] were nourished types and characters of sombre myth and legend which persist in weird literature to this day. . . . The shade which appears and demands the burial of its bones, the daemon lover who comes to bear away his still living bride, the death-fiend or psychopomp riding the night-wind, the man-wolf, the sealed chamber, the deathless sorcerer—all these may be found in that curious body of mediaeval lore which the late Mr. Baring-Gould so effectively assembled in book form. (D 371)

Lovecraft owned a copy of *Curious Myths of the Middle Ages* and mentions it in "Suggestions for a Reading Guide" (CE 2.193).

Lovecraft must have enjoyed this work as an imaginative stimulus, as he did Skinner's *Myths and Legends of Our Land* and Fort's *The Book of the Damned*. As with these works, Lovecraft used *Curious Myths of the Middle Ages* as a fictional sourcebook as well.[1] One chapter of Baring-Gould's work resembles aspects of Lovecraft's "The Rats in the Walls" enough to rule out coincidental similarity, while another seems to have been a more peripheral influence on the tale.

The most important and striking correspondence is between Lovecraft's fictional Exham Priory and Baring-Gould's legend of St. Patrick's Purgatory. Baring-Gould writes:

> In that charming medieval romance, Fortunatus and his Sons, . . . is an account of a visit paid by the favored youth to that cave of mystery in Lough Derg, the Purgatory of S. Patrick.
>
> Fortunatus, we are told, had heard in his travels of how two days' journey from the town, Valdric, in Ireland, was a town, Vernic, where was the entrance to the Purgatory; so thither he went with many servants. He found a great abbey, and behind the altar of the church a door, which led into the dark cave which is called the Purgatory of S. Patrick. (230)

Exham Priory is also a medieval religious house set over a mysterious cavern entered by way of an altar. Both Lovecraft's creation and St. Patrick's Purgatory are located in the British Isles, in England and Ireland, respectively.

The abbot of the Purgatory tells Fortunatus of its origin, "many hundred years ago," when the area was a "howling wilderness." A hermit named Patrick discovered the cave and got lost inside when he wandered in too far. There he heard "piteous cries issuing from the depths of the cave, just such as would be the wailings of souls in purgatory." With the help of prayer, Patrick found his way out of the cave, and after his death was made a saint. "Pious people, who had heard the story of Patrick's adventure in the cave, built this cloister on the site" (231–32). As the site of a prehistoric temple built over a cavern, Exham Priory has an equally ancient origin.

The abbot continues: "Some have affirmed that they have heard a bitter crying and piping therein; whilst others have heard and seen nothing. No

---

1. George T. Wetzel, in "The Cthulhu Mythos: A Study" (90), points out that HPL obtained elements of "The Shunned House" (1924) from Skinner's work. William Fulwiler, in "Mu in 'Bothon' and 'Out of the Eons'" (20), suggests that the idea of extraterrestrial mining colonies on earth found in "The Whisperer in Darkness" (1930) had its source in Fort's book. The general influence of Fort's work on HPL was pointed out as early as Matthew H. Onderdonk's "Charon—in Reverse" (1948).

one, however, has penetrated, as yet, to the furthest limits of the cavern" (232). This last sentence is the kind of thing that appealed to Lovecraft's imagination, and in describing his grotto he tells of its "apparently boundless depth of midnight cavern where no ray of light from the cliff could penetrate. We shall never know what sightless Stygian worlds yawn beyond the little distance we went, for it was decided that such secrets are not good for mankind" (*DH* 43).

Baring-Gould goes on to relate the story of Sir William Lisle, one of many who made a pilgrimage to the Purgatory.

> [Lisle] said that when he and his companion passed through the gate of the Purgatory of S. Patrick, that they had descended as though into a cellar, and that a hot vapour rose toward them and so affected their heads, that they were obliged to sit down on the stone steps. And after sitting there awhile they felt heavy with sleep, and so fell asleep, and slept all night. . . . [Lisle said] that they had been oppressed with many fancies and wonderful dreams, different from those they were accustomed to in their own chambers; and in the morning when they went out, in a short while they had clean forgotten their dreams and visions; wherefore he concluded that the whole matter was fancy. (240–41)

This scene parallels the one in "The Rats in the Walls" in which the narrator and Norrys spend a night in the sub-cellar and the former is plagued by strange dreams:

> Couches were brought down. . . . We decided to keep the great oak door—a modem replica with slits for ventilation—tightly closed; and, with this attended to, we retired with lanterns still burning to await whatever might occur.
>
> The vault was very deep in the foundations of the priory. . . . As we lay there expectantly, I found my vigil occasionally mixed with half-formed dreams. . . . These dreams were not wholesome . . . (*DH* 37)

The descriptions of the two caverns also bear similarities. Lovecraft's grotto is lighted, "not [by] any mystic phosphorescence, but [by] a filtered daylight which could not come except from unknown fissures in the cliff that overlooked the waste valley" (*DH* 41). In Baring-Gould's tale of the Knight Owain, the latter was "locked in the cave, and he groped his way onward in darkness, till he reached a glimmering light" (236). In the twilit grotto, "there were buildings and other architectural remains" (*DH* 42). Knight Owain, likewise, came out into an underground land, where was a great hall and cloister" (236).

Sir Owain goes further into the cave and sees many places where souls are being tormented in various ways. Among these places are pits of molten metals, in which are "men and women, some up to their chins. . . . The knight was pushed by the devils into one of these pits, and was dreadfully scalded, but he cried to the Saviour, and escaped" (236–37). This is echoed by Lovecraft's "accursed infinity of pits in which the rats had feasted" and his narrator's similar mishap: "Once my foot slipped near a horribly yawning brink, and I had a moment of ecstatic fear" (*DH* 44). But Delapoer inhabits a less forgiving Lovecraftian cosmos: there is no salvation.

In Owain's tale and others, the Purgatory contains an evil area where demons hold sway over tormented souls; Baring-Gould notes:

> Unquestionably, the story of S. Patrick's Purgatory is founded on the ancient Hell-descents prevalent in all heathen nations; Herakles, Orpheus, Odysseus, in Greek Mythology, Aeneas, in Roman, descend to the nether world and behold sights very similar to those described in the Christian legends just quoted. . . . In ancient Keltic mythology the nether world was divided into three circles corresponding to Purgatory, Hell and Heaven. (245, 248)

This reminds us of Delapoer's remark that the twilit grotto was "the antechamber of hell" (*DH* 42).

The general situation of St. Patrick's Purgatory, that of a very old abbey in Great Britain built over an infernal cavern, undoubtedly served as a model for Lovecraft's Exham Priory. The more specific similarities were perhaps subconsciously employed by Lovecraft, the tale likely written years after he read *Curious Myths of the Middle Ages*, when he remembered only vaguely the particulars of the Purgatory story. In a letter to Rheinhart Kleiner of May 1921, Lovecraft wrote his address as "St. Angell's Priory," which suggests he was reading Baring-Gould's book at the time (*SL* 1.131).[2]

A more general influence on "The Rats in the Walls" may have been the chapter of Curious Myths entitled "Bishop Hatto." This chapter focuses on tales in which huge swarms of rats attack and devour a human being, usually a ruler who mass-murders the sick and poor of the community. The archetypal tale is one of Bishop Hatto, who during the famine of Germany in 970

---

2. I owe this observation to David E. Schultz.

a.d. is said to have wearied of the cries of the famished and invited them all
to his barn, ostensibly to feed them from his great store of grain.

> Then, when he saw it could hold no more,
> Bishop Hatto he made fast the door,
> And while for mercy on Christ they call,
> He set fire to the barn, and burnt them all.
>
> . . . .
>
> So then to his palace returned he,
> And he sat down to dinner merrily,
> And he slept that night like an innocent man;
> But Bishop Hatto never slept again.
>
> In the morning, as he enter'd the hall,
> Where his picture hung against the wall,
> A sweat, like death, all over him came,
> For the rats had eaten it out of the frame.

Then there came a man to him from his farm, with a countenance pale
with fear, to tell him that the rats had devoured all the corn in his grana-
ries. . . . The Bishop looked from his window, and saw the roads and fields
dark with the moving multitude; neither hedge nor wall impeded their progress as they made straight for his mansion. Then, full of terror, the prelate
fled by his postern, and, taking a boat, was rowed out to his tower in the river. . . .

> He laid him down, and closed his eyes;
> But soon a scream made him arise.
> He started, and saw two eyes of flame
> On his pillow, from whence the screaming came.
>
> He listen'd and look'd—it was only the cat;
> But the Bishop he grew more fearful for that,
> For she sat screaming, mad with fear,
> At the army of rats that were drawing near.

Here, as in Lovecraft's story, a cat gives warning of rodent manifestations.
The rats swim across the river to Hatto's tower:

> And now by thousands up they crawl
> To the holes and windows in the wall.
>
> . . . .

And in at the windows, and in at the door,
And through the windows by thousands they pour,
And down from the ceiling, and up through the floor,
From the right and the left, from behind and before,
From within and without, from above and below,
All at once at the Bishop they go.

They have whetted their teeth against the stones,
And now they pick the Bishop's bones.
They gnaw'd the flesh from every limb,
For they were sent to do judgment on him. (448–50)

This swarm of rampaging, man-eating rats is reminiscent of Lovecraft's rats, which he, too, refers to as an "army":

> And, most vivid of all, there was the dramatic epic of the rats—the scampering army of obscene vermin which had burst forth from the castle . . . the lean, filthy, ravenous army which swept all before it and devoured fowl, cats, dogs, hogs, sheep, and even two hapless human beings before its fury was spent. Around that unforgettable rodent army a whole separate cycle of myths revolve, for it scattered among the village homes and brought curses and horrors in its train. (*DH* 31)

The reference to the "whole separate cycle of myths" might be an allusion to the group of tales recounted by Baring-Gould.

Lovecraft's remark that "The Rats in the Walls" was suggested by "the cracking of wallpaper late at night and the chain of imaginings resulting from it" (*SL* 5.181) seems to indicate the origin of the rats motif; the Hatto myths probably influenced the manner in which the motif was developed. The physical aspect of Exham Priory, however, is most assuredly founded on that of St. Patrick's Purgatory. Furthermore, the pronounced similarities of the altar entrance, strange dreams, subterranean structures, demonic pits, and limitless depths associated with the Purgatory to details in Lovecraft's tale indicate that these particulars at least subliminally influenced the author. Such are the correspondences between *Curious Myths of the Middle Ages* and "The Rats in the Walls." Lovecraft made these elements wholly his own, seamlessly joining them with the theme of man's ancestral curse and creating what has been called "a nearly perfect example of the short story" (Joshi, *H. P. Lovecraft* 46).

Lovecraft's "Elizabethtown"

Though much has been written about H. P. Lovecraft's celebrated "New York Exile," little attention has been paid to the time he spent in neighboring Elizabeth, New Jersey. Lovecraft was very fond of this "pure Georgian city," which he "haunt[ed] continually" during his stay in New York (*SL* 2.16). Indeed, he even considered making Elizabeth his home.[1] Our interest in Elizabeth stems from its role in the composition of two of Lovecraft's stories.

Lovecraft first discovered Elizabeth, which lies west of Brooklyn beyond the North New York Bay, Staten Island, and Newark Bay, in November 1924. This was some seven months after his ill-fated elopement to New York. His letters of the period begin to mention his explorations of the city, most notably in connection with the neighborhood around the City Hall. During Lovecraft's first visit, on Friday the 10th, two houses in particular caught his fancy:

> The Andrew Joline House, built in 1735, is wholly hidden from the street by shops, but stands in a spectral courtyard, with its back to the river. And on the northeast corner of Bridge Street and Elizabeth Avenue is a terrible old house—a hellish place where night-black deeds must have been done in the early seventeen-hundreds—with a blackish unpainted surface, unnaturally steep roof, and an outside flight of steps leading to the second story, suffocatingly embowered in a tangle of ivy so dense that one cannot but imagine it accursed or corpse-fed. It reminded me of the Babbitt House in Benefit Street, which as you recall made me write those lines entitled "The House" in 1920. Later its image came up again with renewed vividness, finally causing me to write a new horror story with its scene in Providence and with the Babbitt house as its basis. (*SL* 1.357)

---

1. "I wish to have my room in Elizabeth, N.J., where rent is less, and the atmosphere more colonial and American." HPL to Lillian D. Clark, 17 November 1924 (*Letters from New York* 92).

The Babbitt house (135 Benefit Street) was a large old farmhouse in Providence where Lovecraft's aunt Lillian Clark had resided in 1919–20. Lovecraft did not conceive the tale immediately, however: the following Wednesday, while riding home to 259 Parkside Avenue in Brooklyn from a lunch in Manhattan with his wife, Lovecraft "was struck with the memory of weird things I had seen in the twilight in Elizabethtown, and other weird things of longer ago—and at once I realised that I was about to write a horror story" (SL 1.359).[2]

Elizabeth, then, indirectly inspired "The Shunned House,"[3] since the nameless house on the corner of Bridge and Elizabeth Streets moved his imagination to the creation of a horror tale. The tale itself is not set in Elizabeth, but the latter was an important factor in its composition. Such is also the case regarding a tale Lovecraft penned almost exactly one year later.

At that time Lovecraft had been living by himself for eight months in a one-room apartment at 169 Clinton Street, in the same seedy Brooklyn neighborhood that inspired his "Horror at Red Hook" (1925). Unable to find a job, and with his marriage less than successful with his wife gone to Cincinnati and Chicago to take up job offers, Lovecraft was under a great deal of stress. To add insult to injury, a robbery in May 1925 deprived him of nearly all his presentable clothes, further impeding his search for work. The city of New York itself, with its dirt, foreign faces, and alien mores, he could hardly bear.

The latter sentiment, of which he later wrote that he "had to get out of town in order to get it into coherent words" (SL 3.101), forms the core of the story "He" (1925). Lovecraft had again gone to Elizabeth to get away from the clangor of the city, and this time found his rest in a more bucolic setting:

> At a small shop I bought a dime composition book; and having a pencil and pencil sharpener . . . in my pocket, proceeded to select a site for literary creation. Scott Park . . . was the place I chose; and there, pleasantly intoxicated by the wealth of delicate un-metropolitan greenery and the yellow and white colonialism of the gambrel-roofed Scott house, I settled myself for

---

2. HPL here uses the colonial name of the town, as he did for Providence and others.

3. The relative importance of the nameless house in the composition of "The Shunned House" was the subject of an exchange between myself and William Fulwiler in the letter column of *Crypt of Cthulhu*, Nos. 19, 22, and 23. Fulwiler made a case that HPL had a tale revolving around the Babbitt house in mind as early as February 1924 (under the provisional title *The House of the Worm*), thus minimizing the importance of the Elizabeth site save as a sort of imaginative reminder. I now accept Fulwiler's hypothesis.

work. Ideas welled up unbidden, as never before in years, and the sunny actual scene soon blended into the purple and red of a hellish midnight tale—a tale of cryptical horrors among tangles of antediluvian alleys in Greenwich village—wherein I wrote not a little poetick description, and the abiding terror of him who comes to New-York as to a faery flower of stone and marble, yet finds only a venomous corpse—a dead city of squinting alienage with nothing in common either with its own past or with the background of America in general. (*SL* 2.23)

On the face of it, "He" would seem to have less to do with Elizabeth than "The Shunned House," since no specific site in New Jersey inspired the former tale. There is in "He," however, an important autobiographical element relative to Lovecraft's visits to Elizabeth.

The first sentence of the story reads, "I saw him on a sleepless night when I was walking desperately to save my soul and my vision" (*D* 266). The startling fact is that this is precisely what Lovecraft had done the night before he retreated to Scott Park to pen his story. His diary entry for 10-11 August 1925, is as follows:

Rose late—wrote in afternoon & evening—dinner—out on jaunt for impressions—Chelsea-Greenwich—Greenwich St—Alden Hall—kitties—Pearl St—Battery—(stay up) ferry 5 am for Staten Island—dawn—car for Eliz[abeth] Ferry—sunrise—Eliz[abeth]—copybook—write story "He" in Scott Pk.—return. (CE 5.165)

The autobiographical element in the story, then, is even stronger than previously thought. The fact that Lovecraft had also stayed up all night walking makes it likely that he was *emotionally compelled* to do so, in the manner of the narrator. Perhaps Lovecraft exaggerated this duress for rhetorical effect, but the kernel of the similarity remains.

Visitors to Elizabeth today will find that little remains of what Lovecraft saw. The Andrew Joline house, which stood at 1110 Elizabeth Avenue, is no longer standing. The nameless house at the corner of Elizabeth Avenue and Bridge Streets (now 1099 Elizabeth Avenue) is also gone, replaced by a gas station. It is left to our imagination to see it through Lovecraft's description.

Right down the street from this intersection is Scott Park, opposite City Hall. It is a small park, about the size of one city block, and it now has no benches. Lovecraft evidently was positioned at the north end of the park, for there across East Jersey Street at number 1105 stood the Scott House. This building was demolished only two years after Lovecraft penned his tale.[4]

But by that time Lovecraft was happily back in his native Providence, writing some of the best stories of his career.

---

4. My thanks to Ms. Catherine Craig of the Union County Historical Society for this information.

On the Emergence of "Cthulhu"

On an afternoon in May 1920, the twenty-nine-year-old H. P. Lovecraft sat writing in the apartment he shared with his mother at 598 Angell Street in Providence, R.I. Exhausted, the great American fantaisiste put his head down on his arm; and, dozing, experienced the following strange dream:

> I was in a museum of antiquities somewhere in Providence, talking with the curator, a very old and very learned man. I was trying to sell him an odd bas-relief which I had just modelled myself from clay. The old man laughed at me, and asked what I meant by trying to sell a new thing of my own workmanship to a museum of ancient things. . . . I said:
> "Why do you say that this thing is new? The dreams of men are older than brooding Egypt or the contemplative Sphinx, or garden-girdled Babylon, and this thing was fashioned in my dreams."
> Then the curator bade me shew him my product, which I did. It was of old Egyptian design, apparently portraying priests of Ra in procession. The man seemed horror stricken, and asked in a terrible whisper—"WHO ARE YOU?" I told him that my name was H. P. Lovecraft . . . He replied, "No, no—*before that!*" I said that I had no other memories before that save in dreams. Then the curator offered me a high price, which I refused; because I saw from his face that he meant to destroy my sculpture as soon as it was his—whereas I wished it hung in the museum. My refusal clearly perturbed the man, who asked me to name my own price. Humorously, I cried "One million pounds sterling!" . . ., when to my amazement the old man did not laugh, but looked only more deeply worried. . . . Then he said in a perplexed, baffled, frightened tone, "I will consult with the directors of the institution—please call a week from today." (Letter to the Gallomo, [April 1920]; *Letters to Alfred Galpin* 87–88)

Somewhat over four years elapse, Lovecraft in the interim moving to New York to marry and look for regular work. On the evening of 28 February 1925, he was relaxing in his rented room at 169 Clinton Street in Brooklyn. Two friends, George Kirk and Samuel Loveman, had just taken their leave.

Suddenly, at 9:32 PM, the two-story edifice was shaken by a powerful earthquake, one that was felt as far away as Toronto. In New York, lamps fell from tables and mirrors from walls; walls themselves cracked, and windows shattered; people fled into the street.[1] This shock was to have farther-reaching repercussions, however; for it set Lovecraft's imagination in motion, prompting the emergence of his most exemplary contribution to literature.

Both these events, so different in scope and so distantly separated in time and space, were to become part of "The Call of Cthulhu," one of Lovecraft's greatest tales. The lengthy development of the story is an interesting example of how the Providence writer modified and expanded germinal plot ideas and images before composition. "Cthulhu" was the first of a series of works (such as "The Whisperer in Darkness" and "The Shadow out of Time") to take an exceptionally long period to come to fruition, and the saga of its development lends insight into Lovecraft's creative imagination.

In the tale as it was finally written, the strange sculpture fashioned in a dream and the February 1925 earthquake—"the most considerable felt in New England for some years" (*DH* 129)—would take on a common source, as portents of the rising of the prehuman citadel of Cthulhu from beneath the Pacific. But before we get ahead of ourselves, let us look at the other events leading to the story's writing.

A few years after Lovecraft dreamed he was a sculptor, he made two entries in his *Commonplace Book* (under the date of 1923) which show the first thematic indications of what was to come:

> [110] Antediluvian—Cyclopean ruins on lonely Pacific Island. Centre of earthwide subterranean witch cult.

> [111] Ancient ruin in Alabama swamp-voodoo. (CE 5.225–26)

These entries, made one after the other, play important parts in "Cthulhu." The first might be called the plot-germ, even if it makes no indication of how the tale would be developed or from what angle it would be told. The second was folded into the first, Lovecraft changing the locale from Alabama to Louisiana and making the voodoo ritual a branch of the "earthwide witch cult." The concept of the witch cult is certainly derived from Margaret A. Murray's *Witch-Cult in Western Europe* (1921), which Lovecraft read around the time these entries were made.[2]

---

1. HPL, [Diary: 1925], CE 5.153; *New York Times* (1 March 1925): 1.
2. HPL's letter to Clark Ashton Smith of 9 October 1925 shows HPL had read *Witch-*

After these entries, there undoubtedly were many other images and incidents that found their way into or influenced the tale. One we know of is the 1925 earthquake. One inevitably wonders if this startling event inspired strange dreams in Lovecraft that night, as he had it inspire the sculptor Wilcox in his tale.

About six months of Lovecraft's life elapse following the tremor; we then hear of another event in the writing of the story. Having been left largely to himself in New York by his wife's absence in the Midwest on business, Lovecraft spent much time with his friends discussing literary matters; and—despite his growing depression over his inability to secure a position—he experienced a small burst of creativity, penning the long "Horror at Red Hook" on 1–2 August 1925, and another story of New York horror, "He," a mere ten days later. Though these tales are by no means among Lovecraft's best, his flare-up of imagination was not quite finished. On waking up the day after writing "He," Lovecraft read some of the ethereal phantasy of Lord Dunsany "to stabilise my recovered creativeness of mood";[3] that night he went to a gathering of his friends at Rheinhart Kleiner's apartment. It was a lengthy session, where the Kalems (so called because the last names of the original group all began with "K," "L," or "M") "talk[ed] avidly" until 4 a.m. ("[Diary: 1925]," *CE* 5.164). We will never know what was among their topics of conversation, but when Lovecraft left his mind was brimful with ideas—reaching back at least as far as 1919 and his strange dream-for yet another weird tale:

> Thence I went home—but not to bed, for I had much to write. A new story-plot—perhaps a short novel—had occurred to my awakening faculties, and it was imperative to get it down in skeletonic details whilst it was fresh. This, of course, was a matter of hours, since I adopted my complete development scheme in full. The writing itself will now be a relatively simple matter—it's to be called "The Call of Cthulhu". . . . This new thing—if it turns out as long as I expect from a mere survey of the ground—ought to bring in a very decent sized cheque—it'll be in three or four parts. (Lovecraft to Lillian D. Clark, 13 August 1925; *Letters from New York* 172)

We can draw several conclusions from this letter excerpt. First, of course,

---

Cult by September 1924 at the latest (*SL* 2.28). Another nonfiction influence on "Cthulhu" is documented in Robert M. Price's "HPL and HPB."

3. HPL to Lillian D. Clark, 13 August 1925 (*Letters from New York* 172). In "Dunsanian Influence on Lovecraft Outside His 'Dunsanian' Tales," *Crypt of Cthulhu* No. 76 (Hallowmas 1990): 3–4, Robert M. Price speculates that "A Shop in Go-By Street" was among the Dunsany stories HPL read that day.

Lovecraft had both conceived and named Cthulhu, the octopoid "god" from another cosmic realm. He apparently spent a significant part of these "hours" working out the details of his "god"; years later he recalled: "I spent enormous pains thinking out *Cthulhu*" (Lovecraft to August Derleth, [31 August 1928]; *ES* 1.154). Second, in light of the amount of time his work took, he had written either a synopsis or an outline of great length and detail. Also, the structure of the narrative had in some sense been decided upon, since the final product was indeed in three parts or chapters.

What is the "complete development scheme" Lovecraft refers to here? It is likely an embryonic version of his essay "Notes on Writing Weird Fiction" (1933), which suggests that a synopsis of events in order of narration be prepared only after a synopsis of events in order of their chronological occurrence is written (*CE* 2.176). Lovecraft, then, perhaps wrote two synopses late that night in August 1925, and the details of the plot were largely in place.

The writing of the story itself, however, was till a long time to come. In fact, a full year elapsed before Lovecraft undertook composition. He was occupied elsewhere, first and foremost with the writing of his celebrated essay "Supernatural Horror in Literature." He likewise evidently felt unable to devote the time and attention required by his "short novel," for he penned two short and rather conventional tales—"In the Vault" (18 September 1925) and "Cool Air" (March 1926) (Joshi, "Chronology" 36–37) before he sat down to write of Cthulhu.

He did, though, plan to write the story at several junctures over the months; once saying in a letter to Clark Ashton Smith under the date of 4 November 1925: "The tale of the sunken continent will probably be written during the coming week, and you shall certainly be the first to see it."[4] Another letter of the following week shows that the tale was indeed much on Lovecraft's mind at this time:

> Yes—that submerged city in the Caspian is much like the sunken towers which I and other fantastic authors love to write about. I hope to read further reports on it—though I am quite certain they will reveal none of the horrors which will come out of my submerged Pacific city of L'yeh [*sic*]— which is older than mankind. (Lovecraft to Lillian D. Clark, 14–19 November 1925; *Letters from New York* 247)

Note that Lovecraft emended the name of the dead city where Cthulhu waits dreaming in the story to "R'lyeh."

---

4. HPL to Clark Ashton Smith, 4 November 1925 (ms., JHL).

Perhaps Lovecraft was inspired to try finally to write out his tale at the above juncture by his reading of Arthur Machen's *The Three Impostors* and "The Great God Pan," which he began on November 1st and 9th respectively. S. T. Joshi and David E. Schultz have speculated that an episode of the *Impostors*, "Novel of the Black Seal," influenced "Cthulhu" in that both stories employ the gradual piecing together of information from disparate documents and subnarratives. Internal evidence alone shows this to be true: Lovecraft's narrative is woven of "the queer bas-relief, . . . [and the] disjointed jottings, ramblings, and cuttings" (*DH* 127) found in a locked box, Machen's from "a lump of black stone, rudely annotated with queer marks and scratches . . . a sheet of manuscript, and . . . some cuttings from obscure local journals" (80) found in a locked bureau. This leaves us to wonder exactly how much of the structure of "The Call of Cthulhu" had been fleshed out in the writing of the synopsis (or synopses) three months before.

Indeed, the fact that Lovecraft was reading all sorts of weird fiction for the purposes of writing his essay on that subject between the writing of the synopsis and the writing of the story makes for perhaps hundreds of diverse possible influences on his product. One strong influence rarely mentioned by commentators, for example, is Guy de Maupassant's "The Horla." At the broadest level of parallel, the French writer's classic tale of an invisible being that sways men's minds contains much philosophical musing on man's tenuous place on this planet: "We are so weak, so defenceless, so ignorant, so small, we who live on this particle of mud which revolves in a drop of water" (465). This is a less eloquent, though no less affecting, version of Lovecraft's cosmic perspective as expressed in "Cthulhu." But as Maupassant's story progresses, he writes with more intensity:

> Now I know, I can divine. The reign of man is over, and he has come. He who was feared by primitive man; whom disquieted priests exorcised; whom sorcerers evoked on dark nights, without having seen him appear, to whom the imagination of the transient masters of the world [i.e., man] lent all monstrous or graceful forms of gnomes, spirits, genii, fairies and familiar spirits. After the coarse conceptions of primitive fear, more clear-sighted men foresaw it more clearly. . . . They called it magnetism, hypnotism, suggestion—what do I know? (466–67)

The last sentence reveals another tie-in, for Cthulhu also exerts a mental influence over human beings. Note how Wilcox's dream of a "voice shouting monotonously in enigmatical sense-impacts uninscribable save only as gibberish" (*DH* 129) is paralleled by the way Maupassant's narrator perceives the name of his antagonist:

> He has come, the—the—what does he call himself—the—I fancy that he is shouting out his name to me and I do not hear him—the—yes—he is shouting it out—I am listening—I cannot—he repeats it—the—Horla—I hear—the Horla—it is he—the Horla—he has come! (467)

Finally, the scope of Maupassant's horror, like Lovecraft's, is global. Both authors use the idea of news items from widely separated locales describing related events to show the pervasiveness of the horror.

"The Horla," then, is only one of many stories Lovecraft read—and was influenced by—beginning in November 1925 as he prepared to write "Supernatural Horror in Literature." But "Cthulhu" was again delayed, and not wholly by the task of essay-writing. Lovecraft's deteriorating emotional state, a result of being without work and away from his New England background, certainly affected his ability to write such a demanding tale. Finally returning home to Providence in April 1926, he experienced an astonishing rejuvenation of his story-writing faculties, and "The Call of Cthulhu" was the first in a series of some of his finest works. He probably did not finish it until September 1926, some eighteen months after the earthquake which must have set his imagination working, and six years after his dream of the newly wrought yet ancient sculpture. On 12 October 1926 he wrote Smith: "I've written two new tales, one of which is the sunken-land thing I described in advance last year" (*SL* 2.77).

The joy Lovecraft felt at being back in his native city, which so colored 1927's *The Case of Charles Dexter Ward*, is also apparent in "The Call of Cthulhu." Providence locales (notably picturesque Thomas Street, where Lovecraft set the quarters of the sculptor Wilcox) are featured as the starting point for its explorations of trans-cosmic horror. Lovecraft likewise gave his narrator Thurston a praenomen and nomen taken from Brown University past president Francis Wayland (1796–1865).

The story certainly gains from these small touches of local color, and the same may be said in a more general sense of the many other images and ideas known and unknown which Lovecraft collected for his story over the long period of its gestation. In a sense it is well that Lovecraft never undertook the writing of "Cthulhu" while in New York, for the story is richer in incident and detail for having been written after his return home and concomitant renewed spirits and creative ability.

The Subversion of Sense in "The Colour out of Space"

The writing in H. P. Lovecraft's "The Colour out of Space" (1927) is rich in subtle contradictions that enforce its theme. A colour is not a colour. A messenger becomes, instead, a message, but later is a messenger again. A forest is said to be dark, though it glows at night. An object that is said to be large is described as small a few sentences later. These contradictions are not an indication of careless composition—indeed, Lovecraft's description of the story as an "atmospheric study" (SL 2.127) shows that he spent even more than his usual extreme care with the style. Instead, they help convey Lovecraft's theme of the apparent violation of natural law. The motif of opposition strengthens the overthrow of logic, the subversion of sense, that takes place in the story. Nothing may be taken for granted, not even the simplest of statements, in a universe where chaos is the only given.

The opening paragraph sets the tone and begins to establish the motif of opposition—hills and vales, natural and man-made, temporary and permanent:

> West of Arkham the hills rise wild, and there are valleys with deep woods that no axe has ever cut. There are dark narrow glens where the trees slope fantastically, and where thin brooklets trickle without ever having caught the glint of sunlight. On the gentle slopes there are farms, ancient and rocky, with squat, moss-coated cottages brooding eternally over old New England secrets in the lee of great ledges; but these are all vacant now, the wide chimneys crumbling and the shingled sides bulging perilously beneath low gambrel roofs. (DH 53)

In contrast to the famous opening paragraph of "The Call of Cthulhu" (1926), this paragraph is not exposition but description. Instead of a discourse on the problems of knowledge, we have an ostensibly straightforward depiction of scenery. But it is evident—if only from deft use of sonorant consonantal sounds (the *l*, *w*, and *r*)—that this paragraph is the more stylistically controlled of the two. In the first sentence, a compound, Lovecraft uses syntax in onomatopoeia. The sentence reads like that which is described—the first section abruptly "peaks" with the doubled *i* in "rise wild," then gradually descends (as if into the valleys) in the second part to the final middle and back vowel sounds in "ever cut." The aural descent continues with melodious but solemn long vowels at the end of the paragraph—"now," "but," "crumbling," "bulging," "low," "roofs." This finely-modulated paragraph represents Lovecraft the stylist at his best.

The verb forms of the paragraph, reiterated in parallel, first establish a temporal stasis: *there are* valleys, *there are* dark narrow glens, *there are* farms. But the apparent timelessness of the farms is contravened by the second half of the last sentence. The farms, though first presented as "ancient" and "eternal," are in fact crumbling. This reversal is characteristic of the entire story, in which opposition is used to signify the defiance of rationality and the violation of natural law.

Over the course of the story this contravention is taken even further—it is not merely the man-made objects that are crumbling, but the very fabric of the seemingly ageless hills and valleys themselves. Reality itself is disintegrating. This is foreshadowed in the fifth paragraph, where amid more landscape description the narrator states: "Upon everything was a haze of restlessness and oppression . . . as if some element of perspective or chiaroscuro were awry" (*DH* 54). This "restlessness"—which contrasts with the stasis conveyed in the opening paragraph—is the meteorite's invasion of all organic life in the vicinity, and is later reflected in the movement of treetops when there is no wind and even the figurative (again) "restlessness . . . in the air" (*DH* 62) at the Gardner place. Similarly, despite the fact that the woods around the ruins of the Gardner farm are said to shine at night (*DH* 81), the area is still described in terms such as "dark ancient valleys" (*DH* 56) and "dark realm" (*DH* 80).

The use of the word "chiaroscuro" calls for comment, since it is uncommon and occurs nowhere else in Lovecraft. Denoting the use of light and dark elements in pictorial art, it is derived from the Italian *chiaro* (light) and *oscuro* (dark), in turn derived from the Latin *clarus* (clear) and *obscurus* (obscure). We again see the disparity which Lovecraft plays on throughout the tale. Later on another unusual word, "frore"—describing the wind that sweeps down at the story's climax. It is a single word that contains its own contradiction: it signifies a cold that burns like fire.

Lovecraft's word choice as he describes the behavior of the meteorite in the scientists' laboratory also encourages the impression of conflict. First, "the wise men talked of the strange stone's affinity for silicon" (*DH* 58). "Affinity," used here in the chemical sense of a force that causes the atoms of one element to combine with those of another, also has a positive connotation of "attraction," or common similarity. This connotation is resoundingly reversed several paragraphs later, where among the specimen's identifying features is its "attacking silicon compounds with mutual destruction as a result" (*DH* 59).

The nature of the meteorite is itself also described in opposing terms—it is a "messenger" (*DH* 58), a "message" (*DH* 60), and again a "messenger" (*DH* 81). It is both "against Nature" (*DH* 75) and "beyond all Nature" (*DH* 81). For one as stylistically fastidious as Lovecraft, we can be sure these variants represent auctorial intent rather than sloppy self-editing. Note, too, how the meteorite is first called a "visitor" (*DH* 57), though "the last faint remnant must still lurk down there in the well" (*DH* 79). This visitor never leaves.

The second paragraph of the story hints of the effects of the colour, as it describes why foreigners shun the area: "It is not because of anything that can be seen or heard or handled" (*DH* 53). It is not through the senses—sight, sound, touch—that the bizarreness of the region is perceived. Yet despite this assertion, the family most severely afflicted by the meteorite's influence—the Gardners—systematically seeks to comprehend the visitor through these sensory channels. After the advent of the meteorite to their farmstead, "the entire Gardner family developed the habit of stealthy listening, though not for any sound they could consciously name" (*DH* 62). Soon after, "the Gardners took to watching at night-watching in all directions at random for something . . . they could not tell what" (*DH* 64). Later, after the insanity of Mrs. Gardner and the deaths of two children, Nahum insists that something is "waiting to be seen and felt and heard" (*DH* 68). The first-hand experience of the Gardners directly contradicts the initial pronouncement.

We may also note the grotesque humor in this most serious and terrifying of Lovecraft's tales. The adjective "grotesque" itself, denoting that which is "characterized by formal distortions of the natural to the point of comic absurdity [or] ridiculous ugliness" (Holman 245), is used twice in the story. Once it occurs in regard to the decimated landscape, and once in regard to the tales the McGregor boys tell of a woodchuck whose "face had taken on an expression which no one ever saw in a woodchuck before" (*DH* 61).

Can a woodchuck really have a facial expression, in the sense of the aspect of the countenance or face? Or does Lovecraft write "expression" in the sense of a manifestation, in the sense of something pressed or squeezed out (i.e., the vital force), or in the sense of a sign or token?

The use of this type of humor is not inconsistent with Lovecraft's purpose. Instead, humor is arrayed against the horror to expand upon the theme of the overthrow of the normal by the incomprehensible.[1]

When the meteor is repeatedly struck by lightning, "digging had borne no fruit" (*DH* 60). But the fruit will be found soon enough, and the pun becomes apparent only two paragraphs later: "Then came the time of fruit and harvest" (*DH* 60). The meteorite has infected the soil and rendered the seemingly excellent crop inedible. This ghastly metaphor is pursued to the denouement, as the narrator, musing upon the nature of the interstellar visitor, concludes that it "was no fruit of such worlds and suns as shine on the telescopes . . . of our observatories" (*DH* 81).

Another compelling motif that Lovecraft works is the Greek πνεῦμα, (pneuma), oscillating among contrapositive meanings: wind, breath, and bodiless (unclean) being. Soon after the advent of the meteor, Mrs. Gardner is horrified to see the limbs of a tree shaking: "The boughs surely moved, and there was no wind." The verb "winded" means "out of breath." When Ammi tries to enter the room in which Mrs. Gardner is being consumed by the colour, he has to "retreat to another room and return with his lungs filled with breathable air" and feels himself "himself brushed as if by some hateful current of vapour." After her death the narrator states that the source of this movement, the colour out of space, is "no breath from the skies whose motions . . . our astronomers measure."

As the effects of the tainted soil and water progressively attack the Gardner family, it appears to their neighbor Ammi Pierce that "they walked half in another world between lines of nameless guards to a certain and familiar doom" (*DH* 66). This serves as a terrible negation of Nahum Gardner's belief, expressed two pages later, that "he had always walked uprightly in the Lord's ways, so far as he knew" (*DH* 68).

Soon Nahum's son Merwin, who has shown signs of mental illness, jumps down the well where the colour lives. Nahum tells Ammi that the boy had

---

1. The materialist Lovecraft apparently follows Darwin's *Expression of the Emotions in Man and Animals* (1872) in which the scientist says: "The young and the old of widely different races, both with man and animals, express the same state of mind by the same [facial] movements," due to a shared human and animal ancestry. Darwin was contesting Charles Bell's theist-based arguments in *Anatomy and Philosophy of Expression* (1824) claiming God created unique human muscles to express unique human feelings.

"been going to pieces for days" (*DH* 68), a figurative expression that presages Nahum's own literal disintegration from the meteorite's effects soon after.

On Ammi's final visit to Nahum, the latter calls for more wood on the fire, and asks if his guest is warmer though no wood has been put on. "The stoutest cord [not literally—a cord of wood—but figuratively] had broken at last" (*DH* 69). Finally, after the climactic eruption at the farmhouse, Ammi "looked back an instant at the shadowed valley of destruction so lately sheltering his ill-starred friend." Given the source of Nahum's demise, the last adjective is grotesquely appropriate.

Of all the paradoxes of the tale, none is more central than that featured in the title itself. "It was just a colour out of space" (*DH* 81), the narrator concludes of the fallen meteorite. Before we proceed, let us examine the qualifying adjective "just," which is a masterful stylistic touch. Lovecraft would not have used the word in the sense of "merely," for that would seem to minimize the seriousness of the horror. It would also go against his dictum that "Over and above everything else should tower the stark, outrageous monstrousness of the one chosen departure from Nature" ("Some Notes on Interplanetary Fiction," *CE* 2.179). Instead, the adjective "just" in this context is rich in ambiguity and consistent with Lovecraft's overall theme of opposition. The word can denote both "precisely" ("just right") and "possibly" ("we just might win").

But what, precisely, is a "colour out of space"? Early in the story, when the meteorite is being examined, Lovecraft first raises the issue of the "colour," as he continues his pursuit of incongruity. When professors from the local university split apart the meteor, they uncover "a large coloured globule" (*DH* 59). This globule disappears when smashed with a hammer, leaving only a "hollow spherical space about three inches across"—a dimension which blatantly contradicts the earlier adjective "large."

A more challenging and important conundrum is the description of the globule itself: "The colour . . . was almost impossible to describe; and it was only by analogy that they called it colour at all." Lovecraft resorts to a literary term—analogy—to convey the verbal difficulty of describing the indescribable.

It is yet another contradiction—the colour is not actually a colour. Analogy is here not just another word for "resemblance." Instead, it conveys a recognition of *differences* between two objects, and a focus on the relations that link one object with the other (Brown 66f.). Analogy is always translatable into the form of a proportion; that is, "*a* is to *b*, as *x* is to *y*":

$$a:b::x:y$$

Here the analogy is as follows:

> The characteristics of light described in terms of hue, luminance, and purity by which the individual visually perceives an object (*a*) is to a natural object (*b*) as [the indescribable] (*x*) is to the globule (*y*).

The reader now has some insight into the globule and its effects, but not so much that it becomes mundane. Lovecraft's brilliant gambit of analogy is successful, and he can proceed with his tale without being forced to overexplain the horror.

Also important in the title is Lovecraft's choice of the prepositional phrase "out of" (i.e., coming from beyond or outside) instead of simply using the preposition "from" (which denotes a starting point or origin). The concept of something coming "from outside space" is a paradox, since astronomical space is infinite.

It is significant that Lovecraft chose this key phrase as his story's title. It turns out that the colour is not really a colour, nor is it really out of space. Lovecraft's continual use of contradiction and opposition throughout the story—in his presentation of dwellings (eternal yet temporary), landscape (static yet restless, light yet dark), the meteorite (messenger yet message), the perception of the meteorite's effects (not sensory yet sensory), as well as his handling of tone (serious yet grotesquely humorous)—help convey the strangeness of the intrusion from outside. These skillful touches add impact to the horror borne of the negation of reason, and of the negation of the well-ordered laws of science, that is at the core of the story.

Tightening the Coil: The Revision of "The Whisperer in Darkness"

In "Notes on the Writing of Weird Fiction" (1933) H. P. Lovecraft advises the aspiring weird writer to "change incidents and plot whenever the developing process seems to suggest such change, never being bound by any previous design. . . Insert and delete whole sections if necessary or desirable, trying different beginnings or endings until the best arrangement is found" (MW 114). "The Whisperer in Darkness" (1930) is a striking example of this principle in practice. Lovecraft made some interesting and significant revisions to the story—including a late substitution of a drastically different ending—in an attempt to heighten its dramatic effectiveness.

In a 1935 letter to Alvin Earl Perry, Lovecraft recalled the origins of the story:

> [B]ehind "The Whisperer in Darkness" lay two initial impelling concepts: the idea of a man in a lonely farmhouse besieged by "outside" horrors, & the general impression of weirdness in the Vermont landscape, gained during a fortnight's visit near Brattleboro in 1928. (SL 4.201)

He took approximately seven months to write the tale, the longest he spent on any single work of fiction. The autograph manuscript, housed at Brown University's John Hay Library, records the dates of writing on the last page:

> Begun Providence, R.I., Feby. 24, 1930
> Provisionally finished Charleston, S.C., May 7, 1930
> Polishing completed Providence, R.I., Sept. 26, 1930

Lovecraft's extensive travel over this period did much to delay the story's completion. It also contributed, indirectly, to the degree that he later would change the text.

190

In his letter to Perry, Lovecraft outlined the process of writing the "Whisperer": the conception of the story plot; the creation of a chronological synopsis of events; the creation of a synopsis of events in the order of narration; the writing of a provisional draft; and finally, the revision and polishing. Lovecraft's synopsis of events in the order of narration is still extant as a series of notes on the last page of the 52 page final version of the A.Ms.:

    I. Introduction
    II. Opening of action (correspondence)
    III. Appearance of tangible factors—record—blk stone loss—
    IV. Tightening of coil—letters
    V. Transition—strange letter
    VI. Personal entry—journey—
    VII. Contact with the Whisperer
    VIII. Conclusion—final scene & climax

The final version of the story adheres very closely to this scenario; though, as we will see, there were considerable changes within Chapter VIII.

As we have seen, Lovecraft put pen to paper on 24 February. On 14 March, he wrote to James F. Morton: "I am still stall'd on [manuscript] p. 26 of my new Vermont horror" (SL 3.129). This is early in Chapter V, at the point of the false letter sent by "Akeley" (i.e., the Outer Ones). On the very same day the front page of the *New York Times* announced the discovery of Pluto by Clyde Tombaugh (Joshi, "Topical References" 262).[1] Lovecraft's letter of 1 April to Elizabeth Toldridge is his first published epistolary mention of the new planet. He exclaims gleefully: "I think I shall suggest its being named *Yuggoth!*" (SL 3.136).[2]

One of the most remarkable revisions Lovecraft made to the "Whisperer" is the inclusion of this discovery as a plot element. Pluto becomes a convenient outpost for the winged Outer Ones. We can look backward from page 26 in the manuscript (Chapter V) to see how he interpolated references to Yuggoth in the partially completed manuscript after Pluto's discovery.

The origin of the Outer Ones is alluded to in Chapter I: "the Winged

---

1. Joshi notes that Tombaugh discovered Pluto on 23 January 1930 but that the discovery does not seem to have been announced until 14 March.

2. HPL had previously made ambiguous references to Yuggoth in the sonnet sequence *Fungi front Yuggoth* (December 1929-January 1930) and the revision of Zealia Bishop's "Medusa's Coil" (May 1930). In neither instance is it clear that Yuggoth is a planet.

Ones came from the Great Bear in the sky" (*DH* 212). In Chapter II, Akeley's first letter reveals that "[t]he things come from another planet" (DH 217) but does not provide further details. Later in Chapter II, on page 12 of the A.Ms., we find the first mention of Yuggoth, inserted after the fact into a laundry list of Mythos names (as indicated by underlined text):

> I found myself faced by names and terms I had heard elsewhere in the most hideous of connexions—Yuggoth, Great Cthulhu, Tsathoggua, Yog-Sothoth, R'lyeh, Nyarlathotep, Azathoth, Hastur, Yian, Leng, the Lake of Hali, Bethmoora, the Yellow Sign, L'mur-Kathulos, Bran, and the Magnum Innominandum—and was drawn back through nameless aeons and inconceivable dimensions to worlds of elder, outer entity at which the crazed author of the Necronomicon had only guessed in the vaguest way. (*DH* 223)[3]

Similarly, there is a later emendation to one of the exhortations on the strange phonograph record (A.Ms., page 15): ". . . (Nyarl)athotep, Great Messenger, bringer of strange joy to Yuggoth through the void, Father of the Million Favored Ones, Stalker among . . " (*DH* 226).

The most obvious retrofitting of the Pluto discovery into the story, however, is this addition to page 17 of the A.Ms.:

> The blasphemies which appeared on Earth came from the dark planet Yuggoth, on the rim of the solar system; and this in itself merely [sic] a populated outpost of a frightful interstellar race whose ultimate source must lie far outside even the Einsteinian space-time continuum or greater know cosmos. (*DH* 228)

Lovecraft, we can conclude, did not have the plot detail of Yuggoth/Pluto in mind during the conception of the tale or the writing of its first four chapters. He may have never mentioned Yuggoth in the tale if not for the opportune timing of Pluto's discovery.

Lovecraft wrote more of the story before 24 April, when he left on a two month trip around the eastern seaboard. He probably finished Chapter VI: it includes adapted portions of his essay "Vermont—A First Impression" (1928), and it is not likely he transcribed this while into the manuscript while traveling.

Lovecraft's itinerary included stops in New York, Charleston, Richmond,

---

3. In this and subsequent citations from the "Whisperer" text, A.Ms. additions are indicated by underlining; deletions are indicated with strikeovers. Citations follow the A.Ms. text, which differs slightly from the unseen T.Ms. and the published version.

Kingston N.Y., and Athol and Worcester MA.[4] He provisionally finished the story in Charleston on 7 May. The A.Ms. then consisted of 58 pages (HPL to August Derleth, 24 May 1930; *ES* 1.263). Lovecraft did not plan to undertake "polishing" until after his trip was completed.

The story at this point in time was very different than the version we know today. This difference is largely due to comments made by Bernard Austin Dwyer, whom Lovecraft visited in early June 1930. Writing to August Derleth from Dwyer's home in Kingston N.Y., Lovecraft stated:

> My "Whisperer in Darkness" has retrogressed to the constructional stage as a result of some extremely sound & penetrating criticism on Dwyer's part. I shall not try to tinker with it during the residue of this trip, but shall make it the first item of work on my programme after I get home—which will no doubt be in less than a week now. There will be considerable condensation throughout, & a great deal of subtilisation at the end. (HPL to August Derleth, 7 June 1930; *ES* 1.265)

What exactly did these changes entail? There is an important clue in a memoir penned in the mid-1940s by Lovecraft's close friend Frank Belknap Long. Lovecraft visited Long in New York City after the author had provisionally finished the "Whisperer" in Charleston, but prior to visiting Dwyer. As he subsequently did for the Dwyer, Lovecraft read aloud the story for Long. Among Long's recollections is: "Howard's voice becoming suddenly sepulchral: 'And from the box a tortured voice spoke: "Go while there is still time—"'" ("Some Random Memories of H.P.L." [1944], in Cannon, *Lovecraft Remembered* 186).[5] With this clue, in combination with Lovecraft's comment

---

4. During the period of writing, HPL's itinerary was as follows: February–24 April: in Providence RI; 24 April: to New York NY; 28 April: to Charleston SC; 9 May: to Richmond VA; 20 May: to New York NY (two weeks); 2 June: to Kingston NY; [c. early June]: to Athol & Worcester MA; c. 13 June–14 August: in Providence (amateur convention in Boston, 2–4 July); 15–17 August: Onset MA with Frank Long; 17–29 August: in Providence; 30 August–1 September: to Quebec. See Faig 21 and *SL* 3 passim.

5. Long's notoriously faulty memory places the reading at Christmas rather than late Spring. However, HPL didn't even spend Christmas 1930 with the Longs; he spent the only the 1932–35 holidays in New York City with them (Faig 21–22). Long also quotes HPL as remarking that both W. Paul Cook and James F. Morton had positively received the story, yet neither could have possibly seen it by the time HPL got to New York City on his return leg. Despite these problems, I maintain that Long's recollection of the original ending is likely in light of HPL's comments in his 7 June 1930 letter to Derleth ("There will be . . . a great deal of subtilisation at the end") and his 17 October 1930 letter to Long ("The final version was changed, especially at the very end" [*SL* 3.186]).

to Derleth, we can propose that the climax of the first version of the tale—the version Lovecraft read to Long and later to Dwyer—was radically different from the published version's. In the first version, it seems, the canister containing Akeley's brain spoke to Wilmarth as he fled from the farmhouse.

Let us examine this theory of an alternate original ending in light of evidence in the text itself. In Chapter VII Lovecraft hints that Akeley's brain is in the cylinder attached to two instruments, apparently visual and audio input devices, on the study table. In the next and final chapter, Wilmarth overhears voices drifting up from the study beneath his bedroom. One of these is a mechanical voice "in a position of subordination and pleading" (*DH* 266): obviously a speech output device has been attached to Akeley's cylinder. The pivotal passage comes when Wilmarth descends the stairs and turns his flashlight upon the now-mute cylinder whose voice he had heard from his room:

> It must, I thought, be conscious of my presence even now; since the sight and hearing attachments could not fail to disclose the rays of my flashlight and the faint creaking of the floor beneath my feet. But in the end I did not dare meddle with the thing. I idly saw that it was the fresh, shiny cylinder with Akeley's name on it, which I had noticed on the shelf earlier in the evening and which my host had told me not to bother. Looking back at that moment, I can only regret my timidity and wish I had boldly caused the apparatus to speak. God knows what mysteries and horrible doubts and questions of identity it might have cleared up! But then, it may be merciful that I let it alone. (*DH* 270)

Based on Long's recollection, in the first version of story Wilmarth was indeed bold enough to hook up the speech apparatus to Akeley's cylinder at this point in the narrative. Akeley then admonished Wilmarth to flee: "[g]o while there is still time." Read in this light, the revised passage above is amusing in its coy understatement: "But in the end I did not dare meddle with the thing. . . . But then, it may be merciful that I let it alone."

One revision, an insertion added later in pen, also supports the theory: Lovecraft has the alien say to Wilmarth as the latter picks up a brain cylinder: "Heavy? Never mind. Be sure of the number—B-67. Don't bother than fresh, shiny cylinder joined to the two testing instruments—the one with my name on it" (*DH* 258–59). The words "fresh, shiny cylinder" recur yet a third time in the penultimate paragraph, to cinch the concept that Akeley's brain had indeed been observing—mutely—the entire bizarre colloquy.

If the original climax of the story was Akeley's verbal warning, what of the final version's climactic confirmation that the thing in the chair was actually an Outer One in disguise? I find it unlikely that Lovecraft would have included both these climaxes in the first version. (The double climaxes in "The Dunwich Horror," "The Shadow over Innsmouth," *At the Mountains of Madness*, and "The Shadow out of Time" occur in separate chapters, so I do not think they may be considered evidence to the contrary.) The first version of the story, then, did not end with the gruesome discovery of the "face and hands of Henry Wentworth Akeley." Instead, the reader was simply left to *draw the inference* that the whisperer in darkness had not been human—a more profound if less forceful ending.[6]

It took a long time for Lovecraft to incorporate Dwyer's comments into the manuscript. Returning to Providence on 19 June, he found himself too busy to devote attention to the story. In fact, he did no polishing until after his September trip to Quebec (HPL to August Derleth, [c. 16 October 1930]; *ES* 1.280). The story was finally finished on 26 September (A.Ms.).

As mentioned, the provisionally finished manuscript—the one that Lovecraft completed in Charleston and read to Frank Belknap Long upon arriving in New York City on 24 May—had been 58 pages. The final A.Ms. is 52 pages, reflecting Lovecraft's excision of six pages as he revised and polished the story. Besides the major revision of the story's ending mentioned above, the A.Ms. reflects other examples of the "subtilisation" the author sought in his final version.

Lovecraft wrote the story on the back of correspondence to him dated between 28 August 1927 and 16 June 1930. Some insight into the revision's

---

6. This change may account for an apparent discrepancy in the text, as pointed out to me by Robert M. Price (pers. comm.). In the transcription of the phonograph record it is said that Nyarlathotep shall wear a "waxen mask" (*DH* 266); yet in the climax as it stands HPL implies that the mask is fashioned from the flesh of Akeley's actual face (e.g., the allusions to "prodigious surgical . . . skill" and the use of the word "identity" in the final sentence [*DH* 271]). Perhaps in the *first* version HPL meant to convey that the thing in the chair merely had on a mask, but added the more gruesome suggestion to heighten the new climax of the *second* version. HPL may have then missed the inconsistency during the revision process; the transcription of the phonograph is on A.Ms. page 15, a holdover from the first version. Cf. his 1935 letter to Perry: "I insert or delete whole sections when I deem it necessary or desirable, trying different beginnings & endings until the best is found. But I always take infinite pain to make sure that all references throughout the story are thoroughly reconciled with the final design" (HPL to Alvin Earl Perry, 4 October 1935 [*SL* 4.203]).

scope can be gleaned from examining the dates of the versos correspondence.

A.Ms. pages one and two are written on correspondence dated September 1927. These are holdovers from the first (provisional) version. Pages three through nine, which introduce the action and contain Akeley's first letter to Wilmarth, are relatively free of emendations. This part of the story seems to have been cleanly recopied from a heavily edited and condensed first attempt into the final version. (This is borne out by pages five through seven, whose versos date to *after* Lovecraft left on his trip.) Page nine, near the end of Chapter II, describes the narrator's reaction to Akeley's letter: "It would be difficult to describe my sentiments upon reading this strange document for the first time" (*DH* 219).

A.Ms. pages 10–12, written in a different pen, are carryovers from the first version. They have been renumbered: 10 had been 12, 11 had been 13, and 12 had been 14. The renumbering shows that Lovecraft's "condensation" occurred primarily in Chapters I and II: he removed at least two pages of text in the introduction and first Akeley letter.

That Lovecraft shortened the letter is somewhat ironic. During the composition of the story he had remarked to August W. Derleth: ". . . I'm now about 10 pages into that new Vermont horror. . . . One of the things Brother Farny [*Weird Tales* editor Farnsworth Wright] won't like about that [*sic*] is a decidedly long letter by one of the characters—but I've decided that this is the best way to introduce the main action, & if he doesn't like it he can reject it" (HPL to August Derleth, [late February 1930]; *ES* 1.251). Perhaps Dwyer's criticism or Lovecraft's need for the *Weird Tales* income caused the author to rethink his position and abridge the two introductory chapters.

A.Ms. page 13, which begins Chapter III with the arrival of the strange phonograph record, has been recopied for the final version. Interlineations begin again on page 14 with the description of the playback itself ("Before trying the record" [*DH* 225]). Among the most heavily touched-up portions of the narrative subsequent to this (apparently retained from the first attempt) are the paragraphs surrounding the three false communications from the aliens (the first telegram in Chapter IV and the letter and second telegram in Chapter V). These changes show Lovecraft struggling to bolster the credibility of Wilmarth's reaction to the false communications, and to buttress the reasoning behind his acceptance of Akeley's (i.e., the Outside Ones) invitation to visit Brattleboro.

Wilmarth's gullibility has been scathingly cited by a number of commentators. His refusal to see through what the reader perceives as an obvious ruse has spoiled the story for many readers. (The first of these, apparently, was among the first to hear the story—Bernard Dwyer.) Lovecraft himself recognized this fault. Upon receiving comments from Derleth, he responded: "My own objection to the tale is . . . an impression that the intended effect, that of an out-reaching & in-sucking horror manifest in ever-tightening coils of bondage, is not perfectly realised" (HPL to August Derleth, [7 November 1930]; ES 1.284). Interestingly, Lovecraft uses the same phrase in the letter as he did in his synoptic outline on the A.Ms.: "tightening of coil." The autograph manuscript shows Lovecraft trying to address this criticism, inserting sentences that attempt to rationalize Wilmarth's reactions.

These attempts, unfortunately, come across as feeble afterthoughts. One example is the insertion on A.Ms. page 20 just prior to the first false communication, a telegram sent by the Outer Ones posing as Akeley: "The thing was *reaching out* so. Would it suck me in and engulf me?" (*DH* 232). (Note again how Lovecraft echoed this wording in his letter to Derleth.) Among the extensive revisions in the text surrounding the second false communication, a letter sent by the Outer Ones signed by Akeley, is this eleventh-hour insertion in pencil (A.Ms. page 28):

> Yet in another way the letter seemed quite characteristic of Akeley. The same old passion for infinity—the same old scholarly inquisitiveness. I could not for a moment—or more than a moment—credit the idea of spuriousness or malign substitution. Did not the invitation—the willingness to have me test the truth of the letter in person—prove its genuineness? (*DH* 242)

Donald R. Burleson (*Critical Study* 164) has already commented on the "oddly specious logic" of the rhetorical question. Likewise, Lovecraft added a similar sentence in pencil after the final alien telegram: "Receipt of this message in direct response to one sent to Akeley . . . removed any lingering doubts I may have had about the authorship of the perplexing letter."

Worse yet, in the A.Ms. both the second false communication (the letter) *and* the third false communication (the second false telegram) are incorrectly signed "Henry W. Akely" (A.Ms. page 28) and "AKELY" (A.Ms. page 29) with Lovecraft's notations "Retain misspelling" and "Retain variant spelling," respectively. Thankfully, Lovecraft later realized that having Wilmarth accept the second *and* third false communications as genuine in the face of the Outer Ones' successive misspellings of Akeley's name was stretching credibility too far. He used the misspelling only in the first false communication, allowing the correct spelling in the second and third false communications when he prepared the typescript.

Lovecraft also inserted references to the Outer Ones' mesmeric powers, apparently to shore up the rationale for Wilmarth's trip to the farmhouse. How these powers could act on Wilmarth from a distance, unfortunately, remains unclear. On A.Ms. page 19, in the episode of the lost package containing the black stone, Lovecraft added: "He [Akeley] spoke of the undoubted telepathic and hypnotic powers of the hill creatures and their agents" (DH 231). On A.Ms. page 26, during the false letter from the Outer Ones, he inserted the sentence beginning "Telepathy is their usual means of discourse" (*DH* 240).

The last significant changes Lovecraft made during the polishing are deletions from the fragmentary conversation that Wilmarth overhears as he lies in bed above Akeley's study. The parties involved are Akeley (the speech-machine), Nyarlathotep (the first buzzing voice), a subordinate Outside One (the second buzzing voice), Noyes, and another human agent whose voice is not transcribed. Lovecraft crossed out several phrases to lessen the substantive information the passage contained (A.Ms. page 48):

(THE SPEECH-MACHINE)

". . . ~~S'pose I~~ brought it on myself ~~the way I poked into your affairs~~ . . . sent back the letters & the record . . . ~~written him in my name~~ . . . end on it . . . taken in . . . ~~on the shelf,~~ seeing & hearing . . . damn you . . . impersonal force, after all . . . ~~your name~~ . . . fresh, shiny cylinder . . . great God . . ."

(FIRST BUZZING VOICE)

". . . time we stopped . . . small & human . . . torture . . . Akeley . . . brain . . . saying . . ."

(SECOND BUZZING VOICE)

". . . Nyarlathotep . . . Wilmarth . . . record & letters . . . cheap imposture . . . ~~puerility~~ . . ."

(NOYES)

"... (an unpronounceable word or name, possibly *Ngah-Kthun*) ... harmless ... peace ... couple of weeks ... ~~real stuff~~ ... ~~distinctly~~ theatrical ... told you that before ..."

(SEVERAL VOICES AT ONCE IN INDISTINGUISHABLE SPEECH)

(FIRST BUZZING VOICE)

"... no reason ... original plan ... effects ... Noyes can watch ... Round Hill ... fresh cylinder ... Noyes's car ..."

(NOYES)

"... well ... all yours ... down here ... ~~sleep~~ rest ... ~~mail-man~~ ... place ..."

(MANY FOOTSTEPS, INCLUDING THE PECULIAR LOOSE STIRRING OR CLATTERING)

(A CURIOUS SORT OF FLAPPING SOUND)

(THE SOUND OF AN AUTOMOBILE STARTING AND RECEDING)

(SILENCE)

With this added information we can attempt to explicate this passage. Akeley's speech is straightforward in content, expressing anger at being taken in by the feigned objectivity of the Outer Ones, regret at having involved Wilmarth, and horror at having silently witnessed the deception. Nyarlathotep (the first buzzing voice) expresses impatience with the deception—which has evidently been engineered by Noyes—and expresses a desire to torture Wilmarth, apparently to assess what he knows about the Outer Ones.

The subordinate Outer One (the second buzzing voice), addressing Nyarlathotep by name, concurs. Noyes then attempts to hold his ground, reminding the others of the element of mockery ("distinctly theatrical") in the deception and perhaps implying that the incident will be forgotten by Wilmarth in a "couple of weeks" if they release him without revealing their ploy. However, Nyarlathotep insists on reverting to their "original plan," sending the silent human agent to Round Hill in Noyes's car for a fresh cylinder for Wilmarth's brain.

The excised reference to the "mail-man" is more difficult to explain, which May be why Lovecraft cut it. Akeley's instruction to send mail in care of General Delivery in Brattleboro (DH 229) earlier in the story may imply collusion on the part of the mail carrier. (This reading would make the latter's teasing of Wilmarth about the wild local rumors [DH 237] blackly ironic indeed.) Perhaps Lovecraft meant to imply the human who left to fetch the cylinder was himself the mailman. Or, it may simply be taken to mean that the operation of placing Wilmarth's brain into the cylinder had to be done before the next day's mail arrived.

It is apparent that the writing and revision of "The Whisperer in Darkness" was a long journey—both literally, as the manuscript traveled for seven months around the east coast with Lovecraft, and figuratively, as the text saw major changes in content and detail. Lovecraft clearly struggled with the story. He was aware of the shortfalls that many have since pointed out, and made attempts to correct them. The alteration he made to the ending, too, was unusually extensive. We will never know if the original finale was more satisfactory than the one we now have, or learn exactly what it was that Akeley conveyed to Wilmarth as the latter fled from that alien-ridden Vermont farmhouse.

Lovecraft's Role in "The Tree on the Hill"

In examining Duane W. Rimel's "The Tree on the Hill" for evidence of Lovecraft's hand, it is important to attempt to distinguish which aspects of the tale reflect Lovecraft's influence upon Rimel and which aspects are from Lovecraft's own pen. Lovecraft's work was an understandably powerful influence upon his young correspondent, and the story bears many echoes of HPL's earlier tales. Fortunately, a letter of Lovecraft's hints at his role in the story, and internal evidence somewhat helps better to define his contribution.

Rimel was among the many aspiring young writers whom Lovecraft encouraged, praising and often touching up their efforts. While Lovecraft was visiting Robert Barlow in Cassia, Florida, in the spring of 1934, Rimel sent him a long poem and "The Tree on the Hill" for comments, and on 13 May Lovecraft replied:

> I read your "Tree on the Hill" with great interest, & believe it truly captures the essence of the weird. I like it exceedingly despite a certain cumbrousness & tendency toward anticlimax in the later parts. I've made a few emendations which you may find helpful, & have tried a bit of strengthening toward the end.[1]

Beyond proving that Lovecraft did in fact have a hand in the story, this passage gives a fair indication of how extensively he revised it. His participation was greatest in the concluding section of the narrative, and he made some additions and corrections in the earlier parts. We may safely assume that the story's theme, setting, and plotting, and most of the prose in the first two sections are Rimel's, in spite of the fact that all these elements show a strong Lovecraftian influence.

Thematically, the notions of strange dimensions impinging on our own,

---

1. HPL to Duane W. Rimel, 13 May 1934 (ms., JHL). This letter was unearthed by S. T. Joshi.

and vast, epochal cycles of time bringing the return of outside forces are present in much of Lovecraft's work. Tales such as "The Call of Cthulhu" and "The Dreams in the Witch House," among others, feature similar themes.

The importance and aspect of the setting in Rimel's story are again derived from several of Lovecraft's most famous tales. The characteristic opening paragraphs describing landscape details bring to mind the. beginnings of "The Colour out of Space" and "The Dunwich Horror." The appearance of a strange sterile area, seared yet not by any fire of earth, is of course modeled upon the Blasted Heath of the former tale. This similarity between Rimel's story and Lovecraft's earlier work is the most obvious, and Lovecraft must have been both amused and flattered upon encountering it.

Rimel's plot elements are also familiar to Lovecraft readers. A lone walk in the woods; a disquieting geographical area; cosmic visions; a narrator's companion versed in strange lore; an ancient and obscure book of arcana; a staying, perhaps temporary, of an Outside encroachment; objective evidence of supernormal occurrences; and permanent mental and physical damage resultant from a horrific encounter—all turn up in at least one previous Lovecraft story.

I suspect that the most Lovecraft may have done to the tale's plotting was to restructure the ending; having the narrator get merely an ambiguous glimpse of the weird photograph immediately before the finish. My only reason for this conjecture is that young authors of horror fiction tend to show too much, and the structure of the finale is characteristic of Lovecraft's approach to that problem.

It is more difficult to be dogmatic regarding Lovecraft's contribution to the story's prose. From the quoted letter and internal evidence such as characteristic language, phrasing, and punctuation, it seems certain that almost the entire third section is Lovecraft's writing. Also, there are specific echoes of phraseology from Lovecraft's earlier tales in both the third section and the earlier ones where Lovecraft probably inserted sentences.

Interestingly, many sentences in the third section actually foreshadow phraseology that would crop up again a year later in Lovecraft's "The Haunter of the Dark." The following passages seem to have been written into Rimel's story by Lovecraft, and then unconsciously echoed by him in his own tale not long afterward:

> The touch of the glass fragment seemed curiously warm and electric, and I could scarcely bear to put it out of my sight. (*HM* 408)

This stone . . . exerted upon Blake an almost alarming fascination. He could scarcely tear his eyes from it. (*DH* 102)

The snapshot I handled with a disconcerting mixture of emotions. (*HM* 408)

Hand and handkerchief soon revealed the truth, and Blake gasped with a baffling mixture of emotions. (*DH* 102)

Even after I had replaced it in the envelope with the rest I had a morbid longing to save it and gloat over it and rush out and up the hill towards the original. (*HM* 408)

At the same time, however, [Blake] displays the dangerous extent of his fascination, and admits a morbid longing—pervading even his dreams—to visit the accursed tower and gaze again into the cosmic secrets of the glowing stone. (*DH* 107)

A parallel passage from the tales is also found in Rimel's quotation from his imaginary book, Yergler's *Chronicle of Nath*: "[Send back the shadow] none could do save through the Gem; wherefore did Ka-Nefer the High-Priest keep that gem sacred in the temple" (*HM* 405). Lovecraft must have added this aside, for Ka-Nefer is mentioned in a 1930 entry in the *Commonplace Book*. He switched the name back to its original form, as used in "The Outsider," in his history of the Shining Trapezohedron: "The Pharaoh Nephren-Ka built around it a temple with a windowless crypt, and did that which caused his name to be stricken from all monuments and records" (*DH* 106).

Echoes of earlier Lovecraft tales present in the third section of "The Tree on the Hill" include the following. "[Theunis] spoke fragmentarily of 'refraction,' 'polarization,' and 'unknown angles of space and time'" (*HM* 407). This brings to mind similar passages from "Nyarlathotep" and *At the Mountains of Madness*: "I . . . mumbled a trembling protest about 'imposture' and 'static electricity'" (*MW* 33); "[Danforth] has on rare occasions whispered disjointed and irresponsible things about 'the black pit,' 'the carven rim,' . . ." (*MM* 105–6).

An exclamation of regret is typical of Lovecraftian protagonists; first, in Rimel's story: "Would that my ignorance might have remained complete!" (*HM* 409). And from "The Rats in the Walls" and "The Whisperer in Darkness": "I knew now why my ancestors had had such excessive gardens—would to Heaven I could forget!" (*DH* 42–43); "Would to Heaven I had quietly left the place before allowing that light to rest again on the vacant chair" (*DH* 270).

Lovecraft closed the revision with the sentence, "But the sketch was hasty, and I could not be sure" (*HM* 409), consciously or not reprising the refrain from "The Hound": "But the autumn moon shone pale and weak, and we could not be sure" (*D* 175).

There are other passages from the earlier parts of the revision that Lovecraft must have inserted, for they too closely echo his earlier work; for example, the sentence "The leaves on the thing were too lush for the work of any sane nature, while the trunk bulged and knotted in the most abhorrent shapes" (*HM* 404) recalls, among others, "The Colour out of Space," "The Dunwich Horror," and "The Lurking Fear":

> The trees grew too thickly, and their trunks were too big for any healthy New England wood. (*DH* 54)

> The trees of the frequent forest belts seem too large. (*DH* 156)

> The ancient lightning-scarred trees seem unnaturally large and twisted. (*D* 180)

There are other, less obvious examples. But the sentences quoted here are so close to the originals that Rimel would not have written them thus. They are characteristic of Lovecraft's writing, and must have been unconsciously rewritten by him upon revising Rimel's tale.

In conclusion, we may say that the third section of Rimel's "The Tree on the Hill" is almost exclusively Lovecraft's work. He wrote nearly all the prose and plotted most of it as well. In the earlier sections, he probably revised and inserted sentences but did little else. Rimel cannot be faulted for following his mentor's approach so closely, for any young writer must choose a model, just as Lovecraft sometimes chose Poe and Dunsany. Indeed, Rimel chose an impeccable source of inspiration in Lovecraft; in fact, his story became a peripheral part of the Lovecraft canon itself.

Some Antecedents of the Shining Trapezohedron

The Shining Trapezohedron, that fascinating centerpiece of one of Lovecraft's finest tales, has many literary antecedents. In tracing the influences upon the author's conception of this "window on all time and space," we will find that no single source was the major influence: many sources diffused and blended over time contributed to its characteristics. Most importantly, we will see that the Shining Trapezohedron is differentiated from all its forerunners in its reflection of Lovecraft's uniquely cosmic imagination.

The sole appearance of the Shining Trapezohedron in Lovecraft occurs in his last major tale, "The Haunter of the Dark" (November 1935). The protagonist of the story, the *fantaisiste* Robert Blake, discovers it in an abandoned church steeple: "The four-inch seeming sphere turned out to be a nearly black, red-striated polyhedron with many irregular flat surfaces; either a very remarkable crystal of some sort, or an artificial object of carved and highly polished mineral matter" (*DH* 102). Blake later deciphers a cryptographic notebook discovered in the vestry room of the church and transcribes into his diary the history of the Shining Trapezohedron:

> Of the Shining Trapezohedron, [Blake's diary] speaks often, calling it a window on all time and space, and tracing its history from the days it was fashioned on dark Yuggoth, before ever the Old Ones brought it to earth. It was treasured and placed in its curious box by the crinoid things of Antarctica, salvaged from their ruins by the serpent-men of Valusia, and peered at aeons later in Lemuria by the first human beings. It crossed strange lands and stranger seas, and sank with Atlantis before a Minoan fisher meshed it in his net and sold it to swarthy merchants from nighted Khem. The Pharaoh Nephren-Ka built around it a temple with a windowless crypt, and did that which caused his name to be stricken from all monuments and records. Then it slept in the ruins of that evil fane which the priests and the

new Pharaoh destroyed, till the delver's spade once more brought it forth to curse mankind. (*DH* 106)

The notebook reveals that gazing into the stone awakens what the Starry Wisdom sect, the cult which had occupied the deserted church, calls "the Haunter of the Dark."

Beyond this, the Shining Trapezohedron is very similar to the crystal ball of popular folklore. Upon gazing into it, Blake experiences a series of strange visions: figures, buildings, and cosmic vistas. There are many objects in literature that reveal strange images when gazed into, some of which Lovecraft encountered in the course of his voluminous reading. These objects doubtless influenced certain aspects of the Shining Trapezohedron, so it is well to examine the sources which we know Lovecraft did in fact read.

Lovecraft was a great devotee of the *Arabian Nights* when he was a child; at age five he "formed a juvenile collection of Oriental pottery and objets d'art, announcing [himself] a devout Mohammedan" (*SL* 1.299). In the 292nd Night of the volume we read the story of young Tarik Ibn Ziyad, who sacked the city of Lebtait in Spain. Among the treasures he finds there is an item vaguely reminiscent of Lovecraft's later creation, "a marvellous great round mirror of mixed metals, made for Solomon, son of David (on whom be peace), wherein whoso looked might see the very image and presentment of the seven divisions of the world" (*SL* 3.321–322). This is apparently an early prototype of the crystal ball. An even earlier example is found in another work Lovecraft read, the *True History* of Lucian:

> I must just mention one other thing that I saw in the King's palace [on the moon]. It was a large mirror suspended over a fairly shallow tank. If you got in the tank, you could hear everything that was being said on the Earth, and if you looked in the mirror, you could see what was going on anywhere in the world, as clearly as if you were actually there yourself. (19)

These objects are mirrors rather than crystals or stones, but all three media have traditionally been used in crystal-gazing (or scrying) over the centuries. Lovecraft read about "crystallomancy" in Lewis Spence's *Encyclopaedia of Occultism*, which he owned: "The crystal most in favor among modern crystal gazers is a spherical or oval globe about four inches in diameter, and preferably a genuine crystal. . . . The crystal, as well as the stand on which it rests, must be inscribed with sacred characters" (111). Details are similar in Lovecraft's tale—recall the "egg-shaped or irregularly spherical object some four inches through" which turns out to be the Shining Trapezohedron, and the small stone pillar covered with "bizarre, crudely incised and wholly unrecognisable hieroglyphs" (*DH* 101–2) upon which it rests.

A few pages later in Spence's book is an article on John Dee, himself a famous scryer. Lovecraft had some interest in Dee, ascribing him as one of the translators of the *Necronomicon*. Spence tells how the angel Uriel appeared to Dee in 1582: "Uriel smiled benignly upon him, gave him a convex piece of crystal, and told him that when he wished to communicate with the beings of another world he had but to examine it intently, and they would immediately appear and reveal the mysteries of the future" (115). Like the Shining Trapezohedron, this crystal not only gives glimpses of other times but also puts one in contact with entities from another planet.

Two stories by Lovecraft's contemporaries seem to have had an influence upon him. H. G. Wells's "The Crystal Egg" documents the demise of mild-mannered Mr. Cave consequent to his purchase of "a mass of crystal, worked into the shape of an egg and brilliantly polished." As in Lovecraft's tale, the crystal exercises a "curious fascination" upon the protagonist. After an interval Mr. Cave sees in the object "a clear and consistent picture of a wide and peculiar countryside" inhabited by batlike beings. He soon deduces he is viewing the surface of Mars. A month later Mr. Cave's companion hears of his death: "He had been found in his shop in the early morning . . . and the crystal had been clasped in his stone-cold hands. His face was smiling . . . He must have been dead five or six hours when he was found." The story concludes: "the terrestrial crystal must have been—possibly at some remote date—sent hither from that planet, in order to give the Martians a near view of our affairs" (111–25).

Resemblances to "The Haunter of the Dark" are obvious. There is, though, a great difference in the respective approaches of the two authors to their material, as may be seen from these analogous passages. First from Lovecraft: "[Blake] was conscious of some formless alien presence close to him and watching him with horrible intentness . . . something which was not in the stone, but which had looked through it at him" (*DH* 104). And from Wells, typically succinct: "And a series of observations . . . convinced both watchers that . . . on one occasion at least one of these inhabitants of this other world had looked into Mr. Cave's face while he was making these observations" (121). This parallel brings to mind Lovecraft's remark about Wells's *Thirty Strange Stories*: "Magnificent plots, but how prosaically handled when one compares them to Machen's work!" (*SL* 1.287).

Wells's story also influenced Clark Ashton Smith's "Ubbo-Sathla," which appeared in *Weird Tales* for July 1933. Smith's opening scene, in a cluttered curio shop, is a virtual rewrite of Wells's; but Smith went further than Wells, having his protagonist regress via the crystal into the primal past of earth.

Smith's and Lovecraft's stories thus share a common influence in "The Crystal Egg." Smith's version, in turn, also influenced Lovecraft in its more blatantly horrific treatment of the crystal-gazing motif and employment of vaster reaches of time. The regression of Smith's protagonist somewhat parallels Lovecraft's history of the Shining Trapezohedron—at one point the former mentally becomes "one of the serpent-men who reared their cities of black gneiss and fought their venomous wars in the world's first continent" (60–61). Recall how the Shining Trapezohedron was salvaged from the Antarctic ruins by the serpent-men of Valusia.

Turning to Lovecraft's own work, we can see how elements of the Shining Trapezohedron seem to have developed over a long period of time. He had worked with similar objects in his original tales and in revisions, and mentions others in extant notes and fragments.

In the case of the collaborations and revisions the other authors involved apparently conceived the objects, though Lovecraft did much to flesh out details. The Whitehead-Lovecraft collaboration "The Trap" (1931), for example, revolves around a mirror which is in fact a portal to "spatial recesses not meant for the denizens of our visible universe" (*HM* 386). Embedded in this mirror is a small oval object called "Loki's Glass," made, like the Shining Trapezohedron, of "some polished fusible mineral" and having "magical properties which include the divination of the immediate future and the power to shew the possessor his enemies" (*HM* 398). There are few other parallels between the devices, for Whitehead's object is a physical rather than mental gateway.

Lovecraft's revision of Duane W. Rimel's "The Tree on the Hill" (May 1934) features an ancient glass lens or prism called "the Gem." This lens, which Rimel invented, and which plays a minor role in the story, shows ultra-dimensional secrets lurking within photographs of an immense tree. Similarity to the Trapezohedron is again limited; however, a quotation from the book consulted by the tale's protagonists sounds familiar: "[Send back the shadow] none could do save through the Gem; wherefore did Ka-Nefer the High Priest keep that gem sacred in the temple" (*HM* 405). We know from a 1930 entry in the *Commonplace Book* mentioning Ka-Nefer that this antecedent is Lovecraft's. He reverted to the original form ("Nephren-Ka," as in "The Outsider") when he used it in a similar context in "Haunter."

In the round-robin story, "The Challenge from Beyond" (Lovecraft's section written August 1935), we see the immediate precursor of the Shining Trapezohedron. C. L. Moore's commencing section introduced a "strangely energized [cube] of a curious crystal" ([8]) which captures the attention of a camper. In the third section, Lovecraft developed the origin and purpose of the cube. It was sent through space by the beings of a distant world to gather information from the minds of the inhabitants of the planet it encountered. Parallels here include the extraterrestrial origins of the objects; their physical aspects, each a glowing mineral nearly spherical in shape; and their effect on human consciousness, that of a "strange, hellish hypnosis or nightmare" ([6]). The stone from Yuggoth, though, was created to subjugate life-forms in a more sinister manner—Lovecraft's development of the Yekub cube has more of a science fiction feel to it, closer to the recently completed "The Shadow out of Time."

The influence of his contribution to this story upon the Shining Trapezohedron should not be underestimated, perhaps, for "The Haunter of the Dark" was written only three months afterward. In addition to Lovecraft's revisions and collaborations, his original fiction anticipates certain aspects of the Shining Trapezohedron. The name of the device itself brings to mind the "little polyhedron" (MM 289) encountered by Walter Gilman in his otherdimensional travels in "The Dreams in the Witch House" (1932). Lovecraft implies that this object is the semi-human witch's familiar Brown Jenkin in transfigured form. (The word "trapezohedron," incidentally, was not coined by Lovecraft; it is defined as a crystalline form whose faces are trapeziums, quadrilaterals with no two sides parallel.) "The Whisperer in Darkness" (1930) also features the notion of an oddly angled stone brought to earth from Yuggoth:

> The thing, as nearly as one might guess, had faced the camera vertically with a somewhat irregularly curved surface of one by two feet; but to say anything definite about that surface, or about the general shape of the whole mass, almost defies the power of language. What outlandish geometrical principles had guided its cutting—for artificially cut it was—I could not even begin to guess; and never before had I seen anything which struck me as so strangely and unmistakably alien to this world. (DH 222)

This stone does not reveal any distant vistas. It is, instead, a specimen of the rock from which the cities of Yuggoth are constructed.

There are, though, other objects in Lovecraft's original work of a more revelatory nature. Among the "Basic Underlying Horrors" which preface the Commonplace Book is this: "Magical telescope (or cognate device) shows the past when looked through" (*CE* 2.172). The date of writing and source (if any) of this entry is unknown. Two entries from the body of the *Commonplace Book* seem pertinent also, the first dated 1926: "Any very ancient, unknown, or prehistoric object—its power of suggestion-forbidden memories" (*CE* 5.228). A later entry has more specific similarities:

> Pane of peculiar-looking glass from a ruined monastery reputed to have harboured devil-worship set up in a modern house at edge of wild country. Landscape looks vaguely and unplaceably *wrong* through it. It has some unknown time-distorting quality, and comes from a primal, lost *civilisation*. Finally, hideous things seen through it. (*CE* 5.231–32)

This entry is derived from Lovecraft's sonnet "The Window" (December 1929–January 1930), one of several of the *Fungi from Yuggoth* he evidently planned to rewrite as stories. Because the idea is so similar to "The Trap," Lovecraft must have recorded it before his involvement with the Whitehead tale. Perhaps Lovecraft, finding this entry too similar in retrospect to "The Trap," changed it slightly when he used it in "Haunter."

Lovecraft's notes for an unwritten story (now in the John Hay Library) feature the most important prototype of the Shining Trapezohedron yet mentioned. Unfortunately, these notes (now known as "The Rose Window") cannot be fitted into the antecedent schema with any degree of confidence since their date of writing is unknown. They tell of an old house in Kingsport, and of a strange carving above a bookcase within it. This carving depicts an octopuslike thing with a circular glass mirror as its great single eye. This mirror possesses many characteristics of the Shining Trapezohedron:

> Glass itself also baffling. Opaque—evidently convex mirror like many in old houses—but curiously devoid of reflective power. [. . .] What one sees in it is generally only cloudy light. This light seems to shift oddly, and one acquires a perverse tendency to keep staring at the thing as if one expected something to appear. Suggestion of self-luminousness at night. [. . .]
>
> Is lens prism, or mirror reflecting vision from other dimension or dimensions—time or space? Or rather, reflecting obscure rays not of vision but operating on vestigial and forgotten extra senses. Constructed by outside Entities in effort to inspect human world— [. . .]
>
> Outer beings peer through it. Influence humans by opening up other senses and dimension-perceptions possibly including hereditary memory. [. . .]
>
> Principal effect, perhaps, to hold the attention and make mind susceptible to outside influence. (*CE* 5.254)

The references to other senses in these passages bring to mind Blake's notation of "senses transfigured" (*DH* 115) in the diary entry that concludes "The Haunter of the Dark."

Though we can easily list some of the antecedents of the Shining Trapezohedron, it is more difficult to decide how these bits and pieces were synthesized into the object in its final form. Lovecraft knew the *Arabian Nights* by the age of five, and probably also read Lucian as a youth.[1] In the 1920s he encountered Spence[2] and Wells.[3] Smith's "Ubbo-Sathla" Lovecraft read in manuscript in March 1932 (Smith, *Letters to H. P. Lovecraft* 33). During the 1930s, he wrote of similar objects in the sonnet "The Window" (1929–30), "The Whisperer in Darkness" (1930), "The Trap" (1931), *Commonplace Book* entry #195 about the "pane of peculiar-looking glass" (c. 1933), "The Tree on the Hill" (1934), and finally "The Challenge from Beyond" (1935). We can only speculate where the most similar antecedent, the notes called "The Rose Window," fits in.

Perhaps Lovecraft wrote the notes for the unwritten story shortly before "The Haunter of the Dark" was written; but because he had to whip up a tale quickly in response to Bloch's "The Shambler from the Stars," he felt he did not have a proper amount of time to develop the idea as planned in the notes. Instead, he simplified them for the occasion. This will remain a surmise until the time the notes are dated, if ever.

We may say, though, that Lovecraft bettered all these antecedents in the Shining Trapezohedron. He imbued the object with a cosmic vision not present in any of its forerunners. Though Smith's crystal had spanned earth's history, Lovecraft's enabled the awesome prospect of viewing any scene in the universe for an infinite span of time extending both before and after our own. This is indeed a frightening thought, reinforcing as it does the notion

---

1. HPL does not mention the *True History* in any work or correspondence I have seen. He was familiar with Lucian, however, as a passing mention in a letter to James F. Morton (30 October 1929; *SL* 3.41) attests. Also, he owned an essay on "Lucian" in H. D. Traill's *The New Fiction and Other Essays on Literary Subjects* (New York: Amsterdam Book Co., 1898; *LL* 891). S. T. Joshi ("H. P. Lovecraft and *The Dream-Quest of Unknown Kadath*" 31) has made a case for the influence of the *True History* on HPL's novel.

2. This volume was published in 1920, and HPL mentions Spence in a letter of 20 November 1928 to Elizabeth Toldridge (*SL* 2.253). I suspect HPL acquired the volume when he was living in New York City; one of his numerous bookseller friends may have brought his attention to it. That he sought background information on conventional occultism is reflected in "The Horror at Red Hook" (1925).

3. HPL read *Thirty Strange Stories* in January 1924 (see *SL* 1.287).

of mankind's total insignificance in the cosmos. This theme is, of course, central to Lovecraft's philosophy, and the Shining Trapezohedron thus another example of the unity of his thought and work.

Aside from this, Lovecraft's treatment of the crystal-gazing motif is more terrifying and atmospheric than any previous incarnation. The Shining Trapezohedron comes alive because the details of its physical aspect, origin, history, purpose, and so forth are thoroughly thought out; one can sense that Lovecraft had the concept in its entirety in mind before he ever put pen to paper. The fantastic imagery the crystal evokes, too, and the subtlety with which the frightful mental bond with the creature is shown, combine to create a powerful effect on the reader. These things make the Shining Trapezohedron truly memorable.

III. Reviews

The Corrected Texts of Lovecraft's Tales

H. P. Lovecraft. *The Dunwich Horror and Others.* **Selected by August Derleth; Texts Edited by S. T. Joshi. Sauk City, WI: Arkham House, 1984.**

The appearance of Arkham House's sixth printing of *The Dunwich Horror and Others* is the single most important event in Lovecraft studies since the same publisher issued its epochal *The Outsider and Others* in 1939. The latter probably saved Lovecraft's weird work from an undeserved literary oblivion; the 1984 *Dunwich Horror* is, I believe, the important first step in securing that work its permanent position as an important contribution to American literature. The new volume is the first to present Lovecraft's fiction as he intended us to read it, and the evident care with which it has been prepared clearly conveys that Lovecraft is an author worthy of serious consideration. Missing, in happy opposition to past editions, are the painful misprints, garish cover, and slovenly design which did much to reinforce the misconception of Lovecraft as an inconsequential pulp fictionist. In the concrete, all readers now—some fifty years after his death—have access, for study and reflection, to what Lovecraft actually wrote; in the abstract, all approaching Lovecraft for the first time are met with the implication that his work is one worthy of conscientious presentation. Arkham House plans to follow this publication with corrected versions of *At the Mountains of Madness and Other Novels* and *Dagon and Other Macabre Tales* later this year.

This milestone is due to the diligence of leading scholar S. T. Joshi, who since 1977 has consulted original manuscripts and other primary source materials in an attempt to reconstruct Lovecraft's writings. Numerous textual errors, he found, had crept into the published versions of the tales over the decades through both willful editorial changes and encrusted typographical errors perpetuated and compounded by reprinting from inaccurate texts. These many errors were mainly of an individually minor sort—punctuation and spelling—but at times encompassed dropped words and sentences, reparagraphing, and other more important divergences; all of which cumulatively sapped much of the coherence and effect of the stories. Of all Joshi's invaluable contributions to the field—which are indeed too numerous to detail here—the publication of the results of his textual research must be counted as his greatest achievement thus far in an absolute sense; for had he not determined to undertake the task, scholars might not have had the definitive Lovecraft for yet another fifty years.

In an evident attempt to continue August Derleth's questionable 1963 copyright, the content and order of the first edition of *Dunwich Horror* (1945) has been retained; the resemblance between the two volumes ends there, however, and this would have been more fittingly called a new edition rather than a "Corrected Sixth Printing" (iv). The text has been entirely reset in the readable and gracefully modern typeface used in the firm's *New Tales of the Cthulhu Mythos* (1980), and sports a new dust jacket, a brief textual introduction by Joshi, and a reprinting of Robert Bloch's introduction to Ballantine's *The Best of H. P. Lovecraft*. The latter piece, though an able defense of the horror genre, says too little about Lovecraft's life and work for the amount of space it takes up; but certainly it is aeons removed from the hardened clichés of Derleth's introduction to the 1963 edition. One is at a loss to know why the publishers did not have Joshi, certainly the keenest commentator on Lovecraft's work, add the introduction as well.

The dust jacket of the book is green with a grey decorative typefont for the author and title names, the front cover featuring a subdued realistic painting by Raymond Bayless depicting Cthulhu emerging from R'lyeh. The endpapers are likewise slate-green, and opposite the title page, which is also set in the cover's display face (as are all the titles in the book), we find a nice surprise: a frontispiece of the 1934 Truesdell portrait of Lovecraft.

There are many other such pleasant surprises. On the contents page, for example, we find the date of composition after each title; this touch, which makes it clear to the uninitiated that it is well to consider Lovecraft's tales as they were written, is typical of the volume.

Among the immediately noticeable textual restorations is the dedication to C. W. Smith of "In the Vault," missing since the first appearance in the *Tryout* in November 1925. "The Thing on the Doorstep" now has seven chapter divisions instead of five. Readers of "The Whisperer in Darkness" may now note an entire line of text restored between the two words in paragraph one—"deep things," as it read in previous editions. And the long-omitted subtitle of "The Call of Cthulhu" is restored. A most attractive change is the use of reduced type as specified by Lovecraft in such things as the news item "Mystery Derelict Found at Sea" in "The Call of Cthulhu" (with correct paragraphing restored) and the Akeley correspondence in "The Whisperer in Darkness." The latter story, finally presented as it was written—with the correctly printed transcriptions of the horrible record and the half-heard conclave at the Akeley place—is a thing beautiful to behold, and forms perhaps the aesthetic high point of the volume's design.

If the other textual corrections present in the book are less immediately obvious, they are no less important in their cumulative effect; for horror fiction succeeds or fails largely on small details that are at first intangible. Certainly, though, certain changes are evident in the course of even a quick perusal. In "Whisperer," for example, the narrator now wishes of Akeley (after his first conversation with him): "If only he wouldn't *gloat* so about Yuggoth and its black secrets!" (225). But in the 1963 version there was no italicization, and thus no subtle hint as to the strength of—and real motivation behind—the pseudo-Akeley's malicious delight in his whispered descriptions of the black planet. Similarly, Nahum Gardener's death-speech in "The Colour out of Space" now tells of the destruction by the extracosmic being not of "Thad an' Merwin," but of "Thad an' Mernie" (77); this odd contraction of the name being one more deft touch of the local color which supports the tale's devastating supernatural realism. In "Cthulhu" Castro now lays the ritual murders to "Black Winged Ones" (140) instead of "Black-winged Ones"; the entities described in this new reading can now perhaps be tied in with the night-gaunts of *The Dream-Quest of Unknown Kadath*. A more extensive textual change is in all the colloquial dialect (i.e., the title story and "The Shadow over Innsmouth"), which is now rendered as Lovecraft wrote it. The many other such corrections, taken together, will prove a boon not merely to students of Lovecraft's style but to all scholars in the field.

Indeed, the whole volume fosters the latter implication—that Lovecraft is an author who ought to be studied—and in a general sense this is the most important thing about it. Joshi's textual introduction, though necessarily brief, references one of his best articles ("Textual Problems in Lovecraft") in the distinguished journal *Lovecraft Studies* (No. 6, Spring 1982: 18–32); this mention well serves to tie the book to the world of Lovecraft scholarship. The fact that such a world exists has not been implied in any previous edition of Lovecraft; and between this, the corrected texts and their careful presentation (plus such touches as dates in the table of contents), and the attractive design of the book, the reader approaches the material with a perception that Lovecraft's work is one of substance and value. Lovecraft wrote carefully and thoughtfully—this, thanks to Joshi and also to James Turner of Arkham House, is evident in the volume's whole approach—and henceforth we will be able to study with equal care and thoughtfulness exactly what he wished us to read.

H. P. Lovecraft. *At the Mountains of Madness and Other Novels.* **Selected by August Derleth; Texts Edited by S. T. Joshi. Sauk City, WI: Arkham House, 1985.**

S. T. Joshi's painstaking quest to reconstruct what H. P. Lovecraft actually wrote is by now well known to all readers; and doubtless all will be pleased to hear that the second Joshi-edited installment of the three Arkham House Lovecraft fiction volumes has now emerged, and exhibits the same high level of quality as *The Dunwich Horror and Others*. At the Mountains of Madness and Other Novels is a fine example of the bookmaking art, with excellent design and production values. The blue dust jacket features a striking painting by Raymond Bayless, depicting a scene from *The Dream-Quest of Unknown Kadath*, and a "new" photograph of Lovecraft (this one taken by Robert Barlow) graces the frontispiece.

Despite the attractiveness of the book (something that is in itself rarely seen in English-language editions of Lovecraft), the important difference in the volume from its previous edition lies in the content. Derleth's error-filled introduction has been replaced by James Turner's sensitive "A Mythos in His Own Image," which discusses the progressive "humanization" of the author and his work and cites many important passages on philosophy and aesthetics from Lovecraft's letters. It is something of a relief to find these pivotal passages finally used to introduce the fiction. Though one may quibble with one or two of Turner's points—Lovecraft's early Haeckelian monism was neither simplistic nor outmoded (cf. the recently published *In Defense of Dagon*), and he continued to adhere largely to its essentials late in life (see, for example, *SL* 2.263 and *SL* 5.352)—Turner's intelligent essay is more than anyone could ask for as an introduction.

From the very first page of the text proper, where the first paragraph is no longer divided in two, changes are evident throughout. Corrections of all sorts are perhaps most visible in *The Case of Charles Dexter Ward*, where some major problems have been addressed. Striking changes appear here, for example, in the antique correspondence of Curwen and his associates. Lovecraft's remarkable recreation of eighteenth century prose has been restored from the autograph manuscript, and now displays all the idiosyncrasies—the "ff" for an "F," the use of "u" for "v" (e.g., in "Prouidence"), and so on—that Derleth was unable to carry into print. The thorn character used for "ye" adds to the authenticity, and there are other emendations that help make these passages seem very much like unnatural survivals from the past. In the narrative itself there are many other corrections, one of the most amusing being a change in the name of the captain of the *Forteleza* from "Harry Leshe" to the rather more convincing "Charles Leslie" (133)!

The cumulative effect of these small emendations is an undeniable strengthening of the coherence and impact of the tales. There are, though, larger (one might even say startling) differences evident in this edition. A restored passage in *At the Mountains of Madness* makes better sense of the surrounding text (39), while a reinserted line in the second paragraph of "The Silver Key" restores the meaning that had been subverted by the line's absence (409). In "The Statement of Randolph Carter" we are likewise treated to a few new sentences—a description of a graveyard with very "Lovecraftian" imagery and cadence—not found in the 1964 volume (303).

"Statement" also shows notable differences in italicization. Carter's remark about Warren's theory "why certain corpses never decay, but rest firm and fat in their tombs for a thousand years" is now in italics, and its iambs ring out more as a threat than a hint. Warren's comments over the phone are also italicized, and the celebrated twist tag line "You fool, Warren is DEAD!" is now in all-caps italic (an effect I consider actually less sensational—no more yelling "BOO!"—and more effective than the previous misreading). Another newly restored emphasis of note is the revelation of the last sentence of Chapter 11 of *Mountains*.

Other changes of great visual impact are the use of reduced type for radio messages from Lake's camp in *Mountains*, which help emphasize the different "voice" of the sender. Indeed, the whole of pages 20-21 are now taken up by the lengthy radio descriptions of the discovered Old Ones, and the new layout seems somehow to help enforce the authority and convincingness of the content. Such is also the case with certain letters in *Ward*, which in their smaller typeface feel even farther removed in time from the contemporary narrative.

One notices that there are certain inconsistencies in the way the correspondence in *Ward* was set—most are in reduced type, but a few are in regular-sized—and this is a mere hint of the hard choices editor Joshi had to make in establishing his text of the novella, which Lovecraft never prepared for publication. Though following Lovecraft in this and most other instances, Joshi had to make certain emendations that were obviously indicated. For example, Ward's letter on p. 181 must be dated 8 February 1928 (not 8 March 1928, as Lovecraft left it in the autograph manuscript), since Willett received it and went to the Ward house on 9 February (183), too late to prevent Charles's murder. Joshi also faced difficult textual problems in *Mountains:* he had to work from the *Astounding Stories* appearance and decide which divergences there from the autograph manuscript were made by Lovecraft in the missing typescript and which were intentional alterations by *Astounding*'s editors.

This sort of thing at times makes one wish that a full textual apparatus had been provided—but in light of the fact that S. T. Joshi is the best-qualified person in the world to make such decisions, we can surely use the texts with confidence enough. All Lovecraftians must again extend their thanks to Joshi and to Arkham House for putting before us the most faithful version of Lovecraft we are ever likely to see.

H. P. Lovecraft. *Dagon and Other Macabre Tales.* **Selected by August Derleth; Texts Edited by S. T. Joshi. Sauk City, WI: Arkham House, 1986.**

Very little need be said in defense of *Dagon and Other Macabre Tales*—the new edition from Arkham House makes a fitting capstone to the new textually corrected trilogy of Lovecraft's fiction. This volume differs even more radically from the previous edition than either of its two companion volumes, for aside from the attractive production and accurate texts it features a few surprises.

One immediately notices, for example, that the first story in the volume is no longer the title story, but "The Tomb"! This is because the contents—save the early tales (including the not-so-early "Transition of Juan Romero"), the fragments, and "Supernatural Horror in Literature"—are now presented in chronological order. This is a great boon, if one keeps in mind the items that were placed in the other two volumes. These items (beginning with 1919's "Statement of Randolph Carter") were excluded because August Derleth grouped the tales by quality and not chronology; they remain in this grouping because of the copyright problems that would result for Arkham House from a more extensive rearrangement.

But it is easy for us to track the order in which the stories were written, thanks to the inclusion of textual editor S. T. Joshi's comprehensive chronology of Lovecraft's fiction, handsomely set in small caps, at the back of the volume. This replaces Derleth's spurious chronology in the previous edition. He simply arranged in alphabetical order the titles for each year, not even making note of this approach—a perfect example of the lazy scholarship that also contributed to the corruption of the texts. Conversely, Joshi's chronology (first printed in his *H. P. Lovecraft: Four Decades of Criticism* [1980] in a more cluttered format) covers everything from "The Noble Eavesdropper" (1897?; non-extant) to "The Night Ocean" (with R. H. Barlow; Autumn? 1936). It includes all Lovecraft's fiction and revisions, even such obscure items as "Old Bugs" and "Sweet Ermengarde."

The main attraction, as usual, are the texts themselves. Joshi has added a more detailed textual introduction to this volume than he did to the others, listing the manuscript sources for each item. As exhaustive as the list is, it only hints at the amount of work that went into the project, for Joshi does not detail the difficult choices and painstaking word-for-word collation of all other manuscripts and relevant publications that had to be accomplished for each work. One wishes for a full textual apparatus here, so that we could see how Lovecraft revised his texts and what decisions Joshi made in arriving at his definitive versions. The editor covered some of this in his "Textual Problems in Lovecraft," and perhaps we can hope for a similar article from him on this topic in the future.

Some of the textual changes here are striking. "Facts concerning the Late Arthur Jermyn and His Family," "Under the Pyramids," and "Celephaïs" (with dieresis; note similarly the restoration of diacritical marks on words such as "Argimēnēs" and "Meroë") have finally been graced with their proper titles, and "The Tomb," "Beyond the Wall of Sleep," and "The Tree" again have epigraphs. A more amusing restoration is the footnote to "Juan Romero": "AUTHOR'S NOTE: Here is a lesson in scientific accuracy for fiction writers. I have just looked up the moon's phases for October, 1894, to find when a gibbous moon was visible at 2 a.m., and have changed the dates to fit!" (As hilarious as this is, it does reflect Lovecraft's lifelong concern with accuracy in his fiction; his letters to Derleth, for example, are full of long notations of geographical and other errors in the latter's tales.)

Another thing that jumps out at the reader is the typographic devices Lovecraft used for emphasis in certain tales, especially in the last line of "The Alchemist" (which, in addition to the four exclamation points dispersed throughout, goes into italics and then into all caps) and "The Beast in the Cave" (where the last word and its accompanying three exclamation points are now in bold). Lovecraft never quite lost his juvenile fondness for such things, but, happily, became slightly more subtle as he progressed. In "The Temple," the dramatic dialogue of the mad Klenze is one step more emphatic, with the addition of underlining—"_He_ is calling! _He_ is calling! I hear him! We must go!"; likewise for "The Other Gods," where Atal now cries in horror of "The _other_ gods! The _other_ gods!"

Because most of the stories here were first printed in pulp magazines, many had been reparagraphed for "easier" reading until this edition. A notable example is "The Hound," where the many divided paragraphs and two sensational one-sentence paragraphs ("Then terror came" and "Then he collapsed, an inert mass of mangled flesh") have now been put right. _Weird Tales_, perhaps because of Lovecraft's early injunction that they print his stories only on the condition that they follow his texts, actually treated the stories better than did some others. "The Doom That Came to Sarnath," which appeared in _Marvel Tales_, was almost as horribly butchered as the men in that story are. Notice things like the last sentence; before:

> But half buried in the rushes was spied a curious green idol; an exceedingly ancient idol chiseled in the likeness of Bokrug, the great water-lizard.

and after:

> But half buried in the rushes was spied a curious green idol of stone; an exceedingly ancient idol coated in seaweed and chiseled in the likeness of Bokrug, the great water-lizard.

Only six words omitted from the sentence in the previous edition—but unfortunately this amounts to one-fifth of the sentence! (The rest of the story was equally corrupt, prompting Joshi to call it "a textual nightmare.")

A very special part of this volume is "Supernatural Horror in Literature." We can for the first time read Lovecraft's great essay (generally accepted as the finest critical survey of weird fiction ever written) as he intended us to. Joshi notes in his introduction that this piece presented particular textual problems of its own; indeed, the text originally was prepared as a project in itself: a critical edition that never saw print. Joshi used the text from the _Recluse_, the _Fantasy Fan_, and _The Outsider and Others_ to compile his version, and presents the most complete and definitive version yet printed. He has even gone back to the original sources (like Samuel Loveman's introduction to _Twenty-one Letters of Ambrose Bierce_) from which Lovecraft cited and cleaned up transcription errors in the passages he quoted. The essay is made even more useful by the index (yes, an index in an Arkham House book!) that is supplied.

The book is topped off by a 40-page introduction by leading weird fictionist T. E. D. Klein. Klein reviews Lovecraft's literary and personal fondness for

Lord Dunsany, his New York "exile," and his literary techniques and themes. The latter discussion is quite comprehensive, if somewhat discursive, and touches on many important facets of Lovecraft's work—things like the use of the dream-city, and the themes of degeneration, fear of the impermanent, and adventurous expectancy. Among Klein's many insights is that Lovecraft's early stories are often "miniatures" of his later, greater works. This is strikingly evident on rereading the stories in this volume. In varying degrees, "The Moon-Bog" has much in common with "The Rats in the Walls," "The Nameless City" with *At the Mountains of Madness*, "The Tomb" and "The Alchemist" with *The Case of Charles Dexter Ward*, and "Facts concerning the Late Arthur Jermyn and His Family" with "The Shadow over Innsmouth." In all, the introduction contains a tremendous amount of information and will be an especial help to the new reader of Lovecraft. Klein (who has a compulsive fondness for Lovecraft's letters) uses copious quotations to let the Providence dreamer do as much of the talking as possible, and this gives the reader a good sense of Lovecraft's personality.

Since this is the last volume of the definitive fiction, it is appropriate to congratulate once more S. T. Joshi on his rediscovery of the "real" Lovecraft. His achievement will stand as a lasting monument to his many contributions to Lovecraft studies. James Turner of Arkham House, who saw Joshi's work to print, should also be singled out. On reflection, it is a sad and astonishing realization that it took fully forty years after Lovecraft's death for the event to come to pass. There are more intangible benefits, also. These volumes will do much to speed the continuing progress of Lovecraft from pulp hack to American artist. Anyone who approaches them will not encounter the garish, shabby, and none-too-coherent editions which have previously been the rule. Instead they will see the scholarly care, effort, and editorial interest befitting an author of literary merit and philosophical depth.

H. P. Lovecraft. *The Annotated Revisions and Collaborations of H. P. Lovecraft.* Edited by S. T. Joshi. Welches, OR: Arcane Wisdom (Bloodletting Press). Volume I: *Medusa's Coil and Others* (2011), 475 pp. Volume II: *The Crawling Chaos and Others* (2012), 350 pp. Limited edition hardcovers signed by the editor and numbered on a custom signature sheet featuring artwork by Zach McCain.

This is a beautifully edited, illustrated, and produced two-volume set. The publisher promotes it as including "the best" of Lovecraft's revisions and collaborations. This is a bit like promoting "the best of the worst." If there is little to recommend here on the merits of the stories themselves, there are at least several powerful items, plus the critical apparatus, that combine to make the set worth owning. S. T. Joshi again breaks new ground by providing a brief overview of each story, determining the definitive texts, outlining the details of the writing and Lovecraft's likely contribution, and annotating the material. The many of the never-before-published annotations, in particular, shed new light on these works and the author's creative process.

For the Lovecraft scholar, the revisions and collaborations represent a vexing question: why are they so bad? Lovecraft only wrote about fifty or sixty stories, and after enjoying these amazing creations we naturally go looking for more. Several generations of hopeful Lovecraft addicts have eagerly sought these stories out, in the hope of a further fix of the intoxicating elixir distilled into "The Call of Cthulhu" or "The Colour out of Space." What they have found is less like an elixir and more like an emetic. Even after reading and studying Lovecraft for many years, one comes away from these stories appalled and confused regarding how it all went to so horribly wrong. No matter how you approach this body of work, the bulk of it remains dross, with which we would be better off without. There are a few gems mixed in, but precious few.

Joshi's excellent introduction and notes go a long way toward sorting a lot of the confusion regarding this material. He unwinds all the details and makes the facts of who, what, and where easy to understand. And he also confronts the second big question regarding the revisions—what the hell was Lovecraft thinking? Lovecraft, who never had a nine-to-five job, apparently decided he could make an income by providing revisory services to struggling writers. Fair enough. However, it seems he only helped writers who were really, really struggling. And he only helped writers who were writing weird fiction—really, really bad weird fiction. And he only helped writers who had no means to pay him.

Re-reading these stories after a long period of time, it may be affirmed that none of the co-authors represented had any talent. At least one, Zealia Bishop, appears to have been borderline illiterate. Taking pen in hand, this is all she could choke out: "There is an Indian mound near here, which is haunted by a headless ghost. Sometimes it is a woman." Not exactly Zola or Proust, or even Seabury Quinn. Lovecraft conceived the notion that he would spun this out into the 30,000-word novella "The Mound." And he somehow came up with a story that is better than some of his signed work (including the "The Dunwich Horror" [1928]). But perhaps there *was* a method to Lovecraft's madness: reverse psychology. Bishop later recalled: "The stories I sent him always came back so revised from their basic idea that I felt I was a complete failure as a writer."

Another perplexing issue: why were so many of Lovecraft's revision clients female? The roster sounds like a women's softball team, and despite Joshi's scorecard there remains a lingering suspicion they are the same person. After all, their stories all equally appalling, and their names sound pretty much interchangeable: Winifred Virginia Jackson, Winifred Virginia Jordan, Zealia Brown, Zealia Brown Reed, Zealia Reed Bishop, Anna Helen Crofts, Sonia Haft Greene, Elizabeth Neville Berkeley, and Hazel Heald. Why did Lovecraft not supply Heald, a valued client, with a middle name? Could he not have borrowed one from Ms. Bishop? Joshi confides that Heald, a divorcée residing in Somerville, Mass., was romantically attracted to Lovecraft. Coming back from a trip to Quebec, Lovecraft told a friend "he was going to take a midnight bus to Providence after dinner in Somerville." Did Lovecraft ever actually get on that bus, and if he didn't, how long was Hazel held? Joshi wisely leaves this question to future scholars. One hopes the story "Midnight Bus to Providence," as by Hazel Winifred Neville, remains undiscovered in the pages of *Thrilling Love* magazine.

The tales are presented in chronological order of writing. The first volume contains eighteen items written up to 1930, plus four items to which Lovecraft contributed relatively less content. There are several stories worth reading here. The Winifred V. Jackson items are redolent of Edgar Allan Poe—the Poe of "The Colloquy of Monos and Una" and "Shadow—A Parable." "The Green Meadow" (1918/19) has an introduction in Lovecraft's realistic style, and a theme that anticipates "The Colour out of Space." "The Crawling Chaos" (1920/1921) has a compelling frisson, in part because of a nebulous connection with "Nyarlathotep" (1920). Both were written around the same time; the two items share little beyond the memorable phrase "the Crawling Chaos," certainly one of the most Lovecraftian of all Lovecraft's locutions. Pioneering Lovecraft scholar George Wetzel saw the two Jackson tales, plus "Poetry and the Gods" (with Anna Helen Crofts, 1920) as part of a "trilogy of quasi-Greek stories" that Lovecraft wrote. Wetzel's argument that the Cthulhu Mythos was influenced by Greek mythology is unconvincing, but he makes the interesting point that the stories in this cluster end with a kind of cosmic apocalypse that is a distinctively Lovecraftian trope.

"Under the Pyramids" (with Harry Houdini, 1924), long considered as part of the Lovecraft cannon proper, towers above the other items here as the

Pyramids tower over the plateau of Giza. This story marks the apex of Lovecraft's early style—incandescent in the manner of Lafcadio Hearn's translations of Théophile Gautier and Gustave Flaubert:

> Mystery attracts mystery. Ever since the wide appearance of my name as a performer of unexplained feats, I have encountered strange narratives and events which my calling has led people to link with my interests and activities. Some of these have been trivial and irrelevant, some deeply dramatic and absorbing, some productive of weird and perilous experiences, and some involving me in extensive scientific and historical research. Many of these matters I have told and shall continue to tell freely; but there is one of which I speak with great reluctance, and which I am now relating only after a session of grilling persuasion from the publishers of this magazine, who had heard vague rumours of it from other members of my family.

This is a classic Lovecraft opening paragraph. It looks back to "The Statement of Randolph Carter" (1919) and forward to "The Call of Cthulhu" (1926)—the first-person narrator suspended between reticence and revelation, the modulated periods, the many parallel constructions, and the suspended syntactical closure. The story is constructed with several sub-climaxes, featuring some energetic bursts of pure Lovecraftian prose:

> Then the mental cataclysm came. It was horrible—hideous beyond all articulate description because it was all of the soul, with nothing of detail to describe. It was the ecstasy of nightmare and the summation of the fiendish. The suddenness of it was apocalyptic and daemoniac—one moment I was plunging agonisingly down that narrow well of million-toothed torture, yet the next moment I was soaring on bat-wings in the gulfs of hell; swinging free and swoopingly through illimitable miles of boundless, musty space; rising dizzily to measureless pinnacles of chilling ether, then diving gaspingly to sucking nadirs of ravenous, nauseous lower vacua. . . . Thank God for the mercy that shut out in oblivion those clawing Furies of consciousness which half unhinged my faculties, and tore Harpy-like at my spirit! That one respite, short as it was, gave me the strength and sanity to endure those still greater sublimations of cosmic panic that lurked and gibbered on the road ahead.

To bask in the white heat of Lovecraft's descriptions of "nighted, necropolitan Egypt" is enough justification to go out and purchase these volumes.

A more modest but no less interesting achievement is the last story in the volume, written with Zealia Bishop in 1929–30. From the low plateau of "The Mound" one can see the titanic peaks of *At the Mountains of Madness*, written a year later. "The Mound" is one of many stories here that really benefit from Joshi's new annotations. A member of Coronado's expedition of 1541, one Zamacona y Nuñez, conducts an expedition to the mound region of Oklahoma. There he hears tales of an underground realm of great wealth beneath a mound, and finds an Indian who will lead him there. Zamacona comes upon the civilization of Xinaian, established by creatures from outer space. These inhabitants possess powers of telepathy and the dematerialization—an ability to dissolve themselves and nearby objects and reconstitute the atoms at a distant location. Zamacona initially finds the civilization has declined both intellectually and morally from a much higher level into decadence. He attempts to escape but suffers a horrible fate. His written record of his adventures is unearthed in modern times by an archeologist, who paraphrases his tale. The story is the first of Lovecraft's tales to utilize an alien civilization as a metaphor for dystopic Western civilization: "Daily life was organised in ceremonial patterns; with games, intoxication, torture of slaves, day-dreaming, gastronomic and emotional orgies, religious exercises, exotic experiments, and the like, as the principal occupations." Very much like modern American, except for the artistic and philosophical discussions. There is a strange thread of sadism and violence in this story like nothing else in Lovecraft:

> As time progressed, [Zamacona] noticed an increasing tendency of the people to resort to dematerialisation as an amusement; so that the apartments and amphitheaters of Tsath became a veritable Witches' Sabbath of transmutations, age-adjustments, death-experiments, and projections. With the growth of boredom and restlessness, he saw, cruelty and subtlety and revolt were growing apace. There was more and more cosmic abnormality, more and more curious sadism, more and more ignorance and superstition, and more and more desire to escape out of physical life into a half-spectral state of electronic dispersal.

Note the closing, prescient allusion to Facebook.

The second volume, which contains thirteen items, continues to appall and confuse. There are fewer thrills and more comedy, all of it unintentional. It becomes progressively impossible to decide at any given moment if Lovecraft is pulling the reader's leg. He *must* be kidding—how could he possibly plagiarize and parody himself so badly without knowing it? Take for example the speech of a black maid in "Medusa's Coil" (with Zealia Bishop, 1930):

> "Iä! Iä! Shub-Niggurath! Ya-R'lyeh! N'gagi n'bulu bwana n'lolo! Ya, yo, pore Missy Tanit, pore Missy Isis! Marse Clooloo, come up outen de water an' git

yo chile—she done daid! She done daid! De hair ain' got no missus no mo', Marse Clooloo. Ol' Sophy, she know! Ol' Sophy, she done got de black stone outen Big Zimbabwe in ol' Affriky! Ol' Sophy, she done dance in de moonshine roun' de crocodile-stone befo' de N'bangus cotch her and sell her to de ship folks! No mo' Tanit! No mo' Isis! No mo' witch-woman to keep de fire a-goin' in de big stone place! Ya, yo! N'gagi n'bulu bwana n'lolo! Iä! Shub-Niggurath! She daid! Ol' Sophy know!'

"The Horror in the Museum" (with Hazel Heald, 1932) and "Out of the Aeons" (also with Heald, 1933), too, have the stench of "Marse Clooloo" hanging about them, but here it is as if the octopoid god has been pickled in formaldehyde. This must have been a truly difficult time for Lovecraft the writer, in between the composition of "The Dreams in the Witch House" and "The Thing on the Doorstep," both signed fictional misfires.

One actual boon for the uninitiated in the second volume is "The Night Ocean" (with R. H. Barlow, 1936), which has the feel of a prose poem and something the manner of Algernon Blackwood's *Incredible Adventures*. Also of note is "The Challenge from Beyond" (with C. L. Moore, A. Merritt, Robert E. Howard, and Frank Belknap Long, 1935), a round-robin tale where one author begins the story, and another author continues the story to a certain point, after which yet another author picks it up, and so on. Lovecraft fares well among his pulpish peers.

In terms of comic rather than cosmic appeal, one of the crown jewels in this volume is "The Diary of Alonzo Typer" (1935). The story was written with William Lumley (yet another illiterate, insolvent client). A diary is found in an old Dutch house in upstate New York near the town of Chorazin. The diarist is an occultist investigating rumors of a haunting. He finds himself unable to leave the premises, trapped by a wall of brambles, and tormented by the spirits and the shadowy presence of something with very large paws. Again, one is unable to tell if Lovecraft is dryly mocking his own style or playing it straight: "I am conscious of several presences in this house. One in particular is decidedly hostile toward me—a malevolent will which is seeking to break down my own and overcome me. I must not countenance this for an instant, but must use all my forces to resist it." During his explorations of the house, he finds a locked door in the basement, the key, and the incantations to enter the mysterious realm of Yian-ho beyond the portal. The ending never fails to amuse, and is one of the most quoted passages in Lovecraft. So here it is again—classic HPL—parody or not, none dare say: "Too late—cannot help self—black paws materialise—am dragged away toward the cellar. . . ."

Lovecraft's Essays, Poems, and Letters

H. P. Lovecraft. *In Defence of Dagon*. Edited by S. T. Joshi. West Warwick, RI: Necronomicon Press, 1985.

The 1921 essays published here for the first time are among H. P. Lovecraft's most eloquent statements on art and philosophy, and lend important insight into the state of his thought at an early date in his fictional career. Lovecraft, of course, discussed his philosophy in surviving letters from the late 1910s and early 1920s, and in certain essays such as "Idealism and Materialism: A Reflection" (1919); but *In Defence of Dagon* is not merely his first really detailed discourse on both metaphysics and the aesthetics of the weird, but also one of the earliest instances where the interdependence of these two facets of his thought is evident.

In Defence of Dagon is comprised of three essays written for the Transatlantic Circulator, a loosely organized group of English and American amateur journalists who exchanged creative material and critical commentary in round-robin fashion. (Details of the group's exact operation remain somewhat obscure, though Lovecraft's mentions of "the Conductor's Notes" and "the General Discussion folio" provide hints.) Lovecraft became involved in July 1920, featuring "The White Ship," which had recently won the Story Laureateship of the United Amateur Press Association. After circulating four more tales and a half-dozen poems, he withdrew in September 1921 due to the pressures of revisory work (and perhaps also the emotional debilitation caused by the death of his mother several months previously). We join the proceedings in January 1921, with Lovecraft replying to criticism not merely of his 1917 tale "Dagon," but also of his penchant for weird fiction and his philosophical outlook in general (evidently the other members of the Circulator were inclined to the traditional!). Aside from displaying exceptionally mature and well-reasoned positions in both aesthetics and metaphysics—in opposition to the commonly accepted view of a dogmatic and book-bound early Lovecraft—the author shows himself to be at the peak of his power as amateur journalist, flinging out many eminently quotable epigrams, posing rhetorical questions, quoting Nietzsche, and exercising the amusing if heavy-handed sense of irony that characterizes his other early amateur productions.

Lovecraft's replies to specific comments on his tales here provide information not to be found elsewhere. We learn, for example, that "Dagon" was at least partly based on a dream, and that "The White Ship" was (like the later "Silver Key") intentionally used as a vehicle for its author's philosophy. Lovecraft also declares that the "gentle" Musides did in fact poison his fraternal rival Kalos in "The Tree," although (as Donald R. Burleson points out in his *Critical Study*) there is no hard textual evidence of this. Equally interesting is Lovecraft's forceful defence of phantasy's integrity as a genre. With the artificiality of romance at one extreme and the banality of realism at the other, phantasy alone, he insists, "exists to fulfill the demands of the imagination." As he would later in both letters and in "Supernatural Horror in Literature," he assails didacticism in literature, saying that the true artist does not construct a commodity for a particular market's needs but instead depicts the imaginative "moods and mind-pictures" that clamour for expression.

Some facets of Lovecraft's own unique aesthetic of weird fiction, many of which would later be expanded and systematized, are also displayed. "To trace the remote in the immediate" is a priority, and in this we may detect an indication of Lovecraft's later belief that effective phantasy is not a negation but an *extension* of reality. So too do we encounter an admission of inability to adopt a humanocentric perspective, even if for the purposes of fiction alone. Lovecraft also expresses his intent to avoid the didactic: "the story is first, and if any philosophy creeps in, it is by accident." Despite his adherence to this, it is by now well known that the best of his tales are unified by a thread of cosmic indifferentism that, by virtue of its strength and coherence, could not help but to make itself evident there.

It is the materialism at the core of Lovecraft's aesthetics to which he devotes most of these essays, his remarks taking the form of a reply to points raised by another, rather disingenuous member of the Circulator, a Mr. Wickenden. Not surprisingly, many of the components of Lovecraft's mature philosophy are already in place here. For example, he is already calling himself a mechanistic materialist, even if as recently as 1915 he could still number himself an agnostic (see SL 1.11). He does, however, mention pessimism as a distinguishing feature of his outlook, which shows that he had not fully formulated his concept of indifferentism at this time.

One especially thought-provoking segment of the book is Lovecraft's deft response to Wickenden's attacks upon one of materialism's most basic (and in some ways its weakest) foundation, that of epistemology. Can we really "know" that religious faith is less valid than scientific fact, since both are essentially interpretations of nature? Fact, Lovecraft counters, is not easily challenged; for it is determined by reason, and "reason has never yet failed." Scientific theory, then, is only that supported by data that are both reproducible and intersubjectively testable. Admittedly, "all theories must indeed be open to scoffing," but "surely those [theories] are weakest which claim most and have least corroboration, while those are strongest which depend most on solid observation." This and similar comments would lead us to conclude that even before the advent of quantum physics Lovecraft's realism was critical rather than naive; that is, he believed that scientific theories are not literal descriptions of nature but merely summaries of data for making predictions about observable phenomena.

Equally impressive is Lovecraft's multipronged assault on the concepts of immortality and the soul. He begins by pointing out that what idealists call the "soul" is simply the sum of consciousness and personality, and, working from pathology, he notes that damage to specific parts of the brain leads to a corresponding impairment of activity in those areas. He also questions the soul's existence on the basis of ontogeny (the "soul" undergoes a continual development throughout the life of the organism, which began as an embryonic cell) and phylogeny (the human "soul" must necessarily be traced back through a long evolutionary series of lesser mammal "souls"). Though the latter aspect of Lovecraft's attack largely follows Ernst Haeckel (especially chapter five of *The Riddle of the Universe* [Eng. tr. 1900]), the keenness of the argument as a whole is not to be denied.

Special mention should be made of the excellence of S. T. Joshi's introduction and notes, which greatly increase the usefulness of the text. The introduction is a fascinating essay in its own right. Joshi first unearths some of the surviving comments on Lovecraft's work by other members of the Circulator (the full text of which would have made a worthwhile appendix), and then makes a brief but enlightening examination of the background behind the philosophical portion of the essays. He also provides much bibliographic data, including a list of the works Lovecraft sent through the Circulator. The annotation is equally helpful, the reader being directed very specifically to works by authors as diverse as Wilde and Chesterton for a greater insight into the influences upon Lovecraft's thought.

Indeed, a reading of this volume cannot but help to instill such insight into Lovecraft as creative artist and thinker, and as such ought to be sought out by all with an interest in him.

H. P. Lovecraft. *Commonplace Book.* Edited by David E. Schultz. West Warwick, RI: Necronomicon Press, 1987.

H. P. Lovecraft used the *Commonplace Book* from 1919 (or 1920) until his death in 1937 as a place to write down images and ideas which struck his fancy, for possible later use in his fiction. It is a document of almost unending fascination, for reading it is the closest we can get to peering directly into the author's imagination. David E. Schultz has undertaken the formidable task of discovering the sources and uses of the entries in Lovecraft's little book. The result is a critical landmark so comprehensive—the breadth of the information here is perhaps unprecedented in Lovecraft studies—that it lends much to our understanding of how Lovecraft's imagination worked and how his imaginings became finished works of art. It will serve as an ideal for future undertakings of a similar kind.

Schultz is a leading Lovecraft scholar, and perhaps the most active critic in amateur journalism—his publications have since the mid-seventies been staples of the amateur press associations devoted to Lovecraft. He was among the first to advocate some of the tenets of what S. T. Joshi has in these pages called "modern" Lovecraft criticism: the establishment of a sound chronology for Lovecraft's tales; the study of those tales in the order in which they were written, to observe the development of important themes and techniques; the explosion of the Cthulhu Mythos; the establishment of a sound bibliography (see his *H. P. Lovecraft: The Anthologies* [Strange Co., 1975]). Schultz has also emphasized the centrality of dreams and dream-motifs in Lovecraft and is currently working on an annotated edition of *Fungi from Yuggoth.* His recent efforts, however, have largely been devoted to the annotation of the *Commonplace Book,* and this Necronomicon Press publication is the fruit of five years of intermittent work. The level of detail and thoroughness of Schultz's product make the reader quickly realize that the editor is by nature a perfectionist.

The book begins with a fine introductory essay describing the history of the *Commonplace Book,* the nature of its entries, the part the latter played in story-writing, and the physical aspect of the book itself (we are even given several charts showing the disposition of leaves and location of entries in the original manuscripts). Schultz refrains from much critical discussion, perhaps because of space limitations—as it is, the introduction is somewhat longer than the text of the *Commonplace Book* itself—but we may hope for future articles from his pen on his interpretation of the importance of Lovecraft's notebook in the creative process. More pertinent to the text is the detailed history of its transmission here. To say that the history is a confusing one is an understatement; but the author has somehow unraveled it and presents a lucid account of his research, lending insight into the Lovecraft scene of the 1940s along the way.

As for the notebook itself, for the first time we have a text that is both complete and accurately rendered. Schultz has taken almost no editorial liberties in his presentation, instead attempting to give us a feel for the autograph manuscript of the notebook. Although this makes reading a bit difficult, it is the next best thing to having the A.Ms. itself: we can see, for example, how Lovecraft centered certain items or made later additions and deletions. Some of the 222 entries are banal, but the majority are fascinating— what we have here is the distilled essence of Lovecraft's fancy, undiluted by short story conventions and other encumbrances.

The annotation of these entries is the main feature of the book, in both bulk (more than four times the length of the text itself) and merit. The notes are concerned with specifically identifying both the sources of the entries— "dreams, things read, casual incidents, idle conceptions, & so on," as Lovecraft put it—and their place of eventual use in Lovecraft's work. Schultz has annotated nearly every entry in Lovecraft's notebook, and in general has succeeded in being plausible and to the point. Unfortunately, this type of project has some necessary evils: it is never quite done, for one is always accidentally coming across new sources (in unpublished letters, typically) and uses; and each reader will undoubtedly recognize some use of the entries in the fiction that the editor has missed. For entry 53 ("Hand of dead man writes"), for example, it might be mentioned that "Cool Air" and "The Thing on the Doorstep" feature similar events. In the end, though, it is at the discretion of the editor about how far to reach for a connection and what to omit.

We may say, however, that Schultz has done an admirable job in walking this fine line and confidently state that his product is about as definitive as possible given these problems. The number and diversity of sources used here is mind-boggling: everything from *Argosy All-Story Magazine* to Baring-Gould's *Curious Myths of the Middle Ages* to Elliot's *Modern Science and Materialism* to (rather embarrassingly) one of Lovecraft's favorites, the 9th edition of the *En-*

cyclopaedia Britannica. Not surprisingly, Lovecraft's letters yield many clues to the sources, and Schultz's primary research in the collection of the Wisconsin State Historical Society has turned up much hitherto unknown information. Extensive consultation with other Lovecraft scholars, in a process that anticipates the execution of Joshi's *Collected Works*, has helped insure that little is overlooked.

The annotation section is so rich, in fact, that one hardly knows what to cite as examples. We learn about how Lovecraft might have developed entries into stories he never got around to writing—entry 133, for instance, about a circus freak whose surgically detached "little anthropoid excrescence" takes on a hellish life of its own (Henry S. Whitehead based his story "Cassius" on this entry), or entries 7 and 9, in which a Civil War surgeon is killed by his own undead creation. Schultz demonstrates, too, that Lovecraft's use of the entries ranged from the incidental to the central. Entry 60 ("Fisherman casts his net into the sea—what he finds" [tentatively dated 1919]), for instance, was casually tossed into "The Haunter of the Dark" (1935), while entry 182 ("In an ancient buried city a man finds a mouldering prehistoric document in English & in his own handwriting, telling an incredible tale" [tentatively dated 1930]) served as the very plot-germ for "The Shadow out of Time" (1934–35).

The reader also gains many small insights into the way Lovecraft's mind worked. For example, entry 155—"Steepled town seen from afar at sunset— does not light up at night. Sail has been seen putting out to sea." This takes on a great deal of force after we learn that one of Lovecraft's favorite ways to experience an atmosphere of antique quaintness was to watch the windows of Marblehead or Providence light up, one after the other, at dusk. Thus, the failure of a town to light up at night would seem to him a horrible perversion of the normal.

Enlightening as all these tidbits are, the real value of this book is in its broader implications on Lovecraft's work. A pattern begins to take shape as Schultz points out the same themes emerging in many entries: displaced identity, the dream-world impinging on the real world, the reanimated dead, the past impinging on the present, the mind shedding the body and wandering through time and space, artifacts that are imbued with cosmic abnormality. These are the actual ideas or experiences that Lovecraft wished to communicate, and this volume helps us become more aware of them. We can reread the author's works with a new recognition of his thematic intent and follow more closely the means by which he embodies his themes in fiction.

Similarly, we begin also to note that Lovecraft's imagination returned again and again to imagery that best expressed his moods—crooked, antique city streets, oily black rivers, strange gardens, forbidden books, buildings that hide terrible secrets, the gateway to supra-reality. This is significant, from a critical perspective, because fictional themes are usually not explicit—that is, they are usually conveyed through imagery and symbolism. Again, in rereading the works, we can pick up on these hints of thematic statement and recognize the associated imagery, thus gradually coming to a fuller understanding of Lovecraft's original vision. Schultz's *Commonplace Book* (and his planned *Fungi from Yuggoth* even more so) shows that there is in Lovecraft a finite set of images that crops up continually in both his poetry and fiction, and the volume will doubtless both incite and assist the work that needs to be done on this approach.

One can hardly hope to do more than touch on the many appealing aspects of this critical study of Lovecraft's notebook. Basically, the vast amount of information in the annotations helps to remind us that Lovecraft's stories did not just spring into being and do not exist only in the pages of an Arkham House book or paperback. Aside from being just plain fascinating reading, the volume helps us understand what Lovecraft intended in his works, what choices he made in their composition, and what effects he sought. This makes it a must for anyone looking for more insight into the imagination and artistry of the twentieth century's finest author of fantastic fiction.

H. P. Lovecraft. *Medusa and Other Poems.* Edited by S. T. Joshi. (*Crypt of Cthulhu* 44.) Mount Olive, NC: Cryptic Publications, 1986.

Lovecraft's poetry is the least controversial aspect of his life and work—nearly everyone agrees that it is bad. But instead of generalizing as Darrell Schweitzer chose to do in his *Dream Quest of H. P. Lovecraft* by opening his chapter on the verse, "The less said about Lovecraft's poetry, the better"—let us be more specific. Real poetic fire is present in some of Lovecraft's verse, autobiographical or historical interest in most of it, and technical perfection characterizes nearly all of it. These are indeed reasons enough to merit the joint effort of Robert M. Price, indefatigable publisher, and S. T. Joshi, indefatigable editor, in bringing us this collection of the remaining unreprinted poetry.

It is not difficult to say why most of Lovecraft's early verse is so poor; many of the poems presented here, in fact, offer the answer quite clearly. We find not the delineation of an alternately awe- and horror-inspiring universe, or the questing for "unformed realms of infinity beyond all Nature as we know it," as we do in the fiction. Instead, we wade through passionless verses on the ethos of New England and the rest of Anglo-Saxondom. Lovecraft himself was well aware of his shortcomings, even at an early date—he signed a revision of 1915 as "Howard P. Lovecraft, Metrical Mechanic"—and when he finally dropped his poetic affectations in the last decade of his life he admitted to a correspondent that he wrote this type of verse "as a means of recreating around me the atmosphere of my beloved 18th century favourites."

So why bother to reprint, or (especially) to read it? One reason is the dazzling facility Lovecraft had with the heroic couplet. His work in this form is mostly flawless in rhyme and shows a masterful command of meter. Lovecraft's defense of the couplet in "Metrical Regularity" (1915) as "capable of taking on infinite shades of expression by the right selection and sequence of words, and by the proper placing of the caesura or pause in each line" is borne out by such efforts here as "Content," "Ver Rusticum," and even "Lines for Poets' Night at the Scribbler's Club," which shifts abruptly from its occasional tone to a dramatic description of Samuel Loveman's poetry:

> Palace and temple, plinth and colonnade;
> Ewer of gold, goblet of carven jade;
> Wing'd brazen lion, sphinx of diorite,
> And marble faun, an ode of living light;
> Ionian moonbeams, bow'rs of Naxian vines,
> Weird trains of Maenads, drunk with Thasian wines,
> Rites that the gods themselves half fear'd to see,
> And fever'd pomps of Phrygian sorcery;
> Vista of cities in the sunset clouds,
> Black halls of Pharaohs in their nighted shrouds; [. . .]

There is music in many of these early pieces, then, but again what is missing is what Lovecraft (echoing Arthur Machen's *Hieroglyphics*) called "a certain degree of concentrated ecstasy in the creator." It is this "ecstasy" that informs "The Music of Erich Zann," "The Colour out of Space," and, yes, certain of the *Fungi from Yuggoth*.

We need not search quite so carefully for the merits of Lovecraft's satiric and humorous verse, well represented here by "Ad Criticos" (printed complete for the first time), the insightful self-parody "On the Death of a Rhyming Critic," "Theobaldian Aestivation," "Medusa: A Portrait," "The Feast," and others. These are amusing mostly because of the way Lovecraft works the grotesque contrast between form and content. We still have the dignified procession of couplets, but now comprised of colloquial language and incongruous imagery. "The Power of Wine: A Satire," one of the funniest things of any kind written by Lovecraft, provides an example:

> How great the pow'r of Wine to beautify
> The manly form, and please th' exacting eye!
> What graceful steps the polish'd drunkard knows!
> How sweetly can he on the road repose!
> The flaming face, the gently leering stare,
> Bespatter'd clothing, and disorder'd hair,
> The od'rous breath, and incoherent voice,
> All charm our fancy, and increase our joys.

Another reason the satiric poetry is so amusing is Lovecraft's use of the couplet form to spring his punchlines (so to speak) when, lulled by the flowing meter, we least expect it. Note, for example, "On the Death of a Rhyming Critic":

> Tho' much by ancient notions marr'd,
> He was a fairly clever bard;
> His numbers smooth enough would roll,
> But after all—he had no soul!

The first three end-stopped lines set up the fourth, with its dash (caesura) and exclamation point for even more "punch."

In this volume there are also a few verses of serious intent worth reading. "Amissa Minerva" was penned during the author's early battle against free verse. In theme it is of a piece with such essays as "The Vers Libre Epidemic," "Metrical Regularity," and "The Allowable Rhyme"; in content it was influenced by Horace's *Ars Poetica* and Pope's *An Essay on Criticism* (for more on this see my essay elsewhere in this volume). There is much poignancy and philosophical interest in "To an Infant," which advises its addressee that "Your dreams are yourself, so tend them as all that preserves you free." The three poems that make up "A Cycle of Verse" have some powerful imagery and evoke more of true fear than most of the pieces in Lovecraft's famous sonnet sequence. In one, "Mother Earth," the narrator explores a familiar Lovecraftian wood, complete with grotesque vegetation and glyph-carved rocks, finally hearing in the trickle of hidden water a warning:

"Mortal, ephemeral and bold,
In mercy keep what I have told,
Yet think sometimes of what hath been,
And sights these crumbling rocks have seen;
Of sentience old ere thy weak brood
Appear'd in lesser magnitude,
And living things that yet survive,
Tho' not to human ken alive."

Though there is less than one might wish in this volume showing the poet feeling as well as rhyming, as do these lines, there is enough of interest to make the book worthwhile for many among us.

H. P. Lovecraft. *Letters to Richard F. Searight.* **Edited by David E. Schultz and S. T. Joshi, with Franklyn Searight. West Warwick, RI: Necronomicon Press, 1992.**

Whenever I happen across the title of C. Alphonso Smith's *Edgar Allan Poe: How to Know Him* (1921) in a bookstore or bibliography, I'm reminded of H. P. Lovecraft's letters. Should one inquire how to "know" Lovecraft, the answer is easy: simply read the thousands of his letters that have been published. Excerpts from around a thousand are available, of course, in five volumes from Arkham House. Readers who have mastered these thoroughly and wish to be on a real first-name basis with E'ch-Pi-El, so to speak, have the option of tracking down other bits of correspondence published in various other volumes. The net effect of reading all these letters to different correspondents—some of whom knew Lovecraft only through the mail—enables us to create a picture of his personality more vivid than any a single correspondent could have known. Indeed, what emerges from this reading is a personality more vivid than many we may know in our own day-to-day interaction with casual acquaintances or colleagues at the office.

David E. Schultz and S. T. Joshi here continue the Promethean task of publishing Lovecraft's uncollected letters, correspondent by correspondent. The Searight correspondence—some thirty-five missives in all—is the largest collection to single individual so far published. They feature a modicum of information of interest not only to those who wish to "know" the enigmatic and charismatic writer, but also to Lovecraft scholars looking for new primary source material.

As a correspondence, the Searight letters fall somewhere in the middle of the spectrum of interest relative to other Lovecraft correspondences. The period covered, 1933–37, has been fairly well saturated by other previously published letters. Lovecraft did relatively little fiction writing during the period, which tends to limit the usefulness of the correspondence for literary critics. Neither did Lovecraft embrace Searight as one privy to his most deeply felt aesthetic and philosophical beliefs, as he did Clark Ashton Smith, Donald Wandrei, James F. Morton, and a few select others.

Lovecraft's role as revisionary consultant to Searight's fiction, however, contributes much of interest to the letters. Richard F. Searight (1902–1975) was employed as a telegraph operator by Western Union and later a bookkeeper and CPA, but he had aspirations as a fantasist and poet. *Weird Tales* editor Farnsworth Wright referred him to Lovecraft in 1933. Much of the initial correspondence is devoted to Lovecraft's critiques and commentary on Searight's fiction. Lovecraft's advice to Searight, "writer to writer," reflects the former's great acumen as literary critic. For example, he immediately takes Searight to task for treating supernormal phenomena as another matter-of-fact narrative episode: "The emotions of normal human beings at sight of anything as incredible as a sign of intelligent extraterrestrial intrusion would be totally different from the matter-of-fact attitude delineated."

This, of course, is the very same rationale behind Lovecraft's own colorful and often condemned prose style. A few letters later, he continues on the thread:

> In tales of epic atmosphere, it seems as if one's prose ought to be written with a sharp ear for harmony in accent & tone-colour—the most desirable effect being that of a subtle, imperceptible rhythm which rises at high moments to the fluency and poetic pulse of actual song. Wilde, Dunsany, & other titans in the field of prose-poetry are worth a close examination.

This very revealing remark, coupled with several similar ones in the *Selected Letters* (cf. *SL* 5.199, 230), shows that Lovecraft was seeking to do something very different from the typical fiction writer. The most poetic passages of his work resemble *symbolisme,* with a richness of meaning unlimited by denotation, and a harmony of sound that has the impact of an incantation. In a later letter, Lovecraft cannily denies Poe was a seminal influence on his style, a conclusion I draw in my essay "H. P. Lovecraft: Consummate Prose Stylist."

Lovecraft's usually insists that art deals with images rather than ideas. He was, however, not above didacticism, as he admits when he calls "The Silver

Key" (1926) "more of an essay than a story." This leads to a long discussion of the philosophical underpinnings of the tale, at one point taking a turn that has particular relevance in today's social climate:

> But what, we may ask, will strengthen popular morale? . . . I fancy that the organised teaching of pure ethics on a basis primarily utilitarian, but with sufficient emotional overtones to catch the enthusiasm of primitive minds, would form the foundation of any successful system. . . . The loyalty & interest of the herd must be caught by some movement which shall seem valid to them—as religion used to do, but as it can (so far as practical results are concerned) do no more. . . . There can be no widespread respect for any morality which impoverishes the many (especially amidst the present plenitudes of resources) while it fabulously enriches the few. Thus a workable morality is bound up closely with the trying & complex issues economic issues of the day.

While this passage alone may not qualify Lovecraft as a great thinker, it puts him ahead of certain candidates for the recent presidential election.

As Lovecraft's relationship with Searight grows, correspondence gains depth. A long, interesting letter covers issues related to ontology and epistemology, concluding that the "least improbable of all theories" is a cosmos of "mutually interacting forces without beginning, ending, meaning, consciousness, or direction. Simply a fixed condition of infinite automatic mutations." We are treated to an excellent discussion—perhaps the most succinct yet published—of the reasons behind Lovecraft's identification with the past, specifically with ancient Rome. There is a suggested reading list for a child—mostly fantasy—which helps us understand what the young Lovecraft found to be most emotionally and imaginatively valuable. The book also offers Lovecraft rehearsing a discussion of aesthetics whose particulars will be familiar to the *Selected Letters* reader. "What is ugly to one," he posits, "is beautiful to another—& certain forms of physical or psychological ugliness possess a perverse & macabre impressiveness which in itself is a shadowy form of beauty."

There is also an important passage that gives us hope for a restored version of "The Shadow out of Time" (1934-35). Lovecraft remarks that paragraphs in the story were broken up when printed in *Astounding*, thereby proving S. T. Joshi's conjecture in "Textual Problems in Lovecraft" (*Lovecraft Studies* No. 6 [Spring 1982]: 18-32]). He continues, "With great difficulty I fixed up 3 copies of each of the 'Mts.' and 'Shadow'—joining broken paragraphs, & careting in missing passages written in fine pencil characters on the margins." Only one such copy is known, and Joshi used it to help derive the current text of "Shadow"; but Lovecraft seems not to have thoroughly corrected it. If the other two copies are extant, they may provide additional information for a further restoration of the text.

The book is rounded out by a touching four-page introduction and memoir of Searight by his son Franklyn, and the usual rigorous annotation by the editors. In all, it is highly recommended to those who wish to know Lovecraft.

H. P. Lovecraft. *Miscellaneous Writings.* Edited by S. T. Joshi. Sauk City, WI: Arkham House, 1995.

For more than a decade, S. T. Joshi has partnered with Arkham House in an effort to renew H. P. Lovecraft's texts. Four volumes of fiction and revisions have already come forth. *Miscellaneous Writings* continues the initiative by correcting and presenting the uncollected fiction and essential nonfiction. This fat, well-designed volume, which runs nearly 600 pages and presents over eighty items, is laid out in nine sections—"Dreams and Fancies" (which includes the excellent prose poems of the 1920s and other fugitive pieces), "The Weird Fantasist," "Mechanistic Materialist," "Literary Critic," "Political Theorist," "Antiquarian Travels," "Amateur Journalist," "Epistolarian" (mostly previously published, but not in the Arkham *Selected Letters*), and "Personal." In addition to many scarce pieces, Joshi also offers some previously unpublished specimens. He adds a detailed introduction to each section and appends a helpful bibliography. The volume is also graced by interesting illustrations—autograph manuscripts, original publications, artwork, and photographs (the one of Lovecraft apparently throttling a tabby cat, facing page 528, is especially amusing).

The book is undoubtedly a treasure-trove for Lovecraft scholars. Having all these items between the same covers makes it easier to understand Lovecraft and easier to cite the material in critical articles. But casual readers and even Lovecraft aficionados may wonder why they should purchase a book that consists largely of what may appear to be rather dry essays. In fact, the best items in *Miscellaneous Writings*—fiction, essays, and letters alike—provide that same unique "Lovecraftian" sensation that draws us to the author's greatest stories.

Take for example the first mature piece in *Miscellaneous Writings*, "A Reminiscence of Samuel Johnson" (1917). This humorous item, the first-person narrative of a 227-year-old man, is an early manifestation one of Lovecraft's primary themes: the persistence of the past. As such, "A Reminiscence" is important in the consideration of "The Tomb" (1917), "The Terrible Old Man" (1920), "He" (1925), and other stories.

But the really fascinating thing about "A Reminiscence of Samuel Johnson" is its effortless and convincing eighteenth-century style of writing. We find this very same style used throughout Lovecraft's prose works. He uses it in the travel essays featured elsewhere in this book. He uses in personal correspondence (see, for example, letters no. 118, 127, 143, 149, 151, 154, and most notably 138 in Arkham House's *Selected Letters 1*). He also uses it in certain other letters: those of the unnaturally aged wizard Joseph Curwen and his associates in *The Case of Charles Dexter Ward*.

In his introduction S. T. Joshi touches glancingly upon this point that the rhetorical element of Lovecraft's writing is powerfully compelling to the reader in all his prose work. The reason why Lovecraft's fiction is so endlessly rereadable; why we devour the *Selected Letters* once we get through the fiction; why we then seek out unpublished Lovecraft letters; and why many of the essays here are so fascinating, is because of Lovecraft's superb and uniquely characteristic rhetorical skill. It is this stylistically driven affect, I suspect, that causes some desperate yet misguided readers seek out "Cthulhu Mythos" pastiches—most of which attempt to ape Lovecraft's style without quite getting it right. The *frisson*—in the sense of shudder or thrill, as the case might be—we get reading Lovecraft's prose, fiction or nonfiction, is one of the author's great distinctions.

In terms of reader response, then, Lovecraft's best essays and letters are similar in effect to his tales. There is the same forceful attempt to persuade the reader (a unique blend of rational, emotional, and ethical appeals), the same rhetorical flourishes (primarily parallelism, antithesis, periodic syntax), and the same careful arrangement of material which cause us to be so affected by the fiction. To prove the point we need only consider that most unique combination of essay and prose poem, "Supernatural Horror in Literature" (included in *Dagon and Other Macabre Tales*). Only Lovecraft could write a monograph about the weird tale *using the manner of a weird tale*. Think of the introductory section: "Men with minds sensitive to hereditary impulse will always tremble at the thought of the hidden and fathomless worlds of strange life which may pulsate in the gulfs beyond the stars, or press hideously upon our own globe in unholy dimensions which only the dead and the moonstruck can glimpse." Joshi has pointed out that many of Lovecraft's plot synopses in this essay are more atmospherically effective than the stories he summarizes.

"Lord Dunsany and His Work" (1922), reprinted here, is another example of the essay-as-metafiction stratagem. Near the end Lovecraft takes off a flight of fancy remarkably similar in effect to passages we find in Lovecraft's Dunsanian fiction. The statements on the nature of art, ascribed to Dunsany but clearly Lovecraft's own, are reminiscent of that essay-disguised-as-a-Dunsanian-story, "The Silver Key."

It is insightful, then, for us to consider all the items in this volume, fiction and nonfiction, from the perspective of reception theory; as Terry Eagleton puts it, "reading is not a matter of discovering what the text means, but a process of experiencing what it does to you." The continuity of effect across all Lovecraft's prose is driven home by the inclusion of an excerpt ("The Very Old Folk") from a 1927 letter to Donald Wandrei recounting Lovecraft's famous Roman dream. This is the "real stuff"—as forceful and thrilling as a Lovecraft tale—because of the panache of the writing:

> And above the nighted screaming of men and horses that daemonic drumming rose to a louder pitch, whilst an ice-cold wind of shocking sentience and deliberateness swept down from those forbidden heights and coiled about each man separately, till all the cohort was struggling and screaming in the dark, as if acting out the fate of Laocoön and his sons.

It is this same stylistic effectiveness that makes the hard-to-find prose poems included here so prized. Especially brilliant is the apocalyptic "Nyarlathotep" (1920), which for all its brevity is surely one of the greatest things Lovecraft ever wrote.

Two rarely-seen humorous pieces—"Old Bugs" (1919), a rather flat morality tale written to discourage a young acquaintance from drinking, and "Sweet Ermengarde" (from the early 1920s), a parody of the Horatio Alger-type story—show a different side of Lovecraft's rhetorical skill. They mix his usual Augustan writing style with colloquialism to very humorous effect. He often pulled the same trick in correspondence to James F. Morton, Frank Belknap Long, and others. (Recently, Peter Cannon outdid Lovecraft himself using a similar approach in the hilarious Lovecraft-Wodehouse pastiche *Scream for Jeeves*.)

Of especial interest among the more obscure items here is "Heritage or Modernism: Common Sense in Art Forms" (1935). This article, which codifies arguments Lovecraft presented to correspondents on the role and meaning of art, is one of the author's most substantial pieces of nonfiction and deserves careful study for its relation to Lovecraft's own art. Parts of this essay, too, read like the fiction; for example, this stream-of-consciousness attack on radical functional forms:

> How, then, can the strained and artificial system of symbolism behind the modern's position be anything but a sorry joke? They launch new decorative designs of cones and cubes and triangles and segments—wheels and belts, smokestacks and stream-lined sausage-molders—problems in Euclid and nightmares from alcoholic orgies—and tell us that these things are authentic symbols of the age in which we live.

Compare the "geometrical forms for which even an Euclid could scarcely find a name" which make up the Old Ones' city in At the Mountains of Madness (1931). Analogous stream-of-consciousness passages appear in many Lovecraft stories: at the end of the Antarctic novella, in "The Hound" (1922), "The Lurking Fear" (1922), "The Rats in the Walls" (1923), "The Haunter of the Dark" (1935), and other tales. Remarkably similar in style is a diatribe in "An Account of Charleston" (1930; a different and more extensive text than previously published versions). After fifteen pages of quaint Queen Anne prose describing the history and environs of the city, Lovecraft suddenly breaks into an impressionistic rant on the decline of the West that could well serve as the climax to "Nyarlathotep":

> Noise—profit—publicity—speed—time-table convict regularity—equality—ostentation—size—standardisation—herding. . . . Emotions grow irrelevant, and art ceases to be vital except when functioning through strange forms which may be normal to the alien and recrystallised future, but are blank and void to us of the dying western civilization. James Joyce . . . Erik Dorn . . . Marcel Proust . . . Brancusi . . . Picasso . . . "The Waste Land" . . . cubes and cogs and circles . . . segments and squares and shadows . . . wheels and whirring, whirring and wheels . . . purring of planes and clicks of chronographs . . . milling of the rabble and raucous yells of the exhibitionist . . . "comic" strips . . . Sunday feature headings . . . advertisements . . . sports . . . tabloids . . . luxury . . . Palm Beach . . . "sales talk" . . . rotogravures . . . radio . . . Babel . . . Bedlam. . . .

Parts of the mesmerizing "Vermont—A First Impression" (1927) were copied almost verbatim into "The Whisperer in Darkness" (1930), again pointing up the identity of effect in Lovecraft's fiction, essays, and letters (conversely, he copied Providence descriptions from the uncirculated Case of Charles Dexter Ward almost verbatim into a 27 March 1927 letter to Donald Wandrei without attribution). And "Observations on Several Parts of America" (1928) concludes with a description of Virginia's Endless Caverns that would not be out of place in "The Rats in the Walls":

> And at the bottom of all—far, far down, still trickles the water that carved the whole chains of gulfs out of the primal soluble limestone. Whence it comes and whither it trickles—to what awesome deeps of Tartarean nighted horror it bears the doom-fraught messages of the hoary hills—no being of human mould can say. Only They which gibber Down There can answer.

Readers of "The Colour out of Space" and other of Lovecraft's best stories will not be unfamiliar with the sensation created by this passage. *Miscellaneous Writings*, it is true, will be of interest primarily to Lovecraft scholars. The availability of all this material in one handy volume may even inspire a whole new wave of criticism. But those of us who are simply Lovecraftian thrill seekers will find much to entertain and amuse here.

Some Lovecraft Scholars

Donald R. Burleson. *H. P. Lovecraft: A Critical Study.* **Westport, CT: Greenwood Press, 1983.**

The publication of Donald R. Burleson's *H. P. Lovecraft: A Critical Study* is something of a landmark in the study of the great American fantasist. Along with S. T. Joshi's recent *Reader's Guide to H. P. Lovecraft,* Burleson's book officially ushers in a new era of Lovecraft criticism, in which it has finally come to terms with the many misconceptions of Lovecraft's work fostered by the late August Derleth. Burleson has written under neither the restricting conditions of encrusted misinterpretation nor (as Joshi was forced to do) of editorial format limitations; and so, more than forty-five years after Lovecraft's death, we at last have a full-length critical volume that treats his imaginative efforts chronologically.

Here, then, is the first volume that has treated Lovecraft's fiction in the order in which it was written, rather than grouping it into "Cthulhu Mythos" and "non-Mythos" tales or other such classifications. The placement of material on the poetry and prose poems where they occur chronologically, rather than relegating them to a separate chapter (or worse, as has often been done, excluding them altogether), is also praiseworthy. This approach, coupled with Burleson's keen insight into the many facets of Lovecraft's art, makes the volume one of the most comprehensive of its kind.

The book begins with a brief biographical overview of Lovecraft which, as one might expect in a critical work, is the most superficial section of the book. We find, though, many fascinating examples of the intimate connection between Lovecraft's life and his work sprinkled throughout the ensuing pages; Burleson has personally visited many of the locales Lovecraft worked into his fiction, and his findings are among the book's most interesting contributions. The first chapter closes with a penetrating took into Lovecraft's aesthetic credo, concluding that Lovecraft's approach to fiction was an "ironic impressionism," by which "the horrors that unfold through the medium of human perceptions and responses are horrors that reduce the very perceiver to utter insignificance."

The second and third chapters of the volume commence the critical reading of Lovecraft's work. The early tales, glossed over by most commentators, are given a gratifyingly serious and detailed treatment. The coverage of the Dunsanian fantasies is particularly notable. In addition to discussions of such much-studied works as "The Outsider" and "The Rats in the Walls" (both of which are examined from a Jungian-archetypal perspective), Burleson treats tales that, though relatively minor, are nevertheless illuminating—"Hypnos" and "The Transition of Juan Romero," for example. In these chapters Lovecraft's prose poems, each a haunting "verbal canvas," are discussed, and shown to be more substantive than their previous lack of critical attention might imply.

In the next two chapters the works of 1924–28 are considered, and we find Burleson refusing to let his obvious respect for Lovecraft's work override his critical faculties. In addition to pointing out the positive aspects of the tales, he notes such things as the odd lapse into conventionality (as in the occult-ritual climax of "The Horror at Red Hook"), intrusively editorializing narration ("In the Vault"), and plot developments of questionable credibility (e.g., Thurston's ease in obtaining the Johansen manuscript in "The Call of Cthulhu"). The fourth chapter closes with a look at a fine, though neglected, poem of 1925, "Primavera." Chapter five, covering the great works of Lovecraft's "homecoming burst of creativity," is full of interesting insights. Burleson's revisionist reading of "The Dunwich Horror," which finds the Whateley twins as the mythic-archetypal *heroes* of the story, is ingenious and unforced. Regardless of whether we ourselves choose to subscribe to it, it is (like Burleson's view of Charles Dexter Ward as a Faustian character) a most enlightening perspective.

The perceptive and in-depth treatments of Lovecraft's late, major tales qualify chapters six and seven as the book's finest. The coverage of "The Whisperer in Darkness" is, like that of "The Dunwich Horror," grounded in Burleson's primary research into Lovecraft's Vermont visit of 1928; we learn, for example, that the Akeley farmhouse of the former story is a faithful description of the house—built, in fact, by one Samuel Akeley—in which Lovecraft stayed, and that a bit of local Indian folklore Lovecraft picked up in talking with neighbors was the genesis of the tale's Winged Ones. The long explorations of *At the Mountains of Madness* and "The Shadow out of Time," if necessarily less concrete, are also good. We are led to a much greater appreciation of "The Thing on the Doorstep" due to Burleson's musing over the *original* source of the demoniac personality of Ephraim Waite—is it, as Lovecraft hints, from some "black abyss"?

Burleson concludes the volume with a chapter on "Major Literary Influences on Lovecraft," covering Poe, Hawthorne, Dunsany, and Machen. Here Burleson notes specific similarities and parallel passages as well as broader, thematic influences. One wishes Machen's work would have received more than three long paragraphs. If it is true that he is the source of Lovecraft's concern with "myth-connected but real survivals from the past," there are also many specific antecedents (such as the painter Arthur Meyrink of "The Great God Pan," who seems to have inspired Lovecraft's Richard Upton Pickman). Likewise, more than passing references to Blackwood, Bierce, and M. R. James (whom S. T. Joshi has shown to be an influence on the structure of Lovecraft's longer narratives) would have been welcome.

Omissions and disproportionate treatments are inevitable in a sense; they reflect less on Burleson than on the very depth of Lovecraft's work. The time and thought Burleson has given to Lovecraft is evident throughout, and his interpretation is, overall, thorough and incisive. His careful attention to detail conveys substantial insight into the artist's mind. All these merits make the book a solid and worthwhile addition to Lovecraft scholarship.

Maurice Lévy. *Lovecraft: A Study in the Fantastic.* Translated by S. T. Joshi. Detroit: Wayne State University Press, 1988.

Maurice Lévy's *Lovecraft: A Study in the Fantastic* is different from other books on Lovecraft's fiction. It does not focus on plot summary, on the Cthulhu Mythos, or even on historical-biographical analysis. Instead, it makes a higher-level examination of Lovecraft using the *exponential* critical approach. It focuses on the *symbols* and *images* that we find in Lovecraft: what they evoke and communicate, how they are woven into patterns, and how these patterns imply *motifs* and *themes*. Because the essential unity of Lovecraft's work differentiates it from all other weird fiction and makes it worth considering seriously, the fiction is well suited to this critical method. The aptness of Lévy's approach, and the brilliance and artistry with which he writes, combine to make this the finest book-length critical study of Lovecraft yet written.

Lévy's book, ironically, was also one of the *first* written about Lovecraft's work. Originally a doctoral dissertation at the Sorbonne in 1969, it was commercially published in 1972. Only now has Wayne State University Press brought S. T. Joshi's English translation to press. The sixteen-year lag represents a hindrance to American critical progress. If this book had been concurrently released in the U.S., perhaps its influence would by now have moved us away from the Mythos concordances, hair-splitting theses, and quibbling articles that are the staples of the fan press and amateur press associations.

After an introductory chapter that briefly places Lovecraft in the perspective of the fantastic tradition, Lévy offers an excellent biographical overview, also touching on Lovecraft's philosophy and his literary influences. This chapter is surprisingly accurate and well-balanced for its time: only the first three volumes of *Selected Letters* were then in print, and L. Sprague de Camp had yet to publish his biography. Even those readers who have read many other accounts of Lovecraft's life will find the chapter fascinating and very perceptive. Lévy concludes that Lovecraft's art was "nourished by neurosis," a notion that he emphasizes (perhaps excessively) later in the book. Admitting up front that Lovecraft's work contains "flagrant defects," he is left to focus on such things as "the importance of images, confirming the role that, in fantastic creation, is played by the sensory element. . . . [These images] should certainly suggest what in the eyes of the author was the essence of the fantastic—the obsessive presence of the unknown, which can at any instant surge from the gulfs."

Titles of later chapters summarize the plan of the book: "Dwellings and Landscapes," "The Metamorphoses of Space," "The Horrific Bestiary," "The Depths of Horror," "The Horrors of Heredity," "Cthulhu," "Unholy Cults," "In the Chasms of Dream," and "From Fable to Myth."

Lévy's final two chapters pull together his thesis. In stories such as *At the Mountains of Madness*, the narrator breaks with "secular time" and merges with "primordial time," returning to the latter's beginning to discover how supernormal entities "brought reality into existence." This process, Lévy notes, places Lovecraft's tales in the realm of myth—myth that is doubly powerful because its author largely *dreamed* it. Lovecraft's dream-images, driven to the surface of consciousness by neurosis, strongly affect us because they are archetypal: "Myth gives depth and efficiency to the fantastic, precisely insofar as [the] return to primordial it involves coincides with a quest for a cure, and also because it permits the irrational to be built on the foundations of the universal psyche." The cults, rituals, and "sacred language" that recur in Lovecraft represent the attempted "reactualization of myth," in which "archaic actions are repeated in order to make history [i.e., the early epochs of the old ones] repeat itself." These rituals and litany represent the unintelligible, and therefore the hideous, and show that for Lovecraft "the fantastic rests on the destruction of all structure, of language as well as those of time and space."

Lévy's observation that the fantastic exists only where the irrational irrupts into the real world leads to his brilliant distinction between Lovecraft's Dunsanian tales and his horror tales. The former are not truly fantastic; here "the inadmissible has lost its aggressive character because it is manifested in an unreal terrain." The Outside entities are often benignant (e.g., the Old Ones in "Through the Gates of the Silver Key"), and "some monsters can be tamed and in these depths it is possible to come to terms with one's demons."

Lévy also discusses Lovecraft's technique of creating a "realistic fantastic." If the fantastic is a transgression, it presupposes a consistent world of immutable laws. Lovecraft's realism provides the necessary foundation upon which the supernormal may occur, and the overall effectiveness of his stories is improved by his ability to create a convincing background. Into this background he places fantastic elements. Imagery gleaned from "a profound level of consciousness" is tempered with skilled literary technique, "arranging and making hierarchical the unrefined data of dream."

Within this framework, it is Lévy's treatment of this imagery that makes his book an achievement. He begins by discussing how Lovecraft's landscapes, cities, and dwellings form a "dream-zone" superimposed on the real New England. Here even such dependable constants as spatial dimensions become disordered, with alterations of perspective and proportion reflecting the suspension of natural law.

Lovecraft's space, he insists, has "a depth," and it is here that the horrors are usually situated. But for Lovecraft the depths are also above: the cosmos may be seen as a "reversed Abysm." Though this distinction may make the reader pause, it makes sense when we consider stories like "The Whisperer in Darkness," "The Colour out of Space," and others, where horrific gulfs are both above and below.

Even time may be considered a gulf into which Lovecraft's characters fall, for descent into the depths is often accompanied by a regression in time—for example, in "The Shadow out of Time." The horrors of heredity likewise arise from the depths within us, from the recesses of our family histories, and through regressive processes we are confronted and transformed by familial antecedents.

There are surprisingly few indications that Lévy completed his book more than a decade ago. The repeated insistence that Lovecraft did not literally believe in his creations (largely a reaction to the work of Louis Pauwels and

Jacques Bergier) is something we now take for granted. It is the uninspired chapter on "Cthulhu" and other entities that most reflects Derlethian critical thought, though Joshi has made some discreet cuts that make the chapter weak rather than inaccurate. There is, by compensation, an interesting discussion in this chapter of why Lovecraft's work is not science fiction—it is essentially "regressive, oriented toward a fabulous past, and rooted in myth," while science fiction is forward-looking.

S. T. Joshi's translation reads well, and he has added an updated bibliography, chronology of Lovecraft's fiction, and a few footnotes. The book is an attractive volume, set in Palatino, and graced with a portrait of Lovecraft by Jason C. Eckhardt on the title page and dust jacket. It is nice to note that it is also available in paperback.

Donald R. Burleson. *Lovecraft: Disturbing the Universe.* Lexington: University Press of Kentucky, 1990.
S. T. Joshi. *H. P. Lovecraft: The Decline of the West.* Mercer Island, WA: Starmont House, 1990.

We are graced in this centennial year of Lovecraft's birth with the two most challenging critical works ever written about him. These works, curiously, take diametrically different approaches to analyzing Lovecraft. Each accordingly lends a different kind of insight into the master fantaisiste, and each has its own strengths and weaknesses.

S. T. Joshi's *The Decline of the West* conducts a philosophical analysis of Lovecraft's worldview as expressed in both his nonfiction (essays and letters) and his fiction. There is a section devoted to each of these two types of prose, with parallel subsections on the metaphysics, ethics, aesthetics, and politics. A brief third section, entitled "The Decline of the West," documents how Lovecraft (influenced by Oswald Spengler and others) believed that civilization is moving in irreversible decline to a state of collapse and barbarism. Joshi touches on how this belief was reflected in the author's view of aesthetics. He then shows its manifestation in the fiction in the form of the themes of regression (collective or individual) into a primitive state, and of a future characterized by sociopolitical decline. This section features Joshi's brilliant reading of the prose poem "Nyarlathotep" as a parable of decline.

The most impressive section of the book, however, is part one, which covers the philosophy. Joshi brings substantial scholarship and erudition to bear on the topic—his own educational background has given him a grounding in

Lucretius and other philosophers that few literary critics can match. But, as in his bibliographic and textual work, his analytical skills are complemented by his industry. Once again Joshi goes further than anyone ever has, hereby being the only scholar ever to have thoroughly familiarized himself with Lovecraft's primary influences—Ernst Haeckel, Hugh Elliot, Santayana, and so on. He is therefore the only scholar able to assess Lovecraft's own claims of philosophical influences. Joshi alone could draw the following point and then go on to expound upon it:

> When [Lovecraft] wrote that "my philosophical position [is] that of a mechanistic materialist of the line of Leucippus, Democritus, and Lucretius—and in modern times, Nietzsche and Haeckel" (SL 2.60), he was being remarkably careless. Only the first two of these thinkers can be called mechanistic materialists, and even they differ so significantly from Lovecraft and all other modern materialists that any resemblance is fortuitous.

This section traces how Lovecraft's worldview evolved from a "cynical materialism" to a "cosmic indifferentism," interspersing many citations from primary sources to support and explicate his case. He notes along the way that Lovecraft, despite his lip service in letters, was never significantly influenced by eighteenth-century philosophy. In fact, of ancient philosophers Lovecraft appears to have read only Lucretius—he absorbed Democritus, Epicurus, and the others whom he was endlessly fond of citing through secondary sources. So too with Einstein, whose work he learned through the popular accounts of Hugh Elliot and others. Joshi summarizes, with a clarity of writing that distinguishes this book, "The entirety of Lovecraft's philosophical career can be seen as a gradual weaning away from the dogmatism, positivism, and optimism of late-nineteenth century science, art, and culture to the indeterminacies of relativity and modernism."

In other subsections, Joshi neatly covers Lovecraft's ethics (including his position on religion), citing Lovecraft's adoption of relative values and his cultural "background." He is the first critic to spend substantial time on Lovecraft's aesthetics, documenting the transition from classicism to decadence to a sort of Epicurean "modified classicism." Joshi's account of Lovecraft's theory of the weird, written in crystal-clear prose, expands upon his analysis in The Weird Tale. It concludes that "Lovecraft's general achievement as an aesthetician was to evolve a theory of weird fiction that could both accommodate his materialist philosophy and be a reflexion of his deepest personal instincts." The section on politics, with Joshi skillfully selecting quotations on a topic very well documented in the *Selected Letters*, is also exceptionally good. This is true also of the parallel section later in the book, showing how Lovecraft incorporated his political beliefs into his fiction. Joshi is on solid ground here, having spent much time on this topic in articles such as "Lovecraft's Alien Civilizations."

In the second section, Joshi deftly demonstrates how the fiction is tied back to the philosophical concepts he examined in section one. Faced with no space limitations, in contrast to his previous work in this area in his Starmont *Reader's Guide* and *The Weird Tale*, Joshi provides many illuminating examples as he examines how Lovecraft's metaphysics, ethics, politics, and aesthetics inform his fiction. For example, he concludes that the characteristics of Lovecraft's "monsters" reflect a sort of modified materialism: "the quasi-materiality of his entities was for him a philosophical necessity, and he in fact had some admirable successes in depicting monsters which, while harmonizing with a modified materialism, nevertheless expand it to its very limits."

This section, though, is less successful than the first, and one gets the sense of the ground-breaking author staggering under the burden of the vast amount of information he needs to assimilate and convey. The book would have benefited from more summarization of conclusions (summaries would have been useful at the end of each section); it abruptly stops as if Joshi had exhausted himself. He seems to have been aware of this, as the comments in the Preface show: "Perhaps another entire book on the subject will be needed in the future." This is less a negative reflection on Joshi than an indication of the depth of Lovecraft's thought, the extent to which it informs his fiction, and the monumental, groundbreaking nature of this book.

Dr. Donald R. Burleson's *Lovecraft: Disturbing the Universe* is equally innovative, but takes a completely different tack than Joshi's book. Burleson extends his recent work in deconstructionist criticism to thirteen of Lovecraft's tales, devoting one chapter to each. The book's success for each particular reader may be proportional to that reader's subscription to the tenets of deconstructionism.

Regardless of one's disposition, though, there are many brilliant insights into Lovecraft here. Stories that have been analyzed to death over the past fifty years suddenly yield startling new interest and meaning, and minor tales are suddenly made valuable. Burleson rarely strays too far into the more questionable analytic techniques of his discipline, and the few doubtful critical claims that result do not damage the book.

Deconstruction, as Burleson explains in his lucidly written introduction, posits that "the meaning of the text can never be totalized or encapsulated or reached, because the nature of language is such that there are always elements of indeterminacy and is such that texts do not have edges or borders." Texts, he states later, "tend to subvert their own apparent 'ruling' logic. It is the purpose of deconstructive reading to discover how this self-subversion comes about."

Burleson's triumphs in the analysis that follows come from a close reading of the text and a probing examination of Lovecraft's word choice and syntax. (This aspect of his work in some ways parallels that of David Halliburton in *Edgar Allan Poe: A Phenomenological Approach*; the latter approach also closely focuses on the text but lacks deconstructionism's more questionable aspects.) In his perceptive exegesis of "The Nameless City," for example, Burleson notes how the descriptions of the city as "inarticulate" and "unvocal" stand in opposition to the fact that the city's murals tell a detailed story of the history of its reptilian inhabitants. This is consistent with one of Lovecraft's central motifs, that of *apophasis*: the denial of an intention to speak of something which is at the same time hinted or insinuated. "The Outsider," Burleson discovers, is in fact both Outsider (from society) and Insider (when he stands alone in the newly deserted mansion). Of "Pickman's Model," a story that is "portraiture of a portraiture," the author asks who or what exactly *is* Pickman's model—is it Pickman, or the subject of his painting, or the painting itself. "The Colour out of Space," Burleson finds, features a pervasive bipolarity of opposites: even the colour itself is both "conduit and barrier." (I arrived at similar conclusions using a different approach in my "The Subversion of Sense in 'The Colour out of Space.'") Other highly successful chapters include those on "The Music of Erich Zann" and "The Statement of Randolph Carter."

It is when Burleson pushes past close textual analysis into the further reaches of deconstruction that his observations become less insightful. Primarily this occurs when he uses one of the central tools of deconstructionism, that of etymology. With this technique, he tells us, "[one] traces words in the text back; often all the way to Indo-European roots, finding that the roots and derivatives entangle themselves in patterns of mutual suggestion, bifurcating and dispersing in ways that produce deep internal differences where there appeared to be only difference." To the layman this seems an arbitrary approach: an exegesis based upon what a word's roots mean, and whether those roots signify a meaning opposite to the word itself, may add little to our appreciation of a short story as a work of art. As Burleson shifts into this mode of analysis in each chapter, his comments carry less value.

For example, the chapter on "Randolph Carter" begins with a penetrating study of the title and the first sentence of the story. Burleson's comments, concluding that this "Statement" is "an infinite self-referential protraction of textual self-rewritings," are truly dazzling, and they renew our interest in a story that on the surface might have seemed quite shallow. But then we come to this analysis of the narrator's first name, "Randolph," which

> derives from the Old English *Randwulf,* where *rand* is "edge" [or] "border" . . . and *wulf* is of course "wolf." Randolph is the wolf of the border, not so much the wolf prowling on the border as the wolf-as-predator . . . of the border, the eater of borders, the gnawer of edges. . . . In being a border-predator or chewer of margins, Randolph Carter is already, even in his name, behaving like text.

This type of discourse may make us smile, or it may make us wince. Either way it adds little to this volume or to our appreciation of Lovecraft.

On balance, Burleson's book succeeds despite the etymological digressions. He remains, however, unable to prove his strangely worded thesis that "Lovecraft's texts . . . richly and intriguingly support deconstructionist readings." This posture—that an author's work "supports" or proves the validity of a critical approach—is a strange one to adopt, and perhaps reflects Burleson's real agenda for the book.

It is most appropriate that these two books are published in the centennial year of Lovecraft's birth. Taken together, they signal a new epoch of Lovecraft criticism: all the "commentary" about Lovecraft has been written, they seem to say; it is now time to address more complex questions—to consider seriously what Lovecraft "means," what Lovecraft's contribution as an artist is to the world. Both Burleson and Joshi achieve this and invite us to do so as well.

Mark Valentine. *Arthur Machen.* Bridgend, Wales: Seren, 1995.
S. T. Joshi. *H. P. Lovecraft: A Life.* West Warwick, RI: Necronomicon Press, 1996.

Reading through these biographies of two great weird writers, one is struck by the many similarities between the men. Both Lovecraft and Machen were born to families of distinguished ancestry that had descended to the "shabby genteel"; endured difficult family situations in childhood; felt mystically close to their native landscape; were thrilled by a copy of the *Arabian Nights* in the family library; were so poor at mathematics that it hindered their education; married older women; conducted informal literary salons; and had absolutely no business sense, suffering lifelong poverty as a result. Most meaningfully, of course, both men were exquisite prose poets with an uncanny sensitivity to the ineffable.

The two biographers are presented, too, with the same challenge: the primary source of their information is their respective subject's autobiographical writings. Mark Valentine, for example, remarks that "[v]irtually all that we know of Machen's childhood and youth is what he chose to reveal." What we know about the latter's adulthood, too, comes largely from his own pen. S. T. Joshi has the same formidable task in *H. P. Lovecraft: A Life*. Lovecraft is one of the most self-documented writers in the history of literature, his correspondence amounting to a detailed, daily diary of the better part of his life.

This lack of independent contemporary sources and still-living acquaintances is a significant drawback for any biographer. The results from the two scholars vary widely: Valentine largely fails to capture the essence of his subject, while Joshi largely succeeds. This is due, in part, to the paucity of secondary material available on Machen as compared to Lovecraft. Valentine is put in the position of having to follow Machen's record—largely his three quasi-fictional autobiographies—as his key source. What we end up getting, inevitably, is Machen's autobiography "as told to" Mark Valentine; a rather superficial and seemly self-serving autobiography from which we get little sense of what kind of a man Machen was. Valentine's book also suffers badly from a complete lack of citation of sources and offers no bibliography, nor even an index.

Joshi, on the other hand, has much more primary source material to work with. Introducing his book by noting that the vast bulk of his information comes from the subject himself, he adds: "I hope that I have also supplied sufficient perspective by which to gauge both the strengths and deficiencies of Lovecraft's view of himself and his world." Joshi succeeds in doing so. He has an almost eidetic familiarity with upwards of 15,000 pages of extant letters, most of which few other scholars have even read. In addition, he has mastered thousands of other documents: juvenilia, commonplace books, a bevy of good memoirs and reminiscences from Lovecraft's contemporaries, mounds of other primary data such as deeds, medical records, death certificates, and so on. Joshi expertly harvests and distills all this information into 704 pages, thousands of footnotes, an annotated bibliography, and, yes, an index.

When we set down Valentine's book, we are left with a sense of Machen as a man who felt a deep connection to nature, particularly to his native Wales; who wrote because "certain places [demand] that a story be written about them" and who believed in the capacity of language to suggest "wonderful and indefinable impressions." And Machen was indeed a mystic, believing, as Valentine paraphrases, that "it is what most people call 'reality,' that is actually the sham: the life of the numinous and wondrous is what we are really here to celebrate."

Yet Machen strikes us as the most unhappy of mystics. His sense of the ineffable did little to assuage emotionally the difficult circumstances of his childhood, early death of his first wife, relative lack of notice for his work, and lifelong penury. Interestingly, it was after his wife died of cancer in July 1899 that Machen, apparently aided by meditative practice, had his most concentrated mystical experience, one that amounted to almost an epiphany. He felt "a singular rearrangement of the world," and later "a rapture of life." But it was only temporary. He soon joined the Order of the Golden Dawn and ended up, of all places, on the stage. At the age of thirty-nine he found himself featured in music hall sketches and melodramas, and it was in this milieu that he met his second wife. Machen claimed the seven years he was involved with the theatre were the happiest of his life, but we get little sense from Valentine regarding how this can be reconciled with the rest of what we know of Machen.

Even if Valentine's book does not succeed as biography, it does serve as an excellent general introduction to Machen. The biographer has a familiarity with the bulk of his subject's writings and justly points us to "The White People," *Ornaments in Jade*, *A Fragment of Life*, *Hieroglyphics*, and *Far Off Things* as the author's best. His treatment of Machen's obsession with the legend of the Holy Grail is interesting, even if we are left wondering exactly how it ties back into Machen's worldview. Valentine has also done good work in identifying the actual locales that inspired some of Machen's works (such as the Welsh estate called Bertholly, featured in "The Great God Pan" and other works). And he treats us to some delightful photographs of Caerleon and other Machen-related landmarks, photographs that do much to bring the author's world to life. Valentine also offers an interesting overview of some obscure precursors of Machen in the fields of prose poetry and *fin de siècle fantasy*, and rehearses the notion (first pointed out, in fact, by Joshi in his 1990 study, *The Weird Tale*) that Machen's blend of fact and fiction in both his tales and autobiographies is a nascent kind of metafiction.

Valentine does less well in characterizing the melodramatic bathos and self-pity that mars books like *Far Off Things* and *Things Near and Far*. He also has some difficulty clearly positioning Machen relative to the Decadent movement: if the latter is "a preference for artificial over natural," how does this fit with Machen's love of landscape? And the biographer's best attempt to summarize Machen's legacy is painfully thin: the work had great influence on such notables as pianist John Ireland, author Paul Bowles, "TV personality" Barry Humphries, and, horror of horrors, L. Ron Hubbard.

The most famous of Machen's disciples, of course, is H. P. Lovecraft, who Valentine claims is "best known for his stories of the 'Cthulhu Mythos,' works in which a race of lurking Elder Gods and monstrosities from the deep are posited." As a remedy to this narrow view, I refer Valentine to *H. P. Lovecraft: A Life*, the finest chapter in S. T. Joshi's crusade to clarify the importance of the man and his work. Over the past two decades Joshi has systematically rehabilitated every major area of Lovecraft studies: primary and secondary bibliography, literary criticism, textual criticism, philosophical exegesis, publication of primary source material, and so on. In this book, he once and for all dismantles misconceptions not only about the Cthulhu Mythos but also about many other aspects of Lovecraft's life and work.

Indeed, *H. P. Lovecraft: A Life* represents the crowning achievement of Joshi's distinguished career. It offers a concise and eminently readable summary of everything he has learned about Lovecraft, in one fat volume. It is not merely the best single book about Lovecraft written to date, but also—and this is not a risky claim—the finest biography of Lovecraft that will ever be written. Specialists may someday exceed Joshi in specific areas: in Lovecraft's genealogy, his childhood, his career as amateur journalist, his personal relations with associates. But it is unlikely that anyone will ever achieve the broad-based mastery of primary sources that Joshi has. Should anyone do so, it is doubly unlikely that they will be better educated, more widely read, or brighter than Joshi, or be able to summarize such a vast mass of material in such an authoritative, comprehensive, and cogent manner. In addition to the material about Lovecraft himself, the book is laden with useful contextual information, including discussions of the history of weird fiction, contemporary politics, philosophy, amateur journalism, and Lovecraft's colleagues. Joshi has gone to great pains to sleuth out the most minute details of Lovecraft-related persons, places, and ideas.

This is not to say that one need agree with Joshi's interpretations of his material and the conclusions that he draws. As he notes in his preface: "Surely we are long past the naive stage of believing that 'objectivity' is either possible or desirable in biography. Even the barest recital of facts is affected by the biographer's biases, prejudices, and philosophical orientation." Overall, Joshi's presentation of Lovecraft's experiences and views is well balanced, but his position is occasionally too sympathetic to his subject. This may be due in part to the fact that Joshi's own outlook has been powerfully shaped by Lovecraft's, who has been his primary intellectual influence since the age of seventeen (he is now thirty-nine).

But to his eternal credit, Joshi is unafraid to pull any punches in presenting the evidence. He courageously quotes the most unflattering of passages from Lovecraft's letters and censures him where he most deserves to be censured: his "contemptible" racism and his "shabby" treatment of his wife. There are forthright accounts, too, of the pathetic circumstances of Lovecraft's poverty, his borderline obsessive-compulsive behavior regarding the selection of dress suits, kerosene heaters, and fountain pens, his bizarre diet, and the fatal cancer whose painful onset he made no attempt to fight.

Joshi also unflinchingly wheels out evidence of what less sympathetic observers will characterize as Lovecraft's severe psychological problems—problems that manifested themselves early on in thoughts of suicide, pathological aversion to human contact (outside his family) from age eighteen to twenty-three, multiple nervous breakdowns, and uncontrollable facial tics and hysteroid seizures. To my mind, Joshi tends to underplay the importance of certain of these disturbing elements.

In particular, the unfortunate events of Lovecraft's childhood, while recounted in vivid detail, are left for the reader to seize upon as pivotal in defining the person he became. When Lovecraft was three years old, his father went mad and was confined to an insane asylum several miles from his home, dying there five years later. My sense is that during this period the precocious, curious, and hypersensitive young child was profoundly and permanently disturbed. One can only imagine the atmosphere of tension and the whispered conversations that characterized his household. But Joshi merely remarks: "Lovecraft probably knew little about his father's illness and death, but I think he wondered a great deal."

Lovecraft's nascent sense of shame and anxiety was, I think, then exacerbated by a string of other misfortunes that occurred prior to his maturity—the death and home funerals of multiple relatives, most importantly that of a beloved grandfather who was a surrogate father figure; the severe emotional crippling he suffered at the hands of an alternately coddling and hypercritical mother who would also later be committed; and the loss of his ancestral homestead and fortune. (As a capstone to this period, Lovecraft's best friend, the one and only pet cat this feline lover ever owned, ran away.)

Born into a large, stable, and affluent family, by the age of fourteen Lovecraft was living alone with his oppressive mother in a duplex a couple of blocks from his old home—deprived of funds, father, grandfather, pet cat, and Victorian mansion with its carriage house, carriage, horses, and coachman, servants, gardens, and statuary. Lovecraft's characterization of this period of time in a later letter is one of the most disquieting non sequiturs in all his correspondence, and brings home the autobiographical nature of his story "The Outsider": "All the air rotted with decay, and the moon itself was putrescent." Is it any wonder that by this time the young Lovecraft was writing "unpleasantly gruesome little stories" (Joshi's phrase) and was beset by screaming nightmares of faceless black winged creatures? Stuart Coleman, though listed as a best friend of this period, later recalled that he "went to [Lovecraft's] home many times and yet not did not know him well" and remarked that Lovecraft "was definitely not a normal child and his companions were few." Joshi's statement that "one's assessment of Lovecraft must be based on last ten years of his life" means more than perhaps even he realizes: in light of his early life, Lovecraft went amazingly far in overcoming his problems through sheer personal courage and force of intellect.

Certainly Joshi could be lauded for avoiding the sort of armchair psychoanalysis I am indulging in here; but he nonetheless might have taken a stronger position on this and certain other issues. One area passed over largely in silence is the mature Lovecraft's strangely framed relationships with younger men. "I see little emphasis of gender confusion in Lovecraft's later life," Joshi remarks, citing as support his subject's prejudice against homosexuals as expressed in correspondence. Lovecraft's attraction to men was a pattern that began when he was in his twenties. His close relationships with Alfred Galpin and Frank Long (each of them eleven years younger than Lovecraft), whom he considered "grandsons," are perhaps innocuous in themselves. But this tendency persisted and perhaps strengthened during the course of Lovecraft's life. In 1934, the forty-three-year-old writer traveled to Florida to spend the summer with his sixteen-year-old protégé Robert Barlow. The visit was repeated the following year, Lovecraft this time casually remarking to a mutual correspondent: "Bob has built a cabin across the lake (I helped him), to which—for the sake of seclusion—he transferred his [printing] press, desk, and various accessories as soon as it was ready for occupancy." Joshi passes over any consideration of this and also leaves unmentioned another of Lovecraft's young male friends, Allan Grayson, to whom he had composed a sonnet a few years prior.

Likewise, the biographer is perhaps too kind regarding Lovecraft's stature as a thinker. As Joshi himself points out in *H. P. Lovecraft: The Decline of the West*, Lovecraft was "remarkably careless" in certain characterizations of the philosophers he claimed to have influenced his thought. Endlessly fond of citing Epicurus, for example, Lovecraft appears never to have read him in the original. He rattles off names like La Mettrie, Diderot, Helvétius, and Hume, whom he appears never to have read at all. He claims Santayana as a major influence, but makes allusions to a correspondent that imply a lack of first-hand familiarity with his work. He appears to have read only one volume each by other "major influences" like Bertrand Russell, Schopenhauer, Spengler, and Joseph Wood Krutch. His thought, instead, seems to have been pieced together mostly from distorted, popularized accounts of major thinkers (e.g., Freud, Darwin, Einstein) or books by second-string thinkers like Hugh Elliot, Ernst Haeckel, and Louis Berman (whose long-forgotten *The Glands Regulating Personality* [1921] was apparently an influence). Lovecraft was also fond of dropping names in letters; making favorable mention for example, of John Dewey, whose brand of pragmatism he would certainly have taken issue with had he really been familiar with it, and elsewhere denigrating Bergson without ever having read him.

While admitting that most of Lovecraft's sources were second-hand, Joshi praises him as a thinker whose views were "well conceived, modified by constant reading and observation, and sharpened by vigorous debates with associates." Less sympathetic observers might contend that Lovecraft, while brighter and far more thoughtful than most, was something of an intellectual lightweight and perhaps even a poseur. His mechanistic materialism became hardened early on and was in fact modified very little. He held fast to the notion that there is a reality that exists independent of the observer and that there is uniformity of natural law. Was this not, after all, his own personal religion?

Lovecraft, I think, also deserves harsher treatment regarding his nearly complete and total disregard of modern art, modern literature, and even mainstream American literature (except for Poe and Hawthorne). I believe Lovecraft's writing suffered from his inability to profit from the work of artists as vital and diverse as Emerson, Melville, Whitman, Eliot, Wallace Stevens, and even Hart Crane (whom he knew).

One of the many areas that Joshi brings to light for the first time is Lovecraft's sense of humor. The biographer rightly takes great delight in this aspect of his subject. His enjoyment is infectious. Lovecraft's wit was of the driest possible kind, so dry that to the uninformed it might merely seem unselfconscious posturing. But Lovecraft, admirably, was his own favorite target of parody. He loved to play the manner of expressing himself against the substance of what he was expressing. (Joshi rehearses, with relish, Lovecraft calling a boiled-egg-and-beans supper "a sumptuous repast.") This tendency, which also permeates Lovecraft's fiction, is highlighted throughout the book as Joshi selects the choicest passages from published and unpublished correspondence. Joshi himself shows high good humor in pointing out the unconsciously comic statements Lovecraft continually made, such as his "acutely embarrassing" remark about Hitler: "I know he's a clown, but by God, I *like* the boy!"

Among the many other triumphs of Joshi's work are the chapters on Lovecraft's marriage and stay in New York City. Using an unpublished diary and consolidating the recollections of Lovecraft's wife and colleagues, Joshi brings to life for the first time an enthralling narrative of the most exciting and disappointing adventure in Lovecraft's external life. First, we hear of the surreptitious courtship and elopement, with the marriage strangely unmentioned for days in correspondence to the aunts; the hope of building a home in Westchester County, and the seriocomic and finally desperate attempts to find a regular job. Then things go horribly wrong: the separation due to Sonia's work out of town; the search for peace in endless antiquarian jaunts around Greenwich Village and remoter points; the all-night meetings with the boys; and the squalor of his solitary Brooklyn apartment. And finally, Lovecraft's near-breakdown: the robbery that left him deprived of a wardrobe; his disintegrating psychological state (near to "screaming in sheer desperation & pounding the walls & floor in a frenzied clamour to be waked up out of the nightmare of 'reality'"); and his escalating hostility towards blacks and Jews ("one feels like punching every god damn bastard in sight"). That his aunts recalled him to Providence at this point may have saved his sanity, even as it ended his marriage.

Another element of the book which is unexcelled is the coverage of Lovecraft's work. Concise, complete information on the genesis of the tales is complemented by finely honed plot summaries and insightful historical-critical remarks. Particularly fine is the coverage of "The Whisperer in Darkness," "The Call of Cthulhu," At the Mountains of Madness, and "The Shadow out of Time." These sections of the book alone are worth the price of admission, but Joshi has accomplished no mean feat: writing a biography almost as fascinating as his subject's best fiction.

Peter Cannon, ed. *Lovecraft Remembered.* Sauk City, WI: Arkham House, 1998.

Lovecraft Remembered forms a worthy pendant to 1996's 700-page biography of Lovecraft by S. T. Joshi. To complement Joshi's portrait of Lovecraft the thinker and writer, Peter Cannon gives us Lovecraft the human being. Editor Cannon has done well in identifying and collecting more than forty first-hand accounts of Lovecraft as remembered by his wife, his friends, and his acquaintances. Many of these pieces are difficult if not impossible to lay hands on, and the value to both scholars and interested readers of having them in one convenient place is incalculable. Most of all, this collection is chock full of insight and interesting nuggets on the man whom Vincent Starrett rightly dubbed "his own most fantastic creation."

As one whose interest in Lovecraft is primarily scholarly, I miss in *Lovecraft Remembered* the apparatus that usually accompanies material of this type: footnotes, a bibliography of original appearances, squibs on the contributors. I also miss running heads with the name of the memoir's author—these pieces begin to blur together after a while, and it is difficult to recall whether it is Edward Cole or Paul Cook reminiscing. I question the inclusion, too, of more than a dozen items by people who knew Lovecraft only through correspondence and critics writing shortly after Lovecraft's death. While it is helpful to have this material here, since much of it not merely excellent but also out of print; I would trade it away to have the long, definitive memoir by Lovecraft's ex-wife Sonia Haft Greene. The latter is the most important record of Lovecraft the person, and while it is in print in a Necronomicon Press edition, its exclusion prevents the volume from being what it could be: comprehensive. The footnotes would serve well to correct certain errors of fact and mysterious allusions present in some of these pieces. Cannon addresses some of these in notes that head the sections, but many others remain.

In some ways, the Lovecraft revealed in this book is even more complex and eccentric than his work. Indeed, there seems to have been two Lovecrafts—the theorist and the man. The theorist was racist, misanthropic, and misogynistic. The man, as depicted here, was cordial, charming, and humorous. *Lovecraft Remembered* reveals a personality who was sincerely loved by, and who sincerely loved, his friends. Again and again throughout the book, the authors convey heartfelt respect and admiration for Lovecraft. But hovering behind this portrait is the Lovecraft we know from his letters—arrogant, judgmental, and conceited. One can only stand back and marvel at the contrast of Lovecraft in theory and in practice, and be grateful the theory so little manifested itself. Indeed, the most remarkable thing about Lovecraft as a person is the extent to which he was able to overcome his emotionally crippling childhood—early deaths of his father and other close relatives, insanity of his parents, loss of his home and fortune—by sheer force of will and intelligence.

The first thing that strikes the reader of *Lovecraft Remembered* is the first thing that struck those who met Lovecraft: his unique personal appearance. His unusual visage is apparent to any who has seen pictures of him, but the impact he made on people bespeaks of one who photographed better that he appeared in person. The classic account is by Alfred Galpin, who recalls "the strange half dead, half arrogant cock of his head weighed down by its enormous jaw, the rather fishy eyes belied by his animated and friendly manner when he began to speak—but with what a strange high pitched voice!" Samuel Loveman notes that Lovecraft's "appearance was frequently a shock to those who met him for the first time." In particular, "the deadly pallor of his skin" is singled out, compared by revision client Zealia Bishop to "old ivory or mummy skin." She continues: "I was not only unprepared but *shaken irreparably* by the peculiar sound of his thin, high-pitched voice" (my italics). The best description of Lovecraft's strange laugh comes from Wilfred Talman: "a ham actor's version of a hermit's laughter."

Any reader of the letters already knows that Lovecraft was intellectually brilliant and widely read, but it is still impressive to be reminded how much information he carried around in his head. As Kenneth Sterling puts it, Lovecraft had "a reasonably thorough competence with almost every area of human knowledge." This is quite a statement, particularly coming from a Harvard graduate. More than one auditor describes Lovecraft's penchant for delivering complete impromptu lectures—structured, detailed, finely reasoned, and delivered in the same modulated periods we find in his writing—on virtually any topic.

One oft-neglected aspect of Lovecraft is his sense of humor. Talman and others emphasize the "sly sense of humor so few seemed to realize he possessed." This also pervades the tales, though few have noticed it. Colin Wilson is typical of literary critics here. He says Lovecraft remained fond throughout his career of phrases like "stark utter horror," but fails to consider that humor partially motivates the use of such phrases. As Muriel Eddy notes, "He chuckled a little when he explained that he liked to use such phrases as 'unnamable monster' and 'eldritch horror.'" There is, in fact, an underpinning of theatricality in all Lovecraft's work, stemming, apparently, from the author's fondness for playacting: "Lovecraft could very easily have become an actor, because he read the manuscript [of "The Rats in the Walls"] with real effect. He imitated the characters, taking on the voices as he pictured them. . . . He even laughed the insane laugh of the cannibalistic character." We know from letters that Lovecraft liked to recite from Shakespeare and even reenacted scenes with his mother. "The whole Kalem group," Talman observes, "realized much of their conversation was play-acting and for some it was competition for center stage."

In light of his upbringing by females and his close companionship with his aunts, Lovecraft's unhappy relations with women may be surprising. According to Rheinhart Kleiner, "he treated [women] with a formal politeness which did not have a touch of gallantry in it" but rather a flavor of "aloofness." Loveman, too, notes that "a certain restraint and progressive hollowness entered into his addresses with the female sex . . . the deferential and overwhelming politeness that he conveyed seemed always strained and faintly artificial." In letters written after Lovecraft's death, Loveman attributed this to a latent homosexuality on Lovecraft's part, but we can as easily ascribe it to simple misogyny. Despite his friendships with Edith Miniter and a few others, Lovecraft tended to consider women an inferior species. His famous statement in a letter to Frank Belknap Long that women "are by Nature literal, prosaic, and commonplace, given to dull realistic Details and practical Things" (SL 1.238) is only half joking. In unpublished letters, particularly those to Lillian Clark now in Brown's John Hay Library, we find a consistent disrespect for the female companions of his friends: Arthur Sechrist's girlfriend is "a lumpish, inane sort of vegetable whose name I don't recall" (11 November 1924), Vrest Orton's wife is "a colourless, stupid, plaintive-voiced little Jew girl devoid of any visible sort of attractiveness or brilliance" (7 May 1928), and so on. The biggest surprise in the book, then, is the near-romance that Lovecraft developed with his revision client Hazel Heald. Heald courted Lovecraft more aggressively than previously revealed, but was rebuffed.

One of the oddest things about Lovecraft was his strange inability to communicate with others regarding his relationship with Sonia. Accounts in this book confirm the impression we get from the letters. Lovecraft eloped to New York and married, but failed to notify his aunts (with whom he lived) until several days later, not mentioning it in correspondence written to them in intervening days. In this collection we learn that Lovecraft never mentioned Sonia to the Eddys, neither on the eve of his elopement nor upon resuming his social calls to them immediately upon his separation and return to Providence.

These first-hand accounts of Lovecraft invite us to assess how his racism, so strong in theory, manifested itself in his interactions with others. It appears that Lovecraft grew more cautious in expressing his opinions as he grew older. As a young man he had a habit of calling Irishmen "micks," according to John Dunn, who encountered the twenty-three-year-old Lovecraft in a writing workshop. In his thirties Lovecraft seemed to temper such verbal invective, though his wife notes that "whenever we found ourselves in the racially mixed crowds which characterize New York, Howard would become livid with rage. He seemed almost to lose his mind." Almost every other contributor, however, presents Lovecraft as the most civil and polite of persons, as exemplified by Loveman's comment in his 1938 account: "I have never known a human being to secrete less envy, malice, morbidity, and intolerance than did Howard." Loveman reversed his position after hearing from Sonia of Lovecraft's anti-Semitism (she blamed the end of their marriage on it) and after being shown letters in which Lovecraft assailed Loveman's Jewish heritage. By the time of a 1975 account (unfortunately not included here) Loveman could write that "Howard's monomania about race was about as close to insanity as anything I can think of." It is likely that Kenneth Sterling's accounts would be less glowing, too, if he had seen letters in which Lovecraft mocked in Yiddish dialect the sincere and respectful Jewish boy who came to him for encouragement and companionship.

Despite this profound flaw in Lovecraft's makeup, his manner was extremely engaging to both friends and acquaintants. The stereotypical young Lovecraft is described by Dunn: he sat "stiffly staring forward" and "didn't have any sense of humor." But the memoirs in this book cumulatively point to the exactly opposite conclusion, that of H. Warner Munn: the mature Lovecraft was "a splendid raconteur" who was very adept socially. As Cole rhetorically asks, "Who could enter more heartily into the discussion of any contemporary problem or participate more effectively and wittily in any gathering?" Lovecraft's conversation, according to Loveman, "takes its place among the masters [sic] of that brilliant but difficult art." E. Hoffmann Price recounts the famous story of how he and Lovecraft were interrupted by a bunch of drunken revelers from the French Quarter: "They came up gaily, and with bottles. . . . [Lovecraft] met the visitors with fine good fellowship. . . . His assurance and poise relieved and delighted me." Lovecraft even mesmerized Houdini: the son of immigrants was undoubtedly envious of Lovecraft's learning and verbal facility. Dining with escape artist, Lovecraft was "in great spirits and bubbled over with good humor, talking a blue streak about every-thing under the sun" while Houdini "gazed on admiringly."

Lovecraft Remembered, then, is an entertaining read and offers the most vivid picture available of Lovecraft the man. Cole's description is representa-tive, depicting one whom many found a fascinating companion: "The driving force of his mind . . . gave his otherwise somewhat somber countenance an animation, a positive luminousness, when he launched upon a subject in which he was truly interested. His manner became thoroughly vitalized; his voice grew vibrant; words poured forth a nervous, high pitched torrent so turbulent that often he almost stuttered because his tongue could not keep pace with his swift thought."

As for Lovecraft the theorist, we can only be grateful that he was—for the most part—beaten into the background. Talman sums it up best, in a conclu-sion that Joshi's biography leaves implicit: "H.P.L.'s extent of genius is most evident in the individualistic personality he made of himself. One of lesser ability, given the handicaps under which he grew up, could well have become a disturbed youth or a crotchety old man. He surmounted this likelihood."

S. T. Joshi. *I Am Providence: The Life and Times of H. P. Lovecraft.* New York: Hippocampus Press, 2010.

I can say with confidence that S. T. Joshi's new biography, *I Am Providence*, is the finest three million characters ever concatenated regarding H. P. Love-craft. But that would be too easy, and not very funny. I could instead say, "S. T. Joshi has written a great book"—but that also would be too easy, and not very newsworthy: he counts many great books among the nearly three dozen he's written. *The Weird* Tale (University of Texas Press, 1990), in par-ticular, comes immediately to mind.

So, a bolder and more accurate statement: *S. T. Joshi has written a classic.*

Or, more precisely, he has re-re-written a classic. The background is this: Joshi knows Lovecraft better than most people know the members of their own nuclear family, and surpasses his subject as a scholar of literature, philosophy, and history. Joshi originally wrote Lovecraft's biography fourteen years ago in 708 pages. That limited edition hardcover went out of print almost immedi-ately and fetches prices exceeding many Lovecraft first editions. A glance on the Internet shows today's market prices: *Dagon and Other Macabre Tales* by H. P. Lovecraft, selected and with an introduction by August Derleth; Arkham House, Sauk City, WI, 1965; 1st ed.; condition, fine in a fine dust jacket:

$250.00. *H. P. Lovecraft: A Life* by S. T. Joshi; Necronomicon Press, W. Warwick RI, 1996; 1st ed.; condition, fine in a fine dust jacket: $600.00.

Necronomicon Press, humanely, issued a paperback of the first version of *H. P. Lovecraft: A Life* in 1996 for $29.95. Five years later, Joshi abridged and revised the original work in a 432-page book published in the UK by Liverpool University Press as *A Dreamer and a Visionary: H. P. Lovecraft in His Time.* Now Hippocampus Press has given us the dreadnought version—nearly 1,300 pages—in which Joshi adds material omitted from the first two versions and provides considerable revision and updates.

The baseline reason the book is so excellent is that Joshi is an expert on the artist and his work. But more than this, the biographer has done outstandingly well in consolidating a massive amount of information and writing a book that reads as easily and fascinatingly as a novel. It is, as the subtitle *The Life and Times of H. P. Lovecraft* states, not just about the author. What the reader gets is not merely a biography but also a rich history of the incredible cultural, political, and literary upheavals that occurred between 1890 and 1937.

Lovecraft, like many authors, did not live an outwardly eventful life. He never held a job, instead living off a small inheritance and sporadic income from stories sold to pulp magazines and from revision work. Nor was he a prolific writer—he composed only 60 or so tales over the three decades of career. Most of his time was spent reading and writing letters (at one point had had nearly 100 correspondents). He liked to walk around in search of colonial architecture and landscape vistas, and took advantage of public libraries and historical society collections to become something of a specialist in New England history.

It could make for a very boring book, but this is far from the case here. Joshi, first of all, is strong on the fiction—deft in summarizing and explicating the fascinating weird tales that bring us to this book. When the reader closes the covers, he or she will have a much-enhanced appreciation of these stories—the finest supernatural horror tales of the twentieth century, a matchless blend of science fiction, fantasy, and existential terror.

Secondly, Joshi has done tremendous research on the *context* of Lovecraft's life, one which divides cleanly into several phases: birth until at age 14; 15 to 23, when he progressively became the reclusive "invalid" (Lovecraft's term) of popular lore; 24 to 32, when he became a minor celebrity in the small world of amateur journalism; 33 to 36, when he made a failed attempt at marriage and workaday employment in New York; and the final decade of his life after his retreat to Providence, when he lived with an aunt, wrote, and did some traveling around the east coast. The biographer is tremendously adroit in using these phases as a framework upon which to interweave Lovecraft's activities, his personal life, his art, his influences, and his thought on political, philosophical, literary, and contemporary happenings. So the book is not only a compelling portrait of the artist, but also a liberal education on the early twentieth century.

Lovecraft's life is one of the most self-documented in literature: for most of his adult life he wrote multiple letters—many of which were preserved by correspondents—every day. In addition to this, we have synoptic diaries Lovecraft intermittently kept—for example, a 1925 pocket agenda with multiple telegraphic entries for each day (he used this as a mnemonic aid in writing letters home to his aunt). So we have a clear idea (perhaps too clear) about his day-to-day activities—when Lovecraft woke up, what he had for breakfast, when he went out, and when he returned; when he slept, what he read, and who he saw. Joshi, happily, does a good job of blurring out the minutiae without losing the essence of the man. He also triangulates Lovecraft's account with other sources and comes up with a well-balanced rendering of events.

It is doubtful that a more complete, accurate, and fluent biography will ever be written. The only thing left for discussion, then, is interpretation; and, as Joshi notes, "judgments of [Lovecraft] will differ in accordance with individual temperament" of the reader. Accordingly, I will mention three areas where future biographers may diverge from Joshi's assessments.

Many a literary biography has been ruined by armchair psychoanalysis. Joshi treads lightly here, but too much so. By the age of eighteen, Lovecraft had experienced a series of personal tragedies that I believe crippled him emotionally even as they provided the themes and the compelling affect that make his fiction powerful.

Joshi paints a candid picture of the really horrifying demise of Lovecraft's father—insanity, confinement, and slow death from tertiary syphilis. The biographer dwells little, however, on the effects this event likely had on young Lovecraft's mental health and the subsequent course of his life. Lovecraft had multiple "nervous breakdowns" prior to age twenty-one, the first at age eight. Joshi does, in fact, mention that the latter might have been related to the circumstances of the father's illness. But there must be more to it than this. Lovecraft was an extraordinarily bright and sensitive child; intellectually curious, and unusually aware of his surroundings (he claimed to have memories going back to before two years old). He was nearly three years old when his father was bought to Providence's Butler Hospital under confinement from a business trip to Chicago. In the years following Lovecraft would have been mindful of household whispers—the affect of shock, shame, and guilt, if not the substance of the matter. Certainly he knew his father was alive, but absent (apparently the child was told his father was unconscious in a coma); nearby, but not available to visit. The five years that passed before Winfield Lovecraft finally died must have seemed a lifetime for the boy Lovecraft, knowing that his father was lying abed only one mile from his house.

Joshi rightly points out that Lovecraft recalled his childhood with fondness, and had a grandfather and uncle as strong father figures. But after the father's confinement Lovecraft's care was left largely to his progressively psychotic mother, who told neighbors her son's face was "hideous." (There is no debate that Lovecraft's later relationships with women were problematic; and Joshi bluntly calls his treatment of his wife "shabby.")

Lovecraft's childhood was overshadowed, too, by other deaths: grandfather George (d. 1895); grandmother Robie (d. 1896); cousin Marion Gamwell (d. 1900); and grandfather Whipple (d. 1904). The latter's demise (at home, apparently) of a sudden apoplectic stroke was followed by the sale of the huge Victorian mansion—complete with stable, outbuildings, carriages, servants, and livestock—in which Lovecraft grew up. The fourteen-year old boy who considered himself an "aristocrat" and his mother removed to a humble duplex about a block away. The lines "I used to sit on the stairs of the house where I was born/After we left it but before it was sold" may appear in a parody of Elliot's *Waste Land*, but cut deeper than anything else in Lovecraft's verse. As if all this was not enough, Lovecraft's much-loved black cat—his best and perhaps only friend—ran away; he never had another pet.

Joshi is correct in giving Lovecraft tremendous credit for going far in overcoming these early issues. But the effects are clearly manifest in much of the author's eccentric behavior, and even more pronouncedly in the stories that speak to the horrors of being abandoned in an uncaring universe and the horrors of existence itself. Another biographer might have used a heavier hand delineating these matters, while still hewing to the facts.

Joshi, to his eternal credit, does not pull any punches on issue of Lovecraft's racism, which he calls "without question, the one true black mark on his character." However, some readers will feel the biographer backs off a little too much at the end of the book when he asserts that "one's final picture of Lovecraft must be based largely upon the last ten or so years of his existence; for it was at this time that he shed many of the prejudices and dogmatisms that his early upbringing and seclusion had engendered. . . . In those ten years I see very little to criticise and very much to praise." A stroll through the last volume of the Arkham House *Selected Letters* tends to refute this. A random example: Lovecraft "would advocate the improvement of backward groups through education, hygiene, & eugenics—nor do I think it especially naïve or ultra-idealistic in me to prefer these conscious & scientific methods to the blind, brutal, & accidental methods of primitive nature, in which real advances are merely the casual by-products of aimless, wasteful forces" (*SL* 5.323). There are others.

Lovecraft, however, did hit the bull's eye when he announced the death of capitalism and predicted the cultural wasteland that American would become:

> Unsupervised capitalism is through. But various Nazi & fascist compromises can be cooked up to save the plutocrats most of their spoils while lulling the growing army of the unpropertied with either a petty programme of *panem et circenses*, or else a system of artificially created & distributed jobs at starvation wages on the C.C.C. or W.P.A. idea. A regime of that sort, spiced with the right brand of hysterical flag-waving, sloganeering, and verbal constitution-saving, might conceivably be as stable & popular as Hitlerism—& that is what the younger & more astute Babbitt's of the Republican party are quietly & insidiously working toward. (*SL* 5.326)

Regarding that last jab—Joshi permits himself a few editorial comments that reveal him as firmly with Lovecraft on the far left. This editorializing is sometimes intrusive, and begs the question as to whether it is simplistic to blame conservatives for problems that stem from not one political party but from a systemically corrupt cabal of business executives, lobbyists, government insiders, and elected officials from both sides of the aisle (see, for example, Janine R. Wedel's recent *Shadow Elite* [Basic Books, 2009]).

A topic that gets little space in the 1,300 pages is Lovecraft's sense of humor—or, more accurately, Lovecraft's sense of *play*. I believe this came from his very solitary childhood, during which he learned to amuse himself in a distinctive way. His sense of humor was truly ludic (the Latin "ludere" means "to play"). One might even go so far as to say that Lovecraft perceived reality itself to be (ahem) ludicrous.[1]

---

1. In the 19th and 20th centuries, various thinkers granted an ever greater role to the imagination in the creation of works of art. For example, German critic Konrad Lange (1855–1921) held play and make-believe to be central to both the making and reception of art. Lange did not explicitly draw the conclusion that works of art are therefore fictions, but he did describe our commerce with them as a kind of lucid or "conscious self-deception" in which we imagine states of affairs while knowing perfectly well that we do not believe in

Lovecraft's unique perspective was complemented by a unique way of expressing himself, verbally and in writing. He became interested in the drama at six years of age; he set up a little toy theatre with hand-painted scenery, and played Shakespeare for weeks. He was taken to many productions at the Providence Opera House. Later Lovecraft expanded his tableau-play by devoting a large tabletop to a scene, which he "would proceed to develop as a broad landscape . . . [and] construct some scene as fancy—incited by some story or picture—dictated, & then to act out its life for long periods—sometimes a fortnight—making up events of a highly melodramatic cast as I went. . . . I kept this up till I was 11 or 12." Lovecraft always had a fondness for *histrionics* in all forms; he enjoyed re-enacting scenes from plays with a fervor that once startled neighbors, and liked to read his own works aloud adding outlandish voice characterizations for what little dialog he used. He was also a skilled mimic, particularly of speech patterns and dialect (one unfortunate manifestation is found in the last *Letters* volume, as Lovecraft uses Yiddish to mock a local fifteen-year-old "Jew boy" fan). Lovecraft found tremendous joy and pleasure in language itself, and we see a great deal of stylistic play in all the prose he wrote. There is very little difference, prosodically, across Lovecraft's stories, letters, and essays. They all use the same bizarre ideolect. Memoirs tell us he spoke the same way.

Similarly, Lovecraft looked at the world around him with a sense of play, constantly on the alert for *prima materia* for his stories. All fiction writers draw upon personal experience in their work; but Lovecraft was exceptional in both the depth and breadth of details he used for the weft of his stories, and the distinctive warp (I use the word advisedly) he placed upon those details. He liked to make fun of himself in his stories. He looked upon everything with a kind of fascination. He often used in-jokes of which only he—or only he and a single disinterested friend—might be aware. In "The Colour out of Space," for example, Lovecraft used real family names (e.g., Nabby Gardner) from the area around Prescott, Mass. But only his friend W. Paul Cook, an amateur journalist with no interest in weird fiction, might have known this. Similarly, his narrator is based upon Frank E. Winsor, who from 1915

---

their actual existence. The artistic artifact, he proposed, is like the toy or other object that is recruited to the ends of a child's imaginative play. A sophisticated and highly influential contemporary exponent of this kind of approach to art and, more specifically, to the philosophical analysis of depiction and fictional content, is Kendall L. Walton (b. 1939); for details, see the latter's *Mimesis as Make-believe: On the Foundations of the Representational Arts* (Harvard University Press, 1990).

to 1926 was chief engineer for the Scituate Reservoir in Rhode Island; it was announced on the front page of the *Providence Journal* for 1 October 1926, that Winsor was resigning to become chief engineer of the Quabbin Reservoir, featured in the story Lovecraft wrote five months later. But only his aunt might have known this. Joshi, David E. Schultz, and Peter Cannon have all contributed to excellent annotated editions of Lovecraft's fiction, thick with examples of this on every page. This *factitious transmutation of the real*, set side by side *with* the real, is another reason why Lovecraft's tales have such impact.

But these are all matters of interpretation and emphasis. The book may be complemented by other perspectives, but not excelled in its factual completeness, level-headed assessments, and sparkling narrative. Joshi—who was influenced by Lovecraft's thought in youth but stands now as his own person, an intellectual equal—is sympathetic to his subject, but not too sympathetic. I leave it to future commentators to speculate on how biographer and subject might have gotten along had they the chance to meet. Each iconoclastic, extremely bright, and extremely opinionated, they might have been fast friends, or mortal enemies.

H. P. LOVECRAFT. *O Fortunate Floridian: H. P. Lovecraft's Letters to R. H. Barlow.* Ed. S. T. Joshi and David E. Schultz. Tampa: University of Tampa Press, 2007.

H. P. LOVECRAFT and AUGUST DERLETH. *Essential Solitude: The Letters of H. P. Lovecraft and August Derleth.* Ed. S. T. Joshi and David E. Schultz. New York: Hippocampus Press, 2008.

H. P. Lovecraft, by virtue of having written so many letters, is someone the interested reader can get to know quite well. The pertinent question here is, how interested are you? S. T. Joshi and David E. Schultz pursue their mad dream of publishing all the Lovecraft letters they can lay their hands on—and apparently they can lay their hands on plenty, for here's another 1,200-plus pages of print. As usual, they've created immaculate editions—well designed, edited, annotated, and . . . appended, if that's the term. The Lovecraft correspondents in question are two youthful fans and authors, quite different from one another. August Derleth (some of whose letters the editors include) comes off as brash and more than a little dim-witted. Robert Barlow seems self-effacing and smart, but seems a little obsequious in his constant proposals to create vanity press editions and his requests for manuscripts, autographs, and photos.

In terms of one's literary legacy, it's more than a little dangerous to reveal so much of yourself in correspondence and have it all collated after the fact—we all tend to shade out positions for a given audience, sometimes to the point of hypocrisy. But Lovecraft acquits himself remarkably well in these letters as a person and a personality. He's funny, interesting, likable, consistent in tone and content with two very different correspondents, and his comments are (on balance) exceptionally well reasoned and informed. The glaring exception, of course, is the racism regarding those "decadent & unassimilable hordes from Southern Europe & the East whose presence in large numbers is a direct & profound menace to the continued growth of the Nordic-American nation we know." Regardless of the tenor of the times, it is hard to pass over asides about a "waddling nigger washerwoman" and "thieving kikes" without a wince. As much as he admires Kenneth Sterling's intellect, he can't help dropping into pseudo-Yiddish dialect when discussing him with Barlow. Nor does he fail to choose the most politically incorrect adjective when (discussing Rhode Island history) he remarks that "Providence was a great slave town."

Here as in other published letters, Lovecraft's ability to judge his own work is shown to be strangely skewed. "Nyarlathotep"—which is one of the greatest things Lovecraft wrote—is "definitely repudiated as below standard," while "The Dunwich Horror"—self-parodying pulp trash—is listed by the author as among his finest. The profound psychological ambiguities of "The Outsider" are overlooked, the force of the tale being instead ascribed to "little more than a meretricious mechanical trick." In December 1926 he writes that "The Strange High House in the Mist" is "by all odds my favorite among my recent yarns"—this despite "The Call of Cthulhu" and "The Colour out of Space" (indisputably greater and more significant stories) having been written during the same period. Lovecraft's comment reflects the magnitude of Lord Dunsany's influence; elsewhere he remarks of the "Strange High House" that it is the exemplar of this influence "in its finally absorbed state."

Lovecraft provides some helpful explication of his tales, especially to the obtuse Derleth. Within this explication we find nuggets that will not be obvious to the most careful reader—as when Lovecraft glosses the final glimpse caught by Danforth in *At the Mountains of Madness* as possibly "a region containing vestiges of some utterly primal cosmic force or process ruling or occupying the earth (among other planets) even before its solidification, & upheaved from the sea-bottom when the great Antarctic land mass arose."

There are a few new (or amplified) clues regarding Lovecraft's creative process and sources. His account of Samuel Casey Jr., an ancestor who was the leading silversmith in Rhode Island in the mid-1700s, makes it apparent that Casey is a source for the villainous Joseph Curwin in *The Case of Charles Dexter Ward*. Casey was jailed for counterfeiting, was liberated when "the local gaol was stormed by a band of men," and then disappeared from sight. The phraseology in the account recalls the wording in the tale, as when Lovecraft writes that "Sam Casey, in truth, was no worse than a vast number of his neighbours—dozens of whom had certainly aided him not only in getting tools & metals, but in circulating his unlawful products." Responding to Derleth's suggestions for revision of "From Beyond," Lovecraft remarks: "I don't know that there's enough in the damn thing to warrant salvaging. The same amount of effort would be spent more advantageously in a wholly new tale. The idea at the bottom of the thing was that of having strange, non-terrestrial sounds filter into a lonely attic—& it could surely find any number of better embodiments than the existing specimen." This sounds remarkably like "The Dreams in the Witch House," written only a few months later. There are hints, too, of stories never written, including the one in which "[w]ill probably begin in Roman times—something will survive one way or another." Sequels to "The Whisperer in Darkness" and "The Dreams in the Witch House" are contemplated.

Lovecraft indicates high regard for specific artists and works, pointing the way for possible critical study on their possible influence. A. Merritt, in particular, comes in for high praise: "The Metal Monster" is singled out as "one of the most striking evocations of absolutely unearthly conditions & experiences that I have ever seen[, p]erhaps the most striking," and again as the "[m]ost effective presentation of the utterly alien & non-human that I have ever seen." Lovecraft even states that "Merritt can weave an air of delirious unreality better than anyone else I know," quite a compliment from an author unexcelled in weaving an air of delirious unreality. Wilde and Cabell are held up as exemplary prose stylists. E. R. Eddison also gets accolades, with *The Worm Ouroboros* touted as "a real work of art—gorgeous fantasy & singing prose which everyone ought to read." Of intense interest is the mention of Ralph A. Blakelock (1847–1919)—an American painter of the fantastic who died in an insane asylum—among a list of artists Lovecraft admires. And Charles Dickens, of all people, should be examined for influence upon Lovecraft. The latter "read him through in youth" and, despite disliking the British author's sentimentality, cites *Barnaby Rudge* and *A Tale of Two Cities* as favorites.

Notable in the Barlow letters is Lovecraft's willingness to open up personally to his correspondent. Specifically, Barlow's father suffered from depression, and in response to the Florida author's comments Lovecraft speaks of his own mental health with candor. At the age of nine years old, he says, "I had a kind of nervous breakdown," and during the period following high school, "when my health was very bad, I often pulled out of breakdown by withdrawing entirely from external contact & vegetating for a period either largely in bed or in an easy-chair with dressing-gown & slippers." (The wording, strangely, is a precise echo the Outer One's behavior in "The Whisperer in Darkness.") The insanity, confinement, and death of Lovecraft's father, combined with the loss of his grandfather and nineteen-room mansion, seems to have given Lovecraft a very serious form of psychosomatic illness.

> My hypersensitive nerves reacted on my bodily functions to such a degree as to give the appearance of many different physical illnesses. Thus I had a very irregular heart action—badly affected by physical exertion—& such acute kidney trouble that a local practitioner would have operated for stone in the bladder had not a Boston specialist given a sounder diagnosis & traced it to the nervous system. . . . Then, too, I had frightful digestive trouble—all, probably, caused by malfunctioning nerves—besides atrocious sick-headaches that kept me flat 3 or 4 days out of every week.

To his credit, Lovecraft is remarkably progressive in his attitude toward mental illness: "The victim can't help himself any more than a victim of indigestion or cardiac trouble can." He is unwilling (or consciously unable) to address the true cause of the problem—his family—and puts it down to heredity and (of all things) the violin lessons imposed upon him. But he does realize that professional help might have alleviated his symptoms: "Undoubtedly, if anyone had known just what psychological shock or exaltation or stimulus to apply to one in youth (unfortunately there is no certain knowledge in this field that one can depend on for results), virtually all of my semi-invalidism might have been sloughed off like a snake's old skin." (Again, a strange echo of wording used to describe Edward Derby's reaction to the death of his mother in "The Thing on the Doorstep.")

Also of interest in the Barlow correspondence is a more extensive discussion of cinema than elsewhere seen, with Lovecraft discussing quite a diverse mix of films. Here he is more positive about horror movies than in other published letters. His disappointment with these films stemmed largely from their diversion from their literary sources (ironic in light of the many failed cinematic adaptations of his own works), but he does admit to enjoying the acting and atmosphere of movies like *Frankenstein* and *Dracula* (both from Universal Studios, 1930).

Lovecraft offers less of himself in the Derleth letters. Derleth was only seventeen years old when the two began corresponding, but the inane comments he makes do not lessen as he matures. It might simply be Lovecraft's poor handwriting that causes Derleth to write of Maturin's famous novel "Welworth the Wanderer," and of Blackwood's wind elemental "the Wendigs." Other blunders are less easy to dismiss. To his credit, Lovecraft treads lightly with his protégé's errors. "[T]he Hudson [River] isn't in New England," Lovecraft writes, prefixing a polite "by the way." The Southern Cross, "incidentally," has four—not five—conspicuous stars. He also notes politely that this constellation can't be seen from the latitude in which Derleth set his tale. "There is," too, "no such title as 'Count' in England." Issues of auctorial judgment come in for a little more direct criticism. "Are presentation greetings & names usually inscribed on kitchen knives?" he asks, apparently remarking on a clue Derleth used in a murder mystery. And when Derleth gives obviously intrusive first names (Phineas and Abner) to some Maryland Protestant characters, Lovecraft can't help needling him. "[Y]ou certainly ought to divest its members of praenomina which unmistakably suggest something else. . . . [S]carcely any reader can fail to notice the glaring incongruity betwixt them & the family in which they are represented as occurring." Derleth deigns to push back, and Lovecraft retorts that his "explanation sounds somehow distinctly strained. Old records do not teem with such hybrid appellations as Adoniram Charles or Melchizidek Dennis." And once again— "Am I to look for stories from your pen in which Sac Prairie families blossom out with such names as Yussuf, Takamoto, Vladimir, Chang, & N'guru?" Lovecraft can't resist one final zinger regarding "the appropriateness of the names of those two old Maryland Papists Krishnamurti & Atahualpa Farway."

The Derleth correspondence is instructive primarily as it reflects Lovecraft's tutelage of a younger writer in the craft of fiction. The maxim that one should "take a great deal of time & care in rearranging the details & hints that [prepare] one for the facing of the mystery" is clearly Lovecraft's own central narrative tenant. There is much discussion of Derleth's use of contrived plot incidents, and of one tale Lovecraft says the Wisconsin writer "suddenly springs an incredible Chinese box of interlocking coincidences so all-inclusive & obvious that the reader is brought perilously & incongruously near to the snickering-point." *Incongruously Near the Snickering-Point*—this sounds like a possible alternate title for some future expanded edition.

Derleth's problematic relationship with Lovecraft's work and posthumous fame adds much interest to this correspondence. After Lovecraft's death Derleth corrupted his vision, misprinted his texts, claimed ownership of his work and even his concepts, and created a kind of hegemony around his publication. But if not for Derleth's efforts, Lovecraft might not have survived obscurity. One can observe Derleth (as David E. Schultz has pointed out) trying to impose his vision of "the Cthulhu Mythos" on Lovecraft's work over a period of time, with Lovecraft repeatedly waving him off: "It's not a bad idea to call this Cthulhuism & Yog-Sothothery of mine 'The Mythology of Hastur'—although it was really from Machen & Dunsany & others, rather than through the Bierce-Chambers line, that I picked up my gradually developing hash of theogony—or daimonogony." And later: "As to grouping certain tales of cosmic forces in a class apart—again I fear that they fall between two stools. Whereas editors think them too uniform when separately considered, they would condemn them as too heterogeneous & perhaps even subtly contradictory if they were expressly offered as a unit."

This becomes more sinister when Derleth makes insistent suggestions for revision and even tries to force Lovecraft to let him revise "The Shadow over Innsmouth"—anticipating the absurd "posthumous collaborations" Derleth published under the Arkham House imprint. Irony abounds in light of Derleth's later claimed (spurious) monopoly on Lovecraft. Regarding his demands for changes to "Innsmouth," Derleth writes: "[D]on't you like the way in which all of us immediately assume proprietory [*sic*] rights over your work and begin criticizing it?" Proprietory, indeed!

But when Derleth inquires about literary executorship and boasts that he could easily secure a Lovecraft book publication, the Rhode Island author gets the last laugh (or snicker) with amazing prescience: "Yes—come to think of it—I fear there might be some turbulent doings among an indiscriminately named board of literary heirs handling my posthumous junk! Maybe I'll dump all the work on you by naming you sole heir. The matter of compiling & placing a book would be a mere bagatelle for you—though it might possibly take a whole afternoon & cut your day's reading quota down to a dozen or so books. So you think if you got hold of Grandpa you could guarantee a book in a half-year? Well, well! that might well be if you had the cash to publish it yourself . . . but persuading other people is another matter."

Anodyne Amusing Appendix

Top Ten Worst Potential Lovecraft Fanzine Names Culled from the Fiction

10. My Cosmic Radio
9. Zadok's Vinous Garrulousness
8. The Luminous *Thing*
7. *More the Same*
6. Unspeakable Congo Secrets
5. Ye Puling Lack-Wit
4. Insane Pleas and Apologies
3. Feeble Little Spits of Immortal Malice
2. Thunder-Croakings
1. Hideous Reptilian Abnormalities Sprouting, Bubbling, and Baking over a Winking Bluish-Green Spectre of Dim Flame in a Far Corner of Black Shadows

Sources:

1.	*D 157*	6.	*D 146*
2.	*DH 196*	7.	*DH 123*
3.	*D 275*	8.	*D 30*
4.	*D 178*	9.	*DH 328*
5.	*D 273*	10.	*D 32*

Top Ten Reasons Why Lovecraft Is "Real" Literature

10. Lost review of *The Image Maker of Thebes* was probably classic.
9. Name sounds like somebody made it up.
8. Not just a bad hack writer who wrote for cheap pulp magazines.
7. Only American author to describe himself as a "star zobo soloist."
6. That neat Cthulhu Mythos.
5. Sang a mean aria from Gilbert & Sullivan if you got him drunk.
4. Disliked plot.
3. Had a cat with a racial slur for a name.
2a. Better than Robert E. Howard.
2b. Better than Clark Ashton Smith.
1. Because S. T. Joshi says so.

A Real Hard Lovecraft Trivia Quiz

1. **According to his wife, with what phrase did Lovecraft express his most profound love?**
   a. "My dear, you don't know how much I appreciate you."
   b. "Umph . . . ungl . . . rrrlh . . . chchch . . ."
   c. "Light my cigarette, bitch!"

2. **By what nickname was Lovecraft known in grade school?**
   a. Professor
   b. Lovey
   c. Gilligan

3. **Of what species did Lovecraft claim to be "inordinately fond"?**
   a. The canidae
   b. The felidae
   c. The young male protégé

4. **What did the members of the famous "Kalem Club" have in common?**
   a. They were all litterateurs
   b. They all had names beginning with K, L, or M
   c. They all had problems finding and keeping a job

5. **Which of the following Mythos entities never appeared in Lovecraft's *signed* fiction?**
   a. Yog-Sotot
   b. Bugg-Shoggog
   c. Booga-Booga

6. **Which of the following lines immortalized Lovecraft in *Bartlett's Familiar Quotations?***
   a. "Life is a hideous thing, and from the background behind what we know of it peer demoniacal hints of truth which make it sometimes a thousandfold more hideous."
   b. "The most merciful thing in the world, I think, is the inability of the human mind to correlate all its contents."
   c. "What, me worry?"

7. **Which of the following repulsed Lovecraft most?**
   a. The Ku Klux Klan
   b. Adolf Hitler
   c. The poems of Edgar Guest

8. **How did Lovecraft often refer to himself in correspondence?**
   a. Grandpa Theobald
   b. E'ch-Pi-El
   c. Tough Guy

9. **Lovecraft's primary dietary staple was:**
   a. Cheese
   b. Chocolate
   c. Eraser crumbs

10. **While travelling, Lovecraft liked to occupy himself by:**
    a. Making antiquarian explorations of Colonial cities
    b. Writing travelogues and postcards to friends
    c. Frequenting strip-joints

Afterword

I read my first Lovecraft story—"The Temple"—in a Berkley paperback anthology my Uncle Don gave me for Christmas: *Hauntings and Horrors: Ten Grisly Tales*, edited by Alden H. Norton. It was an inspired idea on the part of my uncle, who shared with me a love of the old Universal monster movies. I was twelve years old, and the story of the disabled U-boat and the strange undersea city made a strong impression upon me. Submarines were already an interest, with *Wake of the Wahoo: The Heroic Story of America's Most Daring WWII Submarine* by Forest J. Sterling an often re-read favorite. The following summer I discovered the Tower hardcover *Best Supernatural Stories of H. P. Lovecraft* (1945) at the local library, and read it avidly in the New Jersey humidity.

When I went back for it sometime later, however, the volume (mysteriously) was no longer in the stacks or even the card catalogue. Perhaps the librarian had removed it because of its poor condition: the pages were brown and flaking apart, a state which added to the charm of the contents. The *Best Supernatural Stories* had lived up to its title, for the stories—and the book's mummified odor, with its overtones suggesting cassia and cinnamon—lingered large in my memory. But for over a year I had no access to "The Colour out of Space," "The Whisperer in Darkness," and the other classics that subsequently earned Lovecraft a place in world literature.

What I *did* have, soon after, was a series of Ballantine editions of Lovecraft—those black paperbacks whose covers featured grotesque faces and gothic lettering—that contained mostly the lesser tales. Here I read and reread such early favorites as "Beyond the Wall of Sleep," "The White Ship," "The Nameless City," "The Hound," "The Festival," and "He." The strange atmosphere and weird conceits of these minor stories exerted an inordinate fascination upon me. They still do, decades later, though today the charm is tempered by an awareness of their flaws as artistic creations. (Lately, as I realize how poorly written most genre tales—older and newer—are written, I have begun to think even the lesser Lovecraft is greater than 99 percent of other "horror stories.")

Of all the Lovecraft stories I owned, one especially captured my fancy. Contained in *The Tomb and Other Tales* (1973), it was entitled "Imprisoned with the Pharaohs." A small asterisk near the title drew my gaze to the lone footnote in the book: "With Harry Houdini." This astonished me, for independent of my interest in Lovecraft I also had a long-standing obsession with Houdini. Two paperback biographies and some books on magic from the library had left me much impressed with the poor, unschooled immigrant boy from rural Wisconsin who became the world's most famous magician through sheer cleverness and determination. Not having the benefit of L. Sprague de Camp's Lovecraft biography (1975), and not finding any reference to Lovecraft in the Houdini volumes, I wondered idly how the two men could possibly have not merely crossed paths but also come to collaborate on a story. Their personalities were so different—Lovecraft introspective and imaginative, Houdini all brawn and bravura.

"Imprisoned with the Pharaohs" I found exciting on its own merits, in part because I was captivated by ancient Egypt. The stylized art, the architecture and monuments, and the strange culture and mythology of the civilization all absorbed me. Its inhabitants seemed—and continue to seem—to me as alien to our contemporary selves as a race of beings from another planet. In the story, Lovecraft's extravagant descriptions of Egypt, of the vast subterranean chamber where the climax occurs, and of the grotesque composite mummies whose mere existence nearly drive Houdini mad, all struck a chord with my youthful sensibility.

So fond was I of the story that I jumped at an opportunity to cite it soon afterward, in an unlikely venue. At school, one of my eighth grade classes was in "Social Studies" (history, geography, and economics). The students were paired off and asked to prepare a brief "travelogue" on a particular country, describing its culture, environs, and commerce. We were to write our text upon a two-ply "spirit master," which would be duplicated on a Ditto machine by the teacher and distributed to the class. Inevitably, I convinced my partner to choose Egypt as our topic.

Perhaps just as inevitably (this became a pattern for later group projects) I ended up doing all the writing myself. As I neared completion of the paper at home one night, I struck upon the idea of quoting from "Imprisoned with the Pharaohs" as a kind of headnote to the body of the text. (I understand this was a strange idea for a 14 year old. Eighth grade papers rarely have headnotes.) Searching through the tale for something suitable for a travelogue, I carefully transcribed onto the mimeograph master the following passage:

> Old Cairo is itself a story-book and a dream—labyrinths of narrow alleys redolent of aromatic secrets; Arabesque balconies and oriels nearly meeting above the cobbled streets; maelstroms of Oriental traffic with strange cries, cracking whips, rattling carts, jingling money, and braying donkeys; kaleido-scopes of polychrome robes, veils, turbans, and tarbushes; water-carriers and dervishes, dogs and cats, soothsayers and barbers; and over all the whining of blind beggars crouched in alcoves, and the sonorous chanting of muez-zins from minarets limned delicately against a sky of deep, unchanging blue. . . . Antiquity begins to mingle with exoticism.

I realized much later that this passage is highly characteristic of Lovecraft's style. He uses grammatical parallelism to present a fleeting series of images. The result has the effect of a phantasmagoria, here vividly conveying the hec-tic diversity of the Egyptian city. Lovecraft employed this kaleidoscopic tech-nique to superb in many other stories (including "The Shunned House," which he wrote only seven months later), substituting instead the cosmic panoramas so unique to him.

But a less pleasant task lay ahead. In class, there was a surprise an-nouncement that our travelogue on Egypt was to be presented to the other students. At this time I was among that majority of people whose fear of death is exceeded only by their fear of public speaking. Through the haze of the fight-or-flight mechanism, it struck me that I had negotiating leverage. Since I had done all the writing, I managed to coerce my partner into getting up in front of the class to atone for his lack of effort.

Unfortunately, my indolent friend had not even bothered to review the text. And the opening, the most difficult part of any speech, was nothing less than the most intricate kind of Lovecraftian polysyllabics, including words that hitherto had come out of no eighth grader's mouth. My friend's diffi-culty in enunciating the passage above was a little awkward and—in an adoles-cent way—more than a little funny.

It was another seven years before I discovered the world of Lovecraft stud-ies; and even then I never thought to try my hand at criticism until after I had found and read a good sampling of it. In doing so I was delighted to be informed by the work of Kenneth W. Faig that my old favorite "Imprisoned with the Pharaohs" was actually titled "Under the Pyramids." The title under which I knew it for so long had been invented by the editor of *Weird Tales!*

"Under the Pyramids" was a much more compelling title. Far more "Love-craftian" in its implications, it also (as do many titles in the oeuvre) neatly ties back into the text:

> [I]t was curious to reflect how persistently visitors were forbidden to enter the pyramids at night, or to visit the lowest burrows and crypt of the Great Pyramid. Perhaps in the latter case it was the psychological effect which was feared—the effect of the visitor of feeling himself huddled down beneath a gigantic world of solid masonry; joined to the life he has known by the merest tube, in which he may only crawl, and which any accident or evil design might block.

In typical fashion, Lovecraft foreshadows the predicament in which the protagonist ultimately finds himself.

During this period I learned, too, that Lovecraft had probably been influenced in his tale by both the *Arabian Nights* and by a more obscure precursor, Theophile Gautier. The latter shouldn't have surprised me in light of this charming passage from Lovecraft's *Supernatural Horror in Literature*:

> Gautier captured the inmost soul of aeon-weighted Egypt, with its cryptic life and Cyclopean architecture, and uttered once and for all the eternal horror of its nether world of catacombs, where to the end of time millions of stiff, spiced corpses will stare up in the blackness, awaiting some awesome and unrelatable summons.

A couple of years later I found the pertinent volume for sale by mail order: *One of Cleopatra's Nights and Other Fantastic Romances* by Theophile Gautier, "Faithfully Translated by Lafcadio Hearn" (New York: R. Worthington, 1882). This old book remains one of the favorites among my library, and the title story surely shows its influence in "Under the Pyramids", specifically in the plaint of Cleopatra on the oppressive art of Egypt:

> On the right hand, on the left, withersoever one turns, only frightful monsters are visible,—dogs with the heads of men; men with the heads of dogs; chimeras begotten of hideous couplings in the shadowy depths of the labyrinths; figures of Anubis, Typhon, Osiris; partridges with great yellow eyes that seem to pierce through you with their inquisitorial gaze, and see beyond and behind you things which one dare not speak of,—a family of animals and horrible gods with scaly wings, hooked beaks, trenchant claws,— ever ready to devour you should you venture to cross the threshold of the temple, or lift a corner of the veil.

But Gautier was only the first author whose discovery I owe to Lovecraft. Not merely Dunsany, Machen, and Blackwood—as may be expected—but also Baudelaire, Huysmans, de Maupassant, and many more were introduced to me through my readings in Lovecraft. In a way, this is why Lovecraft has been so important to me—through his fiction, poetry, and letters, he has broadened my understanding of literature, art, philosophy, science, history, and numerous other subjects. These subjects are not merely very far afield from "Under the Pyramids," at times often precisely the opposite of Lovecraft's taste and ideology. Someone once said that Lovecraft is a sort of university; beyond the many hours his cosmic flights of fancy have held me captivated, this is how he has most affected my life.

But I should not close, perhaps, without taking this opportunity to apologize to my eighth grade friend.

Works Cited

Abbreviations used in the text and notes:

AHT   Arkham House Transcripts
AT   *The Ancient Track: Complete Poetical Works* (2013 ed.)
CE   *Collected Essays* (5 vols.)
D   *Dagon and Other Macabre Tales*
DH   *The Dunwich Horror and Others*
ES   *Essential Solitude: The Letters of H. P. Lovecraft and August Derleth*
HM   *The Horror in the Museum and Other Revisions*
JHL   H. P. Lovecraft Papers, John Hay Library, Brown University
MM   *At the Mountains of Madness and Other Novels*
MW   *Miscellaneous Writings*
SL   *Selected Letters* (5 vols.)

I. Primary

The Ancient Track: Complete Poetical Works. Edited by S. T. Joshi. San Francisco: Night Shade, 2001. Rev. ed. New York: Hippocampus Press, 2013.

At the Mountains of Madness and Other Novels. Selected by August Derleth; Texts Edited by S. T. Joshi. Sauk City, WI: Arkham House, 1985.

Collected Essays. Selected by August Derleth; Texts Edited by S. T. Joshi. New York: Hippocampus Press, 2004–06. 5 vols.

Dagon and Other Macabre Tales. Edited by S. T. Joshi. Sauk City, WI: Arkham House, 1986.

Dreams and Fancies. Sauk City, WI: Arkham House, 1962.

The Dunwich Horror and Others. Selected by August Derleth; Texts Edited by S. T. Joshi. Sauk City, WI: Arkham House, 1984.

Essential Solitude: The Letters of H. P. Lovecraft and August Derleth. Ed. David E. Schultz and S. T. Joshi. New York: Hippocampus Press, 2008. 2 vols.

The Horror in the Museum and Other Revisions. Selected by August Derleth; Texts Edited by S. T. Joshi. Sauk City, WI: Arkham House, 1989.

Letters from New York. Ed. S. T. Joshi and David E. Schultz. San Francisco: Night Shade, 2005.

Letters to Alfred Galpin. Ed. S. T. Joshi and David E. Schultz. New York: Hippocampus Press, 2005.

Letters to Richard F. Searight. Ed. David E. Schultz and S. T. Joshi. West Warwick, RI: Necronomicon Press, 1992.

Miscellaneous Writings. Edited by S. T. Joshi. Sauk City, WI: Arkham House, 1995.

Selected Letters. Edited by August Derleth, Donald Wandrei, and James Turner. Sauk City, WI: Arkham House, 1965-76. 5 vols.

Uncollected Letters. Ed. S. T. Joshi. West Warwick, RI: Necronomicon Press, 1986.

II. Secondary

Baring-Gould, Sabine. *Curious Myths of the Middle Ages.* Introduction by Leslie Shepherd. New Hyde Park: University Books, 1967.

Barlow, R. H. *On Lovecraft and Life.* Ed. S. T. Joshi. West Warwick, RI: Necronomicon Press, 1992.

Bosky, Bernadette. "In Search of a Mythos Genealogy." *Crypt of Cthulhu* No. 8 (Michaelmas 1982): 16-22.

Bradbury, Malcolm, and James McFarlane, ed. *Modernism 1890–1930.* Harmondsworth, UK: Penguin, 1976.

Brown, Stephen J. *The World of Imagery: Metaphor and Kindred Imagery.* New York: Russell & Russell, 1966.

Burleson, Donald R. *H. P. Lovecraft: A Critical Study.* Westport, CT: Greenwood Press, 1983.

——. *Lovecraft: Disturbing the Universe.* Lexington: University Press of Kentucky, 1990.

——. "A Note on Lovecraft, Mathematics, and the Outer Spheres." *Crypt of Cthulhu* No. 4 (Eastertide 1982): 23-24.

Cannon, Peter. *H. P. Lovecraft.* New York: Twayne, 1989.

Cannon, Peter, ed. *Lovecraft Remembered.* Sauk City, WI: Arkham House, 1998.

Carter, Lin. *Lovecraft: A Look Behind the "Cthulhu Mythos."* New York: Ballantine, 1972.

Chalker, Jack L., ed. *Mirage on Lovecraft*. Baltimore: Mirage Press, 1965.

Conrad, Peter. *The Art of the City*. New York: Oxford University Press, 1984.

Crane, Hart. *Complete Poems*. Ed. Marc Simon. New York: Liveright, 1986.

——. *Complete Poems and Selected Letters*. New York: Library of America, 2006.

Davis, Sonia Haft Greene. *The Private Life of H. P. Lovecraft*. Ed. S. T. Joshi. West Warwick, RI: Necronomicon Press, 1985 (rev. ed. 1992).

de Camp, L. Sprague. *Lovecraft: A Biography*. Garden City, NY: Doubleday, 1975.

Eastman, Richard M. *Style*. New York: Oxford University Press, 1978.

Eckhardt, Jason C. "The Cosmic Yankee." In *An Epicure in the Terrible*, ed. David E. Schultz and S. T. Joshi. Rutherford, NJ: Fairleigh Dickinson University Press, 1991. 45-77.

Eliot, T. S. *Collected Poems 1909-1962*. New York: Harcourt, Brace, 1963.

——. *Selected Prose of T.S. Eliot*. London: Faber and Faber, 1975.

Eysteinsson, Astradur. *The Concept of Modernism*. Ithaca, NY: Cornell University Press, 1990.

Faig, Kenneth W., Jr. *H. P. Lovecraft: His Life, His Work*. West Warwick, RI: Necronomicon Press, 1979.

Feibleman, James K. *The Quiet Rebellion: The Making and Meaning of the Arts*. New York: Horizon Press, 1972.

Feuerlicht, Roberta Strauss. *America's Reign of Terror: World War I, the Red Scare, and the Palmer Raids*. New York: Random House, 1971.

Field, Edward, ed. *State of Rhode Island and Providence Plantations at the End of the Century: A History*. Boston & Syracuse: Mason, 1902. 3 vols.

Fish, Stanley E. "Interpreting the Variorum." In *Reader-Response Criticism: From Formalism to Post-Structuralism*, ed. Jane Tompkins. Baltimore: Johns Hopkins University Press, 1980. 164-84. Cited in the text as Fish 1980a.

Fish, Stanley E. "Literature in the Reader: Affective Stylistics." In *Reader-Response Criticism: From Formalism to Post-Structuralism*, ed. Jane Tompkins. Baltimore: Johns Hopkins University Press, 1980. 70-99. Cited in the text as Fish 1980b.

French, Warren. "The Age of Eliot: The Twenties as Waste Land." In *The Twenties: Fiction, Poetry, Drama*, ed. Warren French. Deland, FL: Everett/ Edwards, 1975. 475-96.

Fulwiler, William. "A Double Dissection: 'The Tomb' and Dagon.'" *Crypt of Cthulhu* No. 38 (Eastertide 1986): 8-14.

——. "Mu in 'Bothon' and 'Out of the Eons.'" *Crypt of Cthulhu* No. 11 (Candlemas 1983): 20-24.

Fussell, Paul. *The Great War and Modern Memory*. New York: Oxford University Press, 1975.

Galpin, Alfred. "The Boat in the Tower: Rimbaud in Cleveland, 1922." *Renascence* (Autumn 1972): 313.

Gayford, Norman R. "The Artist as Antaeus: Lovecraft and Modernism." In *An Epicure in the Terrible: A Centennial Anthology of Essays in Honor of H. P. Lovecraft*, ed. David E. Schultz and S. T. Joshi. Rutherford, NJ: Fairleigh Dickinson University Press, 1991. 273-97.

Gossett, Thomas F. *Race: The History of an Idea in America*. Rev. ed. New York: Oxford University Press, 1997.

Higham, John. *Strangers in the Land: Patterns of American Nativism 1860-1925*. New York: Athenaeum, 1965.

Hoffmann, Fredrick. *The 20s: American Writing in the Postwar Decade*. New York: Free Press, 1965.

Holman, C. Hugh. *A Handbook to Literature*. 3rd ed. New York: Odyssey Press, 1972.

Horton, Philip. *Hart Crane: The Life of an American Poet*. New York: Norton, 1937.

Horton, Rod W., and Herbert R. Edwards. *Backgrounds of American Literary Thought*. 2nd ed. New York: Appleton-Century-Crofts, 1967.

Huysmans, J.-K. *Against the Grain*. Tr. John Howard. New York: Lieber & Lewis, 1922.

Iser, Wolfgang. "The Reading Process: A Phenomenological Approach." In *Reader-Response Criticism: From Formalism to Post-Structuralism*, ed. Jane Tompkins. Baltimore: Johns Hopkins University Press, 1980. 50-69.

Joshi, S. T. "A Chronology of Selected Works by H. P. Lovecraft." In S. T. Joshi, ed. *H. P. Lovecraft: Four Decades of Criticism*. Athens: Ohio University Press, 1980. 27-41.

——. *H. P. Lovecraft*. (Starmont Reader's Guides 13.) Mercer Island, WA: Starmont House, 1982.

——. *H. P. Lovecraft: A Life*. West Warwick, RI: Necronomicon Press, 1996.

——. *H. P. Lovecraft: The Decline of the West*. Mercer Island, WA: Starmont House, 1990.

——. "H. P. Lovecraft and *The Dream-Quest of Unknown Kadath*." *Crypt of Cthulhu* No. 37 (Candlemas 1986): 25-34, 59.

——. "On 'Polaris.'" In Joshi's *Primal Sources: Essays on H. P. Lovecraft*. New York: Hippocampus Press, 2003. 154-58.

———. Review of *H. P. Lovecraft: New England Decadent* by Barton Levi St. Armand. *Lovecraft Studies* No. 3 (Fall 1980): 35–38.

———. "Topical References in Lovecraft." *Extrapolation* 25, No. 3 (Fall 1984): 247–65.

Joshi, S. T., ed. *A Weird Writer in Our Midst: Early Criticism of H. P. Lovecraft.* New York: Hippocampus Press, 2010.

Joshi, S. T., and Marc A. Michaud, ed. *H. P. Lovecraft in "The Eyrie."* West Warwick, RI: Necronomicon Press, 1979.

Klein, Marcus. *Foreigners: The Making of American Literature, 1900–1940.* Chicago: University of Chicago Press, 1981.

Krutch, Joseph Wood. *The Modern Temper: A Study and a Confession.* New York: Harcourt, Brace & World, 1929; rpt. New York: Harvest Books, 1959.

Laney, Francis T. "The Cthulhu Mythology." *Acolyte* 1, No. 2 (Winter 1942); rpt. *Crypt of Cthulhu* No. 35 (Hallowmas 1985): 28–34.

Lawrence, D. H. "The Dragon of the Apocalypse." In *Literary Symbolism*, ed. Maurice Beebe. Belmont, CA: Wadsworth Publishing Co., 1960. 31–32.

Long, Frank Belknap. "Some Random Memories of H.P.L." In Peter Cannon, ed. *Lovecraft Remembered.* Sauk City, WI: Arkham House, 1998. 182–87.

Loveman, Samuel. *Hart Crane: A Conversation.* Ed. Jay Socin and Kirby Congon. New York: Interim Books, 1964.

Lucian. *True History and Lucius, or The Ass.* Tr. Paul Turner. Bloomington: Indiana University Press, 1958.

McDougall, William. *An Introduction to Social Psychology.* New York: J. W. Luce & Company, 1921.

McCormick, John. *The Middle Distance: A Comparative History of American Imaginative Literature, 1919–1932.* New York: Free Press, 1971.

Machen, Arthur. *The Three Impostors.* New York: Knopf, 1923.

Maupassant, Guy de. "The Horla." In Herbert A. Wise and Phyllis Fraser, ed. *Great Tales of Terror and the Supernatural.* New York: Random House, 1944. 447–72.

May, Henry F. *The End of American Innocence: A Study of the First Years of Our Own Time, 1911–1917.* New York: Columbia University Press, 1959.

Milic, Louis T. *Stylists on Style.* New York: Scribner, 1969.

Miller, James E., Jr. "Fitzgerald's Gatsby: The World as Ash Heap." In *The Twenties: Fiction, Poetry, Drama*, ed. Warren French. Deland, FL: Everett/Edwards, 1975. 181–202.

Moore, C. L.; Merritt, A.; Lovecraft, H. P.; Howard, Robert E.; and Long, Frank Belknap. *The Challenge from Beyond.* West Warwick, RI: Necronomicon Press, 1990.

Mosig, Dirk W. "Innsmouth and the Lovecraft *Oeuvre:* A Holistic Approach." *Nyctalops* No. 14 (March 1978): 3, 5.

Munson, Gorham. *The Awakening Twenties: A Memoir-History of a Literary Period.* Baton Rouge: Louisiana State University Press, 1985.

Murray, Will. "The Dunwich Chimera and Others." *Lovecraft Studies* No. 8 (Spring 1984): 10–24.

——. "An Uncompromising Look at the Cthulhu Mythos." *Lovecraft Studies* No. 12 (Spring 1986): 26–31.

——. "Lovecraft and the Pulp Magazine Tradition." In *An Epicure in the Terrible: A Centennial Anthology of Essays in Honor of H. P. Lovecraft,* ed. David E. Schultz and S. T. Joshi. Rutherford, NJ: Fairleigh Dickinson University Press, 1991. 101–31.

Onderdonk, Matthew H. "Charon—in Reverse; or, H. P. Lovecraft versus the 'Realists' of Fantasy." *Fantasy Commentator* 2, No. 6 (Spring 1948): 193–97. *Lovecraft Studies* No. 3 (Fall 1980): 5–10.

Penzoldt, Peter. *The Supernatural in Fiction.* 1952. Extracts in S. T. Joshi, ed. *H. P. Lovecraft: Four Decades of Criticism.* Athens: Ohio University Press, 1980. 63–77.

Peyre, Henri. *What Is Symbolism?* Trans. Emmett Parker. University: University of Alabama Press, 1982.

Price, Robert M. "Demythologizing Cthulhu." *Lovecraft Studies* No. 8 (Spring 1984): 3–9.

——. "Erich Zann and the Rue d'Auseil." *Lovecraft Studies* Nos. 22/23 (Fall 1990): 13–14.

——. "H. P. Lovecraft and the Cthulhu Mythos." *Crypt of Cthulhu* No. 35 (Hallowmas 1985): 3–10. Cited in the text as Price 1985b.

——. "HPL and HPB: Lovecraft's Use of Theosophy." *Crypt of Cthulhu* No. 5 (Roodmas 1982): 3–9.

——. "The Last Vestige of the Derleth Mythos." *Lovecraft Studies* No. 24 (Spring 1991): 20–21. Cited in the text as Price 1991a.

Price, Robert M. "A Lovecraft Taxonomy." *Crypt of Cthulhu* No. 12 (Eastertide 1983): 17–19.

——. "Lovecraft's 'Artificial Mythology.'" In *An Epicure in the Terrible: A Centennial Anthology of Essays in Honor of H. P. Lovecraft,* ed. David E. Schultz and S. T. Joshi. Rutherford, NJ: Fairleigh Dickinson University Press, 1991. 247–56. Cited in the text as Price 1991b.

——. "A Mythos Theogony." *Crypt of Cthulhu* No. 85 (Hallowmas 1993): 28–30. Cited in the text as Price 1993b.

——. "The Revision Mythos." *Lovecraft Studies* No. 11 (Fall 1985): 43–50. Cited in the text as Price 1985a.

——. "What Exactly Is the Cthulhu Mythos?" *NecronomiCon Program Guide*. Boston: Lovecraft Society of New England, August 1993, 17, 19. Cited in the text as Price 1993a.

"Providence." In *Encyclopaedia Britannica*. 11th ed. (1910).

Rank, Otto. *Art and Artist: Creative Urge and Personality Development*. Tr. Charles Francis Atkinson. New York: Knopf, 1932.

Russell, Francis. *A City in Terror: 1919, The Boston Police Strike*. New York: Viking, 1975.

Schwartz, Joseph, and Robert C. Schweik. *Hart Crane: A Descriptive Bibliography*. Pittsburgh: University of Pittsburgh Press, 1972.

St. Armand, Barton Levi. *H. P. Lovecraft: New England Decadent*. Albuquerque, NM: Silver Scarab Press, 1979.

——, and John H. Stanley. "H. P. Lovecraft's *Waste Paper*: A Facsimile and Transcript of the Original Draft." *Books at Brown* 26 (1978): 31–47.

Santayana, George. *The Life of Reason; or, Phases of Human Progress*. One Volume Edition revised by the author in collaboration with Daniel Corey. New York: Scribner, 1954.

Schultz, David E. "From Microcosm to Macrocosm: The Growth of Lovecraft's Cosmic Vision." In David E. Schultz, and S. T. Joshi, ed. *An Epicure in the, Terrible: A Centennial Anthology of Essays in Honor of H. P. Lovecraft*. Rutherford, NJ: Fairleigh Dickinson University Press, 1990. 199–219.

——. "The Lack of Continuity in *Fungi from Yuggoth*." *Crypt of Cthulhu* No. 20 (Eastertide 1984): 12–16.

——. "Who Needs the 'Cthulhu Mythos'?" *Lovecraft Studies* No. 13 (Fall 1986): 43–51.

Searles, Baird, et al. *A Reader's Guide to Fantasy*. New York: Avon, 1982.

——. *A Reader's Guide to Science Fiction*. New York: Avon, 1979.

Sharpe, William Chapman. *Unreal Cities: Urban Figuration in Wordsworth, Baudelaire, Whitman, Eliot, and Williams*. Baltimore: Johns Hopkins University Press, 1990.

Smith, Clark Ashton. *Letters to H. P. Lovecraft.* Ed. Steve Behrends. West Warwick, RI: Necronomicon Press, 1987.

——."Ubbo-Sathla." In August Derleth, ed. *Tales of the Cthulhu Mythos, Volume One.* New York: Ballantine, 1971.

Spence, Lewis. *An Encyclopedia of Occultism.* 1920. Rpt. Secaucus, NJ: Citadel Press, 1960.

The Thousand and One Nights, tr. John Payne. London: privately printed, 1901; 3 vols.

Taylor, John. "Joris-Karl Huysmans as Impressionist in Prose." *Papers on Language and Literature* 8 [Supplement] (Fall 1972): 67–78.

Unterecker, John. Voyager: *A Life of Hart Crane.* New York: Farrar, Straus & Giroux, 1969.

Weber, Brom. *Hart Crane: A Biographical and Critical Study.* New York: Bodley Press, 1948.

Wells, H. G. *The Best Science Fiction Stories of H. G. Wells.* New York: Dover, 1966.

Wetzel, George T. "The Cthulhu Mythos: A Study." In S. T. Joshi, ed. *H. P. Lovecraft: Four Decades of Criticism.* Athens: Ohio University Press, 1980. 79-95.

"What Is the Cthulhu Mythos?" (panel discussion). *Lovecraft Studies* No. 14 (Spring 1987): 3-30. Cited in the text as Panel Discussion.

Widmer, Kingsley. "*The Waste Land* and the American Tradition." In *The Twenties: Fiction, Poetry, Drama,* ed. Warren French. Deland, FL: Everett/Edwards, 1975. 475-96.

Wilson, Colin. "Prefatory Note" to *The Philosopher's Stone.* New York: Avon, 1974.

Wilson, Edmund. "Tales of the Marvellous and the Ridiculous" (1945). Rpt. in S. T. Joshi, ed. *H. P. Lovecraft: Four Decades of Criticism.* Athens: Ohio University Press, 1980. 46-49.

Wimsatt, W. K., Jr. *The Prose Style of Samuel Johnson.* New Haven: Yale University Press, 1941.

Sources

"H. P. Lovecraft: Consummate Prose Stylist." *Crypt of Cthulhu* No. 12 (Eastertide 1982): 5–12 (as "H. P. Lovecraft: Prose Stylist"; abridged). *Lovecraft Studies* No. 9 (Fall 1984): 43–51. [Incorporates "Notes on the Prose Realism of H. P. Lovecraft" (*Lovecraft Studies* No. 10 (Spring 1985): 3–11); in *On the Emergence of "Cthulhu"*; and "Realism in Lovecraft's Early Work" (*Ultimate Chaos* 2, No. 4 [December 1984]: 1–11).]

"Lovecraft's Concept of 'Background.'" *Lovecraft Studies* No. 12 (Spring 1986): 3–12.

"Toward a Reader-Response Approach to the Lovecraft Mythos." In Steven J. Mariconda, *On the Emergence of "Cthulhu" and Other Observations.* West Warwick, RI: Necronomicon Press, 1995.

"Lovecraft's Cosmic Imagery." In *An Epicure in the Terrible: A Centennial Anthology of Essays in Honor of H. P. Lovecraft*, ed. David E. Schultz and S. T. Joshi. Rutherford, NJ: Fairleigh Dickinson University Press, 1991. 188–98. Rpt. New York: Hippocampus Press, 2011. 196–207.

"H. P. Lovecraft: Art, Artifact, and Reality." *Lovecraft Studies* No. 32 (Spring 1995): 12–17.

"H. P. Lovecraft: Reluctant American Modernist." *Lovecraft Studies* Nos. 42/43 (Autumn 2001): 20–32,

"'Expect Great Revelations': Lovecraft Criticism in His Centennial Year." *Lovecraft Studies* No. 24 (Spring 1991): 24–29.

"On 'Amissa Minerva.'" *Etchings and Odysseys* No. 9 [1986]: 97–103.

"'The Hound'—A Dead Dog?" *Crypt of Cthulhu* No. 38 (Eastertide 1986): 3–7.

"'Hypnos': Art, Philosophy, and Insanity." In *On the Emergence of "Cthulhu" and Other Observations.* West Warwick, RI: Necronomicon Press, 1995.

"*Curious Myths of the Middle Ages* and 'The Rats in the Walls.'" *Crypt of Cthulhu* No. 14 (St. John's Eve 1983): 3–7.

"Lovecraft's 'Elizabethtown.'" *Ultimate Chaos* 3, No. 2 (July 190; [1–4].

"On the Emergence of 'Cthulhu.'" *Lovecraft Studies* No. 15 (Fall 1987): 54–58.

"The Subversion of Sense in 'The Colour out of Space.'" *Lovecraft Studies* Nos. 19/20 (Fall 1989): 20–22.

"Tightening the Coil: The Revision of 'The Whisperer in Darkness.'" *Lovecraft Studies* No. 32 (Spring 1995): 12–17.

"Lovecraft's Role in 'The Tree on the Hill.'" *Crypt of Cthulhu* No. 17 (Hallowmas 1983): 10–12, 24.

"Some Antecedents of the Shining Trapezohedron." *Etchings and Odysseys* No. 3 [1983]: 15–20.

"The Corrected Texts of Lovecraft's Tales." Review of *The Dunwich Horror and Others*. *Crypt of Cthulhu* No. 30 (Eastertide 1985): 53–55. Review of *At the Mountains of Madness and Other Novels*. *Crypt of Cthulhu* No. 37 (Candlemas 1986): 53–54. Review of *Dagon and Other Macabre Tales*. *Lovecraft Studies* No. 14 (Spring 1987): 39–41. Review of *The Annotated Revisions and Collaborations of H. P. Lovecraft*. *Lovecraft Annual* No. 6 (2012): 230–36.

"Lovecraft's Essays, Poems, and Letters." Review of *In Defence of Dagon*. *Lovecraft Studies* No. 11 (Fall 1985): 77–80. Review of *Commonplace Book*. *Lovecraft Studies* No. 13 (Fall 1986): 76–78. Review of *Medusa and Other Poems*. *Lovecraft Studies* No. 15 (Fall 1987): 81–83. Review of *Letters to Richard F. Searight*. *Lovecraft Studies* No. 27 (Fall 1992): 32–33. Review of *Miscellaneous Writings*. *Necrofile* No. 17 (Summer 1995): 19–21. "Cthuluism and Yog-Sothothery." Reviews of *O Fortunate Floridian* and *Essential Solitude*. *Dead Reckonings* No. 3 (Spring 2008): 35–41.

"Some Lovecraft Scholars." Review of *H. P. Lovecraft: A Critical Study* by Donald R. Burleson. *Crypt of Cthulhu* No. 18 (Yuletide 1983): 35–36. Review of *Lovecraft: A Study in the Fantastic* by Maurice Lévy. *Lovecraft Studies* No. 16 (Spring 1988): 36–38. Review of *Lovecraft: Disturbing the Universe* by Donald R. Burleson and *H. P. Lovecraft: The Decline of the West* by S. T. Joshi. *Crypt of Cthulhu* No. 76 (Hallowmas 1990): 23–26. Review of *Arthur Machen* by Mark Valentine and *H. P. Lovecraft: A Life* by S. T. Joshi. *Necrofile* No. 24 (Spring 1997): 3–6. Review of *Lovecraft Remembered*, ed. Peter Cannon. *Lovecraft Studies* No. 41 (Spring 1999): 30–33. Review of *I Am Providence: The Life and Times of H. P. Lovecraft* by S. T. Joshi. *Lovecraft Annual* No. 4 (2010): 208–15.

The "Afterword" is previously unpublished.

Index

Jackson, Winifred V., 20, 24, 225. See also Berkeley, Elizabeth Neville

James, M. R., 29-30, 72, 248

Johnson, Samuel, 31–33, 50, 111, 241

Joshi, S. T., 14, 20, 23, 31, 36, 42, 47, 50, 57, 61, 67, 84, 95, 100, 122, 124–25, 129–35, 138–39, 157, 160, 164, 166, 173, 181–82, 191, 201, 211, 215–25, 227, 229, 231, 232, 234–35, 238, 240–42, 246, 248, 251–53, 255–63, 267–71, 273

Joyce, James, 40, 41, 118, 121, 244

Klein, T. E. D., 222–23

Kleiner, Rheinhart, 130, 144, 156–58, 171, 180, 265

Kreymborg, Alfred, 115

Krutch, Joseph Wood, 47–48, 130, 261

Laforgue, Jules, 111

Lamarckism, 49

Lange, Konrad, 271

"Last Test, The" (HPL-de Castro), 59, 66–67, 71

Lawrence, D. H., 63, 127

Leng, 72, 78, 94, 192

Leucippus, 87, 130, 252

Lévy, Maurice, 129, 248–50

Lewis, Sinclair, 111, 121, 156, 206

Library of America, 14

Lindsay, Vachel, 144

Little Review, 111, 154

"Living Heritage: Roman Architecture in Today's America, A," 89

Long, Frank Belknap , 67, 71–72, 87, 130, 155, 157, 163, 166, 193, 195 228, 243, 260, 265

Lovecraft Studies, 129, 132, 137, 160, 217

Lovecraft, H. P.: aesthetics of, 51, 53, 95, 106, 112, 130–31, 163, 166, 218, 229–30, 240, 251–53; and art, 15, 40–41, 51–52, 56, 80–81, 89, 92–127, 143–49, 152–58, 160–67, 185, 206, 209, 218, 223, 229, 232,

239, 241–46, 249, 252, 255, 261, 266, 269, 271, 275; and authorial intent, 13, 15, 16, 20, 60, 69, 81, 97, 101, 110, 133, 155, 159, 161–62, 186, 207, 230, 234, 237; compositional habits of, 16; and concept of atmosphere, 9, 13–17, 20, 26–27, 30, 36–38, 45, 49, 50, 52, 133, 156, 174, 234, 236, 239, 259, 277; and concept of background, 28–29, 46–57, 65, 71, 106; and concept of mood, 44, 62, 120–123, 154, 230, 235; and concept of play, 41, 69, 92, 179, 228, 262, 265, 271–72; humor in, 186, 187, 261–64, 266–67, 271; mathematics in, 85–88, 256; metaphysics of, 34, 46–47, 99, 130, 163, 167, 229, 251, 253; music in, 33, 35, 84, 91, 95, 99, 107–9, 112, 163, 236, 257; and relative values, 46, 48, 56, 252; and symmetry, 32, 38, 51, 85–88, 106–7; use of artifacts, 68, 92–93, 101–5, 109, 217, 234; use of local color, 10, 30, 46, 53–56, 117, 138, 183, 217

Imagery in, 80–91, 107, 122–26, 153, 160, 165, 212, 219, 235, 237, 250

kaledoscopic, 43, 82, 83, 89, 90, 91, 285; geometrical, 85–88; sound, 37, 70, 82, 84, 127, 158, 185, 208, 225, 275, 277–78, 280; pattern, 32, 55, 70, 82, 85, 98, 107, 116–17, 119, 131, 165, 234, 260, 284; rhythm, 15–16, 39, 51, 85–86, 106–7, 239; waste land, 122–24)

Prose style of, 13–34, 41, 45, 72, 98–99, 104, 107, 117–18, 122–28, 134, 145, 158–59, 184, 217, 225–28, 239, 242–44

alliteration, 37, 41; anaphora, 33, 38; assonance, 37, 41; chiasmus, 32, 33; clauses, 25, 40; dialect, 54, 55, 217, 266, 272, 274; narration, 13, 16–27, 29–37, 40–

44, 54, 63, 81–88, 91, 93–99, 102–3, 105–8, 121–22, 126, 128, 131, 133, 134, 138, 156–59, 163, 166, 170, 176, 181–83, 185, 187–88, 191, 194, 196, 201–2, 217, 219, 226, 237, 239, 241, 247, 249, 255, 262, 272–73, 277 (first-person narration, 17, 30, 34, 40, 42–43, 122, 130, 226, 241; interior mono-logues, 40, 42–43, 54); parallelism, 32–33, 243, 285; stream-of-consciousness, 40–44, 153, 243, 244; syntax, 29, 31–32, 38–39, 134, 242, 254; tone, 13–14, 16, 17, 20, 22, 24–25, 27, 29–32, 36, 70, 108, 148, 178, 184, 189, 236, 239, 274; verb usage, 39, 185, 187; vo-cabulary, 18, 25, 29, 31–32, 55

Lovecraft, Winfield Scott, 108, 137, 138, 270

"Loved Dead, The" (HPL-Eddy), 43

Loveman, Samuel, 111–15, 134, 156, 163–64, 178, 222, 236–65, 266, 293

Lowell, Amy, 144, 149, 154

Lucian, 206, 211, 293

Lucretius, 47, 87, 130, 252

"Lurking Fear, The," 27, 34, 43, 122, 204

Machen, Arthur, 32, 72, 110, 130, 182, 207, 236, 248, 255–58, 278

Marblehead, Mass., 53, 234

Marlowe, Christopher, 111

Massachusetts, 21, 49, 53

Masters, Edgar Lee, 119, 121, 149, 154

Maupassant, Guy de, 182–83

"Memory," 292

Mencken, H. L., 115, 124

Merritt, A., 228, 275

Michaud, Marc A., 9, 157, 293

Milic, Louis, 31

Millay, Edna St. Vincent, 115, 116

Milton, John, 60, 148, 151

Miniter, Edith, 265

Modern Science and Materialism (Elliot), 84, 233

Modern Temper, The (Krutch), 47, 293

Modernism, 110–28, 139, 243

Modigliani, Amedeo, 89

Moe, Maurice W., 120, 123

"Moon-Bog, The," 34

Moore, C. L., 115, 209, 228

Morton, James F., 136, 156, 165, 191, 193, 211, 239, 243

Mosig, Dirk W., 59, 61, 134, 294

"Mound, The" (HPL-Bishop), 59, 67, 224, 227

"Music of Erich Zann, The," 34, 84, 162, 236, 254

"Nameless City, The," 34, 86, 105, 134, 254

Narrative of Arthur Gordon Pym, The (Poe), 159

Necronomicon (Alhazred), 22, 37, 66, 67, 70, 73, 78, 89, 192, 207, 232, 238, 255

Necronomicon Press, 100, 137, 157, 229, 232, 263, 268

New Criticism, 10

New England, 10, 23, 30, 46, 49, 51, 53, 54, 55, 56, 135, 160, 179, 183, 184, 204, 236, 250, 277

Nietzsche, Freidrich, 87, 110, 130, 230, 252

Nigguratl-Yig, 58

"Night Ocean, The" (HPL-Barlow), 221

"Noble Eavesdropper, The," 221

"Notes on Writing Weird Fiction," 190

"Nyarlathotep," 34, 42, 58, 59, 71, 72, 83, 89, 121, 122, 128, 192, 195, 198, 199, 203, 225, 243–44, 251, 274

"Observations on Several Parts of America," 244

"Old Bugs," 221, 243

"Old Christmas," 52

Oldham, John, 50

CPSIA information can be obtained
at www.ICGtesting.com
Printed in the USA
BVHW040938120821
614274BV00012B/321